Work and Occupational Psychology
Integrating Theory and Practice

Rachel Lewis and Lara Zibarras

SAGE

Los Angeles | London | New Delhi
Singapore | Washington DC

Los Angeles | London | New Delhi
Singapore | Washington DC

SAGE Publications Ltd
1 Oliver's Yard
55 City Road
London EC1Y 1SP

SAGE Publications Inc.
2455 Teller Road
Thousand Oaks, California 91320

SAGE Publications India Pvt Ltd
B 1/I 1 Mohan Cooperative Industrial Area
Mathura Road
New Delhi 110 044

SAGE Publications Asia-Pacific Pte Ltd
3 Church Street
#10-04 Samsung Hub
Singapore 049483

Editor: Kirsty Smy
Editorial assistant: Nina Smith
Project manager: Jeremy Toynbee
Indexer: Henson Editorial Services
Marketing manager: Alison Borg
Cover design: Wendy Scott
Typeset by: C&M Digitals (P) Ltd, Chennai, India
Printed by: MPG Printgroup UK

First published 2013

Library of Congress Control Number: 2012944265

British Library Cataloguing in Publication data

A catalogue record for this book is available from
the British Library

MIX
Paper from
responsible sources
FSC® C018575
www.fsc.org

ISBN 978-1-44626-069-2
ISBN 978-1-44626-070-8 (pbk)

Contents

Preface
How this book is structured

Part I

Part I of this book focuses on the discipline of Occupational Psychology. In Chapter 1 we present a brief history of the profession and aim to identify what we mean by Occupational/Organisational Psychology in the context of today's work and individuals. We also outline what Occupational Psychology is today and how this might differ from other disciplines such as Human Resources or Management Consultancy. In Chapter 2 we go into greater detail about what Occupational Psychologists are, exploring the different types of jobs they do. We also explain how you can become a registered Occupational Psychologist through the process of Chartership. In Chapters 1 and 2, we introduce the eight key areas in Occupational Psychology, according to the modularisation suggested by the British Psychological Society Syllabus. Each of the eight chapters in Part II of this book focuses on one of those core areas, as described below.

In Chapter 3 we explore the ethical and research skills that Occupational Psychologists need to use in research and practice. We introduce you to key concepts that you will need when studying Occupational Psychology, such as conducting a literature review, research design, and an overview of different qualitative and quantitative research and analysis techniques.

Part II

To give you more of a flavour of the work of Occupational Psychologists and so that you can put into context the theories and models that we introduce in the book, each chapter in Part II includes contributions from leading practitioners and eminent academics in the field. These contributions will not only familiarise you with 'the people to know' in each field, but will provide you with important insights as to what both academics and practitioners do, how their work overlaps, and how both theory and practice inform their work as Occupational Psychologists.

Chapter 4: Employee relations and motivation
By Dr Iain Coyne and Dr Fiona Gavin
Contributions from Professor Rob Briner and Kisane Prutton

This chapter introduces some of the theoretical and practical issues relating to the employer–employee relationship within organisations; structured around the five key areas of employee relations, motivation at work, managing diversity, workplace conflict and workplace bullying.

Chapter 5: Counselling and personal development
By Andrew Kinder, Kevin Nind, Diane Aitchison and Eugene Farrell
Contributions from Professor Frank Bond and Julianne Miles

This chapter is structured in two distinct sections. The first introduces the psychology of work, careers and theories of occupational choice; providing descriptions of methods, approaches and tools used in this area. The second focuss on counselling, moving from the major theoretical positions in counselling, to counselling at work, Professional issues and evaluation of outcomes.

Chapter 6: Career development and appraisal
By Juliette Alban-Metcalfe
Contribution from Professor Beverly Alimo-Metcalfe

This chapter focuses on the meaning and context of career development and appraisal in organisations. The main body of the chapter is an in-depth assessment of performance appraisal in terms of approaches to, design and development of, evidence and impact of bias on, and future directions in performance appraisal systems in organisations.

Chapter 7: Design of environments and work: health, safety and well-being
By Dr Fehmidah Munir and Dr Hilary McDermott
Contributions from Professor Ivan Robertson and Emma Donaldson-Feilder

This chapter begins with an examination of the legal context related to Health and Safety as well as the Equality Act, before introducing the overall problem solving approach and related health and safety procedures. The chapter then moves to an exploration of organisational and contextual issues in the design of work and work environments, particularly focusing on designing and managing workplaces to promote good health and well-being.

Chapter 8: Organisational development and change
By Dr Nigel Guenole and Dr David Biggs
Contribution from Sarah Lewis

This chapter introduces the key concepts of Organisational Development and Change, particularly focused on on models of planned change, the role of Occupational Psychologists as agents or embedders of change, and the impact of change on Organisational culture, processes, structure and strategy; as well and concepts such as decision making, leadership and communication.

Chapter 9: Selection and assessment
By Dr Anna Koczwara and Vicki Ashworth
Contributions from Professor Fiona Patterson and Dr Maura Kerrin

This chapter provides an understanding of the core academic and theoretical principles relating to selection and assessment (S&A); including an overview of S&A, selection systems in organisations, the role of job analysis, assessment methods, principles for designing assessment methodologies, diversity and fairness in selection, candidate experiences, and the future of S&A.

Chapter 10: Training
By Dr Kamal Birdi and Dr Tracey Reid
Contributions by Professor Kurt Kraiger and Alastair Wallace

This chapter explores topics concerning the design, delivery and evaluation of workplace training and development activities, including an introduction to the training cycle, methods of training and development and factors influencing training effectiveness.

Chapter 11: Automation and human–machine interaction
By Dr Varuni Wimalasiri
Contribution by Chandra Harrison

This chapter provides an understanding of the core academic and theoretical principles relating to the area of automation and human–machine interaction; including an overview of the area, display design, control design, learning through interactive procedures, human error and user centred design. The chapter also considers emerging issues within the workplace such as virtual work and AI/robotics and draws implications for the future of automation and HMI in Occupational Psychology.

Important note: Although we have structured and divided the chapters into distinct areas to follow the BPS syllabus, it is important to understand that, in real life, work does not actually fall within these categories and the areas actually all integrate and overlap. Take for example a project Dr Rachel Lewis worked on recently to investigate the reasons behind falling levels of employee

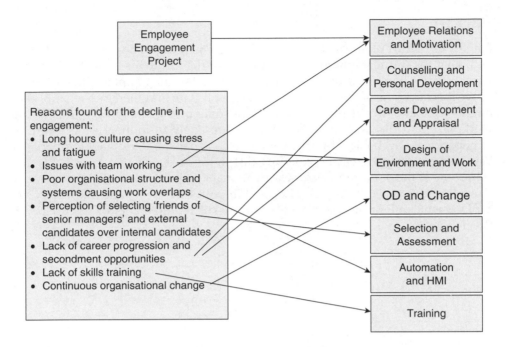

engagement within an organisation. The diagram above demonstrates that although the overall project would be within the area of 'Employee relations and motivation', the reasons found for the falling levels of employee engagement mapped onto all of the eight areas.

Along with specific content relevant to each of the eight areas, and contributions from leading practitioners and eminent academics, each of the chapters in Part II have a number of features, designed to provide the most utility to you as the reader. These include:

- learning outcomes relating to the core BPS syllabus;
- mini case studies, including coverage of ethical and cross cultural issues where possible;
- OP in Practice sections describing the theory in context;
- discussion questions;
- sample essay and examination questions;
- 'Explore further' section, which includes a list of useful weblinks, books and articles;
- 'Day in the life of' section with eminent academics and/or practitioners, to give you a chance to get to know the key people in the field and understand more about the daily working life of an Occupational Psychologist;
- references.

Part III

Finally, in Part III of the book, we focus on the emerging trends in the workplace and what the future might look like, in terms of the future for both Occupational Psychology (Chapter 12) and Occupational Psychologists (Chapter 13). In Chapter 12 we discuss some of the emerging changes in Britain and therefore what Britain might 'look like' in the future. We explore some of the emerging trends in the workplace and discuss how these changes are likely to influence the future of Occupational Psychology. In Chapter 13 we consider the roles that Occupational Psychologists may increasingly occupy due to the recent financial crisis. We discuss some of the opportunities for Occupational Psychologists in the workplace as a result of the emerging trends discussed in both Chapters 1 and 12. Finally we explore what might be some of the future skill requirements of Occupational Psychologists.

About the editors and contributors

Dr Rachel Lewis is a Registered Occupational Psychologist, a lecturer and Course Director in Occupational and Business Psychology at Kingston Business School as well as being a Director of Affinity Health at Work. She combines her academic career with regular conference speaking, consultancy and training, focusing on the links between leadership, management and employee well-being. She has just completed editing a new Wiley-Blackwell *Handbook of Leadership* to be published in January 2013.

Dr Lara Zibarras is a Lecturer at City University London and a Registered Occupational Psychologist. Her key research areas are employee selection (particularly the candidate's perspective); pro-environmental behaviour in the workplace and innovation. She has published widely in academic journals and presented her research at both national and international conferences. Lara has also worked as a consultant for a range of public and private sector organisations in the areas of selection, training, development and psychometric assessment.

Diane Aitchison (along with Kevin Nind) is a Director of All in the Mind Ltd. Established in 2003, working with clients and individuals to achieve of their best. Both Diane and Kevin are Occupational Psychologists, Chartered via the British Psychological Society and Registered with the Health Professions Council. They specialise in leadership and management development initiatives (including training, workshops, development centres and coaching), occupational assessment, stress management and performance management. They have extensive experience in supporting a broad range of clients across all sectors including the Civil Service, automotive, engineering, financial, housing, pharmaceutical, and retail sectors. They work to recruit, develop and support people at all levels from executive to front-line staff. In addition to supporting our clients, They contribute to the on-going success and future of our profession. They work on British Psychological Society Committees to assess and ensure occupational testing training courses meet stringent BPS standards. They also support the Chartership process and coach new psychologists through it.

Juliette Alban-Metcalfe is a Chartered Occupational Psychologist and Chief Executive of Real World Group (www.realworld-group.com). Her particular passion is for increasing employee engagement, diversity and inclusion through leadership. Based on her research with colleagues, Juliette has spoken at international conferences, published numerous papers and articles, and works with organisations globally. She has an MSc in Organizational Psychology from Birkbeck College, University of London, and an MS in Positive Organization Development and Change from Case Western Reserve University, Ohio.

Vicki Ashworth is a Senior Consultant Psychologist for Work Psychology Group and a Chartered Psychologist and registered Occupational Psychologist with the Health and Care Professionals Council (HCPC). Vicki specialises in the fields of assessment and selection for both the corporate and public sector and works in close partnership with clients and stakeholders to ensure that recommended approaches are fit for purpose and reflect cutting edge practice and theory. Her areas of expertise include assessment centre design and evaluation, development and psychometric evaluation of situational judgement tests; and job analyses and competency modeling. She has had her work in these areas published in a number of peer-reviewed papers and presented at national and international conferences. Previously, Vicki worked for the National Policing Improvement Agency (NPIA), an agency that provides assessment solutions within the police service.

Dr David Biggs is the Programme Director for the MScs in Occupational and Business Psychology at the University of Gloucestershire. David as a consultant has provided training, recruitment and research services and still completes associate work in this field. David's research interests lie in non-traditional employment, the use of technology at work and in consulting. More recently, David has examined management in terms of worker relations, leadership and organisational change.

Dr Kamal Birdi is a Senior Lecturer at the Institute of Work Psychology, University of Sheffield and also a Chartered Occupational Psychologist. He has researched and advised extensively for over 20 years on evaluating and improving the impact of employee training and development interventions, developing employee creativity and assessing the influences on organisational innovation. In 2010, he was given the B.P.S. Division of Occupational Psychology Academic Contribution to Practice Award for his efforts to improve organisational practices

Dr Iain Coyne is Associate Professor in Occupational Psychology at the Institute of Work, Health and Organisations, Nottingham University; a Chartered Psychologist and a Registered Occupational Psychologist. At Nottingham, Dr Coyne lectures on employee relations and motivation, but his research interests are specifically in bullying and productive/counterproductive behaviour at work. He has written a number of peer-reviewed papers and has presented at national and international conferences on these topics as well as co-editing a book on bullying in different contexts.

Eugene Farrell has over 25 years experience in public and private healthcare and for the past 15 years has specialised in the development and provision of employee support services, including integrated healthcare, absence management, employee assistance, wellbeing and occupational health services. He has authored articles and research on stress, absence, presenteeism, financial wellbeing, health wellbeing and EAP effectiveness. Former Chair of the UK EAPA, International Director of the US-based Global EAP Association, and board member of Employee Assistance European Federation.

Dr Fiona Gavin is a Chartered Occupational Psychologist and is currently a Lecturer in Occupational Psychology at the University of Nottingham; her research interests focus on workplace diversity and 'modern' forms of discrimination. Collaborators include public-sector, private-sector and charitable organisations, including those with national and international profiles. Having completed a diversity audit for the Council of Europe in Strasbourg, Fiona has recently collaborated with the European Parliament on research into the implication of European Enlargement on employees from the widest possible range of European nations.

Dr Nigel Guenole is a lecturer in work psychology and programme director for the MSc Occupational Psychology at Goldsmiths University of London. He is the director of research for Kenexa High Performance Institute in London. Dr Guenole's work focuses on psychological profiling for personnel selection and development, developing leader capability, and organizational performance. His research has been published in international journals and he is a regular presenter at international psychology conferences.

Andrew Kinder is a Chartered Counselling and Chartered Occupational Psychologist. He is the Past Chair of British Association for Counselling and Psychotherapy's Workplace Division (www.bacpworkplace.org.uk) and was recently awarded with a Fellowship from BACP for his contribution to workplace counselling. He is Vice Chair of the EAPA UK. He works for a large occupational health/counselling provider as their Chief Psychologist and has published widely with an active interest in personal resilience, coaching, stress management, trauma support and EAPs/workplace counselling. Further information at http://www.andrewkinder.co.uk

Dr Anna Koczwara is a Registered Occupational Psychologist with particular expertise in the areas of selection, assessment, and organisational development. She was awarded a PhD from the University of London for her research into the identification of leadership potential in the financial services industry. In 2009 Anna was named the British Psychological Society Occupational Psychology Practitioner of the Year. Anna held the role of Associate Director at Work Psychology Group whilst contributing to this book and has since moved to become Deputy Head of Assessment with Royal Bank of Scotland Group.

Dr Hilary McDermott is a Lecturer in Psychology within the School of Sport, Exercise and Health Sciences at Loughborough University. Her research expertise concerns health and well-being with a strong emphasis on injury prevention, particularly within the context of work and the work environment. Her current work focuses on the occupational health and well-being of those working as activity leaders within the outdoor leisure industry. She has published her work in a number of peer-reviewed journals within her field.

Dr Fehmidah Munir is a Senior Lecturer in Psychology within the School of Sport, Exercise and Health Sciences at Loughborough University. Her research expertise lies in understanding and managing ill-health at work; design and management of work to enhance occupational health and well-being; understanding the influence of individual and organisational factors on presenteeism, sickness absence and return-to-work outcomes. She has written numerous academic articles, book chapters and reports.

Kevin Nind (along with Diane Aitchison) is Director of All in the Mind Ltd. Established in 2003, they work with clients and individuals to achieve of their best. they are Occupational Psychologists, Chartered via the British Psychological Society and Registered with the Health Professions Council. They specialise in leadership and management development initiatives (including training, workshops, development centres and coaching), occupational assessment, stress management and performance management. They have extensive experience in supporting a broad range of clients across all sectors including the Civil Service, automotive, engineering, financial, housing, pharmaceutical, and retail sectors. They work to recruit, develop and support people at all levels from executive to front-line staff. In addition to supporting our clients, They contribute to the on-going success and future of our profession. They work on British Psychological Society Committees to assess and ensure occupational testing training courses meet stringent BPS standards. They also support the Chartership process and coach new psychologists through it.

Dr Tracey Reid has more than 20 years experience working in Human Resources for a variety of organisations including Local Government and is currently providing Stress Management and Management Training within the Care Home Industry. She has worked as a Teaching Associate at the Institute of Work Psychology, University of Sheffield and as a Teaching Fellow at the University of Hull. Her research primarily focuses on the areas of stress, health and well-being, with a particular emphasis on the effect on-call working has on the individual in relation to these outcomes. She is a regular presenter at the European Academy of Occupational Health Psychology Conferences.

Dr Varuni Wimalasiri is a Chartered Occupational Psychologist and lecturer at Exeter University Business School. Her research interests are in the area of Human Factors and Creativity. Her related work has focused on understanding and enhancing decision making in high risk work environments. She has collaborated with other Human Factors academics and practitioners to develop interventions to help improve error-prone (or risky) organisational systems. Varuni writes journal papers and reports, and gives conference presentations for academic and practitioner audiences based on her research work. She also teaches postgraduate students at Exeter University Business School undertaking modules in her specialist area.

Companion website

Be sure to visit the Companion Website (http://www.uk.sagepub.co.uk/zibarras) where you will find additional teaching and learning materials for lecturers and students.

Resources for lecturers

PowerPoint slides
Additional exercises
Case studies

Resources for students

Online readings
Tips and hints
Occupational Psychologist podcasts

Part I

Introduction to work and Occupational Psychology

1 What is Occupational Psychology?

Lara Zibarras and Rachel Lewis

Learning outcomes

On completion of this chapter you should:

- have an overview of the history of Occupational Psychology in the UK;
- understand the key changes that have taken place in the work environment over the 20th century and into the 21st century;
- understand what Occupational Psychology is today, with an overview of the broad areas covered;
- appreciate how Occupational Psychology differs from other areas, such as human resources and management consultancy.

Introduction

The area of applied psychology relating to people at work and in organisations has a number of different labels. Within the UK we generally tend to use the term *Occupational Psychology.* This is the official title and is protected by law. However, you may also come across the labels *Organisational Psychology, Business Psychology* or *Work Psychology*. Elsewhere, such as in Europe, it is common convention to use the term *Work Psychology*; while in the USA, it is commonly labelled *Industrial and Organisational Psychology* (or *I/O Psychology*).

So, what is Occupational Psychology? Broadly speaking, it is the branch of applied psychology concerned with human behaviour in work and organisational settings. As defined by the British Psychological Society (BPS), Occupational Psychology is about *applying the science of psychology to people at work*; where work is generally considered to be paid employment. That said, some researchers and practitioners have increasingly been exploring the links between work and non-work, such as the increasing blurring of boundaries between work and non-work hours (Brough and O'Driscoll, 2010).

In this chapter, we first explore the history of Occupational Psychology from its inception during the early part of the 20th century, through to modern day Occupational Psychology. Next, we consider some ways in which the work environment has changed during the latter part of the 20th century and the early 21st century, and the influence this might have had on Occupational Psychology. Finally we consider some key ways in which Occupational Psychology might differ from other, seemingly similar, areas.

A brief history of Occupational Psychology

The following sub-sections outline the history of Occupational Psychology. You may question why you need to know about the history of our profession; the answer is that to understand contemporary Occupational Psychology, it helps to know how we got here. This brief account of the history of Occupational Psychology is by no means an exhaustive historical account, but instead draws out some of the key developments in and changes to the profession over the previous one hundred years or so. Our aim is that you, as a student, will understand the context of where we are today in Occupational Psychology, by understanding the history of the profession. It may surprise you to see that much of what we think of as 'contemporary' issues in Occupational Psychology were discussed and researched in the early 1900s.

Occupational Psychology: the early years

It was as early as 1915 in the UK, during the First World War, when applied psychology studies began: for example, investigating industrial fatigue and the factors influencing health and efficiency of workers in munitions factories. These studies were conducted by the Industrial Health Research Board (IHRB) and in the 1930s the IHRB reported on topics such as hours of work, industrial accidents, vision and lighting, vocational guidance and selection, time and motion study, and methods of work and posture. Although, as Shimmin and Wallis (1994) note, these research studies did not attract a huge amount of interest, and so many of these reports were soon out of print. Unfortunately, the IHRB did little to publicise its research and it was rarely presented to those who might have been able to use the results.

In 1921 a key institution in the history of Occupational Psychology was founded by Charles Myers (considered one of the most significant British psychologists from this time) and Henry Welch, an important industrialist (Kwiatkowski et al., 2006). This was the National Institute of Industrial Psychology (NIIP) and its primary aim was to 'promote and encourage the application of the sciences of psychology and physiology to commerce and industry by any means that may be found practicable' (Shimmin and Wallis, 1994: 4). The NIIP was conceived to bring practical psychology to industry and it was run as a not-for-profit scientific association. Thus it was dependent on fees earned for diagnostic investigations and work carried out for firms to improve their working conditions and performance. By 1930, many organisations were associated with the NIIP, such as the Bank of England, the Rockefeller Fund, the City of London Corporation, Lloyds Bank and many others (Kwiatkowski et al., 2006). At the time, the NIIP was well known and considered to be extremely influential.

So for a time, in the UK there were two main bodies (the NIIP and IHRB) conducting research and practice in the area we now know as Occupational Psychology. The work conducted by the NIIP during the 1930s was equally as diverse as that conducted by the IHRB, focusing on issues such as job analysis, psychological testing, interviewing and personnel selection, paving the way for much of contemporary thinking (Kwiatkowski et al., 2006). For example, what Occupational Psychologists currently refer to as emotional intelligence or 'EQ' (Goleman, 1998) was explored over 80 years ago within the concepts of mood, emotion and temperament (Myers, 1920); what we currently refer to as 'culture' in an organisation was then explored using the term 'atmosphere' (Miles, 1928). The concept of 'work–life balance' was explored as early as 1937 (Myers, 1937); and from a methodological perspective, the use of work samples and diary study research methods were also being explored at this time (Wyatt and Western, 1920). However, since the NIIP gave guidance to fee-paying individuals or organisations, the participants in their research came largely from professional backgrounds. Other research on broader, more diverse, populations was generally in association with the IHRB (Frisby, 1970).

Yet the socio-economic challenges of 1930s were such that the results of these pioneering studies became obscured. After 1921 the post-war boom diminished: many firms were struggling to survive; many people were out of work, and since there was no welfare state there were no interventions to alleviate the hardship. Additionally, the industrial regions of the country, such as the centres of coal-mining, shipbuilding, iron and steel, were badly affected and increasingly became depressed areas. Given such an unfavourable situation it is perhaps somewhat remarkable that British industrial psychologists survived, especially considering their reliance on consultancy work (Rose, 1975).

The Second World War years

It is notable that the expansion of Occupational Psychology after the Second World War may not have happened at all had it not been for pioneers working in bodies such as the NIIP (Hearnshaw, 1964). Nevertheless, it was during the Second World War (1939–45) that selection procedures in the military were transformed and War Office Selection boards were set up. By the end of the war, three million recruits into the Army, Navy and the Air Force had been through at least a partial psychological assessment procedure, and around two million men and women had experienced a battery of tests on intellectual and educational abilities. Additionally, many recruits were also interviewed and assessed on biographical data along with these test scores. Vernon and Parry (1949) outline in detail the process and outcomes of psychological assessment and selection in the three services, and this is considered to be one of the earliest technical accounts of the application of differential psychology on a large scale in the UK, which included follow-up data to demonstrate effectiveness (Shimmin and Wallis, 1994). Indeed, the success of the psychologists working within the services was recognised by an Expert Committee report that recommended psychologists should be represented on scientific, advisory and other committees concerned with personnel (Shimmin and Wallis, 1994). This endorsement signified a great achievement by psychologists.

Meanwhile, the Cambridge Psychological Laboratory began work on human skill and performance, which had a lasting influence on applied psychology and the emerging field of ergonomics, in particular the study of acquisition of skills and human–machine interaction at work. A distinguishing feature of the work conducted at Cambridge was its theory-drive approach, as opposed to the somewhat pragmatic approach of personnel selection within the services (Shimmin and Wallis, 1994).

Post-war psychology in the government

Since psychology had been successfully applied to wartime problems, conditions were favourable for it to be applied during peacetime. Life in the years following the Second World War was dominated by its consequences: the newly elected Labour administration was embarking on national reconstruction while facing human, technical and economic problems (Marwick, 1982). There were difficulties integrating ex-service personnel into civilian life, combined with the threat of the Cold War; this meant that in addition to civil reconstruction there was a need to sustain the military forces.

However, applied psychology was recognised as having the potential to help tackle these problems, and this had far reaching consequences for the development of the area of Occupational Psychology in the post-war years and the subsequent decades. Particularly influential was the establishment of psychologists practising within government; although, given the constraints of security (the Official Secrets Act), much of the work conducted within the government by these psychologists was not widely disseminated (Shimmin and Wallis, 1994). Nevertheless, many of the activities of the government psychologists paved the way for what we see as Occupational Psychology today. For example, the foundations of the modern-day assessment centre were laid by psychologists working in government, based on the British War Office Selection Boards (Murray, 1990). Refinements of the assessment centre method were made by the Civil Service Selection Board (documented in some publications, such as Jones et al., 1991). Indeed, one consequence of assessment centres being used within government departments was that this provided large datasets of psychological measures and assessments, along with selection decisions and follow-up information. Since psychologists were able to show the benefits of assessment centres, they were soon taken up by other bodies and organisations.

Another significant development in the civil service was that in 1950 a separate job category of 'Psychologist' was established. This provided the opportunity of a professional career for people wanting to specialise in applying occupational, experimental or social psychology in the workplace. From the outset, this attracted many applicants, although they were not required to have any higher degree nor were they required, ironically, to go through a rigorous selection process (Shimmin and Wallis, 1994).

Psychology was also applied to civilian employment and training through the central department responsible for national employment policies. Initially the department was known as the Ministry of Labour, but in 1967 it was rebranded as the Department of Employment and Productivity with powers of intervention in aspects of employment, vocational training and industrial relations. The first Ministry of Labour psychologists worked in employment rehabilitation units, which were originally established to enable the return to work of people who had suffered disabling industrial accidents. These psychologists were the first in the UK to participate in a nationwide service offering support to disadvantaged people. This support mostly involved personal assessment and vocational guidance, but by 1968 over 12,000 injured or disabled people had been helped to gain employment (Shimmin and Wallis, 1994). The Ministry also allocated some psychologists to give professional support to vocational and career guidance staff who gave advice to school leavers, through what was then named the Youth Employment Service (later known as the Careers Service). They were able to provide important advice, in particular in evaluating the assessment methods used to identify occupational interests and preferences.

Post-war research and application in industry

Alongside the developments of Occupational Psychology within the government, there was also an expansion of industrial field studies and other research designed to help British industry adapt in a rapidly changing world. These changes included both the technological advancements made during the war, which led to new jobs and new forms of communication, and also changes in people's expectations and aspirations (Shimmin and Wallis, 1994). The post-war era also witnessed significant changes in the composition of the labour force. There was increasing participation by married women working on both full- and part-time bases, and also by immigrant workers from the former UK colonies, for whom jobs became available due to labour shortages in some industries, such as textiles.

Initially during the 1950s, recovery from the war and the adaptation to changed social economic and political conditions dominated. This was followed by reasonable prosperity as new production techniques reduced the prices of consumer goods and made higher wages possible (Marwick, 1982). In fact, the year 1957 marked the time when post-war restrictions and controls finally came to an end and the word 'affluence' made its way into common language (Marwick, 1982).

Into the early 1960s there were changing attitudes and behaviours. Within social welfare, education, employment and industry there seemed to be optimism about the possibilities and benefits of planned interventions and improvements, such as 'planned organisational change' which later became known as organisational development (Shimmin and Wallis, 1994). Taken as a whole then, the 1960s were a period of change in the emphasis and balance of the activities of Occupational Psychologists: there was continuing work in personnel selection and vocational guidance, ergonomics and training. However, many of these developments in Occupational Psychology throughout the 1960s were not published. This was in direct contrast to other branches of psychology where the research was published to a great extent. As Nelson (1971) points out, this is because much of the work conducted by Occupational Psychologists within organisations was not actually released for publication and, similarly, work conducted by consultancy firms was generally kept confidential; added to this, access to the work conducted within the armed services or civil service was restricted.

There were significant changes in the Occupational Psychology *profession* during this time too. The constitution of the NIIP was altered in 1951, while under the directorship of Frisby, to 'encourage and develop the science of industrial and Occupational Psychology' (Kwiatkowski et al., 2006: 185): the concept of the 'practical application' had been dropped and the focus was on science instead. The NIIP also briefly attempted to compete with the better resourced universities by seeking status as an industrial research association in 1956; and it also continued competing with the more commercially aware consultancies. However, it is claimed (Kwiatkowski et al., 2006) that along the way the NIIP lost its energy and impetus and eventually in 1977 it was closed down. Guest (2006) suggests that, by its end, it was a troubled organisation that was badly run, struggling to find the funds to survive.

Another establishment important in the history of Occupational Psychology is the Tavistock Institute, which was set up after the Second World War in 1946. Although the Institute's emphasis was more clinical psychology than occupational (Guest, 2006), it nevertheless had a major influence on thinking in the field of Occupational Psychology. For example, through debates on job design and the quality of working life (Emery and Thorsrud, 1976), the Institute affected industry and government policy. The Tavistock's approaches had a theoretical underpinning, providing a strong intellectual basis for their work. Indeed, their work provided the basis for systems thinking, the result of the Tavistock's previous coal-mining studies (Trist et al., 1963). This led to the theory of organisations as open, socio-technical systems, representing one of the first multi-level frameworks for considering individuals, groups and organisations. Other systems thinking included the organisational development movement and the rationale underlying action research. All these ideas and theories have been very influential and widely disseminated. Indeed, a key feature of the work by the Tavistock Institute is that it is evidence-based, engaging academia and practice through the use of relevant theory and evidence (Guest, 2006).

By the 1970s, the UK saw an increase in strike activity in both public and private sectors at the same time as the industrial base shrank. There was rising inflation, increased unemployment and a struggle to compete in world markets against Europe and the Far East (Marwick, 1982). Later, there was a short 'boom' in the 1980s, particularly in the financial, technology and service sectors, during which the government sought to cut costs and contain borrowing. This meant that, for organisations that depended on government funding, such as universities, research councils and hospitals, there was a tremendous squeeze on resources. In general, the 1980s were a period of great social and economic change, which saw companies in the UK relocating their manufacturing overseas to countries such as Thailand, Malaysia and Mexico, and expanding into new market economies in Eastern Europe following the collapse of communism. The UK experienced rapid economic growth, in part due to its adoption of laissez-faire economic policies.

During the 1980s, the economic and organisational landscape in the UK was such that it led to increased opportunities for Occupational Psychologists, particularly through consultancy activities. Many of the well known Occupational Psychology consultancies were founded, developed and expanded during this time. In 1984, Peter Saville (then a founding partner of Saville and Holdsworth Limited SHL) published the Occupational Personality Questionnaire (OPQ).

Also in the 1980s the term *Occupational Health Psychology* (OHP) was coined, which emerged out of health psychology, occupational/organisational psychology and occupational health. OHP is concerned with the workplace characteristics that influence the development of physical and mental health-related issues in employees. The field advanced in 1987 when the journal *Work & Stress* was founded and later, in 1999, the European Academy of Occupational Health Psychology (EA-OHP) was established.

The 1990s may be characterised as the *Information Age*. It was during this decade that many technologies became available and commonly used by the general public. This resulted in the ability of people to transfer information freely and instantly, and to have access to knowledge that might have previously been unavailable or difficult to find. This expansion of information may have been due to a combination of factors, including globalisation and widespread use of new media such as the Internet (Patterson, 2001). It was also during the 1990s that the terms *war for talent* and *talent management* were established (Michaels et al., 2001). With shortages in some labour markets, organisations increasingly recognised that there was increasing competition among companies to recruit and then retain competent employees: a war for talent (Lievens et al., 2002).

We end our formal historical section here, since the continuing evolution of theory and practice in Occupational Psychology will be picked up in the chapters that follow in Part II. Each of these chapters will focus on a more specific area of Occupational Psychology (for example, employee selection, organisational development and change), so you will be able to understand how that specific area has evolved and is developing today. Additionally, in Part III we discuss some contemporary concerns and emerging trends in the workplace, including issues such as the recent global recession, globalisation and so forth. Before we move on, we leave with some general points about how Occupational Psychology has changed since its beginnings.

The changing nature of Occupational Psychology

From its inception, Occupational Psychology (or what was then termed industrial psychology) was mainly about the study of individual differences (Shimmin and Wallis, 1994). The emphasis was on investigating and explaining attributes that relate to performance at work, such as a person's ability, skills, traits and personality. The concept of individual difference is what underpins work in selection, assessment and vocational guidance since the individual is focused on as the main unit of analysis. Despite the fact that initial research conducted by the IHRB and the NIIP explored the influence that working conditions had on people at work (with such observations leading researchers to adopt more social psychological perspectives), students in the 1940s were trained to be scientists and thus approached the study of human behaviour using a positivist, classic, scientific paradigm (Shimmin and Wallis, 1994). The methodology in Occupational Psychology therefore emulated the natural sciences, which aimed to describe and explain various phenomena in a way that would allow generalisations to be made. This assumes well-defined problems, the ability to control variables and measurements, all with objectivity and scientific detachment. Further work on individual differences was later expanded through the development and refinement of factor analytic models of personality during the 1950s.

Thus for the most part, the formulation of solutions in Occupational Psychology were for a while focused on the individual as the unit of analysis, based on an individual's performance, but measured in isolation from their working environment. Increasingly, from the early 1960s, the potential limitations of the view of scientific detachment and objectivity were more widely recognised. There was an influx of ideas from social psychology and interventionist approaches began to come into prominence (such as action research [Lewin, 1954]). So, there has been a shift of approach in Occupational Psychology during the 20th century: from a focus on the individual in his or her job role where the employing organisation was taken as given, to an approach that accounts for the organisation as a whole and considers the wider social, economic and political environment in which it functions. Some of these changes are reflected in the ways in which the work environment has changed over this time.

We now turn to a brief overview of some of the key changes that have taken place in the workplace and consider some of the research and practice in Occupational Psychology that has taken place as a result of these changes.

Key changes to the work environment

There have been a number of significant changes to the work environment in the past few decades and these have significantly influenced the context in which people work. Changes such as the increasing globalisation of business, the Internet revolution and the rapid pace of change have impacted the way in which individuals work (Cascio and Aguinis, 2008). Organisations may be increasingly relying on team working and contract workers, while rapidly changing work roles require flexibility, adaptability and innovation (Herriot and Anderson, 1997). The following sections outline some of the key ways in which the work environment has changed.

Technology

Over the preceding hundred years or so there have been significant and rapid changes in technology. Sparked by new technologies and, in particular, the Internet, organisations have undergone far-reaching transformations (Cascio and Aguinis, 2008). This has led to considerable changes in job content, with very few roles untouched by electronic technologies (Patterson, 2001). Across different industries and sectors some job roles have increased in complexity while for others the result has been a redundancy of some skills. For example, in manufacturing firms machines and robots have replaced jobs that may previously have been done by humans; this can lead to employees becoming equipment monitors rather than technical experts (Patterson, 2001).

Millions of workers use computers every day along with other aspects of the digital age – email, mobile phones, the Internet and so on. This is enhancing the opportunity to share vast amounts of digital information and to gain access to this information from anywhere at any time. As the use of technology has increased, so has the occurrence of telecommuting (where individuals can work from home via a computer and the Internet, rather than being physically present in an office [Gajendran and Harrison, 2007]), or the creation of 'virtual' teams of people or offices. It has been pointed out by Cascio and Aguinis that the increasing use of remote access and mobile technology to work 'on-the-go' or at home means that:

> the twenty-first-century organisation must adapt itself to management via the Web. It must be predicated on constant change, not stability; organised around networks, not rigid hierarchies; built on shifting partnerships and alliances, not self-sufficiency; and constructed on technological advantages, not bricks and mortar. (2008: 135)

As a result of many of these technological changes, there has been an increase in research focusing on user-friendly equipment and operations systems (see Chapter 11, 'Automation and human-machine interaction', for further research in this area), developing training methods to develop new skills (see Chapter 10, 'Training') and redundancy counselling for those displaced from jobs because of technological developments and change (see Chapter 5, 'Counselling and personal development').

Changes in patterns of working

With the birth of new technologies there has been an increasing change in patterns of working, including the possibility of job sharing and flexible working (Patterson, 2001). Along with this, there has been an erosion of the working week: many employees are expected to continuously monitor and respond to email via mobile devices, which may lead to an inability to disengage from work.

Furthermore, since the 1980s, organisations have sought to reduce employee numbers, increasingly relying on outsourcing contracts and/or relying on temporary or semi-permanent staff. While this might reduce employment and staffing costs within organisations, there may be less tangible losses, such as reduced organisational commitment and job satisfaction (Rousseau, 2001). The number of people in self-employment has also increased significantly, and the concept of the portfolio worker has emerged, where an individual often works for more than one company at a time on specific projects. This is known as the 'portfolio approach' (Bradley et al., 2000).

Generally, working hours have increased in most occupations (Sparks et al., 2001). This is often due to employer demands for greater flexibility of work schedules to cover extending opening hours. This has resulted in longer working hours for most employees and the decay of the working week. Being able to effectively manage work and non-work demands can significantly influence employees' health and performance. All these changes in the patterns of working have resulted in an increased interest in the possible physical and psychological effects of working anti-social hours and shift-working patterns. Within the last decade in particular there has been an explosion in work–life balance research (Brough and O' Driscoll, 2010). Indeed, research suggests that extended working hours actually have a negative effect on employees in terms of fatigue and reduced performance (Poissonnet and Veron, 2000).

Alteration of labour force and globalisation

The labour force in the UK today looks dramatically different to how it did just a few decades ago. There have been considerable demographic changes in the workforce, with a significant increase in the numbers of women, ethnic minority groups and older workers. These changes have resulted in research and action by psychologists relating to the implementation of equality legislation and issues faced by workers (often women) in relation to combining work and home responsibilities.

Since the 1970s legislation has changed to protect certain workers in the workforce. It is unlawful to discriminate against people on the grounds of gender, ethnicity, disability and so on. Discrimination occurs where a person who is a member of a particular group is treated less favourably than a person not in that group as a direct result of that group membership. The following pieces of legislation have been brought in since the 1970s:

- Sex Discrimination Act 1975
- Sex Discrimination (Gender Reassignment) Regulations 1999
- Race Relations Act 1976 (amended 2000 and 2003)
- Disability Discrimination Act 1995 (amended in 2005)
- Working Time Regulations 1998
- Part-time Workers Regulations 2000
- Fixed-term Employees Regulations 2002
- Employment Equality (Sexual Orientation) Regulations 2003
- Employment Equality (Religion or Belief) Regulations 2003
- Equality Act 2010 (described in more detail below)
- Agency Worker Regulations 2010

In October 2010, the Equality Act 2010 became law. This replaces most of the previous legislation listed above, and was intended to be a law ensuring consistency and fairness within the workplace. In addition to this the public sector Equality Duty came into force in April 2011. This Duty applies to public bodies and functions and surrounds the development and delivery of policies and services related to the Equality Act. The Equality Act covers the same groups that were included within existing legislation (age, disability, gender, gender reassignment, race, religion or belief, sexual orientation) but also extends some of the protections and strengthens some aspects; for instance introducing associative discrimination and disability arising from discrimination. The Agency Worker Regulations came into force in October 2011 and give agency workers (temporary and contract workers) entitlement to the same treatment as employees; that is, paid annual leave, rest breaks, national minimum wage and so on. They must complete a qualifying period of 12 weeks work in order to qualify for this regulation. The implications and ramifications of this Act are described in more detail in Chapter 4.

In addition to the legislation implemented in the UK, increasing globalisation has led to growing unification of the world's economies by reducing barriers, such as international trade tariffs and export fees. In organisations, this has generally resulted in an increase in material wealth, goods and services through international divisions of labour. As the world of work brings together many different cultures and nationalities, it has been important for Occupational Psychologists to examine how this might impact the work environment. The tendency in many workplaces in the UK is that many different cultures are brought together, either physically in offices, or virtually (think for example of UK-based organisations that outsource call centre operations to India). The challenge then becomes one of developing human resource systems (such as selection, training, motivation) that are compatible with many different cultures and ethnicities (Landy and Conte, 2009). It seems that being part of a multicultural environment is just one aspect of working and living in the 21st century. In your working life, it is extremely likely that you will work with co-workers, managers or those you must directly report to who have different cultural values and beliefs to your own.

Changes to organisational structure

Recent years have witnessed some significant changes in organisational structures. On the one hand, there has been a focus, since the 1980s, on downsizing and de-layering in organisations, with redundancies on a large scale; while on the other hand some organisations have become much more complex due to mergers and acquisitions. A further transformation in today's workplace is the number of small- to medium-sized enterprises (SMEs, classified as having less than 250 employees) that have emerged over the previous two decades (Anderson et al., 2004; Wyatt et al., 2010). It has been estimated that in the UK, over 99% of organisations may be classified as small or medium and account for over one-half of private-sector employment and turnover (BERR, 2008). SMEs hold substantial value for social and economic growth in the UK. More discussion on organisational structure and culture follows in Chapter 8.

Owing to the cost-cutting and downsizing regimes of the 1980s and 1990s (and indeed, in much more recent years due to the recent economic downturn), there has been a breakdown of the old employment relationship. The concept of a 'job for life' does not generally tend to be part of young workers' careers (Loughlin and Barling, 2001). Thus, many employees now have to focus on developing their own personal career plans and portfolios to increase their marketability and employability, rather than seeing their employer as permanent. This has resulted in less employee commitment and loyalty to specific organisations and, indeed, loyalty and commitment is rewarded less in organisations (Wilkinson et al., 2001). Personal development and career theories are discussed in more detail in

Chapter 5. Similarly, employer's demands have changed: they generally emphasise employee flexibility, adaptability and innovation (Patterson, 2002) since those are the employees that embrace change and are more likely to flourish in today's turbulent organisations. Consideration of the employee–employer relationship, encompassing employer demands and employee choice, has generated substantial research focusing on the *psychological contract* (Conway and Briner, 2005; Guest, 2004; Rousseau, 2001). The psychological contract is thought to 'capture the spirit of the times' (Guest, 1998: 659) and reflects the individualising of the employment relationship. The psychological contract is discussed more fully in Chapter 4.

There has also been a new form of worker emerging – the knowledge worker (Wilkinson et al., 2001). The notion of corporate commitment has to some extent been redefined to one in which maintaining the intellectual capital of an organisation, that is the knowledge, experience and ideas of employees (Wilkinson et al., 2001) or 'corporate memory', relies on employee commitment and satisfaction.

Contemporary Occupational Psychology

Most commentators agree that there is good reason to be optimistic about Occupational Psychology as a profession (Guest, 2006; Patterson, 2001). Taking the last few decades as a whole, there has been an increase in the opportunities for Occupational Psychologists, and these are unlikely to diminish even during the current economic downturn. The field of Occupational Psychology is flourishing, with academic and practitioner expertise having had a major influence on the way in which organisations operate, from large multinational companies to public sector organisations (Patterson, 2001). Indeed, contemporary Occupational Psychology has seen a vast growth in knowledge (Guest, 2006), the diversity of research areas and applied practice is noteworthy, which may be considered a sign of health in the field. Not only has there been growth in the field, but there has also been a growing demand for Occupational Psychology services in government and industry. Additionally, the adoption of ideas from Occupational Psychology by policymakers has resulted in the advance of evidence, theory and practice (Guest, 2006).

So, how do we know that the profession, field and demand for Occupational Psychology is growing? The BPS appointments memorandum continually lists vacancies within the field, and journals that cover Occupational Psychology topics continue to flourish, indicating that there are continuing academic developments within the field. The ever increasing areas covered by Occupational Psychology may be seen and reflected in the types of topics covered in the BPS annual Division of Occupational Psychology (DOP) conferences. For example, in 1970, the third annual conference lasted one and a half days and papers presented were mainly on topics related to selection and industrial relations. Many years later, the 2012 conference was almost three days long and had 80 papers running in seven simultaneous streams. The range of topics was immense, including (among others) innovation, technology, environmental sustainability, risk tolerance, work–life balance, stress and well-being, candidate perspective of selection and psychological contracts. A recent addition has also been the postgraduate Occupational Psychology conference, which now runs alongside the main conference – this is primarily aimed at MSc students and those who have recently completed their studies. Membership of the DOP has continued to grow year on year, and the number of BPS accredited MSc courses offering Occupational Psychology has increased significantly from around 10 in 1990 to over 25 in 2012.

In the last decade we have also seen a proliferation of related courses focusing on the study of behaviour at work, with courses such as organisational behaviour, work psychology, business psychology and so on. Further, we are seeing Occupational Psychology (or related modules) increasingly being added to undergraduate courses, such as psychology or business management, and also into postgraduate courses such as MBA and human resource management programmes. This suggests that both the interest in, and reach of, Occupational Psychology is growing within the UK.

Occupational Psychology has had a significant influence on the world of work. In fact, many concepts developed by Occupational Psychologists, such as performance appraisals, ability tests and attitude surveys, are regularly used in organisations today. It is possible to see this via the Workplace Employee Relations Survey (Kersley et al., 2004), which is an account of the state of employee relations and working life within UK organisations. The most recent survey carried out in 2004 indicated that 42% of organisations use attitude surveys; 78% use performance appraisals; 46% use ability tests; and 19% of organisations use personality measures. In advocating the use of evidence-based research and practice, Occupational Psychologists have had an opportunity to have significant input into national and corporate policy and practice, and there are many accounts of influential work in which Occupational Psychologists have had this type of positive impact (see the following papers for examples of significantly influential work: Michie and West, 2004; Patterson et al., 2009; Silvester and Dykes, 2007).

So, what are the areas of Occupational Psychology in which research and practice take place? As outlined by the BPS, there are eight areas of Occupational

Psychology that are collectively known as the *Knowledge Dimensions*. These eight areas are:

1 human–machine interaction;
2 design of environments and work, health and safety;
3 personnel selection and assessment;
4 performance appraisal and career development;
5 counselling and personal development;
6 training;
7 employee relations and motivation;
8 organisational development and change.

As we outlined in the Preface, you will notice that this text is split into chapters with headings along similar lines. As you progress through your training as an Occupational Psychologist you will come to see that these areas are not necessarily distinct and separate areas. Indeed, you will often find significant overlap between areas; nonetheless, these distinctions will help guide your learning in this area of applied psychology.

What is Occupational Psychology's unique selling point?

So, what is it about Occupational Psychology research and practice that makes it different and what might be considered its unique selling point (USP)? There are a number of aspects of Occupational Psychology that make it unique as a discipline and we describe these here. We have also included some quotations from key academics and practitioners in the discipline regarding their thoughts on Occupational Psychology's USP.

Julianne Miles, Independent Practitioner, Director of Career Psychologists

‘ I think that the USP of Occupational Psychologists is the credibility derived from our professional training and our evidence-based practice. Our 'brand' is that of highly trained specialists with an in-depth understanding of people at work. This is why it is essential for us to be scientist-practitioners and to stay up to date with current behavioural science research findings and to integrate this learning into our day-to-day work. We can also offer clients the reassurance derived from the professional standards of the BPS, in particular the code of ethics and conduct. '

Professor Beverly Alimo-Metcalfe, Professor of Leadership, Bradford University School of Management and Group Chief Executive of Real World Group

' As Occupational Psychologists we have a strong commitment to conduct rigorous research to real life challenges, and to 'make a difference'. Also, the fact that many researchers also work in the field of consultancy, and use data gathered from their experiences to form the basis of 'ground-breaking' research ... '

First, and perhaps most importantly, there is a *scientific basis* to Occupational Psychology. If you think back to the beginning of the chapter, you will remember that the BPS definition of Occupational Psychology is about 'applying the science of psychology to people at work'. During your training as an Occupational Psychologist you will become familiar with key psychological models, theory and research, and these will form the basis of your work as a practitioner. That is, research is used to address problems or issues in the workplace. You will be trained to become a *scientist-practitioner* and thus it will be important that, as an Occupational Psychologist, you stay up to date with current findings in the literature so that your practice is informed by the latest research. Similarly, many researchers and academics who primarily work and carry out research in universities are also practitioners, conducting important consultancy work in organisations. This means that key links between research and practice can (and should) be maintained. In fact, it has been argued vociferously (Anderson et al., 2001; Hodgkinson et al., 2001) that the scientific evidence base underpinning our practices is the fundamental difference between Occupational Psychologists and other professionals that might also aim to enhance productivity in the workplace. Thus the scientist-practitioner model is our unique selling point.

Professor Frank Bond, Professor of Occupational Psychology, Head of Psychology Department, Goldsmiths, University of London

' I might be expected to say this, as I am an academic, but I believe the single most important USP of Occupational Psychology is its scientific foundation, and, in particular, the applied benefits that stem from sound scientific theory, in-depth analyses, and evidence-based conclusions. What we can offer over and above other disciplines is the application of the scientific theory and methods to addressing the needs of clients, whether it is in selecting a psychometrically sound test, conducting a rigorous job analysis, or examining the impact of work design on health and performance. '

Professor Kurt Kraiger, Professor of Industrial Organisational Psychology, Colorado State University

' I have always emphasised the role of Occupational Psychology in *conducting research to help organisations make better decisions about their human capital*. HR (as an internal function) is often driven both by legal concerns or habit – what's been done in the past. Management consultants are too often driven by what has worked for them in the past. The Occupational Psychologist can recommend interventions based on a body of evidence or applied research in that particular company. '

During your initial training you will learn how to critically analyse and evaluate the research you come across so that you are using an *evidence-based* approach. By casting a critical eye on the research you will then be able to judge for yourself how useful a model or theory will be in a specific work context. Then, using that particular model or theory, you will learn how to diagnose problems, conduct needs assessments, formulate solutions and then evaluate the output to make sure that you are having a positive impact through the work that you do. It is important to remember that the evidence base within a particular area will grow and change according to research findings, making it important to stay informed of new research and literature.

Professor Ivan Robertson, Professor of Organisational Psychology, Leeds University Business School and Director of Robertson Cooper Ltd

' For me the unique selling point for Occupational Psychology rests on two pillars: the scientific basis of the discipline and the technology involved in assessing and changing human behaviour.

Psychology in general is clearly a hybrid discipline and I think it can be unhelpful to compare psychology too closely to the physical sciences. However, a key selling point for psychology is the fact that there is an evidence-base – and that this evidence grows and changes according to the findings of research. The measurement precision that psychologists can bring to bear is perhaps most easily seen in the area of psychometric testing and it is no accident that this is the largest single area of activity for professional Occupational Psychologists. Although formal psychometric measurement is useful and important the whole approach that psychologists bring to understanding, assessing and influencing behaviour represents a uniquely valuable contribution. '

Another important aspect of Occupational Psychology is the *multi-level perspective* that Occupational Psychologists take in conducting research or formulating solutions in practice. From a research perspective, one of the unique aspects of Occupational Psychology is that field-based studies are often conducted using a multi-level framework, that is, the importance of individual, team and organisational factors are taken into consideration. In using good research designs, combined with sophisticated multivariate analyses and statistical modelling, Occupational Psychologists are able to work out causality between variables. This is particularly important in evaluation research so that we can establish direct links between, for example, stress management interventions and employee well-being.

It is true that much of our work in practice can, and is, done by HR professionals or management consultants – for instance, the design of selection systems, change management interventions, design of training or performance management systems to name but a few. This means that, if we list the roles that Occupational Psychologists occupy, and the interventions and projects that we undertake within organisations, the list would potentially be very similar to that of other disciplines. This can make it quite hard for clients, and for those unfamiliar with Occupational Psychology, to see where our unique place in the market lies.

From the insights above, it is clear that it may not be the *work itself* that is unique but rather *our approach* to that work – in other words how we go about addressing an issue or a need in an organisation. Where other disciplines may follow a case study or use a process that they have used in the past, we will base our work on empirical evidence and theory – and in so doing, be able to recommend the most effective methodology. This is perfectly put by Dr Maire Kerrin, Director of the Work Psychology Group:

‘ I think our USP has got to be to do with the word 'psychology', it's what gets people interested when we talk about our work. Our major challenge though is that HR and management consultants often do what we Occupational Psychologists do, and HR/ Management consultants can talk with a lot of credibility around some of the areas in which we work. However, I really do think that one of the things that we do as Occupational Psychologists is that we can take a theory, collect data and test the theory, making links between variables and so on. Essentially we work out a hypothesis and then test it. HR and management consultants don't do this – they often use case studies as examples of their work, whereas we are using our strong evidence base to inform our decisions. ’

Summary

This chapter started with a brief overview of the history of Occupational Psychology in the UK, finishing with some of the key changes that have taken place in the work environment into the 21st century. We then considered how the research and practice in Occupational Psychology has been impacted as a result of these changes. We briefly introduced what Occupational Psychology is today, and this will be expanded on in Chapter 2. Finally, we ended the chapter with some ideas as to the unique selling point of Occupational Psychology and how this might differentiate the area from others such as human resources and management consultancy.

Explore further

- Shimmin, S. and Wallis, D. (1994) *Fifty years of Occupational Psychology in Britain.* Leicester: British Psychological Society. This can be downloaded from the BPS website (and is free if you are a member of the BPS): http://www.bpsshop.org.uk/Fifty-Years-of-Occupational-Psychology-in-Britain-P1435.aspx

---
Discussion questions
---

1 What do you perceive as the most significant changes in the working environment since the middle of the last century?
2 Think about what working life might have been like without email and computers – in what ways would it be different? How would it be easier or harder to conduct a day-to-day job?
3 How would you describe the field of Occupational Psychology to a friend?

References

Anderson, N., Herriot, P. and Hodgkinson, G. (2001) 'The practitioner–researcher divide in industrial, work and organisational (IWO) psychology: where are we now, and where do we go from here?', *Journal of Occupational and Organisational Psychology*, 74 (4): 391–411.

Anderson, N., Lievens, F., van Dam, K. and Ryan, A.M. (2004) 'Future perspectives on employee selection: key directions for future research and practice', *Applied Psychology*, 53 (4): 487–501.

BERR (2008) Small and Medium Enterprise Statistics for the UK and Regions. http://stats.berr.gov.uk/ed/sme/smestats2007-ukspr.pdf (accessed 23 September 2011).

Bradley, H., Erickson, M., Stephenson, C. and Williams, S. (2000) *Myths at Work*. Oxford: Blackwell.

Brough, P. and O'Driscoll, M.P. (2010) 'Organisational interventions for balancing work and home demands: an overview', *Work & Stress*, 24 (3): 280–97.

Cascio, W.F. and Aguinis, H. (2008) 'Research in industrial and organisational psychology from 1963 to 2007: changes, choices, and trends', *Journal of Applied Psychology*, 93 (5): 1062–81.

Conway, N. and Briner, R.B. (2005) *Understanding Psychological Contracts At Work: A Critical Evaluation of Theory and Research*. Oxford: Oxford University Press.

Emery, F.E. and Thorsrud, E. (1976) *Democracy at Work: The Report of the Norwegian Industrial Democracy Program*. Leiden: Nijhoff Social Sciences Division.

Frisby, C. (1970) 'The development of industrial psychology at the NIIP', *Occupational Psychology*, 44: 35–50.

Gajendran, R.S. and Harrison, D.A. (2007) 'The good, the bad, and the unknown about telecommuting: meta-analysis of psychological mediators and individual consequences', *Journal of Applied Psychology*, 92 (6): 1524–41.

Goleman, D. (1998) *Working with Emotional Intelligence*. London: Bloomsbury.

Guest, D.E. (1998) 'Is the psychological contract worth taking seriously?', *Journal of Organisational Behavior*, 19: 649–64.

Guest, D.E. (2004) 'The psychology of the employment relationship: an analysis based on the psychological contract', *Applied Psychology*, 53 (4): 541–55.

Guest, D.E. (2006) 'In praise of contemporary occupational psychology: a response to Kwiatkowski, Duncan and Shimmin', *Journal of Occupational and Organisational Psychology*, 79 (2): 207–11.

Hearnshaw, L. (1964) *A Short History of British Psychology: 1840–1940*. Oxford: Barnes and Noble.

Herriot, P. and Anderson, N. (1997) 'Selecting for change: how will personnel and selection psychology survive', in P. Herriot and N. Anderson (eds) *International Handbook of Selection and Assessment*. Chichester: Wiley-Blackwell. pp. 1–34.

Hodgkinson, G., Herriot, P. and Anderson, N. (2001) 'Re-aligning the stakeholders in management research: lessons from industrial, work and organisational psychology', *British Journal of Management*, 12 (S1): S41–S48.

Jones, A., Herriot, P., Long, B. and Drakeley, R. (1991) 'Attempting to improve the validity of a well-established assessment centre', *Journal of Occupational Psychology*, 64 (1): 1–21.

Kersley, B., Alpin, C., Forth, J., Bryson, A., Bewley, H., Dix, G. and Oxenbridge, (2004) *First Findings from the 2004 Workplace Employment Relations Survey*. London: Routledge.

Kwiatkowski, R., Duncan, D.C. and Shimmin, S. (2006) 'What have we forgotten and why?', *Journal of Occupational and Organisational Psychology*, 79: 183–201.

Landy, F.J. and Conte, J.M. (2009) *Work in the 21st Century: An Introduction to Industrial and Organisational Psychology*, Vol. 3. Hoboken, NJ: Wiley-Blackwell.

Lewin, K. (1954) 'Group decision and social change', in G.E. Swanson, T.N. Newcomb and E.L. Hartley (eds), *Readings in Social Psychology*. New York: Holt, Rinehart, and Winston. pp. 459–73.

Lievens, F., van Dam, K. and Anderson, N. (2002) 'Recent trends and challenges in personnel selection', *Personnel Review*, 31 (5–6): 580–601.

Loughlin, C. and Barling, J. (2001) 'Young workers' work values, attitudes, and behaviours', *Journal of Occupational and Organisational Psychology*, 74 (4): 543–58.

Marwick, A. (1982) 'Print, pictures, and sound: the Second World War and the British experience', *Daedalus*, 111 (4): 135–55.

Michaels, E., Handfield-Jones, H. and Axelrod, B. (2001) *The War for Talent*. Boston, MA: Harvard Business School Press.

Michie, S. and West, M.A. (2004) 'Managing people and performance: an evidence based framework applied to health service organisations', *International Journal of Management Reviews*, 5–6 (2): 91–111.

Miles, G.H. (1928) 'The wide scope of psychology. In how psychology enters into the institute's factory investigations – a symposium', *Journal of the National Institute of Industrial Psychology*, 4 (1): 3–17.

Murray, H. (1990) 'The transformation of selection procedures: the War Office Selection Boards', in E. Trist and H. Murray (eds), *The Social Engagement of Social Science*. London: Tavistock Institute. pp. 45–67.

Myers, C.S. (1920) 'Psychology and industry', *British Journal of Psychology*, 10: 177–82.

Myers, C.S. (1937) *In the Realm of Mind*. Cambridge: Cambridge University Press.

Nelson, D. (1971) *Bibliography of British Psychological Research, 1960–1966*. London: HMSO.

Patterson, F. (2001) 'Developments in work psychology: emerging issues and future trends', *Journal of Occupational and Organisational Psychology*, 74 (4): 381–90.

Patterson, F. (2002) 'Great minds don't think alike? Person-level predictors of innovation at work', *International Review of Industrial and Organisational Psychology*, 17: 115–44.

Patterson, F., Baron, H., Carr, V., Plint, S. and Lane, P. (2009) 'Evaluation of three short-listing methodologies for selection into postgraduate training in general practice', *Medical Education*, 43 (1): 50–57.

Poissonnet, C.M. and Veron, M. (2000) 'Health effects of work schedules in healthcare professions', *Journal of Clinical Nursing*, 9 (1): 13–23.

Rose, M. (1975) *Industrial Behaviour: Theoretical Development since Taylor*. London: Allen Lane.

Rousseau, D.M. (2001) 'Schema, promise and mutuality: the building blocks of the psychological contract', *Journal of Occupational and Organisational Psychology*, 74 (4): 511–41.

Shimmin, S. and Wallis, D. (1994) *Fifty Years of Occupational Psychology in Britain*. Leicester: British Psychological Society.

Silvester, J. and Dykes, C. (2007) 'Selecting political candidates: a longitudinal study of assessment centre performance and political success in the 2005 UK general election', *Journal of Occupational and Organisational Psychology*, 80 (1): 11–25.

Sparks, K., Faragher, B. and Cooper, C.L. (2001) 'Well-being and occupational health in the 21st century workplace', *Journal of Occupational and Organisational Psychology*, 74 (4): 489–509.

Trist, E., Higgin, G., Murray, H. and Pollock, A. (1963) *Organisational Choice: Capabilities of Groups at the Coalface Under Changing Technologies*. London: Tavistock Publications.

Vernon, P.E. and Parry, J.B. (1949) *Personnel Selection in the British Forces*. London: University of London Press.

Wilkinson, A. Dundon, T. Marchington, M. and Ackers, P. (2001) 'Changing patterns of employee voice: case studies from the UK and Republic of Ireland', *Journal of Industrial Relations*, 46 (3): 298–322.

Wyatt, M.R.R., Pathak, S.B. and Zibarras, L. (2010) 'Advancing selection in an SME: is best practice methodology applicable?', *International Small Business Journal*, 28 (3): 258–73.

Wyatt, S. and Western, H.C. (1920) 'A performance test under industrial conditions', *British Journal of Psychology*, 10 (4): 293–309.

2 What are Occupational Psychologists?

Lara Zibarras and Rachel Lewis

Learning outcomes

On completion of this chapter you should:

- have an overview of what Occupational Psychologists are and where they work;
- appreciate the importance of ethics in Occupational Psychology research and practice;
- understand the areas of knowledge that underpin Occupational Psychology;
- appreciate the options for studying Occupational Psychology and the route to becoming a chartered Occupational Psychologist;
- be able to identify whether the route to chartership is the right option for you;
- have an overview of the types of skills needed to become an Occupational Psychologist.

Introduction

The aim of this chapter is to provide you with an overview of what Occupational Psychologists are. We hope to bring this to life through 'day in the life' quotes which will give you a flavour of the types of work that Occupational Psychologists do. You will also find further information about this at the end of each chapter in Part II, just before the References section. We will also outline how you can begin the process of becoming a chartered Occupational Psychologist, first through gaining relevant knowledge and then through applying this in practice. Finally, we outline some of the key skills you will need in order to become an Occupational Psychologist or work in a related area.

What are Occupational Psychologists? What do they do?

As you will have seen in Chapter 1, the field of Occupational Psychology has become increasingly broad with many different and complex topic areas. It touches on a range of different areas from personnel selection, ergonomics and organisational change and development. As such, you will often find that Occupational Psychologists tend to specialise in one or a few areas of research or practice.

Broadly, Occupational Psychology is concerned with people at work and how employees, teams and organisations function. Therefore Occupational Psychologists apply psychological theories in a real-life context to issues in the workplace. Often the aim is to increase organisational effectiveness and ensure the satisfaction of people at work. Work can be in consultant and advisory roles, teaching and research roles, and in some cases more technical or administrative roles.

So what might a typical day of an Occupational Psychologist be? The quotes here are examples of a 'day in the life of' from two practitioners and one academic.

Professor Rob Briner, Professor of Organizational Psychology, University of Bath

'The research part of my job might be done almost anywhere at any time: From a conference to a coffee shop to train or a plane. A lot of research work involves reading, thinking and writing so a laptop and internet access is often all that's required. Typical research-related tasks include collecting and analysing data, negotiating access to organizations, writing and revising papers for publication, acting as a reviewer for peer-review journals, preparing conference presentations, writing grant applications, talking to practitioners, and so on. The teaching part of my job is more physically and temporally fixed. Lectures tend to be in lecture theatres though a lot of research supervision takes place elsewhere and often via Skype and email.'

Alastair Wallace, Managing Director at Brainfood Ltd

'There is not really a typical day for me! Let me give you a flavour of a typical week instead which should give you a clearer idea of the type of work that I do and the sheer diversity. On Monday I facilitated a workshop with a small communications agency in London to help them think through the requirements and key performance indicators for their new ERP (enterprise resource planning) system. Quite challenging as the group are very senior and have very definite ideas about what they want! On Tuesday I was working from home. Completing the design of a performance appraisal system, and then process mapping the employee and manager's journey before designing an interactive training session to communicate and test it out. On Wednesday and Thursday, I flew to Nice to deliver a two-day conflict management training course for a large IT firm. Twelve delegates from eight different countries – varying abilities of spoken English! I wrote up the evaluation report and course refinements on the flight home. On Friday I was carrying out psychometric assessments for a large international drinks manufacturer and giving feedback as part of a development centre." '

Dr Maire Kerrin, Director at Work Psychology Group

' This really varies from day to day. It could be that in the morning I am office based where I have a team meeting, then perhaps a meeting with the accountant, or finance or HR, and then in the afternoon I'm at a client like Saint Gobain where I'm giving one to one feedback to senior managers, and then I'm back in the office writing a tender or a proposal for an organisation. There really is no typical day, but I guess my role in the organisation is that I have some internally focused activities and also some outward-focused activities. Also within our organisation there is a cyclical nature to our business where certain times of year are particularly busy, for example, September to November and then January to March. That's because we do a lot of repeat work with clients who have recruitment and selection rounds at these times of year so we have a particularly busy time organising and running these activities. But overall, it's really different from day to day. '

Where do Occupational Psychologists work?

Work opportunities exist for Occupational Psychologists in a broad range of companies including both the public and private sectors. It is likely that salaries will vary enormously depending on the type of job role. Most Occupational Psychologists work within one of four job settings:

1 As an internal consultant (whereby they work for one organisation within that organisation) in large private companies (such as Royal Bank of Scotland, Ford or Boots), or government and public services. In the UK, the Civil Service is one of the largest employers of Occupational Psychologists, including the Home Office, the Department for Work and Pensions and Ministry of Defence. Within this, Occupational Psychologists may work alongside other professionals, such as human resources, training managers and specialists from the organisation or particular industry in which they are working.

2 As an external consultant, meaning that they work for a consultancy but within a range of different organisations and environments. In this, the Occupational Psychologist will be delivering projects and solutions for a number of different clients from both the public and private sector. They will work for consultancies that range from large test publishers (such as SHL or OPP), to smaller private consultancies (such as the Hay Group, Saville Consulting, Pearn Kandola, Work Psychology Group or Affinity Health at Work). Often consultancies will specialise in the type of projects they undertake and work they do for clients – for instance, the Work Psychology Group are specialists in selection and assessment solutions and Affinity Health at Work are specialists in occupational health.

3 As an independent practitioner – either as an associate (where you work on temporary contracts for other consultancies or organisations), as a sole trader (where you work under your name) or as a limited company (where you have set up your own consultancy). In actual fact, the vast majority of Occupational Psychologists fall within this bracket.

4 As an academic/researcher. This could be as a lecturer in a psychology department or business school, or it could be in a number of research roles that may or may not be within a university. Examples include researchers within organisations such as The Work Foundation, or IES.

Why aren't Occupational Psychologists always called Occupational Psychologists in their job roles?

Although you may be an Occupational Psychologist by profession, for only a minority does their job title actually reflects this. Within organisations, it is very rare for there to be an actual Occupational Psychology team or department. Occupational Psychologists who work internally tend to work within human resources or assessment services or business strategy – or within a variety of other organisational functions or services. As a result, we tend to occupy 'other' titles more commonly; for instance human resources manager, head of talent, assessment services manager, learning and development manager, director of engagement, and so on. It may be that the HR manager that deals with you during a selection process for an organisation is actually an Occupational Psychologist by training or profession.

Further, you may often find that within consultancies (even specialist Occupational Psychology consultancies) Occupational Psychologists are called work psychologists, organisational psychologists or business psychologists. This reflects the fact that, for those that are not familiar with our profession, there is often a confusion in terms between Occupational Psychologists and occupational therapists (who do VERY different types of work), and therefore using 'work', 'organisational' and 'business' can improve clarity for clients.

It is really important to state at this point that 'Occupational Psychologist' is a protected title. As Occupational Psychologists, we are regulated under the Health Professions Council or HPC (as are doctors, for example). In order to use the title 'Occupational Psychologist' we must be registered with the HPC and as such be registered psychologists. How you become a registered psychologist is explored later in this chapter, but in short it involves going through a process of work experience (which may be paid or unpaid) called the chartership process after you have completed your Masters in Occupational Psychology. The chartership process is run by the BPS. Once the chartership process has been completed and passed, individuals are then able to register as an Occupational Psychologist with the HPC. This is also a key factor explaining why the term Occupational Psychologist is less common than you might expect in the world of work. What it does mean is that if you see someone using the title Occupational Psychologist, you can be assured that they have attained a high standard of performance and experience in their profession.

What skills do I need to become an Occupational Psychologist?

It is important to remember that you will not graduate from your MSc with the full skill set needed to be an Occupational Psychologist. This skill set will be something that you develop over time. It is possible that during your MSc you will learn some of the technical skills needed, such as how to conduct a job analysis, a critical incident interview or focus group, and also many of the research skills you will need (this will be explained in more detail in Chapter 3). However, it is likely that you will continue to develop your skill set as you continue your training as an Occupational Psychologist and work within the field. It is also probable that you will need some important skills, such as team work and critical thinking skills. The following is a brief overview of some that are likely to be useful and the following quotes outline some of the skills put forward when key Occupational Psychologists were asked what skills are needed.

Emma Donaldson-Feilder, Independent Practitioner, Director of Affinity Health at Work

'
A reflective practice and continuing to learn from both one's own professional experience and the literature (research, theory, models, others' experience, case studies, etc.). '

Professor Ivan Robertson, Professor of Organisational Psychology, Leeds University Business School and Director of Robertson Cooper Ltd

'
Keeping up to date with research is an important aspect of being a good OP. A good grasp of up to date research methods and data analysis procedures is essential as well – achieving this involves continuous training, reading and development. I also feel that developing a good appreciation of business skills and consulting skills is also something that is useful regardless of what specific role someone holds. '

To some extent the level of technical skills that you will need will depend on the area in which you specialise. However, some practical or technical Occupational Psychology skills might include: interviewing skills; the use of the 'ORCE' model for assessing purposes – that is, observe, record, classify and evaluate; conducting focus groups; using stress audits or risk assessment tools; analysing survey data; conducting validation analyses and so on. You may have also gained your certificates in occupational testing, becoming a competent user in either cognitive ability type tests or personality type assessments. During your MSc it is likely that you will learn a range of quantitative and qualitative research skills, for example, you might learn how to design a questionnaire or run statistical analyses using SPSS (correlations and regressions). You might also develop your qualitative research skills, such as content and template analysis (these research skills will be explored further in Chapter 3). During your MSc you will learn how to critically evaluate theory, research and practice so that you can compare and contrast different approaches. This will be an important skill as you develop in the field of Occupational Psychology in order to make informed decisions about the type of methods and models you use. Being able to critically evaluate information will enhance your problem-solving abilities ensuring that you develop and evaluate options and implement appropriate solutions for your clients.

Professor Rob Briner, Professor of Organizational Psychology, School of Management, University of Bath

'I think Occupational Psychologists need to develop skills in three areas. First, a much deeper level of critical thinking: critical thinking about research, about their own practice, and the problems and issues they see in organizations. Second, skills around reviewing and using existing research evidence is essential: in particular learning the skills required to undertake systematic reviews of existing evidence that address practice questions of relevance to organizations. Third, the data analysis skills necessary for making sense of the often large quantities of data organizations already have but don't use to help make informed and evidence-based decisions.'

Related to this, it will be important as a practitioner to keep up to date with the latest research in your area. As outlined in Chapter 1, Occupational Psychology advocates the use of the scientist-practitioner model. This is because scientific (psychological) research often stems from real-life practical issues in organisations; also, practice would have no accountability unless it was based on scientific research and theories. As Anderson et al. (2001) maintain, Occupational Psychologists should strive for *pragmatic science*, which has a rigorous and theoretically informed basis, while being relevant to practice.

It is extremely likely that during your career you will work in multidisciplinary teams. As we mentioned earlier in this chapter, Occupational Psychologists may work alongside other professionals, such as human resources and training managers, and specialists from the organisation or particular industry in which they are working, thus they need to develop good team working skills. You will also need to communicate effectively with a wide range of audiences – both in terms of written and spoken interactions with others. As discussed above, most psychologists work as consultants, and therefore consultancy skills such as negotiation and sales skills, report writing and analysis are absolutely essential.

Finally, and perhaps most importantly, it is also important for Occupational Psychologists to develop a reflective practice so that they can critically and constructively reflect upon their own professional, intellectual and personal development within the context of their Occupational Psychology training.

Table 2.1   Examples of core skills needed to work as an Occupational Psychologist

Critical Thinking Skills: ability to use logic and reasoning to identify the strengths/weaknesses of different solutions, conclusions or approaches to problems
Problem Solving Skills: ability to identify problems, review related information and to develop/evaluate options and implement solutions
Consultancy Skills: ability to work through a consultancy cycle from negotiating agreements with the client; to identifying and analysing the needs and problems in a project; to developing, implementing and reviewing solutions; and finally to reporting, reflecting and evaluating outcomes
Communication skills: communicating (both speaking and writing) effectively to a different range of audiences
Data management and analysis skills (e.g., knowledge of SPSS and/or qualitative research)
Scientist-practitioner model: using evidence-based research to inform practice and solve problems
Working with people: ability to work effectively in a team and build positive relationships with clients and colleagues
Planning and organising: ability to think and plan ahead, to prioritise and manage time effectively
Active listening skills: give full attention to what others are saying, taking time to understand the points being made, asking questions as appropriate, and not interrupting
Relevant technical skills (depending on level and area of expertise) such as: Test User certificates in occupational testing, interviewing skills, use of stress audits or risk assessment tools; analysing survey data; conducting validation analyses and so on

Where does ethics fit into the work that Occupational Psychologists do?

Early British applied psychology was humanistic in orientation and respect for human dignity was thought to be of great importance. In fact, the National Institute of Industrial Psychology NIIP (which we discussed in Chapter 1) pioneered joint consultation involving users and customers in the evaluation of services. This is often thought of as a recent invention (Kwiatkowski et al., 2006).

In recent years, attention has been turned to focus on values and ethical considerations in research and professional practice. It has been argued that Occupational Psychologists are morally and ethically bound to use their expertise to promote the well-being of individuals and their work-based communities (Shimmin and Wallis, 1994). However, one might contend that since it is often private organisations or public authorities that pay for the professional services of an Occupational Psychologist, it is unavoidable that their interests may take precedence over other social and ethical considerations. However, these two objectives are not necessarily incompatible and it is important that responsible researchers and practitioners find solutions for clients that are advantageous to both the people at work and management alike.

As highlighted by both Professor Ivan Robertson and Professor Fiona Patterson, ethics is integral to the work conducted by Occupational Psychologists.

Professor Ivan Robertson, Director of Robertson Cooper Ltd and Professor of Organisational Psychology, Leeds University Business School

‘ Ethical issues are so central to the work of Occupational Psychologists that they are embedded in our everyday work. Maintaining the confidentiality of individual data, trying to ensure that organisations tackle human behaviour issues in an ethical and professional way, recognising the boundaries and limitations of one's own professional competence – and many other ethically loaded issues are part and parcel of the everyday work of a practicing Occupational Psychologist. ’

Professor Fiona Patterson, University of Cambridge and Director, Work Psychology Group

‘ From a research perspective, everything I do requires ethical approval via various ethics committees, whether that is at the university level or NHS level and so on. As a team at Work Psychology Group, it is central to everything we do; our values are about professionalism and integrity. We also encourage people to become chartered as I strongly believe that this validates your practice. The important aspect of ethics at work is *who* the client is; in large change programs it's often important to protect the rights of individuals. ’

Occupational Psychologists may be faced with ethical dilemmas arising from the conflicting expectations of a psychologist's differing relationships with employees, managers and sponsors and the politics within the organisation itself (Mirvis and Seashore, 1982). Therefore, it is really important that all Occupational

Psychologists adhere to the BPS's Code of Professional Conduct. The Code of Conduct is outlined in greater detail in Chapter 3, and it covers issues such as confidentiality, attitude and behaviours towards clients. In Chapter 3, you will also have an opportunity to explore some ethical issues that you might come across when working in practice.

As you develop as an Occupational Psychologist you will learn that how you deal with questions of values or ethics sits solely with you as the individual researcher or practitioner. Below, Sarah Lewis explains the importance of ethics to her as a practitioner. In Chapter 3 we go into more detail on specific issues you need to be aware of when working in practice.

Sarah Lewis, Managing Director at Appreciating Change

'A clear ethical stance and understanding is very important to me in the work that I do. What I do is not a value free exercise; it is not neutral and un-impactful: I intend to have an effect and I intend for that effect to be benevolent. This means I need to know what I am evaluating my actions against, for example I must have a sense of the ethical bounds of my work. In general terms I would say that, as psychologists, we have powerful knowledge and tools at our disposal. What we say and do affects people's emotional state, sense of self and identity, and their levels of motivation. In organisational terms we interfere with dynamics and relationships that people have to continue to work within after we have moved on to the next assignment. This responsibility needs to be constrained and informed by a clear ethical framework.'

How do I become an Occupational Psychologist?

If you want to become a registered Occupational Psychologist there is only currently (in 2012) one route open to you. This involves first becoming chartered by completing the chartership process with the BPS, and, upon successful completion, registering with the HPC. If you want to go down this route, you need to follow these steps.

Step 1: Obtain a BPS accredited BSc or BA in Psychology (check the BPS website for which courses are accredited).
Step 2: Obtain a BPS accredited MSc in Occupational Psychology (again, details are on the BPS website).

Step 3: Enrol and proceed through the chartership process (QOccPsych) with the BPS in order to become a full division member.
Step 4: Enrol to become a Registered Occupational Psychologist with the HPC.

Details of each step in this route are explained later in the chapter.

Do I need to become a registered and/or chartered Occupational Psychologist?

Prior to 1970 there was no register of Occupational Psychologists working in the field. However, it was thought that the professional standards of Occupational Psychologists were being threatened by the unprofessional practices of those claiming to be able to offer psychological advice; and there was also concern about misrepresentation of psychology in the media (Shimmin and Wallis, 1994).

Currently, it is thought that chartership provides a dual purpose by not only protecting the public (from potential unprofessional practice), but also in helping build public confidence in the profession. Attaining chartered status provides confidence that the individual has reached a high level of competence relating to knowledge-base and skills, and has achieved the BPS standard to practice independently and without supervision. In fact, the title 'Occupational Psychologist' can only be used if you have chartered status and are a full member of the DOP and registered with the HPC. Many consider that it is important and beneficial for people working within the field of Occupational Psychology to work towards chartered status. Figure 2.1 outlines some of the key reasons why chartership may be beneficial to you.

Having said this, not everyone will decide that becoming chartered is for them. For those students that decide to pursue a non-accredited MSc route, it is still possible to work in the field of Occupational Psychology, without being chartered. If you think back to earlier in this chapter, we outlined some of the places where Occupational Psychologists work and what types of job they do.

We must stress that many career routes are still open to those without chartership, so you could end up working in recruitment and selection, talent management, employee relations and so on, without having gained chartership status. Also many students (in fact the majority of students) that *have* completed an accredited MSc decide not to progress through the chartership process. You may use Figure 2.1 to decide for yourself whether it is something you would like to pursue. Whatever direction you choose, your work will be greatly enhanced by the theoretical knowledge gained during your MSc course.

For international students, or UK-based students who decide to move abroad, you may question whether chartership is a worthwhile pursuit if you were to practice abroad. In Figure 2.2 we outline briefly the routes to work as an Occupational Psychologist in both Europe and the USA.

Potential benefits to Chartership	Possible reasons you may choose not to become Chartered
Only by being chartered can you go on to become a Registered Psychologist with the HPC (the regulatory body for Psychologists).	The option is not open to you (i.e. did not complete an accredited undergraduate degree in Psychology and/or accredited Masters).
In some organisations, Chartership is a necessary requisite for working above a certain level as an Occupational Psychologist.	You work within a role where Chartership is not seen as important or essential. Note, this would not just apply to less 'psychology' roles like HR advisor or Learning and Development manager, but very often applies even in Business Psychology consultancies.
For some organisational contracts (particularly public sector), the stipulations of the tender may be that only registered (i.e Chartered) psychologists can work on the contract.	Many clients do not know what Chartership is, and therefore it is not seen as advantageous. Ask your peers and relevant contacts in organisations what they know of the Chartership process or whether they know the possible difference between a registered Occupational Psychologist and a business psychologist.
You are likely to be recognised as competent by employers and potential clients.	Chartership is an expensive process and, without organisational support, many individuals may find the costs involved make the process untenable.
Chartership often comes with additional remuneration (i.e. you may be paid more).	In order to become Chartered, work experience must have been gained (in the main) in the UK. With increasing globalisation, this makes collecting enough work experience difficult for some.
Many practising psychologists acknowledge increased self-confidence and self-efficacy having attained this status.	The process is very time-consuming and therefore takes a high level of personal motivation to complete.
It may be a requirement in order to apply for a professional/practitioner doctorate in Occupational Psychology.	
Without a PhD, it is often seen as an acceptable qualification in order to practice in the US or in other countries.	

Figure 2.1 Should I become Chartered ... or not?

Europe – EuroPsy	USA
• In 2010, EuroPsy was implemented in Europe, having been established by the European Federation of Psychologists' Associations (EFPA). • Essentially, it is the European qualification standard for psychologists awarded only to psychologists who meet a specific list of educational/professional requirements. • The requirements to gain EuroPsy include a University degree in psychology of at least 5 years and at least 1 year of supervised practice. • Applicants must also sign a statement to declare that they will act in accordance with the ethical rules of the profession. • Its main purpose is to facilitate cross-border services for psychologists, while guaranteeing a certain level of professional competence to clients. • However, note that it does not necessarily allow psychologists to *practice* in other counties, but rather it is a European directive that aims to harmonise requirements. However, individual countries may set their own rules regarding practice and so may have certain restrictions regarding whether or not you may practice in that particular country. • To learn more about EuroPsy, go to this link: http://www.efpa.eu/europsy.	• In the USA, you will normally find that someone who calls themselves an Industrial-Organisational (I-O) Psychologist is someone who has completed a PhD. • However, PhD programmes in the USA are generally more structured than they are in the UK, with specific taught components, such as human performance, job evaluation, organisation theory, data analysis and so on. • It is possible to do a Master's level programme in I-O psychology in the USA; however, these are either considered as pre-doctoral training or as practitioner oriented training where the person may work in an organisational setting, but without the I-O psychologist title. (Note that this is similar to the situation here in the UK as outlined on page 28.) • A key difference then between the two routes, as highlighted by the Society for Industrial and Organisational Psychology (SIOP) is that those on doctoral training will be *producers* of knowledge; while those on the Masters training will be consumers of knowledge. • To find out more, the SIOP website outlines these two routes in detail here: http://www.siop.org/gtp/

Figure 2.2   Routes to becoming an Occupational Psychologist in Europe and the USA

Chartership in the UK – the process explained

Note that this section is applicable only to those of you who would like to become a registered and/or chartered Occupational Psychologist.

Recently, there have been some changes to the route into Occupational Psychology. It is possible that changes will continue and so it is worth checking relevant websites in case there are further changes to this process. A key website to visit is the BPS website, specifically their section on careers, education and training. Nevertheless, as it stands presently, in order to become a chartered member of the BPS through the Occupational Psychology training route, you will first need the following qualifications.

Graduate basis for chartered membership (GBC)

You can achieve this by completing an undergraduate psychology degree or a conversion course in psychology that is accredited by the BPS. In order to check if the degree you are interested in is accredited, you can search through the BPS website using the following link: http://www.bps.org.uk/bpslegacy/ac.

Then, you must show competence in the *knowledge dimensions* of Occupational Psychology. You can do this either via an accredited MSc in Occupational Psychology or Stage 1 of the BPS's qualification in Occupational Psychology. Both these are outlined below:

Masters in Occupational Psychology

This must also be accredited by the BPS and there are a number of different universities in the UK that offer accredited MSc courses in Occupational Psychology. However, do note that different universities label their accredited courses in different ways. Some might be called 'MSc in Occupational Psychology' while others might be labelled 'MSc in organisational psychology'. Note that for a course to be accredited it does not have to be called Occupational Psychology and a course in Occupational Psychology is not necessarily accredited. Non-accredited MSc degrees might also be offered, such as 'work psychology', 'business psychology' or 'organisational behaviour'; however doing an accredited course is a pre-requisite for becoming a chartered Occupational Psychologist and so it is always worth checking first to find out whether the course you are interested in is BPS accredited. Again, this can be checked via the BPS website at the same link provided previously.

Different universities and MSc courses will have slightly different entry requirements (for example, some might stipulate a minimum of a 2.1 or higher from an undergraduate degree course and others might require previous work experience). Additionally, some courses may offer one-year, full-time or two-year, part-time courses (or both), and still other courses might offer distance learning opportunities. Your preference for these different options is likely to depend on your personal circumstances; but some students may prefer to do a part-time course so that they can work alongside the course, while others may prefer the flexibility offered by distance learning courses.

Stage 1 of the qualification in Occupational Psychology

This is termed 'QOccPsych Stage 1' and further details can be found on the BPS website (specific links can be found on our companion website). This qualification is assessed by a series of examinations, divided into eight written papers and a research dimension, which focus on the eight knowledge areas of Occupational Psychology. You can register for this process via the BPS.

Both the MSc and the QOccPsych Stage 1 are underpinned by the eight areas of Occupational Psychology which are collectively known as the *Knowledge Dimensions* of the QOccPsych (Stage 1). The titles of the eight chapters in Part II of this book follow these eight areas. This book's structure is designed to facilitate your understanding of the areas of Occupational Psychology as we outlined in Chapter 1.

Competence is also assessed in *research*, since Occupational Psychology is evidence-based and has its roots in science (this idea is elaborated further in Chapter 3). This is achieved either via the MSc or Stage 1 QOccPsych as both contain elements of research methods and statistics. Essentially either option will require you to demonstrate: knowledge of psychological research within Occupational Psychology; an ability to critically evaluate research literature and competence in theory development, hypothesis testing; and data analysis (either qualitative and quantitative analyses).

Becoming a chartered Occupational Psychologist

After you have completed your MSc or QOccPsych Stage 1, it is necessary to complete further professional development. This is called the Stage 2 of the qualification in Occupational Psychology (or 'QOccPsych Stage 2') and further details can be found on the BPS website and our companion website.

QOccPsych Stage 2 requires a minimum of two years supervised practice under a chartered Occupational Psychologist supervisor. Supervised practice is designed so that a trainee Occupational Psychologist can develop the knowledge and skills required to become competent to practice independently as an Occupational Psychologist. With support and guidance from your supervisor, as a trainee Occupational Psychologist you will:

- gain experiences of the realities of professional work;
- develop your practical skills;
- develop your ability to integrate theory with practice.

This approach emphasises the understanding and demonstration of good professional practice in research and consultancy whatever the setting. Note that your supervisor does not have to actually work in the same organisation as you; you will meet him or her on a regular basis, and it is through discussions and visits by your supervisor to your workplace (if you do not work in the same place) that the supervisor 'signs off' the work that you are doing, ensuring that it meets the criteria set out by the BPS.

So, what is the role of your supervisor? Your supervisor will be your main source of support during your training. They guide your work in progress, and offer advice on any potential training needs. They will observe your work, advise you on your logbook completion and general progress, help you to reflect on your learning and practice, and facilitate your integration of theory into practice. It is up to you to establish whether your supervisor is willing and able to hold supervisory events with you during each year (this should be at least quarterly), observe your practice and oversee preparation of your plan of training. Your supervisor should be able to give you appropriately detailed and prompt feedback for your logbook entries and/or progress reports.

In order to demonstrate your competence during Stage 2 of your training to be an Occupational Psychologist, you must keep a record of your practice, which will include reflections on your personal development and supervision within a structured logbook. Within your logbook you will have two main areas, a *breadth* component and a *depth* component. These are outlined in further detail below.

Breadth component

For your breadth component, you must gain practical experience and skill development in at least five of the eight knowledge dimensions (these are outlined on page 41). For each of the five knowledge dimensions you must submit a minimum of two logbook entries (therefore 10 entries or pieces of work) that follow all of the following *process skills*, against which you will be assessed.

- Gathering information or skill – for example, within the knowledge dimension of personnel selection and assessment, this might involve conducting a job analysis.
- Testing or analysing information or skill – for example, within the area of counselling and personal development, this might involve summarising and reflecting back something said by a client.
- Evaluating information or skill – for example, within the knowledge dimension of training, this might relate to developing training evaluation techniques.
- Applying information or skill – for example, within the area of employee relations and motivation, this might relate to conducting performance appraisals.

You need to complete and submit all your breadth entries before working on your depth entries.

Depth component

For your depth component you must submit at least two entries that show competence to practice independently in at least one of the four fields of practice relating to:

- work and the work environment;
- the individual;
- the organisation;
- training.

Note that these fields of practice map onto the eight knowledge dimensions, as outlined in Figure 2.3.

For logbook entries under your depth component you need to have applied all seven stages of the consultancy cycle within a single piece of work or project. The seven stages of the consultancy cycle are as follows:

1 establishing agreements with the customer;
2 identifying needs and problems;
3 analysing needs and problems;
4 formulating solutions;
5 implementing and reviewing solutions;
6 evaluating outcomes;
7 reporting and reflecting on outcomes.

This cycle demonstrates how in organisations Occupational Psychologists progress from establishing initial agreements with a customer or client, through to a diagnostic phase of identifying then analysing the needs and problems. This leads to formulation of the solutions, which are then implemented, reviewed and evaluated. See Box 2.1 for an example of how this might work in practice.

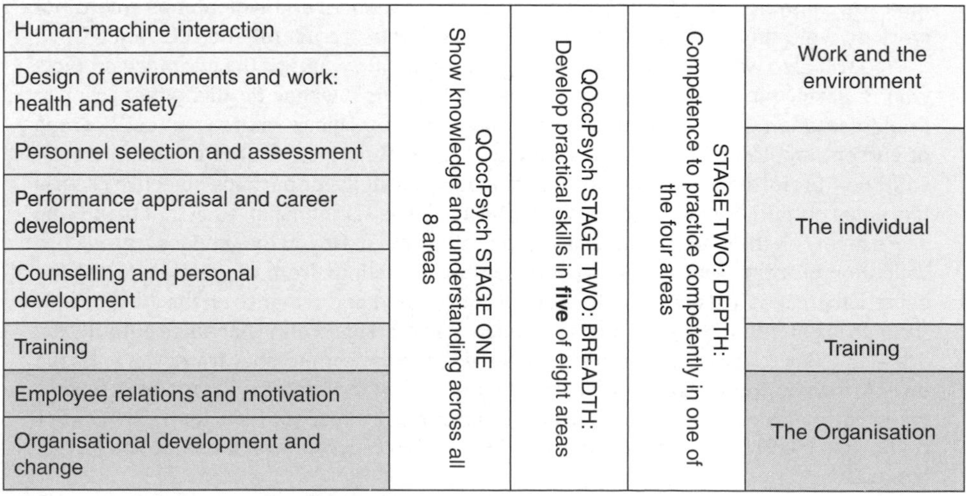

Human-machine interaction	QOccPsych STAGE ONE Show knowledge and understanding across all 8 areas	QOccPsych STAGE TWO: BREADTH: Develop practical skills in **five** of eight areas	STAGE TWO: DEPTH: Competence to practice competently in one of the four areas	Work and the environment
Design of environments and work: health and safety				
Personnel selection and assessment				The individual
Performance appraisal and career development				
Counselling and personal development				
Training				Training
Employee relations and motivation				The Organisation
Organisational development and change				

Figure 2.3 Eight knowledge areas of Occupational Psychology, and how they map onto Stages one and two of QOccPsych

Box 2.1

OP IN PRACTICE
Understanding the consultancy cycle

Imagine you were in the following situation:

You are part of a team of Occupational Psychologists who have been approached by an organisation that wants to develop a competency based interview as part of their selection process; it must reliably predict who will perform well in the organisation.

What would you do and how would you approach this? Let's go through the stages of the consultancy cycle to address this scenario. Through meetings with the managing director you might establish agreements regarding a budget and timing, specifying their requirements for the interview (stage 1). You might also identify that the current problem lies in the fact that the organisation has no standardised interview format to use for their sales team (stage 2). In starting to formulate solutions (stage 4), you may first do a number of analysis activities (stage 3) such as:

- review job profiles and person specifications;
- conduct job analyses interviews with the current sales team. You may also seek input from a variety of other sources (e.g. managers, direct reports, clients and so on);
- develop a competency framework;
- develop competency-based interview questions;
- develop marking criteria to assess the answers to the interview questions.

Before implementing the interview in a live selection process (stage 5), you might pilot the questions you have developed on a group of current employees. This will give you an indication of what interview questions work, and which ones might not work so well; and also whether the marking criteria are useful and relevant.

You will also want to review the process and evaluate whether the interview predicts who is performing well in the organisation (stage 6). You may do this either prior to implementation using a concurrent validation process. This is where you 'test' a group of current employees in the organisation by correlating their scores on the interview with their performance output (such as managerial ratings or perhaps objective criteria like sales output). Hopefully there should be a positive relationship, such that those who score highly on the interview also have high sales output. Or you may choose a predictive validation process. This is when you take interview ratings from candidates during the selection process and correlate these with subsequent performance on the job (possibly three to six months later; and again you might use manager ratings or sales output). You are also likely to review your findings against the initial competency framework. Based on your review and evaluation findings, you may adjust the process, competency framework, interviews or marking criteria. As the project ends, you will then report your results back to the organisation, possibly in a written report or oral presentation format (stage 7).

Finally, you and your colleagues should reflect on the process – what went well, what didn't go well and what would you improve in any future project? Essentially, what have you learnt from this process?

For both the breadth and the depth components, your logbook entries will also be assessed against generic skills and the Occupational Standards for Occupational Psychology. Across all your logbook entries you must show that you have acquired each of the following generic skills:

- questionnaire or survey design;
- interviewing;
- report writing;
- presentation skills;
- statistical or qualitative analysis skills;
- evaluation techniques.

Additionally, across all your logbook entries you must demonstrate how you have acquired the competencies as outlined by four key roles on practice outlined in the Occupational Standards. See Box 2.2 for further details.

Box 2.2

Occupational Standards, in candidate handbook: qualification in Occupational Psychology stage 2

The Occupational Standards identify competence in four Key Roles of practice as being common to all practising psychologists.

The four common Key Roles are used as a basis for the continuing professional development requirements for applied psychologists set by the Society and are to be maintained throughout professional life. Specifically, these denote the ability to:

1 develop, implement and maintain personal and professional standards and ethical practice;
2 apply psychological and related methods, concepts, models, theories and knowledge derived from reproducible research findings;
3 research and develop new and existing psychological methods, concepts, models, theories and instruments in psychology;
4 communicate psychological knowledge, principles, methods, needs and policy requirements.

Writing up your Structured Logbook

The body of your structured logbook entries should be prose accounts of what you actually did in the project or piece of work. It is extremely important that you demonstrate what theoretical framework you have used to inform your practice. You must also reflect on what you have learnt during the experience of the particular project. It is through these reflections that your journey towards increasing professional competence will be assessed. This is an important skill to develop for your lifelong reflective practice as a professional psychologist. It is also essential to consider and address any ethical issues that may have arisen from the piece of work. You will submit your logbooks to the BPS for assessment once a year. In Box 2.3 you will see an extract from an Occupational Psychologist in training's reflections on a specific project.

Box 2.3

OP IN PRACTICE
Reflections from an Occupational Psychologist in training (Antonio Pangallo)

Thinking about this training intervention, one of the main issues I faced was that trainees had varying skills and experience, which were not captured in the needs analysis. E.g. most of the delegates had identified training instruction as a training need, yet about a quarter of the group demonstrated well-developed instructional techniques. This made it difficult to pitch the training to the right level for the entire class, so sometimes I felt the material was either too easy or too hard for a small yet sizeable part of the class. It also meant that I was trying to tailor the training to address individual concerns where possible which interfered with the flow of the programme.

In order to address this issue, I raised this point with my client, to ensure that we re-visited our needs analysis process in future to gain more accurate information prior to training delivery. Whilst I understand my client's competing demands for project implementation, he expressed no real concern about this and I felt the training may have been viewed by my client as more of a 'tick box' exercise. This conflicted with my professional ethics and values, as I would like to be able to think that I am being hired to do a job well and that my client would respect my work enough to take on any feedback I have whilst engaged in the project. In order to address this concern, I thought it best to take more control of the project and in preparation for the next course, I asked my client to provide me with all pre-course questionnaires and a delegate profiles so that I would personally collate and analyse the results. In this instance, my client did the collation and analysis. I believe that this would give me the opportunity to mitigate risk in future courses, so that I can be more fully prepared and more closely meet participant needs.

Another issue I faced which was more ethical in nature was that there were at least three senior government officials appointed to the training for political rather than education purposes. The issue I faced however is that these participants proved to be quite challenging and did not wish to take part in any of the training. This created a divide in the class, and the behaviour of these senior officials was impacting how others in the class were behaving. For example there were constant interruptions, talking amongst themselves, taking phone calls during the training sessions. My dilemma was that as far as my client was concerned the presence of these individuals was good on a stakeholder level, however, it was not helping the training environment. I therefore had to make a decision as to how I would approach this issue ethically and sensitively. I chose to address this directly with the participants concerned in a non-threatening manner and explained (diplomatically) that it was critical for the success of the course that full participation was respected. I referred them back to the learning contract that the class had agreed on in the first session and explained to them that they were free to leave the course at any time they saw fit. This, surprisingly, created a shift in their attitude and it was evident by the end of day two that they were making a concerted effort to participate.

Once you have completed Stage 2 of the BPS Qualification in Occupational Psychology you will be able to use the title 'Occupational Psychologist' and for this you will need to be registered with the HPC (http://www.hpc-uk.org/).

Figure 2.4 shows the relationship between the BPS, HPC and DOP; it may be useful to explain a little more about the HPC and BPS's Division of Occupational Psychology (DOP):

- The DOP is an organisation representing its members. Its main role is to facilitate the continuous professional development of Occupational Psychologists (for example, through attendance of the annual DOP conference and 'learning a living' workshop sessions) and also to oversee the qualification in Occupational Psychology process.
- The HPC is a regulatory body with which psychologists have to register if they want to use the protected title of 'Occupational Psychologist'. The HPC publishes standards of proficiency for psychologists (Practitioner Psychologists, Standards of Proficiency, 2009) and this outlines expectations that are relevant to Occupational Psychologists.

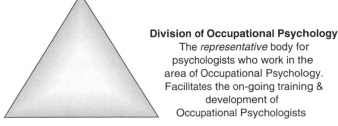

Health Professions Council
Regulatory body for psychologists.
Must be registered as a psychologist with HPC to use title
'Occupational Psychologist'

British Psychological Society
The *representative* body for
psychology and
psychologists in the UK.
Responsible for the promotion
and application of
psychology for public good.

Division of Occupational Psychology
The *representative* body for
psychologists who work in the
area of Occupational Psychology.
Facilitates the on-going training &
development of
Occupational Psychologists

Figure 2.4 Relationship between HPC, BPS and DOP

How can I get a job as an Occupational Psychologist?

In this section we make a few suggestions that will help to start your thinking about how to get a job as an Occupational Psychologist. We have also included some hints and tips from recent MSc graduates that might be helpful.

Antonio Pangallo

'Talk to as many existing contacts as you have got and participate in as many professional networks as you can ... offer your services voluntarily as a way of getting your foot in the door.'

Work experience is a good way to get a better idea and specific insight into a career in Occupational Psychology. In fact, you might have to work initially on a voluntary basis in order to gain enough experience to find paid work; but bear in mind that some voluntary work experience may turn into a paid job; or if not, it will look good on your CV.

Clare Robertson

'I recommend you sign up to the BPS Psychologist jobs alerts; also I found that a lot of recruitment consultants found me via LinkedIn. It is a fantastic networking tool and some companies advertise there that don't put adverts on the usual websites (e.g. Totaljobs).'

Clare Robertson

'Another tip would be to ensure you have keywords in your CV as I have been approached by people looking for someone with experience of a particular software package (like SPSS) or have a qualification, such as Occupational Test User certificates and have found these keywords in a CV search. Keep CVs brief. Typically a recruiter will only read the first couple of lines of each section of your CV, with the volume of applications so high they are ruthless. Make sure you prioritise the most important aspects of your role at the top – imagine they are only going to read two bullet points and ensure this summarises the majority of your responsibilities. Keep the length to no more than two pages.'

Additionally, many organisations that hire Occupational Psychologists also offer internships; these may be anything from one to six months and while you may not be paid particularly well (some places might offer a small stipend, that is, some small amount of remuneration plus travel expenses), this type of work will be invaluable. You could try and find work experience or internships by searching for Occupational Psychologists that work in your area using the Directory of Chartered Psychologists; if nothing else this will give you a good idea of the types of organisations in which Occupational Psychologists work. If you are a member of the BPS, you should receive the monthly magazine *The Psychologist*: this has a psychology appointments section that is also available online: http://www.psychapp.co.uk/.

Gemma Roberts

‘ Meet with as many recruitment consultants as possible so you have the opportunity to describe transferable skills (if you are trying to get into an area you haven't worked in before). Ultimately, they will be selling you to an organisation, so the more they know about what you can do, the better. ’

It is important to network with peers and other Occupational Psychologists. You may be surprised to hear this, but the world of Occupational Psychology is small, and many people may find jobs through word of mouth. A good way to network is by attending conferences and, when you do, it's important to get chatting to people so that you get your name and face known. Early in your career, a good conference to attend is the BPS postgraduate Occupational Psychology conference. It is tailored towards MSc students and recent graduates and provides an excellent opportunity to keep up to date with the latest research, listen to high profile keynote speakers and to attend relevant skills-based workshops. Additionally, the BPS regularly holds events and workshops aimed at supporting your professional development (see this link to identify events in your area: http://www.bps.org.uk/events/search). This is an excellent way to network and meet fellow psychologists.

Clare Robertson

‘ [K]eep an open mind in terms of what you apply for. Flexibility is important, particularly in a tough job market. I once applied for a job and although I wasn't right for it, the agency placed me in another role that was much more suited to my background and qualifications. Sometimes it's just about getting in front of a recruiter, making a good impression and building a relationship. Also, always ask for feedback from interviews, most companies will give you some time if you ask but may not always offer it outright. '

Gemma Roberts

' Start to build contacts during the recruitment process, you may be looking for another role in a few years and may be in a position to call on the contacts you have built up. '

It is also worth bearing in mind that very few people graduate from their MSc and walk straight into a job as a consultant Occupational Psychologist. Many people find that their career path is much more varied than this. Indeed, there are many jobs in HR, learning and development, organisational development and change, and management consultancy where the skills you have learnt during your MSc can be put to use, and where you can start your initial training as a practitioner Occupational Psychologist. So, for your first or indeed subsequent jobs after your masters you may be *working* as an Occupational Psychologist, but without the actual title. Instead you might be a recruitment or training manager or an organisational change consultant. It is worth remembering that you will need to be fairly proactive in shaping your career as an Occupational Psychologist – even if you start in an organisation working in HR you can use your Occupational Psychology skills. You might have to 'sell' your skills to key stakeholders internally in the organisation in which you work so that you can eventually carve out your niche in Occupational Psychology. Use Box 2.4 to help you decide if a career in Occupational Psychology is for you.

Box 2.4

Do I suit a career as an Occupational Psychologist – is it for me?

It's always daunting starting out in a new career or deciding whether it is something for you. We recommend that you ask yourself the following questions to help determine whether this is the career route that you want to take.

Tasks: Are you interested in the kinds of tasks that Occupational Psychologists conduct? Do areas such as stress management, employee selection and development interest you? Are you interested in continual learning; keeping up with and understanding new developments in the profession, such as new data analysis techniques?

Knowledge: Are you interested in developing a knowledge base about the psychology of people at work?

Skills: Do you have, or could you build, the skills that were presented above – i.e. critical thinking skills, problem solving skills and so on?

Abilities: Are you able to listen to, assimilate and understand information and ideas presented to you (through written text or verbally)? Are you able to apply rules or theories to specific problems to produce solutions?

Activities: Do you want to provide guidance and advice to individuals and/or groups of people? Do you want to establish and maintain good working relationships with your clients (both internal and external to the organisation)?

Work context: What kind of context do you want to work in? Would you be happy spending most of your time in front of a computer, answering emails, being on the phone, dealing with clients?

Education: Are you willing to spend the time (and money) to achieve Chartered status? Would you want to work further to gain a PhD? How important is Chartership to you? Spend some time examining Figure 2.1 exploring the reasons why people may or may not decide to go through the process of Chartership and ask yourself: is Chartership for me?

You may find it helpful to explore the answers to these questions with a friend or fellow student to help determine whether a career in Occupational Psychology is for you.

Summary

By the end of this chapter you should now have a clear idea regarding what Occupational Psychologists are, where they work and what they do. We have presented the route to become a chartered Occupational Psychologist, and this should have given you a clearer idea of whether it is something you would like to pursue or not. We have outlined some of the key skills needed to work as an Occupational Psychologist and some tips to finding a job in the field. This will help you to eventually shape a career in Occupational Psychology in a way that suits you.

Explore further

There are many websites and links that provide further information regarding the contents of this chapter. Here is a list of further information you may wish to follow up.

- Further information about accredited psychology courses: http://www.bps.org.uk/careers-education-training/undergraduate-and-postgraduate-psychology/

undergraduate-and-postgraduate-. However, we do recommend that you contact courses direct for more information about content, entry requirements, application procedure and so on.

- Further information about the Qualification in Occupational Psychology, both stages one and two, can be found here: http://www.bps.org.uk/careers-education-training/society-qualifications/occupational-psychology/occupational-psychology. The candidate handbooks for each of these qualifications can be found if you click through the relevant links.
- The BPS – http://www.bps.org.uk/ – and the DOP – http://www.bps.org.uk/networks-communities/member-networks/divisions/division-occupational-psychology/division-occupationa. This will give you access to publications, information about conferences and special interest groups, chat rooms and membership.
- You can find further information regarding developing your skills and career in Occupational Psychology. The best place to visit is section on careers, education and training on the BPS website, http://www.bps.org.uk/careers-education-training/careers-education-and-training. A useful section of this in terms of developing your skill set is the Learning centre and CPD (http://www.bps.org.uk/careers-education-training/learning-centre-and-cpd/learning-centre-and-cpd) where you can find information on workshops and events that might be of interest.
- To find out more about the kinds of work environments/ways of working you would prefer, you might want to try completing a personality measure. Finding Potential has many free psychometrics you could try: http://www.findingpotential.com/
- BPS shop: http://www.bpsshop.org.uk/ – here you will find a range of Occupational Psychology publications through the online shop.

Discussion questions

1 What do you think are the advantages and disadvantages of working as an external consultant compared to working in-house?
2 What do you see as the most important skills to develop immediately, and with a longer term (such as three-year) perspective.
3 Consider the advantages and disadvantages of the chartership route for you personally.

References

Anderson, N., Herriot, P. and Hodgkinson, G.P. (2001) 'The practitioner-researcher divide in industrial, work and organisational (IWO) psychology: where are we now, and where do we go from here?', *Journal of Occupational and Organisational Psychology*, 74 (4): 391–411.

Health and Care Professions Council (2009) 'Practioner psychologists, Standards of proficiency '. Available at: http://www.hpc-uk.org/assests/documents/1000296350p_Practioner_ Psychologists.pdf (accessed 25 November 2011).

Kwiatkowski, R., Duncan, D.C. and Shimmin, S. (2006) 'What have we forgotten and why?', *Journal of Occupational and Organisational Psychology*, 79: 183–201.

Mirvis, P.H. and Seashore, S.E. (1982) 'Creating ethical relationships in organisational research', in J.E. Sieber (ed.), *The Ethics of Social Research: Surveys and Experiments*. New York: Springer. pp. 79–104.

Shimmin, S. and Wallis, D. (1994) *Fifty Years of Occupational Psychology in Britain* . Leicester: British Psychological Society.

3 Ethical and research skills you will need as an Occupational Psychologist

Rachel Lewis and Lara Zibarras

Learning outcomes

By the end of the chapter you will be able to:

- understand the BPS stance and approach to ethics;
- discuss the ethical issues and constraints arising in a number of specific situations;
- understand and use ethical skills in practice, such as the use of contracting, confidentiality agreements and understanding loyalties;
- describe and define different research methods and designs;
- understand how to read, and evaluate, an academic paper;
- describe and define different statistical methods;
- consider when and how to choose the most appropriate statistical test;
- consider the role of qualitative techniques in Occupational Psychology;
- describe and define a number of qualitative techniques.

Introduction

In Chapter 2, the importance of ethics in the daily job of the Occupational Psychologist was introduced. This chapter extends and continues this discussion with an exploration of the ethical skills you may need while working as an Occupational Psychologist and provides an opportunity to discuss the ethical constraints and issues that may arise in a number of situations that could be relevant to your future career. It is also in this chapter that we document both the BPS and the HPC stance on ethics and ethical practice.

The rest of the chapter will focus on research skills, introducing those relevant to your needs as both an academic and a practitioner. It will also explain and demystify some of the key terms and processes surrounding both quantitative and qualitative research. It is important to highlight that this section of the chapter does not and should not replace a methods textbook and a statistics or qualitative textbook. At the end of the chapter you will see a list of recommended texts. Rather this chapter may be useful:

- as a refresher to those who have studied and used research methods and analytical techniques in previous education or undergraduate studies;
- as a 'quick look' reference source to help you to understand key terms and practices used within Part II of this book or within academic papers;
- as an introduction and grounding to those of you who have never formally studied research methods and statistics in previous courses.

Considering ethics

Ethics is central to everything we do whether in research or practice – BPS website, 2011.

In Chapter 2, the discussion of ethics was introduced through an exploration of the contextual meaning and importance of ethics for academia and practice, and also by personal contributions from academics and practitioners. The subject of ethics and ethical considerations is absolutely core to our profession as Occupational Psychologists and will be returned to throughout this book in a number of ways.

Later in this section we will begin to explore the kind of ethical skills or 'tools' needed by practitioners working with Occupational Psychology. You will also see that within each chapter in Part II, you will have an opportunity to explore how ethical considerations emerge in context. First, within the context of projects and work where some of the chapter case studies will include a discussion of the particular and specific ethical considerations involved. Second, in each contribution section (both leading practitioners and eminent academics), authors will respond to the question of what role ethics has in their everyday work and practice.

Considering ethics: the BPS approach

The BPS publishes a comprehensive set of ethical guidelines for researchers, teachers and practitioners. The key document is the Code of Ethics and Conduct (August, 2009) which can be found at the following link on the BPS website. The Code of Conduct (Box 3.1) was first adopted in 1985 by the BPS and is regularly updated.

Box 3.1

The British Psychological Society Code of Ethics and Conduct (2009)

Based on four ethical principles, which constitute the main domains of responsibility within which ethical issues are considered. These are:

1 Respect

Psychologists should value the dignity and worth of all persons, with sensitivity to the dynamics of perceived authority or influence over clients, and with particular regard to people's rights including those of privacy and self determination.

2 Competence

Psychologists value the continuing development and maintenance of high standards of competence in their professional work, and the importance of preserving their ability to function optimally within the recognised limits of their knowledge, skill, training, education and experience.

3 Responsibility

Psychologists value their responsibilities to clients, to the general public, and to the profession and science of psychology, including the avoidance of harm and the prevention of misuse or abuse of their contributions to society.

4 Integrity

Psychologists value honesty, accuracy, clarity and fairness in their interactions with all persons, and seek to promote integrity in all facets of their scientific and professional endeavours.

Taking the lead from the Code of Ethics and Conduct, and the awareness of the types of issues that may arise, the BPS have developed a set of competencies that Occupational Psychologists, or Occupational Practitioners in training, should be able to demonstrate regarding ethical practice. These are held within the so called *Key Roles*. The Key Role relating to ethics is Key Role 1 and includes 'Develop, implement and maintain personal and professional standards and ethical practice'.

There are five learning outcomes for this key role, which include:

1 establish, maintain and develop systems for legal, ethical and professional standards in Occupational Psychology;
2 comply with legal, ethical and professional standards in Occupational Psychology;

3 contribute to the continuing development of oneself as a professional Occupational Psychologist;

4 respond to unpredictable contexts and events professionally and ethically;

5 formulate developments in legal, ethical and professional standards in Occupational Psychology.

Full details of these competencies can be found in Appendix 2 of the Candidate Handbook for the qualification in Occupational Psychology, which we referred to in Chapter 2. This can be downloaded from the BPS website.

It is important to remember that, as described in Chapter 2, the BPS is our representative body, while the HPC is our regulatory body. If you have decided to become chartered, you are then eligible to apply for registration under the HPC. The HPC have their own ethical code, which is called 'Health Professions Council's Standards of Conduct, Performance and Ethics'. This was updated in 2008 and details 14 standards that, as a registrant, you must be aware of, and abide by. In fact, one of the conditions of registration is to sign a declaration to confirm that you will adhere to these standards. Although many are similar to those stated by the BPS, there are additional standards concerning the need to gather informed consent and deal with risks of infection that are worth being aware of. The standards can be found on the HPC website.

What are the ethical skills you will need as a practitioner?

By focusing on the competencies included in Key Role 1 of the BPS guidelines, you will be able to see the broad skills/knowledge that you will need as an ethical practitioner. This tells you what you need to do and consider; but how do you go about working ethically and what tools do you need?

The first stage in developing ethical skill comes with the decision-making process regarding ethics around the project or research you are undertaking. This means deciding what the ethical issues or concerns may be, in order to best decide how to approach them. The BPS (2009) has a useful decision tree to help with this process (Figure 3.1).

You will notice from this tree that much of this process involves talking to others about the possible ethical issues or constraints. This does not just mean talking to your client or research participants, but also to your colleagues, friends and the BPS. Often there is not a simple solution, and ethical concerns may not always be obvious, therefore it is a good idea to get as many 'heads' onto the issue as possible.

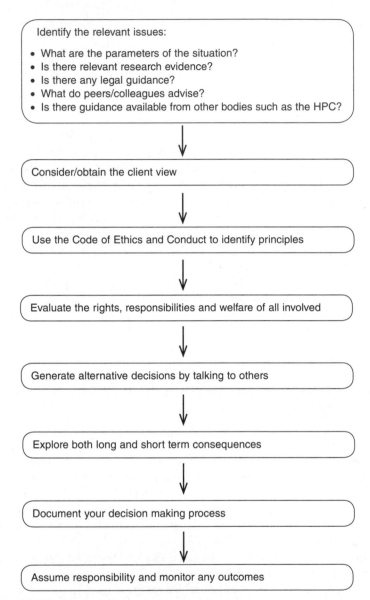

Identify the relevant issues:

- What are the parameters of the situation?
- Is there relevant research evidence?
- Is there any legal guidance?
- What do peers/colleagues advise?
- Is there guidance available from other bodies such as the HPC?

Consider/obtain the client view

Use the Code of Ethics and Conduct to identify principles

Evaluate the rights, responsibilities and welfare of all involved

Generate alternative decisions by talking to others

Explore both long and short term consequences

Document your decision making process

Assume responsibility and monitor any outcomes

Figure 3.1   BPS decision tree

Considering ethics – group project

Have a go discussing the possible ethical issues or constraints of the scenarios in Box 3.2. Discuss in groups of your peers and notice the different perspectives that you gather through this discussion. If you do not have a group to work with, please do spend some time thinking about each scenario before you read on.

Box 3.2

Ethical Discussion Scenario 1:

You are a chartered Occupational Psychologist. You have been asked by a leading UK bank as a consultant to conduct a piece of research to try and show a clear link between the health of employees and their performance at work. The bank believes that healthy employees are better, harder workers. To do this, the organisation is going to give you access to the records of all employees from a number of years, including (but not limited to) absenteeism data, sickness data, hours worked (using clock-in statistics), performance appraisal ratings and sales data (for customer service and sales employees). You are also going to interview some employees from each of the divisions of the bank to find out what they think.

Hint: Have you considered the rights of the employees in terms of use of their data? How will you ensure that this data is used ethically? What might be the implications of the organisation finding links between health and performance?

Ethical Discussion Scenario 2:

You are a trainee Occupational Psychologist and work within a large retail company. The organisation has found that the turnover of employees has increased exponentially in the last two years. This is having a negative impact on the annual cost of training and recruitment (along with other associated costs). You have been asked by the HR Director to find out the reasons for so many employees leaving the organisation. She has given you access to employee exit interview records and told you to work out the reason from these.

Hint: Do you think staff exit interviews would give the full story? Would you be working as an ethical practitioner if you just used these? What else might you need and what might be the implications of this?

Discussion Scenario 3:

You work within a long-established engineering business as a learning and development advisor and counsellor. One of your clients, in the course of a discussion with you, has told you that a member of the board had apparently sexually harassed a number of female staff members (not including the client). The client felt that due to the seniority of the board member, those employees would not be willing to come forward and formally report him – and instead were either finding ways to avoid contact with him, or in some cases leave the company. Your client also felt his behaviour was a reason for some members of his direct team suffering long term sickness absence. This board member happens to be a very good friend of yours and you are shocked by these accusations.

Hint: How do you feel about this information being second hand? Can you ethically ignore it though? What does this lack of disclosure tell you about the culture of the organisation?

In order to guide each discussion, think about the ethical issues in terms of the following questions.

- What ethical issues may arise for the participants/employees of undertaking this work/research? Will the issues be the same for everyone involved?
- What ethical issues may arise for the client/organisation? Do the issues for the client/organisation and participants/employees overlap or work against each other?
- What ethical issues may arise from your work as a practitioner/academic on this?

Also have a discussion in each case about whether you feel that there may be legal checks or issues related to the work. Do not worry at the moment about how you might solve them, but focus more on identifying any concerns or issues.

Hopefully these scenarios will have started to demonstrate how important, and how complicated, a consideration of ethics is while working in Occupational Psychology. Below, two leading practitioners reflect on the importance of ethics to their day-to-day life and work.

Emma Donaldson-Feilder, Director Affinity Health at Work

' Ethics are essential to my practice. This would include issues such as maintaining confidentiality, transparency, doing what you say you are going to do, getting informed consent where appropriate, consultation and participation of individuals on issues that concern them, and integrity in all dealings with clients, individuals, organisations, colleagues ... everybody. It would also mean engaging in reflective practice. '

Julianne Miles, Career Psychologists. Julianne is a leading career counsellor and shows how complicated and key ethics are to her on a day-to-day basis

' Complete confidentiality and a non-judgemental approach are essential to enable my clients to be open and honest and to talk freely about their feelings and concerns. The greatest challenge in my day-to-day practice is maintaining professional boundaries of competence. Given the one-to-one nature of the client relationship, personal issues may come to the fore. I find it particularly important at the screening and contracting stages to distinguish my role as an Occupational Psychologist from that of a counselling psychologist or other type of therapist. The dominant issue for clients may actually be a problematic personal relationship or a debilitating anxiety problem. If I believe from initial conversations that personal or relationship counselling would be more appropriate, I will raise the possibility of a referral elsewhere. Another area of boundaries is counsellor/coach versus advisor. As a psychologist, clients may put me in an expert role and look to be told 'what they should do'. I position myself as a guide who will empower my clients to make their own decisions rather than providing the answers myself.'

You will see from these examples how diverse and complex ethical skills need to be. Below are three key areas that will tend to come up in every project you work on, although do note that this is not an exhaustive list.

Contracting

Contracting should be the first thing you do when working with a client or with an employee. With a client this may involve a formal written contract which details what you will do, how long you will work, who will be involved, what the deliverables will be and what the cost of the project will be. This should also include the loyalty and confidentiality agreements. The contracting stage of the process will often be an iterative one where, together, you and the client will work out how, and the conditions under which, you will work together. With employees, research participants or clients in a coaching/counselling relationship, this contracting will often take place verbally.

Confidentiality agreements

For both work in research and practice you will need to use confidentiality agreements. If you are reading this as a student, your first experience of confidentiality agreements will probably be in your research project (either at BA/BSc or MSc level) where you will need to collect confidentiality agreements from your research participants. As a practitioner, you tend to have confidentiality agreements with a number of stakeholders – both the client/organisation and the employees. You may also be asked to sign confidentiality agreements when you work with organisations in order to have access to privileged information or data.

Important points to remember regarding confidentiality agreements include the following:

- Consider everyone involved in the project/research and to what level confidentiality needs to be upheld.
- Get agreements in writing – it really helps to have physical evidence of what the confidentiality agreements you have made are.
- Research data – what will you do with the data? How can you store it securely to make sure no-one else has access? How can you anonymise the data without losing any of the utility (for instance, if you need to track responses, how will you do this; or if you are going to collect follow up data, how will you contact employees?). How long will you store the data and how will you destroy it?
- Confidentiality of client versus that of the employee – for instance, will the client know who or how many employees responded? Will they have access to group level data if not individual?
- Logistics – make sure if you are working in an organisation, you can use private rooms or telephones to ensure conversations can remain confidential.
- Feedback – how can you give feedback to a client or research participants without breaching confidentiality? Consider this at the beginning of the project rather than when you are creating deliverables.
- Keep checking back – make sure that throughout the project/research, you 'check in' and make sure that you are not breaching any parties' confidentiality agreements. This also applies after the project has ended.

Confidentiality agreements are discussed in much more detail in Chapter 5, where the discussion focuses on the need for confidentiality in workplace counselling interventions.

Understanding loyalties

Who you are loyal to, or who is your client, is one of the first things to try and determine when working with organisations. For instance, if in the course of a discussion with an employee, you find out that particular employees are not working effectively (which may arise from a lack of performance capability or motivation, or from illness for instance), will you pass that information on to your 'client'? There is no right or wrong answer here, but it depends on who you are loyal to.

The important points about loyalties are the following.

- Loyalty is not necessarily to those who pay you. The person/organisation who pays you or hires you does not have to be that to which you show loyalty. Consider where you feel your loyalties should lie as an ethical practitioner. For instance, if you are conducting a developmentally focused 360-degree appraisal system for a client; does the client need to see the ratings that each participant has received?

- Split loyalties – you may be in situations where you know that the solution or intervention you are providing is not going to be as effective as the client hopes. For instance, if you were working as a consultant in an agency, delivering the 'agency' solutions may be what your job is – whether that solution is the best one or not. Would you be happy with this? How might you manage this when your loyalty would be split between your profession, your agency, and the client?
- Get it in writing – often in the course of a project, a client will try to 'push back', asking for information that you had not agreed to provide, or discussed providing. Make sure that the finer points around loyalty are written down and distributed.
- Communicate loyalty agreements to each party. Take the example of the appraisal system above. It is critical that you communicate loyalty, or confidentiality, to all parties so that the client knows what to expect, and in this case so that all participants know under which conditions they are rating/being rated. If, as a manager going through this, you knew that the organisation would not know your individual ratings but would see your development plan, you may be more comfortable and honest in the process.

Considering research

In Chapters 1 and 2, we discussed what Occupational Psychologists do, and how this may differ from other disciplines, such as management consultants and HR professionals. One of the key differentiators is our research skill and focus on evidence-based practice.

You do not have to read much about Occupational Psychology to see reference to the academic-practitioner divide (see, for example, Anderson et al., 2001, for a review on this). This debate is at the forefront of Occupational Psychology; with one side believing academics do not undertake work in practice or develop solutions that would be of use in practice (the ivory tower argument); and the other side believing that practitioners implement solutions and interventions that are not rooted in empirical evidence. It is our belief that, accepting it may not always be the case, it is absolutely critical for practitioners to work with an evidence-based methodology and for academics to consider the practical implications of their research.

Emma Donaldson-Feilder, a leading practitioner, highlights how important this is:

My aim is that everything I do should be underpinned by theory, literature and research – as well as the evidence I have gathered through my own experience. I have always said that I conduct research in order to ensure that my practice is truly evidence-based, but I am a practitioner in order to ensure that the research I do is very practically focused and relevant in practice.

In this book, we have made sure that where theory and academic models have been presented, the practical implications and utility of these are clear. We have also included many examples of both academics and practitioners who do bridge this divide and are working in the direction that Occupational Psychology needs to go in.

Take for instance this quotation from Professor Ivan Robertson, who works both in academia and practice:

> The practical application of my work often provides data and ideas for research. For example (with colleagues) I have recently published a research article that focuses on the extent to which psychological well-being enhances the role that employee engagement plays in productivity. All of the data for this came from surveys that were done directly to meet client needs. In fact the connection between research and practice has been a recurring theme throughout my career. Almost all of my empirical research articles have drawn on data from real organisational settings that have been collected in the course of a live project – rather than data collected for research purposes only. One of the things that I believe in very strongly is that it is healthy for the profession to minimise the barriers between research, practice and teaching in Occupational Psychology.

Having research skills, and keeping up to date with research, is absolutely key for Occupational Psychologists, whether working as an academic or as a practitioner. The rest of this chapter introduces the research skills you need to navigate your way through relevant research and theory. Whether you are training to be an Occupational Psychologist or not, this section should be understandable and of use to you.

Research methods and designs

Each piece of research conducted will have a particular structure. The structure, or design of the research, will influence what results can be gathered and what research questions can be answered – and therefore the design is chosen to match the aim of the study. It is important for researchers to use the most appropriate research design so that the results achieved are reliable, or accurate, and in order that conclusions and implications can be drawn.

Broadly, research fits within two approaches: quantitative research (which uses numerical data to measure results) and qualitative research (which uses verbal data to analyse results, often in an interpretative manner).

Before deciding on your approach to any research, it is important to consider what your belief system around research and measurement might be. We can categorise this belief system into the four major assumptions about social science. As each of these four assumptions is introduced, reflect upon where your philosophical stance sits – which 'fits' with you?

1 Ontology – or the study of the nature of reality:

   a The subjectivist position is that there is no real structure to the world. Whether something exists is dependent on an individual's subjective awareness of the existence.

   b The objectivist position is that the world exists externally – so something can exist regardless of whether we are aware of its existence or not.

2 Epistemology – the study of knowledge; the question being 'how do we know what we know?'

   a The interpretivist position is that knowledge is a matter of interpretation – we all interpret things differently.

   b The positivist position is that knowledge is measurable and can be measured and calculated.

3 Human nature:

   a The voluntarist position is that humans are autonomous and take action under free will.

   b The determinist position is that our actions are determined by the environment or situation in which we are situated.

4 Methodological nature:

   a The qualitative position is that we can understand the world by gaining first-hand knowledge of participants and their subjective accounts.

   b The quantitative position is that the process of measurement is central and methodology involves hypothesis testing, being rooted in scientific rigour.

Later in this chapter, some of the most commonly used analytical procedures associated with both qualitative and quantitative research will be explored. Here we will explore quantitative tests of difference and of similarity, and define qualitative methods including content analysis, discourse analysis, thematic analysis and interpretative phenomenological analysis.

Explaining different research methods/designs

In this section we will explore five different types of research methods and their associated designs. These include:

1 descriptive designs;
2 correlational studies;
3 experimental designs;
4 quasi-experimental designs;
5 reviewing other research.

Remember, before conducting any type of research it is useful to conduct a pilot study – essentially a small version of the intended study.

1 Descriptive designs

Descriptive designs observe and describe. These designs involve observing, describing and measuring behaviour of a participant/s without actually affecting or influencing that behaviour.

Examples of this type of design would include:

- case study – an in-depth study of a particular situation, for instance managerial behaviour in one organisation;
- diary study – providing participants with materials to record daily events, tasks or thoughts/feelings in order to gain insight into their behaviour over time;
- focus group – a facilitated group interview in which participants are asked about their thoughts, opinions or beliefs towards a particular subject;
- interview – a structured discussion in which a single participant is asked by an interviewer about their thoughts, opinions or beliefs towards a particular subject;
- observation – generally this would be obtrusive naturalistic observation, where the participant/s know they are being observed, but where they are observed carrying out their daily tasks (observation is often used for research aims such as analysing jobs and tasks);
- survey – gathering data through questionnaires; this is one of the most common research designs within Occupational Psychology.

2 Correlational studies

Correlational studies determine whether two or more variables are correlated or not; or in other words examining if an increase or decrease in one variable (such as happiness at work) corresponds to an increase or decrease in another variable (such as work performance).

Correlational studies are most commonly either cross-sectional or longitudinal.

- Cross-sectional – gathering data, generally using a survey design, on relevant variables at one time point only. All data is collected at the same time and represents a 'snap-shot' of an organisation or phenomenon.
- Longitudinal – gathering data over a period of time, where measurements of each variable are taken at two or more distinct time points. This can allow the measurement of change. Longitudinal designs can either be time series (where data is collected at regular intervals from an aggregate sample – for instance, employee surveys on successive years) or panel (where data is collected from

the same participants over time in order to measure change at an individual level).

3 Experimental designs

A true experimental design is one in which a single variable is manipulated while all others are held constant in order to see if there is change in another variable. This gives the researcher the opportunity to eliminate alternative explanations for the effect or change, by controlling for confounding variables. The experimental design therefore enables the exploration of cause and effect. The true experimental design must have:

- a random sample;
- a control group (non-experimental group);
- participants must be randomly assigned to control or experimental groups;
- only one variable to be manipulated and tested, and all others must be held constant.

In reality it is incredibly difficult to carry out a true experimental design within Occupational Psychology, not least owing to the fact that there are reactivity effects if participants know if they are in an experiment, and possible ethical issues if they do not. Also, within an organisation, true random sampling is almost impossible because in organisations, you are rarely able to 'randomly assign' people to an intervention.

4 Quasi-experimental designs

Quasi-experimental designs are where one or more of the features of a true experiment are missing. This will include:

- random allocation of participant to conditions and/or;
- full experimenter control over the independent variable.

For instance, a study may be quasi-experimental rather than experimental if, rather than using a random sample of employees, employees from two similar teams are chosen for each experimental group, or, perhaps more commonly, that participants are given the chance to volunteer to take part in the study rather than being chosen by the researcher. What we know from research is that often participants that volunteer to studies are 'different' (for instance, on mental health and personality variables) than those in the general organisational population. An excellent example of a quasi-experimental design in Occupational Psychology is described in Bond and Bunce (2001).

5 Reviewing other research

Two of the most common ways of reviewing other research that you will come across are meta-analysis and literature review.

Meta-analysis is a statistical technique for combining the findings from independent studies. Often lots of separate small studies will have looked at the same variables – for instance, many papers looking at the impact of increasing job control on work performance. Meta-analysis, by combining the data from all the separate smaller studies, allows the researcher to look at effectively a much larger body of evidence and therefore make more robust and accurate conclusions. The strength and validity of the meta-analysis depends upon the researcher having conducted a complete review of the available literature, and using statistically and methodologically similar studies (called heterogeneity). An example of this would be where all the studies used in the meta-analysis used the same measure of job control and work performance.

A systematic literature review is an in-depth evaluation of previous research on a particular area and is presented as a summary of that area of research. It is important to note that a literature review should be an evaluation that presents the different approaches and arguments within a body of research – not just a summary of all the published research. It should also include an evaluation of the quality of the research and therefore the status of the research area (such as the key gaps in knowledge).

Being able to review literature is one of the most important research skills that you need to acquire when embarking on your learning as an Occupational Psychologist – whether your goal is to be a practitioner or an academic. However, academic literature can sometimes seem bewildering with respect to the amount of information available and the complexity of that information. The next section provides some pointers as to how to start to conduct a literature review, and navigate your way around academic papers.

Conducting a literature review

The most difficult aspect of conducting a literature review is deciding whether the literature available to you is appropriate and credible. The choices that you make will determine whether the end product (your literature review or piece of work) is useful or not. One of the most common reasons for students getting low marks in essays and assignments is the quality of the source material used. This next section will aim to help you to make an appropriate choice.

Box 3.3

HOW TO SECTION
If you want to develop your literature research skills, take a look at this!

There are a series of free internet tutorials called 'Virtual Training Suite' developed by a team of UK university lecturers and librarians to help you to develop your internet research skills. Each tutorial will take about an hour, or you can look at a section at a time over the course of sittings. It is an excellent, and highly recommended way, to develop your skills in an interactive way. Each of the tutorials are divided into four sections which enable you to:

— tour the web for your subject area;
— find out how to find information online;
— evaluate which resources are most appropriate for you;
— learn by example.

The following links take you either to the Business and Management tutorial or the Psychology tutorial. Choose whichever is most appropriate to your course of study or area of interest. If you are studying Occupational Psychology though, a recommendation is to have a look at the 'Tour' section on both tutorials as you will then find out how to access both psychology and business journals and articles – and which are going to be available to you.

To access the Psychology tutorial:

http://www.vtstutorials.co.uk/ws//tracking/launchcontent.aspx?cv=36073971-FF61-45A7-B21D-F4667B77EED1&e=A0000&c=209AD8E4-D129-457C-8554-F7EA6C629679&SID=24453c0b-2543-458d-bb95-1068c20b60cb

To access the Business and Management tutorial:

http://www.vtstutorials.co.uk/ws//tracking/launchcontent.aspx?cv=78911681-E697-49D1-B98C-7901B6648D0E&e=A0000&c=19FCBF04-106D-49FB-BAE8-8274A87C680F&SID=24453c0b-2543-458d-bb95-1068c20b60cb

First, what do we mean by literature? One of the important, and unusual, aspects of Occupational Psychology literature is that key relevant information may be found in both psychology literature, and in business or management literature. By 'literature', we generally mean academic or educational literature published in academic journals or books. Generally in an undergraduate course, you will be given a book

Government Websites	Societies/Professional Bodies/relevant organisations	Publications
Key information on legislation, source of statistics and funded reports.	Most provide useful reports, reviews and data in specialist areas.	Most publications are available freely online and are an excellent way to keep up to date with current affairs and news in business and psychology.
– Health and Safety Executive (HSE)	– British Psychological Society (BPS)	– News (online and broadsheet) such as BBC: Business, *Financial Times* and *New York Times*: Business
– Department for Work and Pensions (DWP)	– American Psychological Association (APA)	– *The Economist*
– Her Majesty's Stationery Office (HMSO)	– CIPD (Chartered Institute of Personnel and Development)	– *The Week*
– Office for National Statistics (ONS)	– TUC (Trade Unions Congress)	– *People Management*
– Department for Business, Innovation and Skills (BIS)	– National Institute for Occupational Safety and Health (NIOSH)	– *The Psychologist*
– Business Link	– ACAS (Advisory, Conciliation and Arbitration service)	– PsycPORT
	– Institute for Employment Studies (IES)	– Podcasts such as Money Box
	– The Work Foundation	
	– Chartered Management Institute (CMI)	
	– Business in the Community (BITC)	

Figure 3.2   Sources of information

list with recommended books to buy, or borrow from the library, for each particular course. Lots of books are now available as ebooks, so do make sure you ask before buying! Academic journals will be covered in more detail later in this section.

Psychology, and Occupational Psychology in particular, is a constantly evolving and developing discipline. As you will have read in Chapter 1, the world of work continues to change at a rapid pace, and with that comes implications for our understanding of Occupational Psychology. What this means for you is that it might not always be a good idea to rely on information in books if those books were published a number of years ago (or at least without thinking for yourself what might have changed since publication). This is also why you are often recommended (particularly at the MSc level) to use academic journals as your primary source of literature.

Before focusing on academic journals, however, we would strongly urge you to cast your net wider in terms of gathering information. The Internet is, of course, a brilliantly easy way to keep up with the latest news and information. A good level of business awareness is absolutely critical in order to understand the implications and ramifications of any theory or model you are looking at. Figure 3.2 presents a selection of information sources that can provide interesting information.

In addition, do not forget to use social media as an information source for instance:

- Facebook has many Occupational Psychology groups including BPS Division of Occupational Psychology and *Journal of Occupational Health Psychology.*
- LinkedIn is a great way to network within the industry and also has a huge number of relevant groups including Occupational and Organisational Psychologists, Psychologists in the UK, the Association of Business Psychologists and many more.
- Twitter is great for following key people – have a go at searching for some of the eminent psychologists and practitioners included in this book. Also follow newsfeeds for many of the professional bodies and relevant organisations.
- Blogs. Look out for blogs that might be of interest. There are a huge number out there to suit your interest. Three you might want to look at include 'Pestons Picks' (Robert Peston is the BBC Business Editor), the BPS Research Digest blog and Professor Cary Cooper's blog (Cary is an eminent Occupational Psychologist working within health and performance in the workplace).
- Wikis. Wikipedia can be a useful source of general information (although never use Wikipedia for any assignments you are asked to do) but there is also a proliferation of more specific Wikis that you can access such as 'The Psychology Wiki' and 'Business Essentials on the Web'.
- Video sharing sites. Youtube has some useful lectures and content – have a look at Youtube EDU which contains information from US universities and colleges including Harvard Business School. You can also find content relevant to Occupational Psychology on TED, Fora.TV and Scitalks.

A word of caution regarding using social media: the information is often not validated – therefore you cannot assume it is right. Do not rely too heavily on it and certainly do not use it as the basis for your literature searches. It is however useful to give you an overall idea of the literature or story; and to provide you with an insight to some of the critique and debate around the area of study.

Academic journals

Although it is a good idea to read and assimilate a wide selection of literature, if you are a student, your focus will be upon insights from papers within academic journals (and books). There is a wide selection of academic journals. Each journal is published at regular intervals – this is generally either quarterly or monthly. Generally we rely on peer-reviewed journals. Peer review is a quality control procedure whereby each paper, prior to publication, will have been read and validated by at least one, often multiple, expert, objective academics. This ensures that peer-reviewed journals are of a quality that you can trust. Although journals are published in hard copy, and may be available in your library, in reality, the vast majority of journals are now available to read online. Box 3.4 provides some of the answers to the most common questions around using academic journals and papers.

Box 3.4

How do I find journals and academic papers?

If you are a student, the best place to start is with your library website. Through the library search engine you can find all the literature you need – both journals and books and databases that you will need. There are a number of academic search engines that you can access through your university such as Ingenta and ScienceDirect. These are often available for free from your university. Which journals are available to you will differ depending on your university – make sure you access a tutorial from your learning provider to get best use of this.

If you are not a student, you can access free academic materials via Google Scholar. You can access this through the drop down menu on the Google home page. Google Scholar works by searching a selection of databases from different universities, publishers and societies. Although useful, it is not a comprehensive review and so, if you are a student, you would need to use other sources as well.

Further, The Center for Evidence-Based Management (http://www.cebma.org/about-cebma/) has allowed those who are not students to have online access to ABI/INFORM, Business Source Elite and PsycINFO. To access these databases, you will need to become a member of the Center (http://www.cebma.org/membership/), which provides a unique login and password. The cost of membership at the time of publication is around £120, which is comparatively highly cost effective.

Can I print out and keep these papers when I find them?

It depends. If you are a student, your university will pay subscription charges to some journals. Some of these charges will include 'full text'. If you have full text access, then yes, you can print out the papers. You can also pay (usually £20–30 per paper) if you do not have full text rights.

Through Google Scholar some of the papers will be available to print out. You will see from an icon or a link to the right hand side of the paper if this is available. A good tip is that if the full text paper is not available from your university subscription, it is worth checking on Google Scholar as you might find you can access it from there.

How do I know what is a 'good' paper?

Being able to judge the quality of a paper is absolutely key. It is harder than it seems to be able to do, and much of this is actually a matter of experience.

Three key tips however would be to:

1 Use an academic search engine to find your papers. This will ensure that the papers have gone through some kind of 'vetting' procedure.
2 See if the paper is published within a 'peer reviewed' journal. This is a formal quality control procedure and means that an independent, third party academic who is an expert in the relevant area, has read and checked the paper prior to publication. You can see if journals are peer reviewed by going onto the main website of the particular journal and checking submission procedures.
3 See where the paper has been cited – i.e. who else has used it. If the paper has been cited many times by other authors, it is likely to be a good and useful paper. You can check citations in a number of ways. The most rigorous way is through the ISI Web of Science, but you can also check from your library search engine or through Google Scholar. Please note however that if the paper has been published very recently (for instance in the last year) it may not yet have been cited.

Reading academic journals

There will be a number of key journals that you find crop up again and again on reading lists. What these are will differ depending on what subject you are studying (for example, HR versus occupational psychology courses) and the area within that subject you are studying (for instance, whether it is selection and assessment, or automation and human-machine interaction). Have a look at the reference list at the end of each of the chapters in this book to get an idea of the relevant journals for each particular area.

Reading academic journals can, at the beginning, feel very daunting as they use unfamiliar language, style of writing and analytical procedures. Later in this chapter you will find a section explaining some of the analytical procedures. When you are searching for papers, have a read of the abstract before you embark on the whole paper. The abstract will tell you what the study involved, the aims and objectives of the study, and the main findings. You can use this to ascertain if it is a useful paper for you before you go any further with your reading.

Generally, an academic paper will follow a fixed format. Box 3.5 gives an indication of what you are likely to find in each section. Note this applies to quantitative rather than qualitative studies; although it is a fact however that the vast majority of academic papers are quantitative. This template also does not apply to review articles.

Box 3.5

Title of Article
Authors (along with affiliation)

Abstract: The abstract is generally 100–150 words, and includes a brief description of the study, the aims, the methodology and the results.

Introduction: The introduction sets out the premise for the research and provides a brief review detailing relevant literature and gaps in literature. The introduction sets the theoretical basis for the research. The introduction may also include the hypotheses or research questions to be tested. Usually the introduction includes sub-headings to denote particular areas within the literature review.

Method: This section details what was done to actually conduct the research and generally has a number of sub-headings:

- *Participants:* The sample size, and descriptive statistics such as percentage of females and university graduates within the sample.
- *Measures:* This section describes all the measures, or scales used in the study. It will usually give an example item (such as a question asked) and will give data on how reliable the measure was in this particular sample (via an alpha coefficient).
- *Procedure:* This section describes the design of the study (how the study was actually carried out) such as how participants were selected, what they were provided with, and how many times the data was collected. It should be in enough detail that a reader could replicate the study. The section tends to also provide information on data protection and security.
- *Data analysis:* This section describes the analytical procedures taken as a whole and for each hypothesis/research question.

Results: Generally results will be structured in terms of each hypothesis or research question that was being explored and will describe each analytical procedure taken (in detail if there is no data analysis section in the Method). The results section details what was found, but not the implications of these findings.

Discussion:

- The first part of the discussion will summarise the results from each of the hypotheses, along with the implications of these findings. The findings will be discussed in the context of previous research data and conclusions. The strengths of the research study will also be highlighted here.
- *Methodological issues and limitations:* This section describes the weaknesses in the study in terms of the research design (such as use of cross sectional data), the measures used and/or the sampling. It is useful in order to help you to make a judgement about the generalizability of the findings.

> • *Implications and suggestions for future research:* This section provides not only the theoretical implications of the research, but also implications of the findings for practice (i.e. how the findings are relevant within organisations) and also suggests where future research should focus. The future research section can be useful in order to identify the gaps in research.
>
> **Conclusions:**
>
> This tends to be a short paragraph of around 200 words providing the overall 'take home' message from the study; whether that be a call for more research or reiterating the importance of the findings.

The use of analytical procedures in research

As discussed earlier in this chapter, research in Occupational Psychology can either use qualitative or quantitative research methods. This final part of the chapter describes the types of analytical procedures you may come across in your course or in your reading, both from qualitative or quantitative research. When you study Occupational Psychology or work as a practitioner within the area, you will need to understand, and possibly use, both types of research methods.

Which method you use depends on the research question you are dealing with. For instance, if you are conducting an employee survey, you are going to need to collect quantitative data. This is because you will want to reach a large number of employees in a short amount of time. Analysis of this data could show, for instance, differences in satisfaction by demographic. Imagine the data demonstrated that female employees aged between 25 and 35 were the least satisfied employee group. Although the quantitative data would show that this was the case, it would not be able to explain *why*. Could it be for instance that this age of female employees were the most likely to be managing childcare responsibilities – and this was putting the group under pressure? Or could it be something to do with promotional opportunities for female compared to male employees? There are so many reasons that *could* explain this finding. By using a qualitative method such as a focus group, the practitioner can build on the findings to understand the reasons behind the data. Therefore not only are qualitative methods useful for different studies and research designs, they are also widely used, particularly in practitioner-based research, as complementary methodologies. Professor Andy Field reiterates this point:

> People tend to sit in the two camps and there are strong opinions about which method is 'best'. Asking which method is best is as stupid as asking whether a knife or a spoon is best. If you want to cut something the knife is best, if you want to eat soup the spoon is best. It's the same with quantitative and qualitative methods: they have their strengths and weaknesses. They

can be combined with very powerful results too. Personally (and some will disagree) I think qualitative methods are good for generating hypotheses and quantitative methods are good for testing those hypotheses, but that's probably a controversial statement. Basically, it's horses for courses.

The importance and use of statistics in Occupational Psychology

The amount of statistics in MSc courses (generally up to 20% of the course content in an accredited Occupational Psychology MSc) strikes fear in the majority of potential students. It can sometimes even put students off doing an accredited programme and push them towards non-accredited programmes (which tend to include less statistics) or related programmes, such as business psychology.

So why are statistics so important to Occupational Psychology? Statistics, and statistical skills, are absolutely essential if you want to be a researcher or work as an academic in the field of Occupational Psychology. As Professor Andy Field says 'The practical application of statistics underlies everything I do as a child development researcher. Without statistics I do not have a research career.' That said, it is a *fallacy* that statistical skills are only essential to research scientists. To be an effective, evidence-based practitioner a core understanding of, if not a use of, statistics is a key requirement. For example, statistical skills enable us to:

- understand and disseminate the latest research from journals – this ensures that, as a practitioner, you stay ahead of the game;
- critique research from journals to make sure that results are understood in context (for instance, could this research apply in the organisation/sector/ employee group that you might be working with?);
- explain results to clients effectively and accurately. An example might be when feeding back to a client the results of a performance management process. Manager 1 on that process got a feedback average of 4.75 out of 5 and Manager 2 got a feedback average of 4.5 out of 5. The client may assume that Manager 1 was a stronger performer than Manager 2 – but without using statistics, it would be wrong to make that assumption. You could use statistics to find out if indeed the difference between the two was significant. You can see the implications of this – without statistics potentially the wrong conclusion could have been drawn and Manager 1 could have been seen as a poorer performer – which could then have affected remuneration and reward packages for that manager.

Statistical skills therefore give you power, give you credibility and also, importantly, help to ensure that you are behaving as an ethical practitioner by providing the best advice and services for your clients. Here are some words from Professor Andy Field.

Professor Andy Field, Professor of Child Psychopathology, University of Sussex

" If you do certain kinds of research then statistics gives you the power to answer very interesting questions. I think many students miss this link: they are interested in psychological questions, but they see statistics as a detached discipline that is somehow being taught to them as punishment for crimes they don't remember committing, but assume that they must have. However, a wide and in depth understanding of statistics gives you enormous power. Admittedly not the kind of exciting climbing-walls power that Spiderman has, but power nevertheless. With the right statistical tools you can answer any question that sparks your curiosity; anyone with an inquisitive nature, which most students have, should find that an incredibly liberating and exciting prospect. "

Definition of key terms

This section is not intended to be used in place of a statistical text, but can be used as a quick reference to explain some terms you may come across – particularly if you are reading a paper and want to know what the test conducted was.

If you are studying Occupational Psychology, it is a good idea to buy a statistical textbook. Your course tutor will provide you with a reading list, but, following much experience both as a student and as a lecturer, the most popular, and palatable texts are from Andy Field. We would recommend *Discovering Statistics Using SPSS* (3rd edition). Andy Field also has a website: www.statisticshell.com that includes masses of useful, clear and free information.

When you start a course in Occupational Psychology, or even study psychology as an undergraduate, you will probably be introduced to SPSS. This is the software program that you will tend to use for most of your statistical analyses. There are other programs that you will see referred to, such as SAS, AMOS or LISREL, but these will be for much more advanced techniques.

Key terms: The basics of statistical analysis

Measures of central tendency
These measures tell us about a single most typical or representative score within a group of scores (Box 3.6).

- The mean is the arithmetic average for a group of scores and is the main measure of central tendency. To calculate it we add up all the raw scores of participants and divide this by the number of participants.

- The mode is the most frequently obtained score.
- The median is what may be described as the 'middle value'. To calculate the median we would write down all scores in rank order from lowest to highest then select the middle value.

Box 3.6

Have a go at calculating the mean, mode and median from the following scores.

17 1 7 23 25 7 2 24 17 2 3 15 19 17 12 15 21 5 3 17 15 20

(Hint: To calculate the median you need to write all these numbers down in order and see which number falls in the middle. For the mode, which number appears the most times? For the mean, add up all the numbers and divide by 22 which is the total number of scores)

The answers are below:

Mean: 13.05; Mode: 17; Median: 15

Did you get the same answer?

Measures of central tendency, however, do not give us information about the overall spread or distribution of scores in a group, and therefore we often need to also calculate standard deviation and variance statistics.

The standard deviation is a calculation of how far an individual's score deviates from the group mean. Therefore, when there is a large standard deviation, there is a wide range of scores; and where a small standard deviation, a narrow range of scores. Take for instance an example of a psychology examination. The average (or mean) exam result may be 58. However, if we look at two cohorts (for instance the BSc students compared to those taking psychology as an option), the BSc students group results had a standard deviation of 12, whereas the 'psychology option' students group results had a standard deviation of 26. What does this tell us? As the standard deviation is smaller in the BSc group, it means that the range of scores was smaller – and therefore more students scored similarly (closer to the mean score) in their exam. In the 'Psychology option' group, the standard deviation is larger, so the range of scores was larger – more students might for instance have done very badly or very well in the examination.

Variance is another measure of dispersion, and is calculated by squaring the standard deviation. However, generally we use the standard deviation statistic.

Variables

In studies and papers, you will see variables referred to as either independent or dependent variables. Independent variables tend to be those which you are manipulating, or those that change; whereas the dependent variable is what you observe from the manipulation of the independent variable. Take, for example, a study in which you were examining the effect of working hours on job satisfaction. Working hours here are your independent variable, and job satisfaction your dependent variable. Another way to look at it is the independent variables are your study variables and dependent variables your results, or outcome variables.

Statistical significance

When we are looking at results of statistical analyses, we are interested in whether the test is significant. What we mean by this is whether the result could have been obtained by chance (or whether we can rely on the results that we have found in our study). The level we generally accept is the 0.05 level of significance. This is a test at the 95% probability level, or in other words, means that there is only a 5% probability that the results of our study were achieved by chance/error.

Error

If we take a 0.05 significance level in our study, we are accepting that there is a 5% chance that the results could have been achieved by error; and we are also accepting that there will always be a level of error in our study – but that 5% is an acceptable level. In statistics, we are concerned with two types of error: type 1 and type 2 errors.

- Type 1 errors are when the results of your study are significant (for instance, show that there is a difference between two sets of results), but actually there is not a difference. You can term this as a false positive result.
- Type 2 errors – are when the results of your study are not significant when actually there is really a difference (so you fail to find a difference between two sets of results, for instance). You can also term this as a false negative result.

Parametric versus non-parametric tests

Parametric tests are those in which data can be described by a normal distribution whereas non-parametric tests would be based on data that would not follow any kind of defined distribution. It will only (in the vast majority) be parametric tests that are included and described in journals and therefore these are the only ones defined in the section below. If however in your research you do need to use non-parametric tests (such as Mann-Whitney or Wilcoxon) please refer to a statistics text.

We are able to broadly categorise statistical analyses into two categories:

- Tests of difference in which you are exploring to see if two or more variables are significantly different to each other. Research questions for instance could include 'Do part time workers have higher levels of well-being than full time workers?' or 'Do some departments perform better than others?'.

• Test of similarity in which you are exploring to see if there is a relationship between two or more variables. Research questions for instance could include 'Is performance in exams related to performance in the job?' or 'Is a happy employee more productive?'.

The next section will describe the most common forms of analysis under each of these categorisations. Tree diagrams have also been provided at the beginning of each section to demonstrate decision making processes when choosing an appropriate test.

Tests of difference

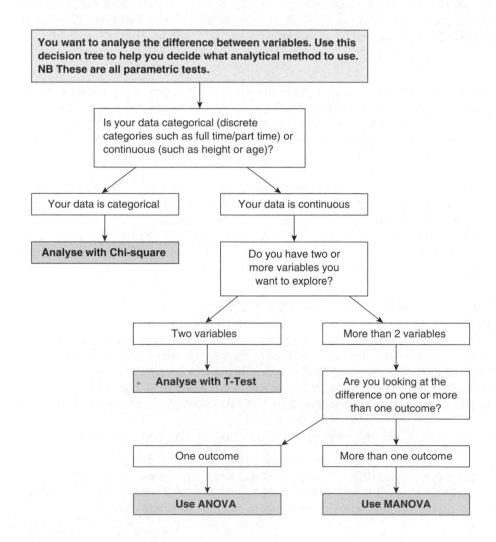

A *t*-test is a test used to establish if two mean scores are significantly different to each other (for instance: are the 2012/13 cohort for the MSc in Occupational Psychology stronger than the previous 2011/12 cohort?). Rather than just looking to see if the figures are different, the *t*-test takes into account the size of each sample (in this example the size of each cohort) and the amount of variation in scores (or in this case, marks) in each group. The test produces a single value which is known as the *t*-test; the bigger the value, the more likely that the test will be significant, or that one of the two groups is actually stronger than the other.

ANOVA (analysis of variance) is another test to establish difference, but can be used to compare more than two groups (as opposed to the *t*-test which is just a comparison of only two groups). An example of use might be, for instance, if you were evaluating performance assessment ratings in an organisation and wanted to see if the ratings were different for departments in the organisation – for instance you might look at ratings for finance, marketing, sales, procurement and so on. ANOVA is calculated based on the relative variance between groups, compared to the variance within groups. The higher the relative difference, the more likely that the best rating will be significant, or that the groups are different to each other. From ANOVA therefore you would see that there are significant differences between departments in terms of performance ratings. A version of the *t*-test is then used to work out which groups differ significantly from each other. Again the test produces a single value – in ANOVA, this is called the *F* statistic.

MANOVA (multivariate analysis of variance). Whereas ANOVA is used to look at the differences between groups on one dependent variable or outcome (in our example this was to look at differences between departments on performance ratings), MANOVA can be used to look at the differences between groups on more than one outcome. For instance we could use MANOVA to see if those same departments differed not just by performance ratings, but also by sickness absence levels and levels of employee engagement. MANOVA also explores the combinations between these outcomes. You may argue that you could just conduct a number of ANOVA tests – that is, looking at whether departments differ by performance ratings, then sickness absence rates, then employee engagement levels. Although this is possible, by conducting multiple tests, you increase the chance of making an error because you are conducting so many tests on the same data.

Chi-square (χ^2) is a further test of difference but is one that can be used when the data that you have falls into discrete categories (categorical data rather than continuous data). If, for instance, you wanted to see if there was a difference in prevalence of part-time working (as opposed to full-time working) in employees in one department compared to another department; you would use the chi-square test. The test is based on a process of tabulation where it compares the likely numbers in each group (part-time department 1, part-time department 2, full-time department 1, full-time department 2). Again, a single value is provided, whereby the bigger the value, the more likely the test will be significant and there will be a difference between the group (in this case that one department would have significantly more or fewer part-time workers than the other).

Tests of similarity

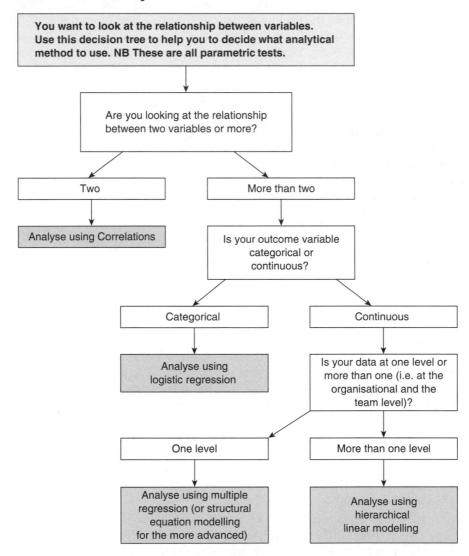

Correlation, rather than being concerned with whether scores differ, calculates whether scores are related to each other (that is, if they covary). There are different ways to calculate a correlation depending on the type of data you have, but the result will always be a correlation coefficient. Correlation coefficients vary between −1 and +1, where a 0 would represent no correlation (or relationship between the two scores). If the test produces a negative correlation (scores between 0 and −1), it means that the relationship between the two scores is such that when one increases, the other one decreases. An example of this could be looking at the correlation between transformational leadership and turnover intentions – the more transformational managers are, the less likely that their employees will intend to leave the organisation.

If a test produces a positive correlation (scores between 0 and +1), it means that the relationship between the two scores is such that when one increases, the other increases. An example of this could be looking at the correlation between age and job satisfaction in employees. Older employees tend to be more satisfied at work; therefore as age of employees increases, so does job satisfaction. You will see correlations referred to throughout this book. The rule of thumb is that the closer the correlation to +1 or −1, the stronger the relationship between the two scores, and the more likely that they are significantly related.

As ANOVA is a more complex form of *t*-test, so multiple regression is a more complex way to look at similarity. Whereas a correlation looks the relationship between two variables, multiple regression enables the researcher to explore the relationship between more than two variables. For instance, you may want to look at what workplace factors are related to job satisfaction in the workplace and so could explore the impact of age, autonomy and transformational leadership (and any others you wanted to look at). Multiple regression enables the researcher to look at the relative importance of each of the variables (by estimating each correlation independently), as well as the overall importance of all the variables. Taking this example, you could see how much of the variance in job satisfaction would be predicted by the age,

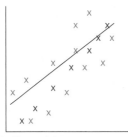

Positive correlation
The variables are positively related

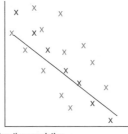

Negative correlation
The variables are inversely related

No correlation
There is no relationship between the variables

X = Perfect/strong relationship (*r* = 1)
X = Weak relationship
X = No relationship

autonomy and transformational leadership – and also which one thing had the strongest relationship with job satisfaction. You may also come across the term logistic regression. Logistic regression is multiple regression where your outcome is categorical.

Multiple regression also enables the researcher to explore moderators and mediators. A moderator is a variable that influences the strength of the relationship between two variables – for instance, age could be a moderator of the relationship between autonomy and job satisfaction in that older employees would be happier taking on more autonomy and responsibility. In this case, age would strengthen the relationship between autonomy and job satisfaction. A mediator is a variable that is linked causally to a variable and the outcome variable – for instance, it could be that transformational leadership results in employees feeling that they had greater autonomy at work, and that this then resulted in them feeling satisfied. In this example, autonomy would be the mediator of the relationship between transformational leadership and job satisfaction. In other words, transformational leadership is related to job satisfaction in employees because transformational leadership increases employees' feelings of autonomy.

Box 3.7

HOW TO SECTION: Tip for remembering the difference between mediation and moderation

Think of a car stereo where the independent variable is the music and the outcome is the sound. The moderator would be the volume knob – it strengthens or weakens the effect – making the music louder or quieter. A mediator would be the power switch – the sound of the music can only be heard when the on switch is pressed.

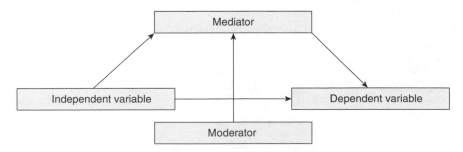

Figure 3.3   Figure to show the affect of mediator and moderators on the relationship between the independent and dependent variable

And finally – more advanced methods

Please note that although you may not use these methods as a student, you will see them used and referred to in journal articles, and therefore having a broad understanding is useful to you.

Structural equation modelling (SEM) is a very complex form of regression. It enables the researcher to see the many different relationships between all the variables. Generally SPSS is not used for this, but rather a program such as AMOS or Mplus.

Hierarchical linear modelling (HLM, also called multi-level modelling) is another more advanced form of multiple regression that enables the research to look at relationships with the outcome at more than one level – for instance, within the same data set, look at the relationships between work conditions and job satisfaction at not just the department level, but also the team level. It therefore needs data to be 'nested' – meaning that employee data would be collected where employees nested within teams that nested within departments that nested within the organisation.

Box 3.8

Test your understanding

For each of these scenarios, which would be the most appropriate analytical technique to use. The answers are all on the online site.

- You want to look at the predictors of engagement in an organisation. You have data on management capability, employee engagement and working hours.
- You have been asked to analyse if part time workers are more effective than full time workers.
- You want to see whether there is a relationship between management behaviour and employee well-being.
- You want to explore whether some selection methods are more useful than others. You use interviews, psychometric tests and references as your methods and you want to check utility against cost, candidate satisfaction and accuracy.

The role of qualitative techniques in Occupational Psychology

Qualitative researchers need to have a thorough knowledge and understanding of the philosophical assumptions underpinning their research. Unlike quantitative researchers, qualitative researchers are often required to defend their position regarding ontology (the study of reality; the question being 'what is it we are looking at?') and epistemology (the study of knowledge; the question being 'how do we know what we know?') and therefore this is one of the initial key skills of a qualitative researcher. It is often assumed that qualitative research is easier and less labour intensive than quantitative research. In fact, the opposite is true if that research is done well.

Data is generally collected by methods such as interviews or focus groups, where the dialogue will often be recorded. The task of the researcher is then to transcribe this data before analysis. In order to analyse qualitative data, the researcher needs to translate a huge amount of textual and/or visual data into theory. Patton (2002) says this involves four key skills and processes:

- reducing the volume of data;
- sifting trivial data from that of significance;
- identifying key themes in the data;
- constructing a conceptual framework.

The coding of the data (which is essentially breaking down the data into identifiable elements) is an early part of the analysis. The researcher is then required to link the coding elements together to form themes (such as common areas) and an overall story. For example, the research might be interested in understanding the reasons behind lack of motivation in the workplace. In this example, themes (or the category of reasons) might include poor working environment, low pay, lack of development opportunities and so on. This requires considerable skill and knowledge of the data. In terms of analysis more broadly, although there are different analytical techniques in qualitative research, the methodology for these techniques tends to be a set of guidance materials more than a set of rules. This means that the researcher has the flexibility and judgement to be able to apply those guidelines and transform the data.

This last point refers to one of the most important aspects of qualitative research, which is reflexivity. Reflexivity involves 'reflecting on the way in which research is carried out and understanding how the process of doing research shapes its outcomes' (Hardy et al., 2001: 533) and essentially refers to how the researcher themselves will affect both the design and outcome of the study.

As it is sometimes difficult to describe qualitative research so succinctly, we have included examples of Occupational Psychology papers that have used each particular methodology in this section. If you are interested in the method, have a look and see how it works.

Interpretative phenomenological analysis (IPA) is a relatively new analytic method developed specifically for psychology. Although used widely in health psychology, it is becoming a more commonplace method in Occupational Psychology. The main emphasis of IPA is upon taking an inductive approach and exploring in detail how individual participants make sense of an object or event – it is not concerned with the production of an objective statement about the event, and neither would there be an attempt to test a predetermined hypothesis. Generally data is collected by in-depth interviews with participants and research will include a small sample. A small homogeneous (similar to each other) sample is generally necessary due to the painstaking case-by-case analysis that is required. The aim is to make some sense of the perceptions and understanding of the group, rather than to make any generalisable claims.

An example of a paper that uses this method is: Millward, L.J. (2006) 'The transition to motherhood in an organisational context: an interpretative phenomenological analysis', *Journal of Occupational and Organisational Psychology*, 79: 315–33.

Content analysis can be defined as 'an approach to the analysis of documents and texts that seeks to quantify content in terms of predetermined categories and in a systematic and replicable manner' (Bryman, 2001: 180). This process involves coding the data and it can be done in one of three ways (Hsieh and Shannon, 2005). First, the conventional method is where the researcher reads the text and devises content categories from it. Second, the directed approach is where the research applies an existing theory or model to the text. Finally, in the summative approach, the data is analysed in terms of occurrence of key words or elements of the text, rather than coding the whole text. In each method the researcher will create a coding framework, which has categorised all the data. It is possible to use content analysis as a quantitative technique by applying a frequency analysis to the coding (for instance, using percentage frequency of mentions of particular themes in the data). An example of a paper that uses this method is: Lewis, R., Yarker, J. and Donaldson-Feilder, E. (2010) 'Using a competency based approach to identify the management behaviours required to manage workplace stress in nursing: a critical incident study', *International Journal of Nursing Studies*, 47: 307–13.

Template analysis or thematic coding can be seen as a technique that sits between content analysis and grounded theory (King, 1998). Like content analysis, it involves the production of codes that relate to themes within the data. The difference is that whereby in content analysis the codes are predetermined and data is analysed against those codes; in template analysis, many of the codes will be defined a priori, but then those codes can be modified, updated and altered as a researcher continues to analyse the data or text. An example of a paper that uses this method is: Dick, P. (2000) 'The social construction of the meaning of acute stressors: a qualitative study of the personal accounts of police officers using a stress counselling service', *Work & Stress*, 14: 226–44.

Discourse analysis focuses on understanding 'discourse' in terms of how and why the individual has used the language that they did. It therefore involves seeking to gain insight about the meaning an individual applies to themselves and the world. There is a huge variation in methods of conducting discourse analysis. From deconstructing the discourse (which could be a conversation, a speech, a letter, a flyer, a piece of gossip and any other forms of discourse), the researcher will seek to explore the meaning throughout and within the text. This could involve analysing length and prevalence of pauses, voice intonations, pronunciation, sentence structure, the organisation of the discourse, or any other aspect of that linguistic behaviour. The perspective taken in discourse analysis tends to be one of social constructionism, which holds that reality is entirely subjective and is defined by the individual through their thought processes and social interactions. An example of a paper that uses this method is: Harkness, A., Long, B.C., Bermbach, N., Patterson, K., Jordan, S. and Kahn, H. (2005) 'Talking about work stress: discourse analysis and implications for stress interventions', *Work & Stress*, 19: 121–36.

Summary

This chapter aimed to continue and build upon the exploration of ethics and ethical skills introduced in Chapter 2 by exploring the ethical skills that you will need as either an academic or practitioner in Occupational Psychology, and exploring the approach taken to ethics and associated standards by the BPS and the HPC. Ethics will continue to be included and discussed within each of the chapters in Part II – remember to look particularly at the practitioner and academic insights at the end of each chapter which asks how each individual embeds ethics into their daily lives.

   In the second part of the chapter the focus was upon research skills, introducing those that you will need both as a student and in your future roles in organisations or in research. The chapter can be used to refer back to explain key terms as you read through the chapters in Part II; and will help you to follow academic papers and journal articles. As you read forward into Part II you will see how important research continues to be to both academics and practitioners – again for concrete examples of this do read the practitioner and academic insights at the end of each chapter. It is intended that this chapter section will have provided an introduction to research skills, methods and analyses. You may need, and may want, to explore further in particular areas. If this is the case, below you will find a list of further reading around methods and qualitative and quantitative analyses.

Explore further

Recommended statistical and qualitative methods texts:

- Barbour, R. and Kitzinger, J. (1999) *Developing Focus Group Research*. London: Sage.
- Boyatzis, R.E. (1998) *Transforming Qualitative Information: Thematic Analysis and Code Development*. Thousand Oaks, CA: Sage.
- Cassell, C. and Symon, G. (2004) *Essential Guide to Qualitative Methods in Organisational Research*. London: Sage.

- Field, A. (2009) *Discovering Statistics Ising SPSS*. Introducing statistical methods series. London: Sage.
- Kvale, S. (1996) *Interviews: An Introduction to Qualitative Research Interviewing*. London: Sage.
- Smith, J.A. (2003) *Qualitative Psychology: A Practical Guide to Methods*. London: Sage.
- Smith, J.A., Flowers, P. and Larkin, M. (2009) *Interpretative Phenomenological Analysis: Theory Method and Research*. London: Sage.
- Strauss, A. and Corbin, J. (1990) *Basics of Qualitative Research: Grounded Theory Procedures and Techniques*. London: Sage.
- Willig, C. and Stainton-Rogers, W. (2008) *The Sage Handbook of Qualitative Research in Psychology*. London: Sage.
- Yin, R. (2009) *Case Study Research: Design and Methods*, 4th edn. London: Sage.
- For more information about Ethics and the Chartership Process: www.bps.org.uk
- To read more about our regulatory body, the Health Professions Council: http://www.hpc-uk.org/
- Online qualitative data analysis site: http://onlineqda.hud.ac.uk/index.php
- CAQDAS: Computer Assisted Qualitative Data Analysis Project – University of Surrey project delivering excellent training courses: http://www.surrey.ac.uk/sociology/research/researchcentres/caqdas/
- Professor Andy Field's statistical analysis site: http://www.statisticshell.com/

Discussion questions

1 How is confidentiality different to anonymity? It is really important to hold this difference in your work in practice or research. Often the terms are used interchangeably and this can create many problems.
2 What belief system do you hold around research and measurement?
3 It is suggested that statistics, and use of statistical methods, is going to become more and more important in organisations of the future. Why might that be?

References

Anderson, N., Herriot, P. and Hodgkinson, G. (2001) 'The practitioner-researcher divide in industrial, work and organisational (IWO) psychology: where are we now, and where do we go from here?', *Journal of Occupational and Organisational Psychology*, 74 (4): 391–411.

Bond, F.W. and Bunce, D. (2001) 'Job control mediates change in a work reorganisation: intervention for stress reduction', *Journal of Occupational Health Psychology*, 6 (4): 290–302.

Bryman, A. (2001) *Social Research Methods*. Oxford: Oxford University Press.

Hardy, C., Phillips, N. and Clegg, S. (2001) 'Reflexivity in organisation and management theory: a study of the production of the research subject', *Human Relations*, 54 (5): 531–60.

Hsieh, H.-F. and Shannon, S.E. (2005) 'Three approaches to qualitative content analysis', *Qualitative Health Research*, 15 (9): 1277–88.

King, N. (1998) 'The qualitative research interview', in C. Cassell and G. Symon (eds), *Qualitative Methods in Organisational Research*. London: Sage. pp. 118–34.

Patton, M.Q. (2002) *Qualitative Research and Evaluation Methods*. Thousand Oaks, CA: Sage.

Part II

Key areas in Occupational Psychology

4 Employee relations and motivation

Iain Coyne and Fiona Gavin

Learning outcomes

By the end of this chapter you should:

- understand the changing nature of employee relations and have knowledge of the psychological contract as a relatively recent approach to managing employee relations;
- be able to distinguish between needs theories, cognitive theories and the job design approaches to the understanding of employee motivation;
- have knowledge of the differing approaches to managing diversity in the workplace and understand the differing ways that diversity can be conceptualised;
- understand organisational conflict from functional and dysfunctional perspectives, and the processes involved in conflict, its management and prevention;
- have knowledge of workplace bullying – its conceptualisation, individual and organisation antecedents and outcomes, and approaches to reducing bullying at work.

Introduction

This chapter considers the employment relationship within organisations and the role psychology has played in helping us understand and manage this relationship. Throughout, we consider the ways in which managers can enhance relationships with employees, with the ultimate aim of improving business performance. We begin broadly, by setting the wider employee relations scene and the move away from a traditional, collective industrial relations philosophy to a more individual employee relations approach. We then outline the psychological contract as an approach to managing this more individual focus based on notions of trust, fairness and reciprocal deals. Next, we highlight employee engagement as an outcome of positive reciprocal deals and examine psychological theories of human motivation and how these may help us understand better how and why employees are engaged or disengaged on the job. We follow this by considering diversity in the workplace and how this impacts on the employment relationship, with particular emphasis on exploring approaches to manage diversity. Since diversity in interests and values is one of the ways that conflict may occur within organisations, we then explore functional and dysfunctional conflict and discuss employee relations in the context of understanding and managing conflict. Finally, we take a particular form of destructive interpersonal relationships – workplace bullying – and detail the extant literature and implications for management interventions.

Throughout this chapter we discuss theoretical developments as well as the applied context through the use of case study exercises, links to podcasts and illustrative examples of occupational psychology in action.

Employee relations

Employee relations (ER) is: 'managing fairly and getting the best out of people'. This quote (cited in Gamble, 2006) describes the approach adopted by a UK organisation operating in China to managing the employment relationship. On reading the rest of this chapter, keep in mind this quote and consider whether ER is simply all about 'being fair' and 'getting the best out of people'.

Typically, ER are managed by the broader human resource management (HRM) strategy within an organisation. ER can include: management of the employment contract; organisation of work; communication between managers, employees and union/non-union representatives; organisation of reward-based structures; management of workplace conflict; development of employee well-being; and retention of talent within the organisation. ER is perceived as a philosophy rather than a management function; it is proactive and concerns building trust, managing complex and fast-moving environments and 'achieving strategy through people' (CIPD, 2005: 2). Ultimately, an organisation's ER approach is designed to ensure employees are committed, motivated and loyal, and that they deliver the business objectives of the organisation.

Historically, the term 'industrial relations' (IR) has been synonymous with this area. IR typically reflected an employment environment of strong union involvement, collective bargaining, industrial action and manufacturing sector jobs (Blyton and Turnbull, 1994). However, as a result of changes to the economic environment, the nature of work and organisations, and to union membership, we do not now tend to observe traditional IR in practice. The 'old deal' of stable, structured employment environments in which job security was assured, time and effort was rewarded, income was related to experience and an individual received fair pay for good performance, has been replaced by a 'new deal' of less stable, flexible employment environments, lacking job security, where results are expected and rewards are based on performance (Hiltrop, 1995; Millward and Brewerton, 2001). Reductions in employee numbers, the flexibility and fragmentation of jobs, the increasing diversity of the workforce and the growth in individualism prompted the development of ER (Guest, 2004). This mirrors the move away from the reactive, low trust, formal, centralised and specialist notion of personnel management (better suited to managing IR) to the more proactive, high trust, organic, flexible and strategic HRM used to manage ER (Guest, 1987).

Figure 4.1 encapsulates chronologically this changing nature of employment relations in the UK. It demonstrates clearly the move from a collective to individualistic focus, from mechanistic to organic organisational structures and from union dominance to steady-state union membership. In recent times the state of ER in the UK has been characterised by stable union membership, more direct communication between managers and employees, an increase in trust and an increase in flexible working (Kersley et al., 2005). Interestingly, projections suggest reduced trust in senior managers, insecure, stressed and worried employees, a period of unstable employee relations and escalating industrial action (CIPD, 2011a, 2011b). See Box 4.1 for some further ideas on the outlook for ER.

Box 4.1

Employment relations outlook

The podcasts below are from the CIPD podcast series, highlighting different individuals' views on the outlook for ER in the UK. Listen to both and consider the main themes advanced by the contributors and how they may impact on ER. Also, are these views supported in the current employment climate?

2008 – http://www.cipd.co.uk/podcasts/_articles/_employeerelations.htm?link=title

2011 – http://www.cipd.co.uk/podcasts/_articles/_hrtrendsfor2011.htm?link=title

---

Although we've focused on the UK context, we must touch briefly on managing ER at an international level. First, one cannot assume that the UK has 'exported' an ER approach to the rest of the world. For example, the Japanese systems of quality circles, teamwork and total quality management influenced ER practices in the UK during the 1980s and 1990s (Leat, 2007). Second, as Sparrow (1996) suggests, we cannot also assume that one set approach operates worldwide. For example, across European countries evidence points to differing ER practices being used (Larsen and Brewster, 2003) and variations in incidences of industrial action – suggestive of the need to approach ER differently (European Foundation for the Improvement of Living and Working Conditions, 2010). So while we have said a new perspective on employee relations has emerged, it is inaccurate to suggest this pattern is reflected worldwide.

1950s	1960s	1970s	1980s	1990s	2000s	2010 +
High union membership and industrial relations approach. 75% of the workforce were covered by national or statutory agreements on pay, hours, conditions and so on.	Industry/national level bargaining increasingly undermined by collective agreements at the level of the workplace. Still a strong union presence.	Height of union 'power' and a peak in industrial action, strikes and conflict.	Decrease in bargaining opportunities, regulations on industrial action and union activities changing. Reduction in industrial action (down 93%).	Development of human resource management approaches to managing employee relations and the influence of the Japanese 'lean production' model. Performance-based management. Emergence of the psychological contract.	Steady state of union membership – dominant in the public sector. Continual decline in industrial action. Growth in direct employee-manager communications and an increase in flexible working conditions. More trust in manager-non union organisations, but an overall perception of good employee relations.	Expectation of unstable employee relations with a pattern suggesting a decline in relationships. Union membership showing signs of increasing (mostly in public sector). Some signs of a worried and stressed workforce. Favourable attitudes to managers, but a lack of trust in senior managers. A focus on employee engagement.

Figure 4.1 Timeline for employment relations in the UK

Source: CIPD (2005, 2011a, 2011b), Guest (1987), Kersley et al. (2005), Leat (2007) and Rousseau (1997).

Therefore, multinational organisations need to consider carefully how they will manage ER in local organisations and whether given differences in cultural values, ER procedures from one country can apply to a different country. Leat (2007) proposes three approaches:

- Ethnocentric – the parent organisation's ER procedures dominate and are dictated to the local organisation.
- Polycentric – ER procedures are devised by the parent organisation but are consistent with the local organisation's cultural values.
- Regiocentric/geocentric – ER procedures are developed at a region or geographical level (for example, Asia).

Leat (2007) highlights that a polycentric approach is more common, although Box 4.2 indicates that an ethnocentric approach can also be effective.

Box 4.2

CASE STUDY: Experiences of human resource practices in China

Gamble (2006) details a case study of employee experiences of HRM practices in a UK-based store (UKStore) operating in China. UKStore operated effectively an ethnocentric ER approach to China. Through interviews and surveys, Chinese employees were asked to compare their experiences of UKStore with their experiences of state-owned enterprises (SOEs).

Perceptions of UKStore and SOE:

- UKStore perceptions: fast-paced, clear division of labour, equal treatment, long-term planning, good (informal) supervisor relationships, sharing of information, ability-based promotion, job security in return for commitment, enhanced opportunities for development and promotion, modern management approach, people centred.
- SOE perceptions: slow-paced, variable treatment, ad hoc planning, formal/limited relationships with supervisors, information not shared, seniority-based promotions, deteriorating security of employment and old management approach.
- In UKStore pay was higher, working conditions were better and satisfaction, commitment and sense of achievement were higher than those seen in SOEs.
- The pace of work was more intense and the work ethic stronger in UKStore than SOEs.

(Continued)

(Continued)

- UKStore had a procedure where employees could voice grievances and outcomes were fed back.

Conclusions:

Gamble concludes that even though UKStore's HRM procedure is contrary to a traditional view of Chinese management practices (e.g. those seen in SOEs) employee perceptions are more positive of UKStore than SOEs. This supports the notion that 'Western' HRM practices can be transferred into a Chinese context. Indeed, he argues that the UKStore approach appealed to the younger, more ambitious Chinese citizen.

Caveats:

Gamble introduces a number of caveats to these findings, which provide ideal discussion questions:

1 UKStore is new and exciting with only has a short history in China. What problems could emerge long-term after this initial excitement has died down? Are perceptions just related to an initial contrast effect with experiences of SOEs?
2 UKStore operates in an economically developed area in China. Would the same findings emerge in less economically developed areas?
3 Will UKStore be able to match employee expectations of job security, higher pay etc., during times of economic uncertainty?

Gamble, J. (2006) 'Introducing Western-style HRM practices to China: shop floor perceptions in a British multinational', *Journal of World Business*, 41: 328–43.

The psychological contract

We have talked about the changing nature of 'deals' in the employment relationship from what Rousseau et al. (as cited in Guest, 2004) term standard deals (collective) to idiosyncratic deals (individual). This has meant a move away from institutional perspectives towards a more individual ER perspective. As a result, psychology has become more relevant to our understanding of this area (Arnold et al., 2005), as psychology can help researchers and practitioners understand why an individual responds in the way they do.

One concept where this is increasingly the case, and reflects the changing nature of 'deals', is the psychological contract (PC). The PC emerged from early work on social exchange theory (Blau, 1964), which posits that relationships between individuals operate through a reciprocal process of abiding by rules of social exchange and, so long as these rules are adhered to, trusting and loyal relationships are maintained. The PC is defined as: 'The perception of both parties to the employment relationship – organisation and individual – of the reciprocal promises and implications implied in the relationship' (Guest and Conway, 2002: 22). It therefore provides employees with a mental model of the employment relationship in terms of what they are required to do in order to meet their side of the bargain, and what they can expect from their employer. Being individualised it synthesises well with newer HRM approaches to employee relations.

Key features of the PC are (Rousseau, 1995):

- beliefs on what an employee and employer are obliged to contribute;
- an expectation of reciprocal relationships;
- a focus on promise fulfilment rather than met expectations;
- underlying notions of fairness and trust in the development and management of the psychological contract.

Rousseau (1995) theorised the PC to range on a continuum from 'transactional' (characterised by short-term, economic exchanges with limited employee involvement and little commitment) to relational (long-term and dynamic, based on mutual trust, loyalty and employee involvement). Rousseau further argued that beliefs can develop from overt promises (such as the provision of training discussed at recruitment) or learning and experience (for example, witnessing other employees' experiences at work). Perceived obligations are not necessarily static or universal rather varying across roles, organisations and changing over time (that is, from the 'old deal' to the 'new deal' discussed earlier). Table 4.1 illustrates some of the main employee and employer obligations identified in previous research. Looking at these and considering the discussion on the change in ER, think about how some of these promises may change in the future.

The formation of the PC occurs over a series of phases (Rousseau, 2001). Before an individual even starts work he or she has beliefs (possibly from previous experience) regarding the nature of work and the organisation that create certain thoughts about joining a specific organisation. Next during recruitment, a potential employee and employer create an initial understanding on what is being offered by both parties. Once in the role, work experiences foster the continuing exchange relationship between employer and employee. Finally, the employee starts to evaluate the relationship to judge whether obligations have been met. When a fair deal has been perceived to be delivered, positive organisational benefits in terms of loyalty, intention to stay (De Vos and Meganck 2009) and engagement in organisational citizenship behaviour (Hui et al., 2004) emerge. However, if there is a belief that one party has failed to live up to its promises, a violation of the PC emerges, which can result in: low trust, job dissatisfaction and staff turnover (Robinson and Rousseau, 1994); a lack of loyalty and failure to do the job properly (Turnley and Feldman, 1999); reduced citizenship behaviour and increased workplace deviance (Restubog et al., 2007).

The PC concept is not without its critics. Arnold (1996) argued that the distinction between transactional and relational contracts is not as clear in practice and that obligations do not map consistently to a transactional and relational framework (for example, training could sometimes be seen as transactional or

Table 4.1 Employee and employer obligations in the psychological contract

Employer obligations	Employee obligations
Provide adequate training	Work to contract
Ensure fair selection and appraisal	Have a strong work ethic
Consult with employees	Be honest
Provide feedback on performance	Be flexible
Promote responsibility in employees	Be loyal and committed
Provide equitable pay	Develop new skills and update old ones
Provide reasonable job security	Come up with new ideas
Provide opportunities for promotion	Work extra hours when required

Source: (CIPD, 2011c; Cross et al., 2008; Herriot et la., 1997).

relational). Further, he suggests that little research has tested whether a contract is solely based on broken promises or whether it also can develop from unmet expectations. Indeed, Montes and Zweig (2009) have shown that PC violation can occur when no promises have been made. Cullinane and Dundon (2006) propose that the PC is not a contract at all as it does not have the same explicit agreement between parties one would expect with a contract. Finally, Sparrow (1996) has questioned whether the PC concept is equivalent in different cultures. He posits that the PC is 'conditioned by national cultures ...' (1996: 484) and will differ across countries as a result of individual factors (for example, differing individual needs across countries), social cues (for example, predominant values within each country) and differing management practices.

As an attempt to extend the PC to provide a framework for understanding the emerging employee relations, Guest (2004) proposes a systems model that considers the contextual and background factors as well as policies that shape the PC, the nature of the PC (for example, what the perceived agreed promises are) and the resultant outcomes. Central to this model is the current state of the PC in terms of whether a fair deal has been delivered and how this impacts on employee-employer trust. These 'states' become mediators between the PC and outcomes (such as job satisfaction, organisational commitment, job performance and turnover intention). The big advantage of this model according to Guest is that it: '... helps to maintain a focus on employment relations and the concerns of employees in a context which is increasingly non-union and where employee "voice" may be restricted ...' (2004: 551).

A model such as Guest's can help research and practitioners better understand how employees view their relationship with their employer and how, in changing economic and employment environments, important it is that managers continually monitor the state of the PC. Effective communication with employees to foster perceptions of trust and fairness become an integral part of this process.

Engagement and motivation at work

In the timeline (Figure 4.1), we introduced the notion of employee engagement and, listening to the podcasts (Box 4.1), you'll already know that employee engagement is seen as a key driver of future ER. Tying it back to the PC, one outcome of the reciprocal deal seen in the PC is employee engagement. Saks (2006), building on social exchange theory, argued that reciprocal beliefs dictate the extent that an individual is engaged or disengaged with their role. He posits: 'employees feel obliged to bring themselves more deeply into their role performances as repayment for the resources they receive from their organisation. When the organisation fails to provide these resources, individuals are more likely to withdraw and disengage themselves from their roles' (2006: 603). Therefore, similar to the PC, engagement is a two-way relationship between the employer and employee.

Kahn defined personal engagement as 'the harnessing of organisation members' selves to their work roles' and personal disengagement as 'the uncoupling of selves from work roles' (1990: 694). When engaged, an employee directs their self into active role performance and becomes engaged physically, cognitively and emotionally. Psychological drivers of engagement include: meaningfulness of the task and role, feeling psychologically safe to be able to voice opinions, line manager style and skills, person-job fit, senior manager vision, supportive environment, effective communication, fairness and challenging jobs (Alfes et al., 2010; Fleck and Inceoglu, 2010; Kahn, 1990; Macey et al., 2009).

Engaged employees are more involved, satisfied, committed, intrinsically motivated, likely to stay and perform better on the job (Rich et al., 2010; Saks, 2006). Further, engagement has a positive impact on return on assets, profitability and shareholder value (Macey et al., 2009). Therefore, it is not surprising that engagement is a hot topic, because as organisations are limited in their ability to use monetary rewards to motivate employees, they need to look to other ways to engage their employees. Although, a word of caution: too much support for engagement (for example, jobs which are too challenging or trust which cannot be reciprocated) may result in disengagement (Macey et al., 2009).

Although there are divergent perspectives on what engagement is – indeed some critics question whether it is a new construct (Newman and Harrison, 2008) – there is growing consensus that engagement is a psychological state with both cognitive and affective components. For example, Fleck and Inceoglu (2010) derive four engagement states based on a cognitive versus affective, and job versus organisational framework:

* cognitive – job = absorption in the work;
* cognitive – organisation = alignment with organisational goals;
* affective – job = feeling energised by the job;
* affective – organisation = emotional identification with the organisation.

If engagement is such a hot topic and if it is seen to be the key driver of employee relations, there is a need to better conceptualise it and to better understand its underlying processes. One such approach offered by Inceoglu and Fleck (2010) is to view engagement within a motivational continuum ranging from dispositional motivation (personality or needs) at one end to situational motivation (motivated behaviours) at the other. Engagement is placed within the middle of this framework and is viewed as state motivation or the feeling of being motivated. Therefore, understanding how individuals experience feelings of being motivated (or engagement) is paramount to developing a high-performance culture within an organisation. Given your ability or capability to perform and an environment that allows you to perform; motivation determines whether you will actually perform or not (Muchinsky, 2006). The ultimate goal for an organisation is to have motivated employees who choose to direct their effort towards organisational goals, who invest maximal effort into their job and who sustain their effort over prolonged periods (Muchinsky, 2006).

Psychology is populated with a plethora of theories purporting to explain human motivation, with each taking a slightly different perspective. The following discussion will detail some of the main theories and assess their empirical support and practical applicability.

Needs theories

Needs theories propose that individuals are driven to satisfy various subconscious needs. As a result, these approaches fit into the notion of dispositional motivation (Inceoglu and Fleck, 2010) as they are relatively stable and provide an explanation as to why an individual feels engaged. Arguably the most famous of these theories is Maslow's Hierarchy of Relative Propotency (1943) – commonly termed Hierarchy of Needs. Maslow suggested a hierarchy of five needs in which an individual is motivated to satisfy, what is at that point, a more important need before she or he can move on to the next need. Once satisfied, the need no longer becomes the focus of the individual's drive and ceases to directly motivate (see Figure 4.2).

At the bottom of the hierarchy are our basic *physiological* needs for food, water and so on. Next is our *security* need for psychological safety and freedom from harm, and following this, our *social* needs capture our desire to be loved or to love. Maslow saw these three levels as deficiency needs, because to be deficient in these results in an individual being unable to progress to the higher levels of the model. The following two needs, *esteem* and *self-actualisation*, are seen as growth needs as they motivate people to seek out new experiences, to develop and to grow. Esteem needs promote our desire for achievement, freedom, recognition, reputation and appreciation. At the highest level the individual has a need for self-fulfilment or self-actualisation and to reach this final level an individual needs to become a 'basically satisfied person' (Maslow 1943: 383).

Maslow's model has intuitive appeal and offers practical utility, yet despite this, empirical support for Maslow's model is limited. Muchinsky (2006) highlights the lack of agreement on the number of needs and the hierarchical progression of need satisfaction as problematic. Interestingly, although portrayed as a strict hierarchy, Maslow actually pinpointed some exceptions to this notion. For example, creative people may appear to be self-actualised even if they seem to lack the satisfaction of basic needs (for example, the poor artist). Indeed, he argued that the hierarchy should be viewed as 'degrees of relative satisfaction' rather than absolutes. Consequently, an individual does not have to be 100% satisfied with a need before moving on to the next. So long as the individual is at a level of satisfaction that they are content with, the drive to satisfy the next need is triggered.

Subsequently, Alderfer (1972) adapted Maslow's model in the development of the ERG needs theory. Here, human motivation is driven by three needs which can be activated at any time and which can all operate at the same time (therefore non-hierarchical).

- Existence needs: these correspond to physiological and safety needs in Maslow's model.
- Relatedness needs: needs satisfied by meaningful social and interpersonal relationships (social).
- Growth needs: needs satisfied by an individual making creative and productive contributions (esteem and self-actualising).

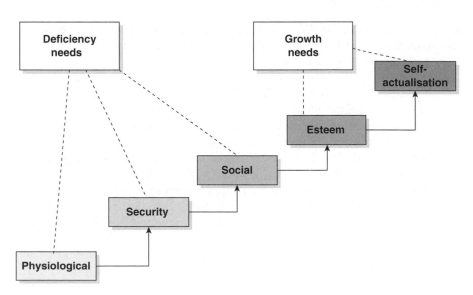

Figure 4.2 Representation of Maslow's hierarchy of needs

McClelland's (1961) theory differs from the previous two in its conceptualisation of needs. Rather than subscribing to the notion that needs are universal, inherent drivers of behaviour, McClelland proposed a trait-based conceptualisation in which individual differences influence the drive to satisfy certain needs. The most commonly researched needs in Occupational Psychology are:

- need for achievement (nAch): the need to accomplish and achieve success;
- need for affiliation (nAff): the need to cooperate with others and develop relationships;
- need for power (nPow): the need to influence others and be in charge.

One advantage of this model over the previous two is the more direct mapping of needs to actual work behaviour (Steers et al., 2004). As an example, Bartram (2005) illustrates how nPow and nAch relate to competency factors in an organisational competency framework. Empirically, nAch has been shown to relate to entrepreneurial success (Collins et al., 2004). Other evidence suggests effective managers are high in nPow, moderate in nAch and low in nAff (McClelland Boyatzis, 1982).

The main drawback to this approach is the use of the thematic apperception test (TAT) to assess for these unconsciousness needs. Expert assessors are required to interpret TAT assessments and projective tests, such as the TAT, have questionable psychometric accountability (Woods and West, 2010).

Cognitive theories

You may encounter needs theories sometimes referred to as content theories. This is because they describe *what* motivates an individual and *why* this individual behaves in a particular way (for example, I am motivated to work longer hours than required to satisfy my need to achieve). As stated they tend to reflect the more dispositional side to motivation. However, they tend to neglect *how* an individual chooses a course of action from a set of alternatives and the processes underlying this volition (for example, why did I choose to work longer hours rather than attending training to update my knowledge?). In the 'golden age' of motivation research (Steers et al., 2004) a series of process-oriented theories emerged which attempted to identify the cognitive processes an individual experiences when making a choice to act in a specific manner. Such theories may help us explain the motivational basis underlying individual engagement, how individuals develop the motivational state of engagement and how they choose motivated work behaviours.

Vroom's (1964) expectancy theory posits motivation to exert effort as a function of an individual's cognitive appraisal of three features (Figure 4.3).

- Valence (V) – the value (from positive to negative) an individual places on the perceived outcomes (reward) of exerting effort.

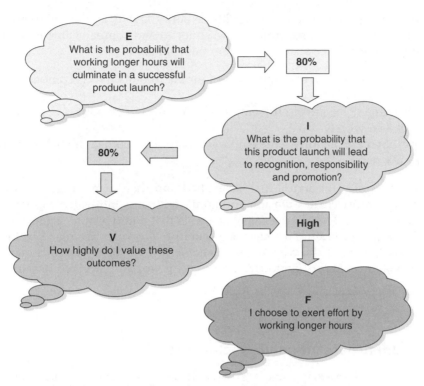

Have a go yourself with the model using your own example

Figure 4.3   VIE process for working longer hours

- Instrumentality (I) – the perceived probability that performance will relate to positive outcomes.
- Expectancy (E) – the perceived probability that effort will relate to required performance.

Vroom combined these features into an equation predicting 'Force to act' (F):

$$F = V \times I \times E$$

Research is generally supportive of the model, with VIE force scores shown to predict ratings of effort and job performance (Pritchard and Sanders, 1973) and job-related attitudes (Van Eerde and Thierry, 1996). Although in both cases, the VIE score was not as strong a predictor as individual factors (for example, V) or other combinations of factors (for example, VE). Additionally, in the latter study the VIE model did not exhibit strong effects for actual work-related behavioural outcomes.

Focusing more on cognitions of perceived fairness, Adams (1963) proposed a theory of social inequity to explain motivation. In this model, an employee evaluates the ratio of their inputs (experience, skills, seniority, loyalty and so on) to outcomes (pay, job security, status, recognition and so forth) and compares this to a referent other (co-worker). Three states result from this evaluation.

- Equity – the employee's evaluation of inputs to outcomes is comparable with that of a co-worker.
- Overpayment inequity – the employee's input-outcome ratio is greater than that of a co-worker.
- Underpayment inequity – the employee's input-outcome ratio is less than that of a co-worker.

In states of equity, the individual is satisfied and there is no motivation to act. However, inequity creates tension and an individual is motivated to reduce this and restore equity. Muchinsky (2006) suggests that equity can be achieved either behaviourally (increasing/decreasing inputs or lowering/raising outcomes) or cognitively (changing the way you see events). Box 4.3 looks how this may work at a national level in relation to UK public-sector worker perceived unfairness.

Box 4.3

The 'unfairness' of public sector cuts

As a result of the banking crisis, in 2010–11 the UK public sector saw cuts in funding with knock on effects to job security and reduced pensions. There was a sense of unfairness in this sector that they were taking the hit for a problem which was the fault of 'greedy bankers'. Let's hypothesise the underpayment inequity perceptions of a public sector worker.

Underpayment Inequity

'It is unfair that I am now being asked to continue to invest my experience, effort and time yet increase my pension contribution and take a pay cut, particularly in comparison to a city banker who is receiving a large bonus this year without any changes to their work, when they caused the problem in the first place.'

Behavioural

'I will reduce my efforts by working to the minimum of my contracted role and will engage in industrial action.'

Cognitive

'Cuts need to be made and it could be worse – at least I have my job. Bankers need to help get us out of the recession.'

Adams advances support for this theory, and more contemporary research has also reported relationships between equity perceptions, job satisfaction and intention to quit (Griffeth and Gaertner, 2001). However, evidence for overpayment inequity is limited and the main practical problem with the model is that inequity can be reduced without promoting an employee to exert more effort (Muchinsky, 2006). This is hardly an ideal situation for an organisation.

More contemporary theorists have expanded on equity theory in their development of organisational justice. Within this framework, fairness moves beyond inequity of outcome to include other forms of injustice:

- distributive justice – fairness of the outcome (equity);
- procedural justice – 'fairness of the procedures used to determine outcome …' (Colquitt et al., 2001: 425);
- interactional justice – fairness perceptions in terms of being treated with dignity and respect (interpersonal) and in terms of how decisions are communicated and explained (informational).

In their meta-analysis, Colquitt et al. (2001) report relationships between all justice dimensions and job satisfaction, commitment, withdrawal and performance. Other research indicates relationships between procedural justice and intrinsic motivation and task performance (Zapata-Phelan et al., 2009) and between procedural injustice and workplace aggression (Hershcovis et al., 2007). We have already seen how fairness (procedural and interactional justice) is inherent within the development and maintenance of the psychological contract.

Goal-setting theory (Locke and Latham, 1990) suggests individuals act rationally to direct their efforts towards the attainment of goals. Principally, specific and difficult goals motivate the individual to achieve higher task performance because they:

- direct attention to goal activities;
- reduce ambiguity in performance expectations;
- enhance persistency on goal activities;
- energise the activity by requiring greater effort to succeed;
- promote the use or development of strategies to achieve the goal. (Locke and Latham 2002)

Through these mechanisms, an individual is motivated to achieve their set goals and will perform more effectively than when no goals or vague goals are set. If satisfied with their performance and the rewards, the individual will commit to new goals. This process is moderated by perceptions of how important or meaningful the goal is, self-efficacy or confidence in achieving the goal, the amount of feedback on goal progression and the complexity of the task (Figure 4.4).

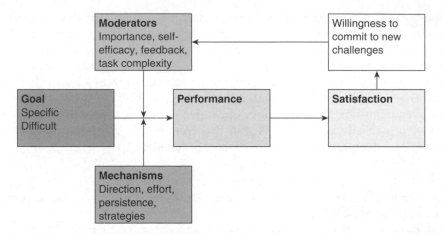

Figure 4.4   Model of goal-setting theory

Source: Locke, E.A. and Latham, G.P (2002) 'Building a practically useful theory of goal setting and task motivation. A 35-year Odyssey', *American Psychologist*, 57 (9): 705–17.

Goal-setting theory is '… among the most valid and practical theories of employee motivation in organisational psychology' (Locke and Latham, 2002: 714). Substantial support is reported for the model (Ambrose and Kulik, 1999) and its relative simplicity allows the development of effective goal-based organisational interventions to enhance employee motivation. Conversely, limitations include:

- Multiple goals induce goal conflict which impedes performance towards one single goal.
- Goals can sometimes lead to increased risk taking.
- Goals can narrow focus to only goal-directed behaviour at the expense of other behaviours.

Work design models

Work design theories focus on features of the job rather than processes within the individual per se which promote motivation. This work has roots in Herzberg's (1966) motivation-hygiene hypothesis, which developed from examining why some people were satisfied and dissatisfied at work. Herzberg identified two factors.

- Hygiene (extrinsic) factors: such as pay, working conditions and quality of supervision do not necessarily motivate, but cause dissatisfaction if not met.
- Motivation (intrinsic) factors: such as achievement, advancement and recognition promote growth, motivation and satisfaction.

To enhance employee motivation, managers therefore need to enrich jobs with involvement, responsibility and career progression that encourages intrinsic motivation. Critics of the model have argued that hygiene factors (especially pay) do motivate effort. However, Sachau (2007) argued this criticism misinterprets Herzberg's original thesis of hygiene factors 'moving' (or extrinsically motivating as we now vision it) an individual. Hence pay is viewed as an extrinsic motivator, although it has a short shelf life and may not satisfy every employee.

Adopting the concept of intrinsic motivation, Hackman and Oldham (1980) developed the job characteristics model (JCT). Theoretically, certain features of the job (skill variety, task identity, task significance, autonomy and feedback) are hypothesised to predict outcomes of intrinsic motivation, work performance, work satisfaction, absenteeism and turnover. This is achieved through three psychological states.

- Meaningfulness – the skill variety, task identity and task significance of the job creates a sense that the job has purpose and importance.
- Responsibility – job autonomy creates a feeling of personal responsibility and freedom to achieve goals.
- Knowledge of results – feedback on the job provides information on how well an individual is performing.

Additionally, they proposed an individual needs component (growth need strength, GNS) that moderates the extent an individual responds to job characteristics and experiences psychological states. They further developed an equation for organisational use to judge the motivating potential (MPS) of a job:

$$\text{MPS} = \frac{\text{skill variety} + \text{task identity} + \text{task significance}}{3} \times \text{autonomy} \times \text{feedback}$$

Meta-analyses endorse a number of the proposed relationships between characteristics and outcomes as well as the influence of psychological states (Fried and Ferris, 1987; Humphrey et al., 2007) – although, the psychological state of meaningfulness has been identified as the primary influencing factor between job characteristics and outcomes. By contrast, relationships between job characteristics and outcomes of job performance and absenteeism are less supported.

Humphrey et al. (2007) expand on the original JCT by including additional motivating characteristics, new social characteristics (for example, social support), new work characteristics (for example, physical demands) and additional outcomes (such as well-being and role perceptions).

The psychology of work motivation has a long and productive history and we can see how some of these ideas are put into practice. Theories range on their intuitive, practical and empirical appeal and focus on *why* people are motivated, *how* they choose a course of action or *what* features in a job promote motivation. Theories do not necessarily contradict each other; rather they focus on different aspects of the motivational process (Locke and Latham, 2004). Indeed, these authors postulate the development of a mega-theory based primarily on a goal-setting ideology, yet inclusive of needs, expectancy, fairness and job characteristics models. We have also seen that these theoretical approaches may provide insight into how and why employees become engaged on the job. Some of the drivers of engagement are reflected within the motivational theories discussed: meaningfulness of the task (job characteristics theory); disposition (needs theories); fairness (equity theory) and challenging jobs (goal setting theory). Theories also help us to understand how employees become motivated to engage: whether as a result of a drive to satisfy needs; a cognitive process based on expectancy or fairness; the energy to achieve specific and difficult goals; or through enhancing intrinsic motivation through meaningfulness, autonomy and effective feedback.

Managing diversity at work

Within the last three decades, there has been increasing emphasis among both academics and practitioners on constructing the notion of difference among employees as something that needs 'managing', apparently for the benefit of both employees and organisations (Harzig et al., 2010). Clearly, changes in the characteristics of the workforce have implications for the nature and management of the employment relationship, especially in terms of how diverse employees view the psychological contract they have with an organisation. Therefore, understanding how diverse individuals or groups work with each other, how to ensure fairness can be achieved in managing diversity and how to realise business performance outcomes from managing diversity are important features of effective employee relations management.

As Chapter 1 explored, various social processes such as increasing globalisation and women's increasing workplace participation have resulted in greater sociological and psychological diversity within contemporary workforces (Harrison and Sin, 2006). However, equality of access to work and equal treatment in the workplace remain challenges that are often debated and difficult to address. Indeed it has been said that organisations are arenas that both reflect and maintain the inequalities that exist in society at large (Priola and Brannan, 2009). The current state of equality in the British workforce has been assessed as part of a wider review of social equality in a recently published report by the Equality and Human Rights Commission; some of the key findings are presented in Box 4.4.

Box 4.4

How Fair is Britain?

First Triennial Review 2010

Employment Rates

- The percentage of low qualified disabled men in work dropped from 77% to 38% from the 1970s to the 2000s.
- 45% of disabled people in their early 20s are neither in employment, education nor training.
- Only 25% of Bangladeshi and Pakistani women work.
- Muslims have the lowest rate of employment of any religious group, with only 47% of Muslim men and 24% of Muslim women in employment.

Occupational and Heirarchical Segregation

- Women occupy 77% of administration and secretarial posts but only 6% of engineering and 14% of architects, planners and surveyors, meanwhile 83% of people employed in personal services are women.
- 40% of female jobs are in the public sector compared to 15% of male jobs, a factor that contributes to the pay gap (see below) since public sector jobs generally command lower salaries than comparable positions in the private sector.
- Despite an increasing number of women entering the workplace, only 1 in 3 managerial jobs in Britain are held by women.

Pay Gap

- Women aged 40 earn on average 27% less than men of the same age.
- Disabled men experience a pay gap of 11% compared with non-disabled men.
- Black graduates face a 24% pay penalty across their life-span.

Discrimination and Harrassment

- People with a disability or long-term illness are over twice as likely to report bullying or harassment in the workplace as non-disabled people.
- Lesbian, gay and bisexual people are twice as likely to be report discrimination and nearly twice as likely to report unfair treatment as heterosexuals.

Source: Equality and Human Rights Commission (2010)

Factors contributing to persistent inequality in the workplace are wide ranging and include:

- stereotyping and assumptions about the skills and abilities of individuals, based on gender, ethnicity, disability or other demographic characteristic (for example, men make good mechanics, women make good receptionists);

- pressure of social and cultural conformity surrounding the acceptability of certain tasks and behaviours (for example, asking for a pay rise being a more acceptable action for a man than a woman);
- intergroup prejudice, where those in power devalue individuals from other demographic groups simply on the basis of their group membership (for example, failing to promote the best person for the job due to prejudice about that individual's sexual orientation);
- inequalities within domestic relationships (for example, designating women as primary carers and men as primary breadwinners);
- the social construction of work-roles (for example, emphasising assertiveness – a stereotypically 'male' trait – as a quality needed by a manager);
- differences in access to education and educational qualifications;
- lack of physical accessibility in terms of premises, equipment and other resources at work.

Equal opportunities and managing diversity

Early approaches to dealing with workforce differences developed in the context of the social and political climate of the 1960s and 1970s and were predicated on the moral imperative of addressing inequalities between groups of people with differing social status (Doherty, 2004). Thus the notion of 'equal opportunities' (EO) was conceived. However, despite being well-intentioned, EO measures have received some heavy criticism.

- Some organisations faced a 'backlash' from majority-group workers (usually white males) resenting what they saw as 'special treatment' for minorities (Doherty, 2004).
- Some individuals became vulnerable to accusations of being rewarded solely on the basis of their minority status rather than on merit (Kalev et al., 2006).
- All groups are encouraged to adopt traditional values and compete within existing patriarchal cultures rather than challenging such cultures (Smithson and Stockoe, 2005).

Partly in response to the failings of EO, a new paradigm of 'managing diversity' (MD) developed in the 1990s, which has a more positive focus and an overarching goal of promoting inclusive working practices that would be relevant to all workers. The main differences between the old and new paradigms are outlined in Figure 4.5.

The business case for diversity

The primary motivation for adopting the MD ethos is a belief in the business case for diversity which has an internal economic focus. This business case suggests, first, that the performance of excluded workers is likely to decrease while

EQUAL OPPORTUNITIES	MANAGING DIVERSITY
Externally driven • Moral / legal obligations • EO = cost	Internally driven • Rests on business case • MD = investment
Operational basis • Concerned with statistics • Piecemeal interventions	Strategic basis • Concerned with experiences • Holistic culture change
Group focused • Group initiatives • Family friendly policies	Individual focused • Individual development • Employee friendly policies
Difference = other • Deficit model • Ethnocentric and heterosexist • Assimilation advocated • Discrimination focused • Harassment = individual issue	Difference = asset • Model of plenty • Celebrate difference • Company adaption advocated • Development focused • Harassment = organisational culture issue

Figure 4.5   Equal Opportunities versus managing diversity

Source: Adapted from Wilson and Iles (1999).

absenteeism and turnover costs are likely to increase. Second, it is argued that a diverse workforce enhances creativity and productivity, and can be more responsive to the needs of its client or customer base.

However, though the business case for diversity has intuitive appeal, there are inevitable complexities that make the reality less than ideal. A benchmarking survey (*Personnel Today*, 2005) found that although 91% of 113 organisations identified a business case for diversity, only 35% could quantify the benefits. Therefore, if a rational economic stance is taken, it could be argued that for the 65% of businesses not finding any quantifiable benefits, focus on MD is merely a cost. This implies that in these cases, a return to the moral argument of the EO ethos is necessary in order to drive action for equality.

Organisational inclusion

Despite the criticisms of the MD paradigm, the concept of organisational inclusion, central to the MD ethos, is a useful starting point for exploring minority groups' experiences at work. A definition of the inclusive workplace is given in Figure 4.6.

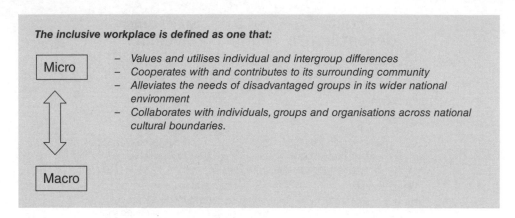

Figure 4.6   Definition of the inclusive workplace

Source: Mor Barak (2000).

While establishing a value base such as that proposed by Mor Barak (2000) may be a useful starting point from which to operationalise DM, there is a considerable body of empirical evidence that suggests this is not sufficient to ensure equality or inclusion. In a recent, large participant sample study across 163 organisations in the hotel industry, Herdman and McMillan-Capehart (2010) explored organisational level predictors of perceptions of diversity climate. They found that there was a positive relationship between existence of diversity programmes and a positive climate for diversity (PCFD), but that this relationship was moderated by several variables, including the 'actual diversity and the collective relational values of the management teams' (2010: 41). In other words, diversity initiatives in themselves were taken to indicate a PCFD, but this relationship was much stronger where the management team itself consisted of a high level of ethnically diverse individuals and where those individuals were perceived as taking an investment or 'relational' approach to employees. The explanation is that individuals utilise multiple cues in perceiving their environment; therefore organisations with diversity programmes but no diversity within the management team would send inconsistent cues regarding the organisations' actual commitment to diversity.

Equality, diversity and UK law

In the last 30 years there has been a growing body of national and international legislation that has sought to protect the rights of minority groups, nevertheless, the global picture remains patchy. Although European regions (for example, the Netherlands and Scandinavia) are among those with the most widely respected approaches to diversity, even within this continent diversity legislation differs according to national guidelines.

In the UK there has been a recent attempt to harmonise equality legislation with the introduction of the Equality Act 2010, which updates and replaces previous legislation such as the Race Relations Act 1976 and the Disability Discrimination Act 1995. The aim of this new act was to achieve a measure of consistency to the legal status of the various protected characteristics and to extend protection to characteristics not previously covered. The legally protected characteristics are now: age, disability, gender reassignment, race, religion/belief, sex, sexual orientation, marriage/civil partnership, pregnancy and maternity.

The legal system in the UK makes a distinction between the concepts of discrimination, harassment and victimisation, all of which are prohibited within the Equality Act:

Discrimination

This is defined as treating someone less favourably than another person because they (a) possess a protected characteristic, (b) are perceived to possess a protected characteristic or (c) associate with someone who possesses a protected characteristic. Indirect discrimination is also prohibited by law, and this is defined as a situation in which a policy or practice is applied to everyone but particularly disadvantages those with a protected characteristic.

Harassment

There are three types of harassment defined within the law:

Type 1: Unwanted behaviour (which can include spoken or written words or abuse, imagery, physical gestures, facial expressions, jokes, etc.) related to 'protected characteristics'.

Type 2: Sexual harassment, which is defined as unwelcome actions or communications (verbal, non-verbal or physical) of a sexual nature that has the effect of violating a person's dignity, or creating an intimidating, hostile, degrading, humiliating or offensive environment for that person.

Type 3: Less favourable treatment because of submission to or rejection of previous sexual harassment or harassment on the basis of gender reassignment.

Victimisation

This is deemed to occur when someone is treated less favourably because they have made or supported a claim under the Equality Act 2010.

The main points of the Act are summarised in Figure 4.7 and there are some examples of how the Act might apply to workplace situations in Box 4.5.

Equality Act 2010

What's new & what's changed: at a glance

acas

Key

Colour	Meaning
	Characteristic covered in existing legislation – no changes
Changes	Characteristic covered in existing legislation – but some changes
New	Characteristic not covered in existing legislation – now covered
	Characteristic not covered in existing legislation – still not covered

	Age	Disability	Gender Reassignment	Race	Religion or Belief	Sex	Sexual Orientation	Marriage & Civil Partnership	Pregnancy & Maternity
Direct discrimination — Someone is treated less favourably than another person because of a protected characteristic (PC)	New	New	New						
Associative discrimination — Direct discrimination against someone because they associate with another person who possesses a PC	New	New	New			New			
Discrimination by perception — Direct discrimination against someone because the others think they possess a particular PC	New	New	New			New			
Indirect discrimination — Can occur when you have a rule or policy that applies to everyone but disadvantages a particular PC	New	New	New						
Harassment — Employees can now complain of behaviour they find offensive even if it is not directed at them	Changes	Changes	Changes	Changes	Changes		Changes		
Harassment by a third party — Employers are potentially liable for harassment of their staff by people they don't employ	New	New	New	New	New		New		
Victimisation — Someone is treated badly because they have made/ supported a complaint or grievance under the Act	Changes	Changes	Changes	Changes	Changes	Changes	Changes	Changes	Changes

Figure 4.7 The UK Equality Act 2010

Source: ACAS Guide for Employers (2011).

Box 4.5

The UK Equality Act 2010

Which part of the Act might apply?

Scenario 1

Sajid is 45 but looks much younger. Many people assume that he is in his mid 20s. He is not allowed to represent his company at an international meeting because the Managing Director thinks that he is too young.

Sajid has been discriminated against on the perception of a protected characteristic.

Scenario 2

Paul, a senior manager, turns down Angela's application for promotion to a supervisor position. Angela, who is a lesbian, learns that Paul did this because he believes the team that she applied to manage are homophobic. Paul thought that Angela's sexual orientation would prevent her from gaining the team's respect and managing them effectively.

This is direct sexual orientation discrimination against Angela.

Scenario 3

June works as a project manager and is looking forward to a promised promotion. However, after she tells her boss that her mother, who lives at home, has had a stroke, the promotion is withdrawn.

This may be discrimination against June because of her association with a disabled person.

Scenario 4

Lydia is pregnant and works at a call centre. The manager knows Lydia is pregnant but still disciplines her for taking too many toilet breaks as the manager would for any other member of staff.

This is discrimination because of pregnancy and maternity as this characteristic doesn't require the normal comparison of treatment with other employees.

Scenario 5

Anne makes a formal complaint against her manager because she feels that she has been treated less favourably since she got married and is therefore claiming discrimination. The complaint is resolved through the organisation's grievance procedures and it seems that there was a level of misunderstanding and miscommunication rather than actual discrimination. Since the complaint, Anne is subsequently ostracised by her colleagues who felt she had been making a fuss over nothing, and her manager is avoiding her because he feels offended by the complaint.

Anne could claim victimisation.

Diversity auditing

One of the practical steps an organisation can take in order to assess the extent to which their organisation is managing diversity effectively is to conduct a diversity audit. This takes the form of an independent assessment of employees' experiences, and ideally should include both numerical equality (that is, quantitative measures) and quality of experience (that is, qualitative measures) – see Box 4.6.

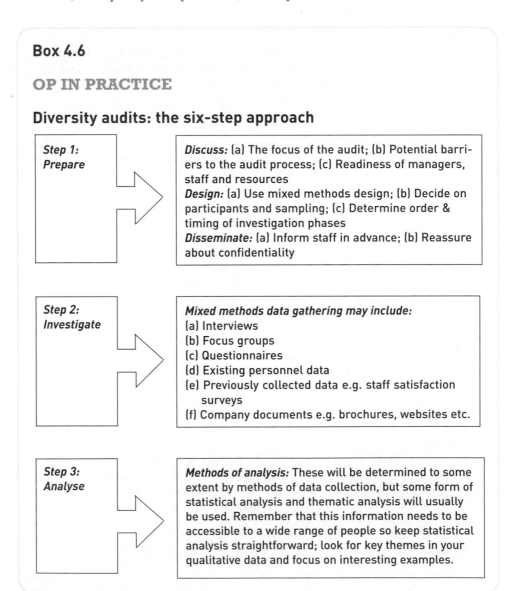

Box 4.6

OP IN PRACTICE

Diversity audits: the six-step approach

Step 1:
Prepare

Discuss: (a) The focus of the audit; (b) Potential barriers to the audit process; (c) Readiness of managers, staff and resources
Design: (a) Use mixed methods design; (b) Decide on participants and sampling; (c) Determine order & timing of investigation phases
Disseminate: (a) Inform staff in advance; (b) Reassure about confidentiality

Step 2:
Investigate

Mixed methods data gathering may include:
(a) Interviews
(b) Focus groups
(c) Questionnaires
(d) Existing personnel data
(e) Previously collected data e.g. staff satisfaction surveys
(f) Company documents e.g. brochures, websites etc.

Step 3:
Analyse

Methods of analysis: These will be determined to some extent by methods of data collection, but some form of statistical analysis and thematic analysis will usually be used. Remember that this information needs to be accessible to a wide range of people so keep statistical analysis straightforward; look for key themes in your qualitative data and focus on interesting examples.

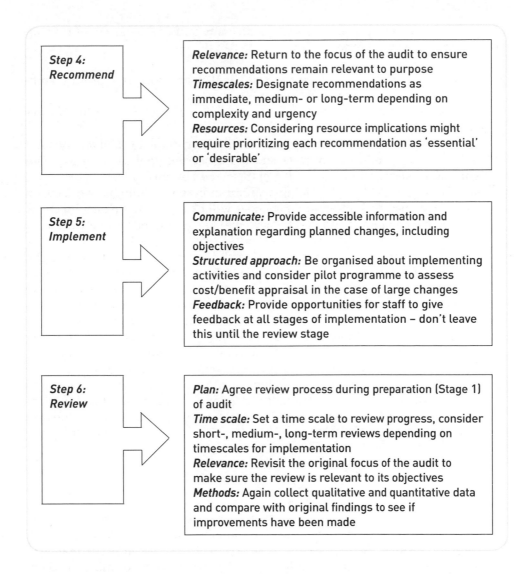

Step 4: Recommend	**Relevance:** Return to the focus of the audit to ensure recommendations remain relevant to purpose **Timescales:** Designate recommendations as immediate, medium- or long-term depending on complexity and urgency **Resources:** Considering resource implications might require prioritizing each recommendation as 'essential' or 'desirable'
Step 5: Implement	**Communicate:** Provide accessible information and explanation regarding planned changes, including objectives **Structured approach:** Be organised about implementing activities and consider pilot programme to assess cost/benefit appraisal in the case of large changes **Feedback:** Provide opportunities for staff to give feedback at all stages of implementation – don't leave this until the review stage
Step 6: Review	**Plan:** Agree review process during preparation (Stage 1) of audit **Time scale:** Set a time scale to review progress, consider short-, medium-, long-term reviews depending on timescales for implementation **Relevance:** Revisit the original focus of the audit to make sure the review is relevant to its objectives **Methods:** Again collect qualitative and quantitative data and compare with original findings to see if improvements have been made

There are many possible reasons to embark on a diversity audit.

- External catalysts, for instance, where there have been changes to legislation and/or concerns about compliance with legislation, an audit may help to identify problem areas.
- Internal catalysts, such as the recognition of persistent or specific inequality within the organisation; a diversity audit can help to pinpoint the problems, identify those most affected and barriers to improvement.
- Intervention as catalyst, for example, where an organisation has recently implemented new policies or practices, an audit can help to explore the impact of these.

Organisations may be resistant to doing a diversity audit for a variety of reasons. Some of the barriers include:

- complacency – where issues relating to equality and inclusion are not sufficiently prioritised in an organisation;
- ignorance – where managers may be unaware of the problems and/or of ways to address them;
- fear of alienation – where managers are afraid that conducting a diversity audit might indicate a minority agenda and are concerned that as a consequence their non-minority employees will feel threatened by this;
- fear of raising expectations – doing an audit indicates a willingness to take on board the results and implies that changes will be made on the basis of these. If the relevant employees don't then perceive changes, morale is likely to suffer.

A diversity audit may be seen as a diversity intervention in its own right, regardless of any contingent recommendations. Such an audit may be viewed as a statement by the organisation that diversity and equality are issues that management endorses. This may help to raise the profile of diversity management within the organisation and also increase retention of 'minority' staff who are directly affected by such issues. Indeed, Chrobot-Mason (2003) discovered that minority employees with higher expectations of fair treatment from their organisation experienced a stronger negative emotional reaction than where expectations were lower. Such reactions were shown to include disillusionment, disappointment and cynicism. It is therefore vitally important that before a diversity audit is operationalised, commitment to address the prospective findings is secured from those in power within the organisation.

Conflict

As we have indicated in the previous section, diverse organisations encompass individuals or groups with conflicting goals, interests and values. This can result in positive outcomes for the organisation, especially if the conflict is managed effectively, However, too much conflict or conflict of a destructive nature can damage relationships and inhibit organisational performance. ER, therefore, is characterised by cooperation and conflict and there is no doubt that those involved in managing the ER strategy in the organisation will have to delve into the world of conflict management. In this section we will identify different forms of conflict and their consequences, and then explore different types of conflict management strategies and their likely outcomes.

A conflict can be defined as an awareness of opposition of goals, values, opinions, or activities by at least one party. A party's action based on a conflict experience is defined as conflict handling. At the point where a party starts to act, the conflict becomes a dynamic process where the conflicting parties influence each other in a vicious circle of action and reaction. (De Reuver and van Woerkom, 2010: 480)

Types of conflict

First, it should be said that current thinking in conflict research posits that conflict is an 'inevitable and commonplace' aspect of interpersonal dynamics in the workplace (Desivilya et al., 2010: 29). Researchers have also differentiated between 'functional' versus 'dysfunctional' conflict, where the former may have certain beneficial outcomes and can aid organisational functioning, while the latter has a negative impact on the performance and well-being of individuals and organisations. This differentiation has been further clarified as the difference between task conflict and relationship conflict. Task conflict relates to differing opinions about aspects of tasks or activities, including ideas, strategies, processes and distribution of resources; this form of conflict has been equated with functional conflict in that it can enhance team performance by improving communication and aiding clarity surrounding concepts and goals (Jehn, 1997). Meanwhile, relationship conflict has been suggested to be a form of dysfunctional conflict based on interpersonal incompatibilities resulting in negative evaluation of others, difficulty in communicating effectively and lowered team performance (Jehn, 1997).

However, researchers have also demonstrated that task conflict may be more problematic than the above description initially implies, owing to its association with relationship conflict. In a meta-analysis, De Dreu and Weingart (2003) found that teams reporting task conflict tended to experience relationship conflict as well. This study also demonstrated, perhaps unsurprisingly, that where correlations between the two forms of conflict were higher, there was more likely to be a negative relationship between task conflict and team performance.

Consider the issue of causality here. Can you think of examples from your own interpersonal relationships where alternately:

1 conflict over an activity has resulted in the deterioration of an interpersonal relationship;
2 relationship conflict has resulted in arguments about how to go about a task.

What was the outcome in each situation and could it have been managed more effectively using a different strategy?

Personal conflict management strategies

Several different ways of handling conflict have been identified and are generally located within the conceptual framework of the 'Dual Concern Model' that was originally developed by Blake and Mouton (1964). The underlying assumption of

Table 4.2   Personal conflict management strategies

Type of conflict management strategy	Concern for self	Concern for other	Related behaviours
Dominating/ competing	High	Low	Forcing other party to accept own view
Obliging/ accommodating	Low	High	Giving in to the wishes of other party
Avoiding	Low	Low	Evading confrontation
Integrating/ collaborating	High	High	Looking for mutually beneficial outcomes
Compromising	Moderate	Moderate	Each party offering concessions

this model is that an individuals' conflict management style in any given situation is determined by two underlying motives: (1) degree of concern for self; and (2) degree of concern for other(s). Five different conflict handling strategies have been identified (Desivilya et al., 2010) based on differing degrees of concern for self and other(s) (see Table 4.2).

A review of research into the outcomes of utilising these various strategies suggests an emphasis on the 'integrating/collaborating' mode as the most productive, with findings showing that it can improve individual and team effectiveness, increase feelings of self-efficacy, reduce the likelihood of further conflict and increase innovation (Cornish et al., 2007; De Dreu, 2006). However, Desivilya et al. (2010) argued that these findings tended to focus on situations that involved task rather than relationship conflict. They suggest that task conflict might be viewed as less personally threatening and might involve less intense emotions than relationship conflict and, on that basis, while collaborating might be a useful approach to resolving task conflict, it might be almost impossible to find mutually beneficial ground between parties experiencing relationship conflict.

Competitive or domination strategies in which one party tries to impose their own will on others is most associated with the escalation of conflict, resulting in negative outcomes for individuals and teams (Van de Vliert and Euwema, 1994). Consider how this type of conflict management might link with the issues highlighted in the section on bullying in this chapter.

There is an interesting caveat to all of the above findings regarding the effectiveness of different conflict management styles: it should be noted that most conflict research focuses on conflict between individuals who work in conventional team contexts. There is a limited amount of research into conflict and its management in virtual teams, though with the increasing use of IT in the workplace, this might represent an area that needs further investigation. In one of the few studies in this area, Montoya-Weiss et al. (2001) found that some conflict management strategies had very different outcomes in virtual teams and in certain situations, and produced the opposite effect of what would be expected in conventional settings.

Conflict-management interventions

Where conflict is having a negative impact on team functioning and cannot be resolved by the members themselves, it is sometimes necessary to involve a third party. This might be someone within the organisation who knows the issues at stake, such as a manager, or it might be an individual with knowledge of conflict management, such as a human resource professional. Where the individuals involved are trade union members, a union representative might be able to assist in the resolution of the matter. Issues surrounding trust, confidentiality and impartiality might lead to a preference for external sources of conflict resolution; this might involve engaging an independent consultant or organisation, such as the Arbitration and Conciliation Advisory Service (ACAS).

There are a variety of processes that can be used to help to resolve conflicts in the workplace, some of which have specifically been designed to avoid the need for legal action. These are generally known as 'alternative dispute resolution processes' and include the following.

- Mediation, which is an informal way of resolving workplace disputes that might avoid the need for formal or legal procedures. An independent third person, a trained mediator, works with the disputing parties to help them reach an agreement which optimises the needs of each party. It usually involves a face-to-face discussion between the parties that is guided by the mediator. It is a voluntary process and the agreement is not legally binding.
- Conciliation, which follows a similar process as mediation but is more likely the term to be used when an employee has brought a complaint about an employer. During the conciliation process the two parties might not necessarily be brought together to discuss the matter and resolution is usually achieved through eliciting concessions from each side.
- Arbitration, which is a process in which a dispute is resolved by an impartial adjudicator whose decision will be final and legally binding.

More information about these processes may be found on the ACAS website, the details of which are given in the list of resources to explore further at the end of this chapter. Furthermore, there is a case study outlined in Box 4.7 relating to a real-world conflict intervention in which an organisation engaged a specialist conflict consultant to resolve a dispute.

Box 4.7

OP IN PRACTICE

Conflict management intervention

Background
A multi-cultural, government team was experiencing unusually high levels of tension. A round of redundancies had just been announced by the department, morale was low, one team member had recently launched a grievance concerning another, sickness absence was creeping up and the supervisor was coming in for criticism from the team for not handling difficult situations promptly. As an internal resource, there was also the pressure to maintain customer satisfaction, particularly under the current threat of cuts and consolidation.

Management recognised this team needed outside help to turn the situation swiftly around and Kisane Prutton, Chartered Psychologist (Occupational), Director of The Prutton Partnership was invited to help.

Proposal
With a very small budget, a pragmatic, cost effective and snappy approach was required. A proposal was accepted that was driven by the question 'How can a healthy culture be created that meets the individual needs of its diverse members, whilst creating a unified whole?'

Aims of the intervention

- To raise morale by reinforcing the team's identity as a successful service provider
- To create a more healthy workplace, thereby reducing the risks of future inter-personal conflict

Objectives

- To identify if there were any outstanding causes for concern that needed addressing
- To conduct a team build in which members create a shared, positive identity
- To generate materials to produce a bespoke handbook comprising (a) Mission, Vision and Values statements, (b) a set of 'Professional Standards', agreed expectations, for the way people work together with team members and with internal customers, (c) behavioural criteria that could be used to adapt existing HR procedures and (d) ways to communicate successes with internal customers

Methodology
Phase 1: All members of the team were invited to attend a confidential, one-to-one, semi-structured interview. The purpose of this phase was to (a) enable each team member to air their concerns and needs in private, in the knowledge that only anonymous, aggregate information would be shared in the Phase 2 workshop, (b) to

collate data that could be used as a catalyst for conversation and action in the workshop and (c) to identify potential inflammatory issues that could spark conflict on the day of the workshop.

Phase 2: All members of the team were invited to a one-day team-development workshop. Small and large group exercises were clustered around the themes 'Concerns, Needs and Aspirations', 'Team Identity' and 'Celebrating and Communicating Success'. Materials generated were to be delegated to volunteers to develop post-workshop into end products.

Outcomes

People were generally relaxed and candid in the private interviews. The workshop was vibrant; people were visibly excited by the creative process, pooling ideas about their shared identity and generating a substantial amount of highly relevant material. Post-event evaluation, confirmed by feedback from management, indicated people appreciated the opportunity to speak in private about their concerns and valued the opportunity to work together on their own internal team-based issues. Significantly, a three month follow-up indicated a reduction in complaints to the union.

Workplace bullying

Workplace conflict can be destructive for individuals and organisations and left unmanaged has the capacity to spiral out of control and manifest itself as workplace bullying. The following section will discuss some of the key research and practice issues in this topic.

Bullying encompasses a variety of behaviours such as setting unreasonable deadlines, persistent and undue criticism of work, spreading rumours and gossip, social isolation, and verbal and physical abuse. Key features professed (although not always agreed on) to disassociate bullying from other forms of conflict include:

- behaviour being repeated over a prolonged period;
- the requirement that the victim must perceive that they are being bullied;
- negative outcomes for the individual;
- power imbalance between the parties involved.

Incidence rates of those experiencing bullying across countries range from: 8% in Denmark (Mikkelsen and Einarsen, 2002), 10.6% in the UK (Hoel et al., 2001) and 28% in the USA (Lutgen-Sandvik et al., 2007). However, some researchers (Cowie et al., 2002) argue that methodological problems in the collection of prevalence data create difficulties in comparing across countries. Others show how different combinations of self and peer reports (Coyne et al., 2003) and different methodologies (Nielsen et al., 2009) produce different victim rates in the same set of data.

Why is workplace bullying of concern?

Empirical findings offer unequivocal evidence that bullying is a severe workplace stressor. Victims of bullying report increased stress (Lutgen-Sandvik et al., 2007), burnout (Bowling and Beehr, 2006), depression (Agervold and Mikkelsen, 2004), cardiovascular problems (Kivimaki et al., 2003) and post traumatic stress disorder (Tehrani, 2004).

Reduced individual and team performance (Coyne et al., 2004), low job satisfaction and commitment (Bowling and Beehr, 2006), increased absenteeism (Kivimaki et al., 2000) and higher employee turnover (Rayner, 1997) indicate the negative impact bullying has on the organisation. In addition, the organisation will face potential costs such as litigation, industrial action, replacement and training costs, as well as reduced morale and motivation in other employees who witness bullying (see Box 4.8). As a result, organisations need to present a business case for dealing with bullying based on direct costs (for example, costs of replacing individuals), indirect costs (lowered morale and productivity) and reputation damage (Rayner and McIvor, 2008).

Box 4.8

The financial cost of bullying

The costs below are taken from a real bullying incident in a UK local authority. The case revolves around a complainant in charge of around 20 people and an accused who was the complainants subordinate, but who had gone for the same job as the complainant prior to the alleged bullying. Escalating behaviour culminating in threats of violence by the accused resulted in the organisation enacting a formal investigation. The accused was suspended on full pay and the complainant had to take sick leave due to the stress of the situation. The accused eventually resigned from his/her position.

? = costs unknown or difficult to assess

Absence	£6,972
Replacement costs	£7,500
Reduced productivity	?
Investigators' time for grievance investigation	£2,110
Local management line-manager time	£1,847
Head office personnel	£2,600
Corporate officers' time (including staff welfare)	£2,100
Cost of disciplinary process (hearing/solicitor)	£3,780
Witness interview costs	£1,200
Transfers	0
Litigation	?(0)
Effects on those indirectly involved	?
Miscellaneous (effects on public relations etc.)	?
Total costs (minimum)	£28,109

Hoel, Einarsen, & Cooper (2003) Organisational effects of bullying. In S Einarsen et al., eds. Bullying and Emotional Abuse in the Workplace. International Perspectives in Research and Practice. London: Taylor and Francis (p.156). Adapted with permission.

Q1. Why is it important to account for those costs indicated as unknown in the table?
Q2. How could these unknown costs be assessed?

Antecedents of workplace bullying

The majority of investigations have focused on organisational antecedents of workplace bullying. Table 4.3 presents some of the principal organisational and individual antecedents of workplace bullying reported (see Coyne, 2011, for a more detailed discussion).

Theoretically, the revised frustration-aggression hypothesis (Berkowitz, 1989) and social interaction model (Felson and Tedeschi, 1993) have been offered as explanations for organisational antecedents (Einarsen, 2000). In the former, frustrations in the work environment may lead to bullying via a mediating effect of negative emotion. In the latter, stressful events change the way an individual behaves, which in turn may result in the person violating work norms of what is acceptable behaviour. This results in them becoming the focus of bullying.

Salin (2003) conceptualised an interactive organisational-antecedent model of:

- enabling processes (power imbalances and poor management style) which provide the conditions that facilitate bullying;
- motivating processes (politicised work environments and organisational norms conducive to bullying) which present the individual with a rationale for bullying;
- precipitating processes (organisational changes, change in management) which provide the trigger mechanism for bullying processes to evolve.

Table 4.3 Organisational and individual antecedents of workplace bullying

Organisational factors	Individual factors
Uninteresting and unchallenging work Strained and competitive environment Poor leadership Poor working conditions Role ambiguity and role conflict Organisational culture tolerant of bullying behaviour Changing nature of work	Victim personality (high conscientiousness, low extraversion, high neuroticism, low assertiveness) Perpetrator personality (aggressive, violent, tyrannical, low self-esteem)

Victim personality has been explained through notions of submissive and provocative victims (Coyne et al., 2000). A submissive victim may be seen as an easy target because of vulnerabilities in his or her disposition. This indicates his or her inability to defend himself or herself, inability to cope, or lack of a peer support network which places him or her in a socially exposed position. Provocative victims provoke aggressive behaviour within another person as a result of envy, being too anxious, being too conscientious and clashing with expected group norms.

The notion of victim characteristics is controversial because critics suggest it focuses on blaming the victim for being bullied. However, if bullying was exclusively a product of organisational factors, why are some employees working in the same organisational environment targeted and others not? Research that focuses on victim characteristics is attempting to address this important question rather than suggesting that victims are to blame. The thesis of this research is that when bullying is on-going, personality may provide some explanation as to why certain individuals are targeted in preference to others.

As a consequence of the victim focus, which pervades this topic, and because of the difficulty in obtaining perpetrator samples, relatively little research has focused on personality as a pre-disposition to perpetrator status. Explanatory mechanisms for perpetrator characteristics include the following:

- Inflated self-esteem or unrealistic view of self. Conflict is perceived as a threat to self-esteem, and to preserve self-esteem bullying is directed towards the threat source.
- A lack of social competencies, low emotional control and low empathy. As a result, anger is vented in an inappropriate manner and with a lack of awareness of the effect such behaviour has on others.
- Competitive, dominant and assertive behaviours to gain power. (Zapf and Einarsen, 2003)

Combining victim and perpetrator disposition, Aquino and Lamertz (2004) hypothesised that the interaction between submissive and provocative victims, and domineering and reactive perpetrators culminates in different types of bullying behaviour. Four outcomes are proposed:

- Submissive victim-dominating perpetrator – as the perpetrator has a desire to control the victim and the victim is an 'easy target', predatory bullying occurs (for example, tyrannical leader).
- Provocative victim-dominating perpetrator – the perpetrator's desire for dominance is resisted by the victim's provocative nature resulting in dispute-related victimisation (for example, clash with group norms).

- Provocative victim-reactive perpetrator – the perpetrator reacts to perceived provocation from the victim (for example, via threatened self-esteem) and dispute-related bullying emerges.
- Submissive victim-reactive perpetrator – as there is no trigger and the perpetrator has no motive to dominate, no or little bullying emerges.

While not yet empirically tested, this model provides insight into how personality may function within workplace bullying and how the dynamic interplay between victim and perpetrator plays out.

Acknowledging that single causal explanations are too simplistic to account for the phenomenon of workplace bullying, a number of theoretical models have emerged which try to capture individual and organisational antecedents (Bowling and Beehr, 2006; Einarsen et al., 2003). Relating back to previous ideas, Parzefall and Salin (2010) introduce a social exchange perspective on workplace bullying with particular emphasis on fairness and the psychological contract. They argue that the perceived interactional fairness of an act may dictate whether an individual views the act as bullying or not and may mediate the relationship between experiencing the behaviour and outcomes. The implication here being that the more an act is perceived as unfair the more it is judged to be bullying and the worse the outcomes will be for the individual. Additionally, bullying can be perceived as breaching fairness and trust principles which results in violation of the psychological contract. This is not only at the victim level; witnesses may also perceive the behaviour as unfair, resulting in a violation of their psychological contract with the organisation.

How do organisations tackle workplace bullying?

Perhaps the most common response to the problem of workplace bullying is to introduce a bullying policy (often termed harassment policy or dignity at work policy). Although early research demonstrated only 55% of UK organisations introduced anti-bullying policies (Woodman and Cook, 2005), more recently an increase to 74% in the use of policies has been observed (Woodman and Kumar, 2008). However, we must be careful not to confuse increased use with effectiveness. Indeed, Beale and Hoel (2011) posit a number of limitations to bullying policies:

1 Their focus is often on avoiding litigation and not on creating a dignity culture.
2 Managers are often the perpetrators of bullying and hence will not wish to enforce a policy within their organisation.
3 They encourage more individual resolution and discourage independent, collective action. As a result a victim may have to try to resolve the problem on their own.

Table 4.4   A framework for workplace bullying intervention

Society level			
Cultural values, legal framework, union/professional body support, guidance from Government, anti-bullying associations			
	Prevention	**Support/intervention**	**Remedial**
Organisation	Risk assessment Change work design Leadership training Culture change Dignity at work	Staff surveys Monitor absences Support from the top Creation of informal and formal networks	Ensure sanctions are implemented Monitor culture change Monitor and evaluate training
Group	Awareness training for groups Diversity training Foster appropriate group norms	Examine in-group and out-group (team network) Facilitate group meetings and group discussions	External meetings to change norms Change the make-up of the team
Individual	Training (emotion regulation, social skills, anger management etc.)	Contact person / buddy system Confidential support and advice Informal and formal procedures	Counselling for victims and perpetrators Support to take a grievance case

Source: Coyne, I. (2011) 'Bullying in the workplace', in C.P. Monks and I. Coyne (eds), *Bullying in Different Contexts.* Cambridge: Cambridge University Press. pp. 157–84.

What is evident is policies alone are not the complete answer to controlling workplace bullying. In an attempt to map out a framework for bullying interventions, Coyne (2011) developed a three-level framework reflecting preventative, supportive or remedial interventions at the organisational, group and individual level (Table 4.4). The organisational level considers initially identifying risk factors for bullying, through ultimately developing a culture of dignity and respect where bullying is evidently not tolerated. Group level interventions focus on changing group norms and values through awareness training and the development of anti-bullying group norms. Individual level interventions include providing training to stop potential victims and perpetrators, informal and formal support mechanisms, and support when taking grievance cases or when re-entering the workplace.

The society level captures the national context in terms of social values, laws (to date there is no specific bullying law in the UK), government guidance/political action and trades unions', professional bodies' and national anti-bullying associations' voice and support. This effectively provides a macro perspective on whether bullying is acceptable which will likely impact on the micro-organisational perspective.

Summary

We have presented a discussion of ER covering the general ER framework, work motivation, the management of diversity, workplace conflict and workplace bullying. One key feature apparent in this area is that anyone researching or practising needs to be aware of the dynamic nature to employee relations. While an organisation may adopt a specific strategy to managing the human resource, internal and external pressures and changes mean any strategy needs to be flexible to respond to such demands. In all areas we have seen changes in approaches – some quite fundamental (for example, the move from collective to individual ER approaches and the change from EO to MD) – which attempt to better capture the employment context at the current time. This suggests the need to create a business case for managing the employment relationship and the need to place ER at the strategic level in the organisation. Getting the case right can engage and motivate employees as well as help to manage diversity and prevent workplace bullying.

Finally, returning to the quote right at the start of the chapter, how well is the notion of ER about 'managing fairly and getting the best out of people' captured in the information we have presented? Although simplistic, this perspective is not a million miles away from effective ER. We have seen throughout how fairness plays a role in the psychological contract, motivation, diversity and (the lack of it) in conflict and bullying. Further, engaging individuals, managing the psychological contract, intrinsically motivating, fostering diverse workforces, developing functional conflict and tackling bullying all can 'get the best out of people'. Underlying these concepts, notions of trust, dignity and respect, and meaningfulness, have been strongly represented throughout the chapter, with a thread throughout the chapter characterising the employment relationship as a social exchange between employer and employee. Clearly, as well as agreeing a legal contract with an employer, employees also experience an individual psychological contract based on reciprocation, trust, fairness, dignity and respect, and engagement in meaningful activities. To 'get the best out of people', it is the role of the ER approach to not only manage the legal contract, but to also create psychologically engaging environments that foster productive social exchanges. And, as we have shown, Occupational Psychology has a lot to offer in this domain.

The next chapter continues the focus on the needs of the employee by exploring how personal development and counselling interventions can meet those needs.

Explore further

- http://www.human-resource-solutions.co.uk/ Provides lots of information about the HR role. Often with free downloads.

- Leat, M. (2007) *Exploring Employee Relations*. Oxford: Butterworth-Heinemann. This is a good general, introductory textbook on employee relations
- http://www.cipd.co.uk/podcasts A great resource for finding out about current employment relations issues.
- http://www.direct.gov.uk A useful place to find information about legal right and responsibilities within UK law
- http://acas.org.uk Informative and practical resource for information on resolving disputes in the workplace

- Christian, J., Porter, L.W. and Moffitt, G. (2006) 'Workplace diversity and group relations: an overview', *Group Processes & Intergroup Relations*, 9 (4): 459–66.
- Einarsen, S., Hoel, H., Zapf, D. and Cooper, C.L. (2011) *Bullying and Harassment in the Workplace*, 2nd edn. London: CRC Press.
- Guest, D.E. (2004) 'The psychology of the employment relationship: an analysis based on the psychological contract', *Applied Psychology*, 53 (4): 541–55.
- Kickul, J., Lester, S.W. and Belgio, E. (2004) 'Attitudinal and behavioral outcomes of psychological contract breach: a cross cultural comparison of the United States and Hong Kong Chinese', *International Journal of Cross Cultural Management*, 4 (2): 229–52.
- Leat, M. (2007) *Exploring Employee Relations*, 2nd edn. Oxford: Butterworth-Heinemann.
- Locke, E. and Latham, G.P. (1990) 'Work motivation and satisfaction: light at the end of the tunnel', *Psychological Science,* 1 (4): 240–46.

Discussion questions

1 Which theories would you include in your 'mega-theory' of motivation?
2 How would you develop a business case for effective employee relations?
3 Will we ever eradicate workplace bullying?

Sample essay question

How important are fairness, trust, and dignity and respect in managing the employment relationship?

> ### Sample exam question
>
> With reference to both theory and practice, outline the challenges and benefits of managing diversity in the workplace.

OP IN PRACTICE: DAY IN THE LIFE OF …

Professor Rob Briner, Professor of Organisational Psychology, School of Management, University of Bath	
What areas of OP do you work within?	I am a researcher, PhD supervisor and lecturer in two main areas: work and well-being (specific topics such as 'stress', moods, emotions, emotional labour) and the psychological contract (specific topics such as psychological contract violations, fairness, the effects of the psychological contract on affect and behaviour). I also have interests other areas including ethnicity at work, the relationships between work and non-work, absence, and evidence-based approaches to practice.
How did you become interested in this area?	I guess my main interest is this area is the psychological contract – the implicit 'deal' between employee and employer. It seems to me that the quality and nature of the employment relationship strongly shapes feelings and behaviour in the workplace. I suppose I became interested in the first place as it seemed that OP had not really paid sufficient attention to the psychological contract. What's really striking is that when people talk about what they love or hate about their jobs and why they want to accomplish something or withdraw effort very often it's about the quality of their psychological contract.
What has been the major academic development in this area?	Apart from developments in psychological contract research, some of the major developments have been around thinking much more carefully about what motivation might mean. Historically it has been defined quite poorly and not broken down in sufficient detail nor thought about as a set of quite complex processes. Another important development is the way in which researchers are elaborating our understanding of what performance might mean by considering ideas such as organisational citizenship behaviours and counter-productive work behaviours.
To what extent does the practical application of your work inform your research?	I do very little practical application in this particular area. What is in some way strange about the psychological contract is that although it seems to give researchers and managers great insights the practical applications of such insights are not obvious.
What role do ethics have in your work?	In terms of my research, the main role of ethics is in providing ethical codes for how research with people should be conducted. More broadly I think ethics is also closely related to evidence-based practice. For example, it

(Continued)

(Continued)

	doesn't seem ethical if OP practitioners recommend or implement an intervention in an organisation without first having a very explicit, systematic, critical and comprehensive understanding of the body of evidence showing the benefits and possible harm that may result from that intervention.
Can you give an example of a day in your working life?	My research part of my job might be done almost anywhere at any time: from a conference to a coffee shop to train or a plane. A lot of research work involves reading, thinking and writing so a laptop and internet access is often all that's required. Typical research-related tasks include collecting and analyzing data, negotiating access to organisations, writing and revising papers for publication, acting as a reviewer for peer-review journals, preparing conference presentations, writing grant applications, talking to practitioners, and so on. The teaching part of my job is more physically and temporally fixed. Lectures tend to be in lecture theatres though a lot of research supervision takes place elsewhere and often via Skype and email.
How has your work changed in the last five years?	The main change has been a sharp increase in my involvement with a whole series of activities around evidence-based approaches to management practice and occupational psychology. I find that I'm doing more and more presenting, writing and training around the topic as well as attempting to build infrastructure which will support evidence-based approaches.
How do you see your work changing over the next five years?	I don't think I see it changing much but I do hope that some of the ideas around evidence-based practice start to appeal more to managers and organisational psychologists and that some tangible strengthening of the links between evidence and practice will occur.

OP IN PRACTICE: DAY IN THE LIFE OF ...

Kisane Prutton, Director of the Prutton Partnership

What areas of OP do you work within?	I specialise in workplace conflict resolution. Workplace conflict arises because a number of unfortunate criteria collide, rather like the Big Bang! Misunderstandings, assumptions, lack of information, perceived threat to one or others' goals, perceived violation of values, perceived lack of respect and perceived lack of fairness are all common features of relationship breakdown and conflict.
	Attending to interpersonal conflict in an organisation naturally opens up the potential for organisational change. It is helpful if organisations are prepared to examine the conditions of the workplace that have allowed the conflict to fester. Organisational culture, communications, management training and development, HR systems are all potential targets for intervention.

How did you become interested in this area?	I was introduced to conflict resolution when I was working for a firm of chartered accountants who specialise in assisting family businesses. There is a higher risk of conflict in family businesses because beliefs may exist and decisions may be taken which are driven by the underlying interests of particular family members. This may be construed as unfair by other family members or employees.
What kinds of organisations are interested in your work and why?	We are beginning to see mediation and the broader concept of conflict resolution considered good practice in resolving disputes. This has been stimulated by a number of Government initiatives aimed at encouraging Alternative Dispute Resolution. ADR provides an alternative to litigation and aims to reduce the number of claims going to court.
	I am finding that both the public sector and the SME market are looking seriously at conflict resolution, but for different reasons. The public sector is, as we know, going through major change and experiencing serious employee dissatisfaction. They seem keen to develop more engaged employees. I have been helping teams in the NHS come to terms with the changes they have undergone and have been working with them to consolidate and develop healthier, more cohesive teams going forward.
	The SME sector is focused more on the 'saving money' argument behind conflict resolution. They are painfully aware that to survive the current economic downturn they need to address anything that drains resources, wasted management time, legal costs, reduced employee productivity and so on. High sickness absence and low morale can make or break a small business.
How is your work informed by theory, literature and research?	I am always on the lookout for new research to develop my thinking and my practice. I have found the following particularly helpful in my work both as a practitioner and an educator/trainer:
	MEDIATION: John Winslade and Gerald Monk (Narrative Mediation);
	Richard Ryan and Edward Deci (Self Determination Theory) and
	Abraham Maslow (Hierarchy of Needs)
	WORKPLACE VALUES AND ORGANISATIONAL CHANGE: Kurt Lewin, Edgar Schein, John Kotter and Geert Hofstede
	HELPING AND CONSULTING: Gerard Egan and publications by McKinsey.
What role do ethics have in your day-to-day practice?	A big one! Because a significant aspect of my work is conducted under the umbrella of employment law, I have to be scrupulous about all forms of communication, my paperwork, what I say and what I do. I am on high alert for not breaching confidentiality, informed consent, voluntary participation and I have to work with other legal privileges such as without prejudice (this concerns any offers, admissions or concessions made during a negotiation and holds that they cannot be carried over into a tribunal should the parties in mediation not reach an agreement).

(Continued)

(Continued)

Can you give an example of a day in your working life?	No two days are alike and my work is either feast or famine. Using the 80:20 rule, I would say I spend 80% of my time 'developing new business', that is, in a non-fee earning, famine mode and 20% of my time feasting on the work that I deliver to clients.
	During the famine stages I tend to break up chores like sorting out invoices, updating my website and following up from networking, with things I enjoy doing, such as rewriting one of my talks, writing an article or a new training programme, attending a CPD event or conducting some desk research on something that I am curious about.
	I have a number of pro bono roles which keep me busy and on my toes all year round. In return, I remain connected and informed on new developments in those fields. To maintain my psychological knowledge, I support the British Psychological Society's Press function and sit on the Division of Occupational Psychology's Occupational Psychology in Public Policy group. In my mediation world, I contribute to the work of the Civil Mediation Council's Communications Committee and the Civil Mediation Council's Workplace Committee.
	I am a director of one business and a partner in another. One is pure me, pure OP and the other is a multi-disciplinary consultancy, comprising me and a small team of ex-accountants turned consultants. I have the luxury of an office at home and an office in Nottingham with my colleagues.
	When I am in delivery mode, I am out on site with the client. Yesterday I spent the morning in the board room with an MD and his general manager, brainstorming ideas to address their problems following the resignation of a shareholder. Tomorrow, I will have to spend the morning writing a proposal for them. Incidentally, I met this client at a breakfast seminar hosted by a law firm where I was the guest speaker. No surprises, I was talking about the impact of conflict on individuals and organisations. Tomorrow I am running the second round of private meetings in a complex mediation involving a team of HR professionals.
How has your work changed in the last five years?	Thanks to European developments in Alternative Dispute Resolution, I have actively pursued a career in mediation which has enabled me to offer services in related areas of conflict prevention and resolution, such as conflict coaching and organisational change.
How do you see your work changing over the next five years?	Commercially, I would like to consolidate my different streams of work. Personally I would like to expand my understanding of neuroscience and what it offers our understanding of changing people's beliefs, attitudes and behaviours.

References

Adams, J.S. (1963) 'Toward an understanding of inequity', *Journal of abnormal Psychology*, 67 (5) : 422–36.

Agervold, M. and Mikkelsen, E.G. (2004) 'Relationships between bullying, psychosocial work environment and individual stress reactions', *Work & Stress*, 18 (4): 336–51.

Alderfer, C.P. (1972) *Existence, Relatedness and Growth*. New York: Free Press.

Alfes, K., Truss, C., Soane, E.C., Rees, C. and Gatenby, M., (2010) *Creating an Engaged Workforce. Findings from the Kingston Employee Engagement Consortium Project*. London.

Ambrose, M.L. and Kulik, C.T. (1999) 'Old friends, new faces: motivation research in the 1990s', *Journal of Management*, 25 (3): 231–92.

Aquino, K., and Lamertz, K. (2004) 'A relational model of workplace victimisation: social roles and patterns of victimisation in dyadic relationships', *Journal of Applied Psychology*, 89: 1023–34.

Arnold, J. (1996) 'The psychological contract: a concept in need of closer scrutiny?', *European Journal of Work and Organisational Psychology*, 5 (4): 511–20.

Arnold, J., Patterson, F., Robertson, I., Cooper, C. and Burnes, B. (2005) *Work Psychology. Understanding Human Behaviour in the Workplace*, 4th edn. Harlow: Pearson Education.

Bartram, D. (2005) 'The great eight competencies: a criterion-centric approach to validation', *Journal of Applied Psychology*, 90 (6): 1185–203.

Beale, D. and Hoel, H. (2011) 'Workplace bullying and the employment relationship: exploring questions of prevention, control and context', *Work, Employment & Society*, 25 (1): 5–18.

Berkowitz, L. (1989) 'The frustration-aggression hypothesis: an examination and reformulation', *Psychological Bulletin*, 106: 59–73.

Blake, R.R. and Mouton, J.S. (1964) *The Managerial Grid*. Houston, TX: Gulf.

Blau, P. (1964) *Exchange and Power in Social Life*. New York: Wiley.

Blyton, P. and Turnbull, P. (1994) *The Dynamics of Employee Relations*. Basingstoke: Macmillan.

Bowling, N.A. and Beehr, T.A. (2006) 'Workplace harassment from the victim's perspective: a theoretical model and meta-analysis', *Journal of Applied Psychology*, 91 (5): 998–1012.

Chrobot-Mason, D.L. (2003) 'Keeping the promise: psychological contract violations for minority employees', *Journal of Managerial Psychology*, 18: 22–45.

CIPD (2005) *What Is Employee Relations?* London: CIPD.

CIPD (2011a) *Employee Outlook. Summer 2011*. London: CIPD.

CIPD (2011b) *Employment Relations*. London: CIPD.

CIPD (2011c) 'The psychological contract factsheet'. Available at: http://www.cipd:co.uk/h-resources/facksheet/psychological-contract.asp (accessed 19 August 2011).

Collins, C.J., Hanges, P.J. and Locke, E.A. (2004) 'The relationship of achievement motivation to entrepreneurial behavior: a meta-analysis', *Human Performance*, 17 (1): 95–117.

Colquitt, J.A., Conlon, D.E., Wesson, M.J., Porter, C.O.L.H. and Ng, K.Y. (2001) 'Justice at the millennium: a meta-analytic review of 25 years of organisational justice research', *Journal of Applied Psychology*, 86 (3): 425–45.

Cornish, F., Zittoun, T. and Gillespie, A. (2007) 'A cultural psychological reflection on collaborative research', *Forum: Qualitative Social Research,* 8 (3): Article 21.

Cowie, H., Naylor, P., Rivers, I., Smith, P.K. and Pereira, B. (2002) 'Measuring workplace bullying', *Aggression and Violent Behavior,* 7: 33–51.

Coyne, I. (2011) 'Bullying in the workplace', in C.P. Monks and I. Coyne (eds) *Bullying in Different Contexts.* Cambridge: Cambridge University Press. pp. 157–84.

Coyne, I., Craig, J. and Smith-Lee Chong, P. (2004) 'Workplace bullying in a group context', *British Journal of Guidance & Counselling,* 32 (3): 301–17.

Coyne, I., Seigne, E. and Randall, P. (2000) 'Predicting workplace victim status from personality', *European Journal of Work and Organisational Psychology,* 9 (3): 335–49.

Coyne, I., Smith-Lee Chong, P., Seigne, E. and Randall, P. (2003) 'Self and peer nominations of bullying: an analysis of incident rates, individual differences, and perceptions of the working environment', *European Journal of Work and Organisational Psychology,* 12 (3): 209–28.

Cross, C., Barry, G. and Garavan, T.N. (2008) 'The psychological contract in call centres: an employee perspective', *Journal of Industrial Relations,* 50 (2): 229–42.

Cullinane, N. and Dundon, T. (2006) 'The psychological contract: a critical review', *International Journal of Management Reviews,* 8 (2): 113–29.

De Dreu, C.K.W. (2006) 'When too little or too much hurts: evidence for a curvilinear relationship between task conflict and innovation in teams', *Journal of Management,* 32 (1): 83–107.

De Dreu, C.K.W. and Weingart, L.R. (2003) 'Task versus relationship conflict, team performance, and team member satisfaction: a meta-analysis', *Journal of Applied Psychology,* 88: 741–9.

de Reuver, R. and van Woerkom, M. (2010) 'Can conflict management be an antidote to subordinate absenteeism?', *Journal of Managerial Psychology,* 25 (5): 479–494.

De Vos, A. and Meganck, A. (2009) 'What HR managers do versus what employees value: exploring both parties' views on retention management from a psychological contract perspective', *Personnel Review,* 38 (1): 45–60.

Desivilya, H.S., Somech, A. and Lidgoster, H. (2010) 'Innovation and conflict management in work teams: the effects of team identification and task and relationship conflict', *Negotiation and Conflict Management Research,* 3 (1): 28–34.

Doherty, L. (2004) 'Work-life balance initiatives: implications for women', *Employee Relations,* 269 (4): 433–52.

Einarsen, S. (2000) 'Harassment and bullying at work: a review of the Scandinavian approach', *Aggression and Violent Behaviour,* 5 (4): 379–401.

Einarsen, S., Hoel, H., Zapf, D. and Cooper, C.L., (2003) 'The concept of bullying at work: the European tradition', in S. Einarsen (eds), *Bullying and Emotional Abuse in the Workplace. International Perspectives in Research and Practice.* London: Taylor & Francis. pp. 3–30.

Equality and Human Right Commission (2010) 'How fair is Britain? Equality, human right and good relations in 2010. The first trienmial review'. Available at: http://www:equalityhumanrights.com/key-projects/how fair-is-britain/faultreport and-evidence-downloads (accessed 24 June 2011).

European Foundation for the Improvement of Living and Working Conditions (2010) *Developments in Industrial action 2005–2009.* Dublin: European Foundation for the Improvement of Living and Working Conditions.

Felson, R.B. and Tedeschi, J.T. (1993) *Aggression and Violence. Social Interactionist Perspectives*. Washington, DC: American Psychological Association.

Fleck, S. and Inceoglu, I. (2010) 'A comprehensive framework for understanding and predicting engagement', in S. Albrecht (ed.) *The Handbook of Employee Engagement: Models, Measures and Practice*. Cheltenham: Edward-Elgar Publishing House. pp 31–42.

Fried, Y. and Ferris, G.R. (1987) 'The validity of the job characteristics model: a review and meta-analysis', *Personnel Psychology*, 40: 287–323.

Gamble, J. (2006) 'Introducing western-style HRM practices to China: shopfloor perceptions in a British multinational', *Journal of World Business*, 41 (4): 328–343.

Griffeth, R.W. and Gaertner, S. (2001) 'A role for equity theory in the turnover process: an empirical test', *Journal of Applied Social Psychology*, 31 (5) : 1017–37.

Guest, D.E. (1987) 'Human resource management and industrial relations', *Journal of Management Studies*, 24: 503–21.

Guest, D.E. (2004) 'The psychology of the employment relationship: an analysis based on the psychological contract', *Applied Psychology*, 53 (4): 541–55.

Guest, D.E. and Conway, N. (2002) 'Communicating the psychological contract: an employer perspective', *Human Resource Management Journal*, 12 (2): 22–38.

Hackman, J.R. and Oldham, G.R. (1980) *Work Design*. Reading, MA: Addison-Wesley.

Harrison. D. and Sin, H. (2006) 'What is diversity and how should it be measured?', in A. Konrad, P. Prasad and J. Pringle (eds), *Handbook of Workplace Diversity*. London: Sage.

Harzig, C., Juteau, D. and Schmitt (2010) *The Social Construction Of Diversity*. New York: Berghahn Books.

Herdman, A. and McMillan-Capehart, A. (2010) 'Establishing a diversity program is not enough: exploring the determinants of diversity climate', *Journal of Business & Psychology*, 25 (1): 39–53.

Herriot, P., Manning, W.E.G. and Kidd, J.M. (1997) 'The content of the psychological contract', *British Journal of Management*, 8 (2): 151–162.

Hershcovis, M.S., Turner, N., Barling, J., Arnold, K.A., Dupré, K.E., Inness, M., LeBlanc, M.M. and Sivanathan, N. (2007) 'Predicting workplace aggression: a meta-analysis', *Journal of Applied Psychology*, 92 (1): 228–38.

Herzberg, F.I. (1966) *Work and Nature of Man*. New York: Thomas Y. Crowell.

Hiltrop, J. (1995) 'The changing psychological contract: the human resource challenge of the 1990s', *European Management Journal*, 13 (3): 286–94.

Hoel, H., Cooper, C. and Faragher, B. (2001) 'The experience of bullying in Great Britain: the impact of organisational status', *European Journal of Work and Organisational Psychology*, 10 (4) : 443–65.

Hui, C., Lee, C. and Rousseau, D.M. (2004) 'Psychological contract and organisational citizenship behavior in China: investigating generalizability and instrumentality', *Journal of Applied Psychology*, 89 (2): 311–21.

Humphrey, S.E., Nahrgang, J.D. and Morgeson, F.P. (2007) 'Integrating motivational, social, and contextual work design features: a meta-analytic summary and theoretical extension of the work design literature', *Journal of Applied Psychology*, 92 (5): 1332–56.

Inceoglu, I. and Fleck, S. (2010) 'Engagement as a motivational construct', in S. Albrecht (ed.), *The Handbook of Employee Engagement: Models, Measures and Practice*. Cheltenham: Edward-Elgar. pp 74–86.

Jehn, K.A. (1997) 'A qualitative analysis of conflict types and dimensions in organisational groups', *Administrative Science Quarterly*, 42: 530–57.

Kahn, W.A. (1990) 'Psychological conditions of personal engagement and disengagement at work', *The Academy of Management Journal*, 33 (4): 692–724.

Kalev, A., Kelly, E. and Dobbin, F. (2006) 'Best practices or best guesses? Assessing the efficacy of corporate affirmative action and diversity policies', *American Sociological Review*, 71 (4): 589–617.

Kersley, B., Alpin, C., Forth, J., Bryson, A., Bewley, H., Dix, G. and Oxenbridge, S. (2005) *Inside the Workplace: First Findings from the 2004 Workplace Employment Relations Survey (WERS 2004)*. London: Economic and Social Research Council/Advisory, Concilation and Arbitration Service/Policy Studies Institute/ Department of Trade and Industry.

Kivimaki, M., Elovainio, M. and Vahtera, J. (2000) 'Workplace bullying and sickness absence in hospital staff', *Occupational and Environmental Medicine*, 57 (10): 656–60.

Kivimaki, M., Virtanen, M., Vartia, M., Elovainio, M., Vahtera, J. and Keltikangas-Järvinen, L. (2003) 'Workplace bullying and the risk of cardiovascular disease and depression', *Occupational and Environmental Medicine*, 60 (10): 779–83.

Larsen, H.H. and Brewster, C. (2003) 'Line management responsibility for HRM: what is happening in Europe?', *Employee Relations*, 25 (3): 228–44.

Leat, M. (2007) *Exploring Employee Relations*, 2nd edn. Oxford: Butterworth-Heinemann.

Locke, E.A. and Latham, G.P. (1990) *A Theory of Goal-Setting and Task Performance*. Englewood Cliffs, NJ: Prentice Hall.

Locke, E.A. and Latham, G.P. (2002) 'Building a practically useful theory of goal setting and task motivation: a 35-year odyssey', *American Psychologist*, 57 (9): 705–17.

Locke, E.A. and Latham, G.P. (2004) 'What should we do about motivation theory? Six recommendations for the twenty-first century', *The Academy of Management Review*, 29 (3): 388–403.

Lutgen-Sandvik, P., Tracy, S.J. and Alberts, J.K. (2007) 'Burned by bullying in the American workplace: prevalence, perception, degree and impact', *Journal of Management Studies*, 44 (6): 837–62.

Macey, W.H., Schneider, B., Barbera, K.M. and Young, S.A. (2009) *Employee Engagement: Tools for Analysis, Practice and Competitive Advantage*. Chichester: Wiley-Blackwell.

Maslow, A.H. (1943) 'A theory of human motivation', *Psychological Review*, 50 (4): 370–96.

McClelland, D.C. (1961) *The Achieving Society*. New York: Van Nostrand Reinhold.

McClelland, D.C. and Boyatzis, R.E. (1982) 'Leadership motive pattern and long-term success in management', *Journal of Applied Psychology*, 67 (6): 737–43.

Mikkelsen, E.G. and Einarsen, S. (2002) 'Relationships between exposure to bullying at work and psychological and psychosomatic health complaints: the role of state negative affectivity and generalised self-efficacy', *Scandinavian Journal of Psychology*, 43 (5): 397–405.

Millward, L.J. and Brewerton, P.M. (2001) 'Psychological contracts: employment relations for the twenty-first century', in I. Robertson and C. Cooper (eds), *Personnel Psychology and HRM. A Reader for Students and Practitioners*. Chichester: Wiley. pp. 377–437.

Montes, S.D. and Zweig, D. (2009) 'Do promises matter? An exploration of the role of promises in psychological contract breach', *Journal of Applied Psychology*, 94 (5): 1243–60.

Montoya-Weiss, M., Massey, A. and Song, M. (2001) 'Getting it together: temporal coordination and conflict management in global virtual teams', *Academy of Management Journal*, 44 (6): 1251–62.

Mor Barak, M.E. (2000) 'The inclusive workplace', *Social Work*, 45 (4): 339–54.

Muchinsky, P.M. (2006) *Psychology Applied to Work*. Belmont, CA: Thomson Wadsworth.

Newman, D.A. and Harrison, D.A. (2008) 'Been there, bottled that: are state and behavioral work engagement new and useful construct 'wines'?', *Industrial and Organisational Psychology*, 1 (1): 31–5.

Nielsen, M.B., Skogstad, A., Matthiesen, S.B., Glasø, L., Aasland, M.S. Notelaers, G. and Einarsen, S. (2009) 'Prevalence of workplace bullying in Norway: comparisons across time and estimation methods', *European Journal of Work and Organisational Psychology*, 18 (1): 81–101.

Parzefall, M.-R. and Salin, D.M. (2010) 'Perceptions of and reactions to workplace bullying: a social exchange perspective', *Human Relations*, 63 (6): 761–80.

Personnel Today (2005) Diversity policies make billions for UK firms. 28 June 2005. Available at: http://www.personneltoday.com/articles/2005/06/28/30552/diversity-policies-make-billions-for-uk-firms.html (accessed 24 February 2009).

Priola,V. and Brannan, M.J. (2009) 'Between a rock and a hard place: exploring women's experience of participation and progress in managerial careers', Equal Opportunities International, 28 (5): 378–97.

Pritchard, R.D. and Sanders, M.S. (1973) 'The influence of valence, instrumentality and expectancy on effort and performance', *Journal of Applied Psychology*, 57 (1): 55–60.

Rayner, C. (1997) 'The incidence of workplace bullying', *Journal of Community & Applied Social Psychology*, 7: 199–208.

Rayner, C. and McIvor, K. (2008) 'Research report on the Dignity at Work Project.', Portsmouth University.

Restubog, S.L.D., Bordia, P. and Tang, R.L. (2007) 'Behavioural outcomes of psychological contract breach in a non-western culture: the moderating role of equity sensitivity', *British Journal of Management*, 18 (4): 376–86.

Rich, B.L., Lepine, J.A. and Crawford, E.R. (2010) 'Job engagement: antecedents and effects on job performance', *Academy of Management Journal*, 53 (3): 617–635.

Robinson, S.L. and Rousseau, D.M. (1994) 'Violating the psychological contract: not the exception but the norm', *Journal of Organisational Behavior*, 15 (3): 245–59.

Rousseau, D.M. (1995) *Psychological Contracts in Organisations.: Understanding Written and Unwritten Agreements.*. London: Sage.

Rousseau, D.M. (1997) 'Organisational behavior in the new organisational era', *Annual Review of Psychology*, 48: 515–46.

Rousseau, D.M. (2001) 'Schema, promise and mutuality: the building blocks of the psychological contract', *Journal of Occupational and Organisational Psychology*, 74 (4): 511–41.

Sachau, D.A. (2007) 'Resurrecting the motivation-hygiene theory: Herzberg and the positive psychology movement. *Human Resource Development Review*, 6 (4): 377–93.

Saks, A.M. (2006) 'Antecedents and consequences of employee engagement', *Journal of Managerial Psychology*, 21 (7): 600–19..

Salin, D. (2003) 'Ways of explaining workplace bullying: a review of enabling, motivating and precipitating structures and processes in the work environment', *Human Relations*, 56 (10): 1213–32.

Smithson, J. and Stockoe, E. (2005) 'Discourses of work-life balance: negotiating "genderblind" terms in organisations', *Gender, Work and Organisation*, 12 (2): 147–168.

Sparrow, P.R. (1996) 'Careers and the psychological contract: understanding the European context', *European Journal of Work and Organisational Psychology*, 5 (4): 479–500.

Steers, R.M., Mowday, R.T. and Shapiro, D.L. (2004) 'The future of work motivation theory', *Academy of Management Review*, 29 (3): 379–87.

Tehrani, N. (2004) 'Bullying: a source of chronic post traumatic stress?', *British Journal of Guidance and Counselling*, 32: 357–66.

Turnley, W.H. and Feldman, D.C. (1999) 'The impact of psychological contract violations on exit, voice, loyalty, and neglect', *Human Relations*, 52 (7): 895–922.

Van de Vliert, E. and Euwema, M. (1994) 'Agreeableness and activeness as components of conflict behaviours', *Journal of Personality and Social Psychology*, 66: 674–87.

Van Eerde, W. and Thierry, H. (1996) 'Vroom's expectancy models and work-related criteria: a meta-analysis', *Journal of Applied Psychology*, 81 (5): 575–86.

Vroom, V.H. (1964) *Work Motivation*. New York: Wiley.

Wilson, E.M. and Iles, P.A. (1999) 'Managing diversity – an employment and service delivery challenge', *The International Journal of Public Sector Management*, 12 (1): 27–48.

Woodman, P. and Cook, P. (2005) *Bullying at Work. The Experience of Managers*. London: CMI.

Woodman, P. and Kumar, V. (2008) *Bullying at Work 2008. The Experience of Managers*. London: CMI.

Woods, S.A. and West, M.A. (2010) *The Psychology of Work and Organisations*. Andover: Cengage Learning EMEA.

Zapata-Phelan, C.P., Colquitt, J.A., Scott, B.A. and Livingston, B. (2009) 'Procedural justice, interactional justice, and task performance: the mediating role of intrinsic motivation', *Organisational Behavior and Human Decision Processes'*, 108 (1): 93–105.

Zapf, D. and Einarsen, S.. (2003) 'Individual antecedents of bullying', in S. Einarsen (eds), *Bullying and Emotional Abuse in the Workplace. International Perspectives in Research and Practice*. London: Taylor & Francis. pp. 165–84.

5 Counselling and personal development

Andrew Kinder, Kevin Nind, Diane Aitchison
and Eugene Farrell

Learning outcomes

On reading this chapter you will understand:

- how work is defined and the psychological significance of working or not working;
- what we mean by the term 'career';
- the challenges that individuals face in achieving fair and equal treatment at work;
- the key models of career development and career choice;
- the distinction between career advice, guidance and counselling;
- the main types of psychometric tools used to help clients make career decisions.
- the role of counselling and employee assistance programmes in the workplace.

Introduction

The overall rationale for this chapter is to understand more clearly the needs of the individual in the world of work and how personal development and counselling interventions can meet these needs. As practitioners, our main focus is on individual clients and employees – improving their skill level, enabling their career progression, maximising their contribution to organisations and society, and helping them cope with adversity, through a range of interventions. This chapter aims to highlight relevant research findings, concepts and practices. The areas in the workplace include:

- up-skilling to meet business needs;
- entering or leaving work;
- handling career transitions including unemployment or redundancy;
- achieving equality of treatment;
- coping with distress.

With the practitioner areas being: career advice, guidance and counselling; personal development programmes; self-development advice; guidance and coaching; organisational policy; and counselling including outplacement. Key in this area of work is the individual and how they can be best supported to fulfil their personal development.

The psychology of work

> If constant organisational change is the new order of the day, constant personal change is the inevitable corollary. (Herriot, 2001: 1)

This section of the chapter focuses on the individual's experience of work and its absence. People have vastly different experiences of work; the work they do, what work means to them, how they choose a job and the career paths they chose to follow. Our responses and choices are made in a challenging context; as explored in Chapter 1, the nature of work and careers have changed dramatically in recent decades with developments in technology, globalisation and associated economic opportunities and pressures.

Definition and meaning of work

Box 5.1

Exercise 1
Consider and answer these questions before you read this section

1 Describe one thing you have done today that you think is 'work'.
   – What made it 'work'?
2 Describe one thing you have done today that you do not consider to be 'work'.
   – Why is this not work?
3 How do you distinguish between 'work' and 'non-work' activities in your life?

Work is not an easy concept to define; what is seen by one person as 'work' may not be perceived that way by others. Rose suggests: '... in a profit-seeking economy, work is regarded as a commodity that is bought and sold in the market. A wage is a sum paid for work' (1988: 8). Yet there are many exceptions to this definition, for instance, people who do voluntary work or unpaid work. Does this mean that their activities are not work? Should the activities of a student at university be considered work? Hence, our adopted definition needs to encompass purposeful activity that is not just for financial reward, but is still engaging and fulfilling.

Another important aspect not yet captured is people's ambivalence to work – we need to work for a variety of reasons, but we do not necessarily enjoy it. Warr defines work as 'an activity with a purpose beyond enjoyment of the activity itself. It can be arduous and/or tedious, involving effort and resistance beyond the point at which it is pleasurable' (2007: 3).

So academics have helped us define the nature of work. As practitioners, it is helpful to explore clients' views of work and its meaning to them; work is purposeful activity, mostly with productive outcomes, that may or may not be remunerated and whether it is perceived to be 'work' depends on the individual.

Unemployment and redundancy

> The most potent lesson of the twentieth century regarding the nature of working life is that while work itself can be good or bad, the absence of work over a sustained period of time represents a serious threat to individual and social wellbeing. (Overell, 2009: 3–4)

In the UK and across Europe, governments' deficit reduction strategies, including 'austerity' measures will inevitably result in job losses; hence dealing with unemployment and its impact will be a more common experience. From an individual perspective, research by Paul and Moser (2009) shows that unemployment can have a serious detrimental impact on mental health. They reviewed a large number of research studies to explore the impact of unemployment on mental health. Unsurprisingly, they found that unemployed people experienced more distress than those in paid employment. Men generally, and those in blue-collar jobs, were more distressed when made unemployed than women and those in white-collar jobs. They concluded that 'unemployment is not only correlated to distress, but also causes it' (2009: 264).

Warr (2007) also concludes that the unemployed experience significantly more negative feelings than the employed. He identified a range of factors that intensify negative feelings: strong commitment to work; having less financial support; being newly unemployed; having existing symptoms of mental ill-health; living in a low unemployment area; and having fewer social contacts. Fortunately, the negative impact of unemployment on psychological well-being need not be permanent; Murphy and Athanasou (1999) found that re-employment had a positive impact on mental health.

In summary being unemployed is likely to have a detrimental effect on mental well-being. As practitioners, our role is to support people through times of distress, uncertainty and transition. The outplacement counsellor or coach provides support with writing CV's, identifying potential employment options, preparing for interviews and conducting job search campaigns. Attending to clients' psychological needs during unemployment, for example, reduced confidence and self-esteem, is also a vital part of the support offered by practitioners.

Box 5.2

Exercise 2

How might the person in the following situations feel? What could a practitioner do to support them?

- A young female automotive assembly worker finding 'lads' magazines with pictures of naked women lying open in the coffee area
- A woman missing a work promotion interview as she had to collect her sick child from school
- A Muslim man not being offered overtime from his supervisor because the last time he turned it down to attend Friday prayers
- A partially deaf man being excluded from a major project at work because it will involve team conference calls

---

Retirement

The effect of retirement on people can be similar to that of unemployment, especially if the individual does not retire willingly (Warr, 2007). Hanisch (1994) found that people with positive, rather than negative reasons for retiring, were more likely to plan for and enjoy retirement. The option of not retiring at all or at a time of one's own choosing is likely to become more popular given discrimination legislation which enables people to work beyond the traditional retirement age.

The challenge of achieving equal treatment

Chapter 4 explored the impact of discrimination on an individual. An individual's experience at work can be affected by their gender, ethnicity or whether they have a disability. Despite more than 30 years of legislation designed to ensure equality at work, equal treatment has not been consistently achieved. One mark of progress is the Equality Act 2010, as described in Chapter 4 (see also Acas, 2011). Practitioners need to be aware of the work challenges faced by women, ethnic minorities and people with a disability, some of which are identified next.

Gender

The profile of women at work has changed over the last four decades; the proportion of women in employment has grown from 56% in 1971 to 70% in 2008 (ONS, 2010). Women in full-time jobs still earned 10.2% less than men in 2010, although the gap was down 2% from 2009, so the challenge of achieving equal pay for the same work is still present. Arnold et al. (2010) highlight that women are more likely to take up less well-paid careers, such as healthcare and teaching, than men, so this may account for some of the pay difference, but not all. Another challenge facing women is managing the demands of work and family life; although there has been an increase in dual-career couples, women still undertake the majority of domestic responsibilities, so overall demands are not equally shared (Barnett and Shen, 1997).

Race and ethnicity

People from ethnic minority backgrounds experience multiple challenges in the workplace. Noon and Blyton (2007) observe that in the UK, ethnic minorities face higher unemployment, are less likely to access government employment training schemes, achieve fewer promotions and experience more harassment, for example, verbal abuse. They conclude that not only do organisational policies and procedures discriminate against ethnic minorities, but that '… the culture of an organisation may perpetuate values and attitudes that exclude certain ethnic groups …' (2007: 291).

Disability

People with disabilities may also be discriminated against, despite legal requirements for organisations to make 'reasonable adjustments' during their employment. The employment-rate gap between disabled and non-disabled people has decreased from approximately 36% in 2002 to approximately 29% in 2010 (ONS, 2002, 2010). However, the overall employment rate for disabled people is still only 48%, which compares unfavourably with 78% for non-disabled people. In addition, Arnold et al. (2010) observe that numerous studies in the 1980s show disabled people tend to work more in lower status occupations, or in lower levels of higher paid occupations.

In summary, achieving equal treatment at work is still a challenge for some groups: women, ethnic minorities and people with disabilities. We all need to challenge organisations' policies and procedures if inequality is encountered, and be sensitive to the additional challenges faced by some due to their background. By working with disability charities, for example, SCOPE, MIND, additional options for employment with appropriate support can be considered for people with specific needs.

Self-employment and portfolio workers

The number of self-employed workers in the UK is growing; in 2008 3.8 million people were self-employed, 12.9% of the workforce (ONS, 2008). Some may have chosen this option, while others do so in response to redundancy or limited employment opportunities. Portfolio workers are self-employed people who work for a number of different customers. Totterdell et al. observe that self-employed and portfolio workers experience greater autonomy and freedom than those in employment, but also may suffer more job stress due to 'inconsistent workflow, limited independence, reduced control and greater insecurity' (2006: 67).

Self-development and employability

In our experience, individuals are expected by their employers to take more responsibility for their development; 'self-development' is now a key part of organisations' learning and development strategy. Even supportive organisations, who may help employees identify needs via appraisals, typically expect employees to drive their development. There are benefits for both parties to self-development; employers do less costly formal development and employees are more in control of how their skills develop thereby boosting their employability. This is explored further in Chapter 6.

As self-employment becomes more popular in the UK, people need to develop a different skills base to those in employment, one more focused on self-motivation, running a business, networking, selling and virtual teamwork. Within organisations too, there is an increased focus on self-development, meaning that practitioners are asked more often to facilitate provision of informal development processes, online resources and remote coaching.

Careers

What is a career?

The *Oxford English Dictionary*'s definition of a career, as a person's 'course or progress through life' fits with our subjective feeling about what we spend a significant proportion of our lives doing. Academics through decades of research have more informed definitions; for instance, Arnold defines a career as being: 'the sequence of the employment related positions, roles, activities and experiences encountered by a person' (1997: 16). This definition captures two important aspects of a career: those that can be objectively defined, for example, job grade, and those related to our subjective experience, for example, highs and lows. This definition also leads us to adopt a more socially inclusive approach, with fewer assumptions about the nature and order of a person's work experiences. Fewer people are pursuing traditional, linear careers in employment, so we need a broader-based definition.

We have also found a definition by Adamson et al. (1998) to be helpful in conversations with clients; careers are not only 'what one does for a living, but about what one has done, does now and might do in the future'. As practitioners, we aim to have meaningful interactions with our clients, including the exploration of the objective aspects of someone's career.

'Boundaryless' and 'protean' careers

Changes in the world of work mean that our experience of a career is likely to be very different to that of our parents. The wider societal context has an impact on what we mean by a career and how we can support clients in developing and managing theirs. 'Boundaryless' careers, described by Arthur and Rousseau (1996), see careers as having a greater independence from a specific profession, organisation or job specific skills. People move across boundaries in their working lives; changing departments, roles and organisations, working flexible hours, becoming self-employed or running a small company. While some enjoy the flexibility of a 'boundaryless' career, others find them confusing and even threatening (Hirsch and Shanley, 1996).

Hall's (2002) 'protean' or person-centred career places the individual at the centre of their career choices. The individual's internal values, ability to direct their work pattern and achieve success on their own terms, are key components of a protean career. The result is a perceived greater degree of control, autonomy and freedom to make career choices.

There is a wealth of potentially useful models published in the academic literature, hence the purpose of this section is to present a brief overview of the most conspicuous models of career development, choice and decision making. Before we do this, we need to define what is meant by personal development.

Personal development

Essentially, personal development enables people to perform at their best; improving their skills and achieving their optimum potential in the light of prevailing demands. It is also a key component of our own professional role. Professional competencies typically identify personal development as a core responsibility in terms of our own development, the development of others and the processes by which employees are developed.

Personal development encompasses a wide range of tools, techniques, processes and approaches aimed at enabling people to become better at what they are doing. Within the workplace, personal development is harnessed to the organisation's mission and goals; investment in employee development is expected to deliver business benefits. Beyond direct employment, people are still motivated to improve themselves, and self-development is supported by a plethora of books, questionnaires, online resources, life coaches and self-help gurus.

Commercially, personal development is a significant sector in the global economy with a US$64 billion industry worldwide. In the UK, professional associations such as the Chartered Institute for Personnel and Development (CIPD), British Psychological Society (BPS) and Institute of Careers Guidance have many thousands of professionally qualified members offering various types of personal development. Practitioners come from a variety of professional backgrounds: human resources, learning and development, occupational psychologists and vocational/careers guidance counsellors.

Theories of occupational choice and career development

There are a range of theories that practitioners can draw on to work with clients in exploring their career issues, dilemmas and challenges. Some can be used to help an individual make a specific career choice at any given point in time, while others help the individual understand the different stages of their career as it develops over time and in relation to their experiences.

Choosing a career

The traditional role played by vocational guidance and career guidance specialists is to help an individual choose the best career for them. As practitioners, we may be asked to help clients make decisions about their career. We can look at their capabilities, their interests and what realistic options are available. Holland put forward a 'person-environment fit' approach to helping clients choose a career. His (1997) most recent version suggests that people seek jobs that match their interests, and that there are six interest types that jobs fit into and that people are interested in. These are:

- realistic – likes practical, hands-on work, has mechanical abilities; less interested in socialising;
- investigative – likes to investigate and analyse concepts, interested in scientific-type jobs;
- artistic – likes to be imaginative and expressive with their emotions; has musical/artistic abilities, may be disorganised;
- social – likes to help others, interested in teaching, social work counselling; has good social skills but may lack scientific ability;

- enterprising – likes to persuade people rather than help them, tends to be ambitious, likes to achieve things;
- conventional – likes structure, order and has organisational abilities, less interested in imaginative or artistic roles.

Holland arranged these types into a hexagonal model, grouping similar types together and found that people describe themselves in terms of the three types most like them (Figure 5.1).

The reader can help clients assess their interests using this model, the self-directed search and the strong interest inventory (see Table 5.1), which are based on Holland's model and can be bought for this purpose. Holland proposes that people make good career choices when there is congruence between what the job offers and the person's job and personality preferences. If the degree of fit is weaker, people try to change either their environment or themselves to improve their fit.

Kidd (2006) points out that although there is research to support Holland's theory of congruence (Spokane, 1985), other research casts doubt on whether congruence results in satisfaction (Tinsley, 2000). She suggests that this could be explained by people considering more what *job* they would like to do, rather than considering what *occupation* suits them best (2006: 16). Arnold (2004) proposed a number of reasons for the poor statistical relationship between congruence and satisfaction. He raises questions about what the 'environment' in 'person-environment' fit might mean. For some the greatest satisfaction may come from their being a close fit with the organisation; for others it could be a specific work group, or even an industry sector.

Arnold et al. (2010) also point out that Holland's model does not describe the process by which an individual makes a career decision. They suggest self-awareness (understanding ones' strengths and development areas, values, likes and dislikes),

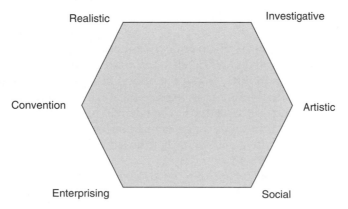

Figure 5.1   Holland's hexagonal model of vocational types

and occupational knowledge (appreciating the range of potential jobs available and what they involve) help individuals make effective career choices. They suggest 'good awareness of self and the world of work is often a consequence of a willingness to engage in exploration, and a cause of successful career decisions' (2010: 625). Other factors that they believe to be important are the quality of a person's decision-making style, the strength of an individual's personal identity and development to date, and a strong self-efficacy, or confidence in their own abilities.

While theories of occupational choice, such as Holland's, can help the practitioner focus their client on their interests and skills at one point in time, they are somewhat static. Kidd (2006) sees developmental career theories as potentially more useful, and describes the 'monumental' shift away from the more static approach. She believes they provide a concept 'of career support with the emphasis of developing the individual's career maturity, particularly of self-awareness, seeking opportunities and facilitating informed decision-making' (2006: 21).

Supporting career development

As well as helping clients choose a career or occupation, practitioners are often asked to support them in exploring or developing their careers. This requires a different approach than simply testing people and suggesting which occupations they should try. There are a number of theories that the practitioner can draw on. Developmental career theories attempt to take account of the processes leading up to making an occupational choice. They suggest that choosing a career and adjusting to work is a continuous process that carries on through life and that concepts from developmental psychology can be used to explain the process of career development (Kidd, 2006).

Stage theories

One approach to understanding career development has been to see it as a series of predictable stages. Erikson (1957, 1980) describes eight stages of ego development throughout life from birth to late adulthood that when successfully negotiated allows the individual to progress to the next stage. Erikson sets life stages in a social context, which requires actions to be taken to resolve the potential conflict during each stage. The adulthood stage can be concerned with passing on something worthwhile for future generations. For those well-established in their career this is often a focus.

Levinson et al. (1978) also considered life stages in *The Seasons of a Man's Life*. Their research, based a small sample of 40 men, led to conclusions similar to Erikson's, that distinct stages or seasons can describe our life cycle. They described three broad stages of adulthood (early, middle and late) each with its own series of transitions. Levinson describes activities that a client can take to help manage their way through these stages, for example, finding a mentor and reviewing achievements.

Developmental theories

Super is the best-known of the developmental theorists. Super (1957) looked specifically at career development and initially identified four age-related career stages. At each stage the individual is concerned about specific issues and there will be certain tasks that they are concerned with. The stages are:

- exploration (15–24 years) of the world of work and of their own preferences to identify occupational preferences;
- establishment (25–44 years) of their career path, settling down and advancing in that chosen career;
- maintenance (45–64 years) holding their own in their career, developing themselves where necessary to do so;
- disengagement (65+ years) decreasing their involvement and planning for retirement.

Although ages are attached to the different stages, it is likely that questions from earlier stages may re-surface in later ones. For example, people experiencing a mid-life crisis and who are in the 'maintenance' stage may also experience some concerns from earlier stages if they are challenging their own views of their career and their contribution. Super also identifies the notion of 'career maturity' which is the individual's willingness to respond to the developmental tasks appropriate to the career stage they are at.

Arnold et al. (2010) highlight that it may not always be easy to identify what stage a person may be in their career, particularly if a person enters a career especially early, or if they change career and start a new one at an older age.

Super's most notable contribution to career theory is that of how our self-concept develops throughout our working lives in light of our experiences. This self-concept is refined over time by the nature of our work experiences and in turn informs our career choices. Kidd (2006) points out that with this self-concept there is a stronger focus on the subjective perspective of the individual in making occupational choices. The role of the practitioner becomes one of enhancing the individual's understanding of themselves and their preferences and skills. Assessment tools are used to facilitate the individual's understanding rather than seeking a perfect individual–environment fit.

Super's model provided a formative basis for future research into professional roles, but has been criticised for not having a broad enough relevance to all types of work and workers. As Kidd (2006) highlights, later stages are not well-defined, do not address organisation-based careers, and do not mention the psychological challenges of adapting to a new job.

Later, Super (1980) acknowledged that linking age to stage may not always be appropriate, so developed a more flexible 'life-career rainbow'. The rainbow strands reflect the roles an individual takes on, and in their adult life they can take on several at one time, for example, student, worker and parent.

Schein's career anchors

Schein's (1993) career anchors look beyond ages and stages, suggesting that we are drawn to certain types of jobs. His career anchors are a mix of the individuals' needs, values, motivation and skills that draw people to specific types of jobs. He identifies eight career anchors: managerial competence; technical/ functional competence; security; autonomy and independence; entrepreneurial creativity; pure challenge; service/dedication to a cause; and lifestyle integration. This idea may sound similar to Holland's type model of occupational choice, but it does go beyond it. Career anchors reflect a much more in-depth consideration of the individual. Schein suggests that your strongest anchor is the one element of your self-concept that you will not give up, even in the face of difficult choices. These anchors, once identified will not necessarily predict the type of job a person does; for example, owners of a small business may have as strong a need for lifestyle integration as they do for entrepreneurial creativity. However, knowing which anchor is the strongest can have a clear influence on the job a client chooses. The practitioner can use this approach to explore the client's strongest anchor and identify jobs that will allow that need to be met. There is an online tool which practitioners can use with clients to identify their career anchors (see Table 5.1).

Practitioners working in organisations should be aware of the range of anchors that their employees may have and that the organisation can satisfy. The authors have worked with a scientific research organisation which had challenges in satisfying the career ambitions of its mostly scientific workforce. The creation of a clear technical career path, in addition to the original managerial one, meant many dissatisfied (and often poorly skilled) managers were able to return to the technical roles they most enjoyed and still satisfy their need to progress in their career.

Career transitions

Nicholson and West (1988) consider the topic of a career from a transition point of view. They explore how an individual copes with the transition in or out of a job, between jobs or even any major change to duties and activities within the same job. Each transition has a four-stage cycle: preparation, encounter, adjustment and stabilisation. Although each stage is distinct, they are interdependent – the effect of one stage can impact the next. Transition cycles can recur and have a cumulative effect, which can lead to cycles of disappointment or satisfaction depending on how they are managed. The benefit of this transition model is that it allows the practitioner to identify and address the emotional response to the transition, and Nicholson (1990) describes career-related tasks that practitioners can use with clients to anticipate change and cope with new situations.

In summary, the practitioner can use these theories to help clients build insight into their career paths and make choices and transitions in a more informed manner. They can also help clients anticipate future challenges and help them to prepare for them. With recent theories there are a series of activities clients can do to manage their career with practitioner support. For further reading on this topic, including a critique of the models, see Kidd (2006).

Career counselling

Kidd (2006) suggests a four-stage model of career counselling that is based on Egan's (2002) model of helping. Kidd's four stages are summarised in Figure 5.2 with associated tasks she suggests the practitioner works through with their client.

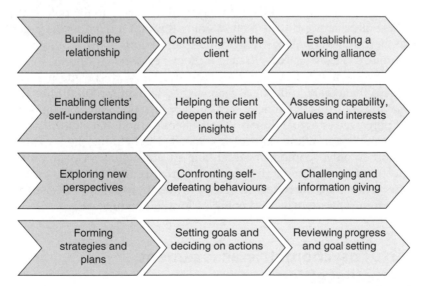

Figure 5.2   Summary of the career counselling process described by Kidd (2006)

Help in the choice process: methods and approaches

The role of a practitioner – advice, guidance and counselling

Before considering the skills required by a practitioner, we need to distinguish between three ways of working with clients – advice, guidance and counselling.

Advice and guidance help clients explore relevant options and make informed choices using tools and professional expertise. When giving *advice,* information is provided tailored to clients' needs, when providing *guidance,* practitioners provide knowledge on the basis of their expertise with a variety of structured tools and then guide them through a process to an agreed end point. This increases clients' insight and helps them make decisions about future directions in a supported manner.

Counselling is different from advice and guidance because of the issues concerned. Counselling is typically sought when clients have problems they cannot cope with and which cause them distress to some extent. A counsellor enables the person to cope better with managing their thoughts, behaviours and emotions. There are different therapeutic approaches that counsellors use, and counselling is described later in the chapter along with coaching.

The skills of a practitioner

Enabling a person to make decisions about their job and career in a supportive and systematic manner is a highly skilled activity, mainly owing to the potential significance of those decisions and the effects of going through the process. A practitioner has to use their professional expertise to interpret various sources of information – some objective, some subjective – to help a client explore their options in an empathetic, yet impartial manner. A client will need support with considering a range of factors to help them make rational decisions, then to plan for the future. The intervention may be occurring at a time of transition or turbulence in a person's life, with significant perceived or actual threats to self-esteem, emotional and financial stability. At such times, counselling skills may be needed to help the client manage their emotions and improve coping, representing an additional level of professional competence for the practitioner. It is important that practitioners are aware of the level of intervention and are prepared to refer onwards, when the nature of a client's problems become too extensive and complex for their competence.

The role of psychometric assessment in career counselling

Essentially, the plethora of tools available for use in career counselling enable practitioners to help clients understand themselves, the world of work and their options, including opportunities they were not aware of. It is through the practitioner's expertise with interpreting results and giving meaningful feedback that thinking and insights are stimulated. Without professional and impartial interpretation, misleading conclusions might be drawn. Without a structured process for integrating information from a variety of sources, the full picture might not emerge.

There are various ways of combining results for personality questionnaires (self-reported behaviours or preferred style), interest inventories (occupational task or activity preferences) and ability tests (performance on specific tests of speed and power). One of simplest and most effective is the 'ship metaphor' – a client's overall suitability is a combination of their:

- 'hull' or personal style (different roles require different styles or personal attributes);
- 'engine' or relevant abilities (certain abilities are needed at certain levels for certain roles);
- 'rudder' or occupational interests (people are drawn towards their interests);
- 'ship's mission' or values (people strive for what they are passionate about or believe in).

Box 5.3

CASE STUDY: A client who is a principled artist

When working with a talented artist, who was questioning whether she needed to change her choice of career, a practitioner explored her abilities, which were well suited to her role – above average spatial and diagrammatic reasoning, excellent hand-eye and fine motor co-ordination and good interpersonal skills. Her personality showed a high degree of 'fit' with her chosen career; highly creative and unconventional, a strong belief in her own ideas, and organised and disciplined in her approach to work. As might be expected her interests were strong to the point of passionate about artistic and creative pursuits. So far, so good. The sticking point came when her values were explored – she did not believe in being commercial, rather letting her pieces 'find their own value'. She then recognised that she needed to get an agent who could help her make a living from her art work.

Tools for enabling occupational choice

There is a very wide range of tools available for the practitioner to use in their personal development career counselling activities. Table 5.1 identifies the main types of instruments available, qualifications required to use them and where they can be obtained from. The BPS Psychometric Testing Centre (PTC) provides reviews on a wide range of psychometric tests from a variety of test publishers.

Table 5.1   Tools to help clients explore their capabilities and career interests

Instrument/tool	Useful for ...	Available from
Ability tests: e.g. verbal, numerical, mechanical reasoning, checking tests, leadership judgement tests, etc.	Establishing clients' level of ability in key work relevant skills.	Psychometric test publishers: SHL, Saville Consulting, Criterion Partnership, OPP, Pearson
Personality questionnaires: e.g. OPQ, Wave, CAL, Identity, Hogan HDS, NEO-PIR.	Exploring clients' preferred ways of behaving in the workplace, e.g. do they: prefer to work on their own, or with others; make decisions based on facts or intuition. Different questionnaires measure different aspects of personality at work.	Psychometric test publishers: SHL, Saville Consulting, Criterion Partnership, OPP, PCL, Quest Partnership, Team Focus, Hogrefe, Pearson
Interest inventories: e.g. Strong Interest Inventory, Self-Directed Search	Exploring clients' preferences for activities associated with specific types of work or professions.	OPP, Self-Directed-Search (PAR)
Strengths questionnaires: e.g. Strengthscope	Focusing on clients' key strengths (as opposed to areas for development) to explore and build-on in development conversations.	Blue Edge Consulting, Capp
Values questionnaires: e.g. self-administered questionnaires or checklists	Helping clients' identify work that matches their values, e.g. do they want to work in a highly profit-oriented environment where good results are rewarded? This goes beyond simply exploring occupational choice.	Self-administered checklists from the Internet; see further reading.
Composite questionnaires: e.g: Schein's Career Anchors, The Campbell Interest and Skills Survey (CISS). Career anchors online surveys.	Exploring a range of factors that can help clients understand their current position and help them choose alternative careers. Such factors can include the individual's attraction for specific occupational areas, with aligned skill scales that provide estimates of an individual's confidence in his or her ability to perform various occupational activities.	Pearson Assessment. Online administered questionnaire from Career Anchors or RapidBI.

All these tools can be used to help people identify transferable skills, preferred ways of working and personal values, when considering their career options and choices. The BPS Level 2 Test User Qualifications in Ability Tests (formerly 'Level A') and Personality Questionnaires (formerly 'Level B') may be needed to use these tools. Personality measures can be helpful tools for personal development, especially where coaches are looking to understand the fit between the individual and their environment. Counsellors tend not to use personality measures but do use various clinical measures instead which focus on clinical symptoms rather than personality traits or preferences. The rest of the chapter focuses on the subject of counselling in the workplace.

Counselling

What is counselling?

Counselling offers a safe and confidential place for individuals to discuss their problems or concerns, things that are troubling them or causing upset, pain or confusion. Such issues may be related to work or personal life or indeed both.

Counselling is delivered by a trained therapist, who will listen and ask questions, allowing the individual to talk. It takes place over a number of sessions and the number and length varies between individuals.

Counselling does not work for everyone and takes time to be effective. Of great importance is the relationship between the client and therapist, and from an individual's perspective it is important to choose a therapist you can really get along with.

There are many types of therapy available such as cognitive, solution focused, person-centred or humanistic and psychodynamic. There are also approaches that combine such approaches.

Counselling may take place at different levels, such as informal counselling by line management through conversation, performance appraisal or personal development as described earlier in this chapter; however, this may be highly variable in its nature and delivery and would rarely have a counselling theoretical or clinical framework. In the workplace, counselling is usually delivered by qualified practitioners who work within departments such as occupational health, welfare or an in-house counselling service. An example of such a service is that provided to the fire and rescue services or policing. Some job roles may also receive counselling for specialist risk roles; such as viewing disturbing images or forensic photography; where regular counselling acts as both supervision and early diagnosis of poor coping.

Organisations may employ one or more counsellors as part of their on-going staff support to assist employees with work and personal issues. The role of the on-site counsellor is one of special trust; they act for the client and for the organisation (see later in the chapter for a discussion on the 'three cornered contract'), and through their employment and physical presence have specialist knowledge of the organisation and its people. Within this role they are able reach out to others, for example line management and HR, to assist the client in their issues. Kinder et al. (2008) highlight examples such as responding to traumatic incidents, suicide and sudden death, bullying and harassment as well as tackling a macho culture.

Counselling has become synonymous with work stress management in the workplace. The very term stress 'has so many different meanings that it is confusing, elusive and heard so often its meaning is frequently distorted and its implications taken for granted' (Arthur, 2005), and for both internal and external programmes this has been an advantage and disadvantage. Stress and mental health in the workplace will be explored in Chapter 7.

Trauma-based counselling is an important part of workplace counselling. This has existed in policing, fire and rescue and related services for many years, yet the increasing awareness of post traumatic stress disorder (PTSD) and indeed post-9/11 terrorism and major incidents has highlighted the need to support the organisation and employees after such events. In 2005, NICE published guidelines on the treatment of trauma and prevention of PTSD, and a major new textbook on trauma in the workplace has recently been published (see Hughes et al., 2012).

Counselling at work

The relationship between the employer and employee

In 1943, Maslow presented his hierarchy of needs that we as humans require (see Chapter 4). While in our modern society the base needs are taken for granted, we retain a demand for the higher needs. Work is important to an individual; realising their needs in respect of esteem and self actualisation; it has meaning for individuals and provides social interaction, a sense of belonging and accomplishment, a place to learn and grow, to feel pride and the feeling that our work might contribute to the well-being of others. While the employee might gain, so too does the employer in terms of labour and output.

The role of the employer is an important one; it goes beyond the simple work for pay relationship, exemplified by constructs such as the psychological contract and employee engagement explored in Chapter 4.

The case study in Box 5.4 illustrates what happens if aspects of the psychological contract related to career development between employer and employee are fundamentally challenged.

Box 5.4

CASE STUDY: Client is a Talent Manager, International Oil Company

James was a respected HR professional working as a Talent Manager in a division of an oil company. Having served successfully with the organisation in various employee assessment and development roles over 10 years, James anticipated developing his

---

career within the organisation over the next few years, achieving his next promotion to senior management within that time frame. At his last appraisal, he had been identified as 'ready for promotion within 2 years' and had planned his development accordingly. A significant business review identified the need to restructure the entire HR function, resulting in all HR staff applying for their own jobs and a headcount reduction of 25%. James was successful in achieving his existing role, but was offered it on the condition of a transfer to the European Head Office. Due to family commitments, James declined the offer and was assigned to a holding role as Talent Development Manager for a UK support function and his promotion path was put on hold. Despite success in his new role over the next year, James decided to accept an offer of a senior level appointment with another European company.

- What models of career and personal development are relevant to this case?
- What factors influenced James' decisions about his career?
- What else could have been done to by the organisation to retain James' services?

While the employer may have a legal duty of care for physical and psychological health, the workplace today sees employers investing in health and well-being products and services that extend beyond the legal requirements. In the context of health and well-being, many organisations have a strong history:

> advancing the health, safety and well-being of our global workforce is an absolute priority … – IBM

> we have provided health services for employees for several decades, starting at a time when it was considered a discretionary benefit – Tate & Lyle

> the general well-being of employees makes a big difference to their engagement and productivity at work – Nokia

The employer's responsibility for employee's personal and family issues is a matter of debate. While employers wish to maintain employee well-being, how is it possible to separate the personal from the work identity of an individual? It could be argued that supporting an individual with their personal issues will benefit working lives. It also works the other way in that their, by assisting employees with work-related problems, they are by default assisting with personal-related issues, and through this intervention they gain better work-related performance.

Definition and origin of employee assistance programmes

An employee assistance programme (EAP) is a strategic intervention designed for organisations to provide support and information to their employees when they have work-related issues, such as high workload demand, pressure and work performance. The programme is purchased by the organisation and provided to employees without cost to them. In the UK there are between 20 and 30 providers with an estimated market size of £50 million (EAPA UK, n.d.).

The origin of EAP is generally accepted to be the USA although the exact historical roots are often disputed. In 1971, ALMACA (Association of Labor-Management Administrators and Consultants on Alcoholism) was formed and it was through this group that the EAP concept was expanded worldwide. In 1981, the National Institute on Alcohol Abuse and Alcoholism (NIAAA) funding was revoked, yet and despite the lack of funding EAPs continue to prevail with a shift toward work-related issues. The term 'employee assistance programme' was popularised in a book titled *The Employee Assistance Programme* by J.T. Wrich (Sonnenstuhl and Trice, 1990), and subsequent to this in 1990 ALMACCA changed its name to Employee Assistance Professionals Association or EAPA, which has a 'branch' in the UK.

In the UK, although there are now many outsourced EAPs, some organisations have adopted different models of EAP provision such as internal, external, outsourced via occupational health, and hybrid EAPs (for an explanation of the advantages and disadvantages of each of these models see Hughes and Kinder [2007], Carroll [1996] and also Cole [2003]).

Growth of EAPs

External outsourced EAPs spread to the UK in the late 1970s and were formed in response to demands for counselling and psychological services. In the UK, programmes quickly added other services, such as legal information, health information and children's and older people's health, and support location services. This positioning came from a more work-life perspective, also with a focus on mental health services.

EAPs really began to expand following a series of high profile occupational stress-related litigation cases beginning with John Walker in 1996. The most important was *Hatton* v *Sutherland* in 2002 where workplace counselling was specifically mentioned within Lady Justice Hale's judgment, stating 'an employer who offers a confidential advice service, with referral to appropriate counselling or treatment services is unlikely to be found in breach of duty'. This provided a backdrop for providers to promote services to employers as being a form of 'insurance' related to duty of care. The economic threat encountered by business has led to outsourcing of many internal counselling services to EAP providers, with EAPs being able to provide a wider offering over and above counselling (see Buon, 2004, for a discussion on the globalisation of EAPs and the increased trend towards outsourcing). The result is that over the last 10 years the counselling landscape has become dominated by the growth of EAPs that play an ever increasing role in the workplace. In a recent survey by *Employee Benefits Magazine,* some 73% of organisations reported having an EAP as a core healthcare benefit; this was the number one benefit growing from 23% in 2002 to 48% in 2007, and 69% in 2010 (*Employee Benefits Magazine* Healthcare Research June 2011).

Structure and services of EAPs

An EAP is essentially a bundle of services that provide support and information to managers and employees accessed through a single telephone number or web portal. EAP providers may employ a number of different specialists to deliver the services, and may outsource some of the services such as psychologists, debt counsellors and lawyers, among others. While telephone counselling can be delivered immediately by the provider's employed counsellors, face-to-face counselling is often delivered by a national network of counsellors contracted to deliver service on behalf of the provider. Such affiliate counsellors may undertake work for several EAP providers.

Typical EAP services could include any of the following:

- telephone counselling;
- face-to-face counselling;
- managerial consultation;
- debt counselling;
- legal information;
- health information;
- government benefits;
- childcare/eldercare location services;
- emergency childcare search;
- organisational management information;
- specialist account management.

Market trends of EAPs

Increasingly EAPs offer web-based services alongside their telephone services as this enables employees to self-serve informational support, such as legal and health. There is also a growth in online counselling being offered both as real time 'chat' (i.e. instant messaging, video/webcam conference) and time delayed, which is more like email exchange. Whatever method, it is important that the online environment is secure, password protected and encrypted.

Entry to EAP is for the most part self-referral with employees able to call the EAP as and when they require support. Organisations may also make management referrals to EAPs in a formal structured way, as well as informally recommending the use of EAPs to employees. The role of line management in identifying and managing behavioural and psychological health changes is an increasingly important one, and the EAP provides an active tool so managers can refer those who need extra support. Hughes and Kinder highlight that 'the counsellor/ service provider can act as a bridge between the client and the organisation (such as via human resources, welfare, occupational health) so that the underlying work-related difficulties can be addressed' (2007: 5). The cost of EAP services is known to have declined significantly over the last 10 years; although there are no official public figures, estimates are in the region of 50% drop in the per-capita rate. This is in part due to the market entry of non-specialists, such as health insurers, and partly due to the application of cost-control measures driven by efficiency and competition.

The utilisation of EAP services by organisations is a somewhat contentious issue, especially as this directly links to the cost for providing the service by the EAP. There are at least six different measures used within the market (http:// www.eapassn.org/files/public/utilisation06.pdf) and this rather confuses the real levels of utilisation. Some providers count all contacts including web hits, while others may exclude the web hits, and others count each case as a piece of work under a single issue where several contacts and services may have been delivered. Clearly buyers and users need to be absolutely clear about the measure being used when comparing services.

Professional issues

Code of conduct

Whether delivered by affiliate counsellors of EAPs or workplace counsellors from an internal service, 'counselling' is a professional activity that requires practitioners to follow a strict code of practice in order to safeguard vulnerable clients and to ensure that the public is protected. There are a variety of different codes of practice available from each professional body, although they all share adherence to various principles of good ethical practice. For instance, within the UK there are three main professional bodies, not forgetting in addition the regulatory body for psychologists, the HPC:

- British Psychological Society;
- British Association for Counselling & Psychotherapy (BACP);
- United Kingdom Counselling & Psychotherapy (UKCP).

There is also a specialist association covering cognitive behavioural therapy (CBT) called the British Association for Behavioural and Cognitive Psychotherapies (BABCP). Psychologists are now regulated by the HPC as applied psychologists within their respective discipline, such as counselling, occupational or clinical.

The ethical codes of practice set by both the BPS and HPC was explained in Chapter 3. The largest counselling organisation is the BACP with almost 40,000 members. They have published the *Ethical Framework for Good Practice in Counselling and Psychotherapy* (2010) which sets out the professional standards that need to be followed, and this code of ethics is available via their website (www.bacp.co.uk).

Complaints and protection of public

Professional bodies need to demonstrate that good clinical standards are being maintained and that there are sanctions for those who fall short and negatively impact clients. Currently the BACP publishes in their journal occasions where counsellors have broken the ethical framework as a means of reassuring the general public that sanctions for bad practice are made and also to educate other practitioners about good ethical practice.

Any organisation involved in delivering counselling needs to have a clear complaints policy so that concerns/issues can be quickly investigated and, if needed, the problem put right. Clients who feel that their issues have not been satisfactorily resolved by the counselling organisation can raise the concern with the relevant professional body.

It is therefore important that organisations providing counselling should ensure the practitioners they employ or contract with are full members of a suitable professional body, such as the BACP, BPS, UKCP or BABCP, to enable further recourse for clients with concerns about poor practice. In addition, practitioners need to ensure they receive training/clinical supervision to ensure they understand how to interpret and follow professional guidelines, and counselling providers need to contract only with these reputable practitioners.

Using a complaints procedure to resolve issues is one aspect of any quality improvement process. However, not everyone wishes to make a complaint given the formality involved. Informal client feedback is just as important for any service provider, and the EAPA have recognised this in their standards for registered members where an EAP should define what is to be regarded as a complaint – which may be considered to be different from 'negative feedback' (EAPA UK, 2011).

Confidentiality

The BACP highlights that confidentiality is at the heart of counselling:

> Respecting clients' privacy and confidentiality are fundamental requirements for keeping trust and respecting client autonomy. The professional management of confidentiality concerns the protection of personally identifiable and

sensitive information from unauthorised disclosure. Disclosure may be authorised by client consent or the law. Any disclosures of client confidences should be undertaken in ways that best protect the client's trust and respect client autonomy. (2012: 7)

However, confidentiality can never be 100% absolute in that there are always exceptions depending on the exact nature of the counselling service being provided and its context. For instance, the following circumstances can mean that a disclosure may be made:

- where there is risk of harm to self or others;
- where there is a serious alleged crime;
- where there is a legal requirement (for example, protection of children or prevention of terrorism);
- where there is a significant threat to the health and safety of those within an organisation.

Any client who makes use of the service should be informed of the limits of confidentiality, that is, in leaflets or websites that publicise the programme as well as when clients make contact with the service. If a disclosure is felt to be needed, the counsellor needs to ensure this is the last resort and should do their utmost to discuss with the client beforehand.

Roles of a counsellor in the workplace

BACP Workplace (a specialist division within the BACP) has published guidelines on being a counsellor within an organisation (Hughes and Kinder, 2007). It makes the case that any counsellor practicing in the workplace needs to be not only competent in the technicalities of their profession but also adept at managing the many different roles that can present themselves when working in an organisation. This is what differentiates a counsellor working as a private practitioner to a workplace counsellor or competent EAP affiliate, where the ability to juggle the different roles and expectations is an important attribute. Schwenk (2006) has highlighted these as:

- advising line managers on approaching troubled employees;
- employee counselling – face-to-face, by phone or online;
- training and health education – proactive intervention;
- advising the organisation on policy matters in relation to welfare and emotional/ psychological health;
- managerial responsibilities – in relation to counselling service provision and operation;

- facilitating organisational change;
- critical incident support and other trauma management;
- advising on equal opportunities and other related employment policies and procedures;
- publicising the service to staff and managers;
- monitoring effectiveness and service evaluation;
- administration of notes and reports to managers from business referrals;
- procedures for referring on;
- mediating between client and organisation.

Such roles apply just as much to internal counsellors employed by an organisation as they do to EAPs, where the service provider takes on these functions.

Coaching/mentoring

Coaching/mentoring is another area which could be added to the list as this is emerging as an important component of an EAP or internal service and is developing into a distinct area of professional practice (for example, the Special Group of Coaching Psychologists [SPCP]). Coaches and mentors are not necessarily qualified as counsellors, although some may be, and an increasing number are psychologists, from the occupational stable, or HR practitioners who have additional training in coaching. There is much debate as to the difference between counselling and coaching/mentoring with various definitions offered. One way of understanding the difference is to imagine a spectrum of coping from '−10', where the individual is unable to cope with work and maybe off sick from work or moving that way, to '0', where the individual is coping but not showing high performance, and then '+10' where the individual is highly effective in their work. Counselling's focuses on moving an individual from −10 to 0, while coaching/mentoring focuses on moving them from 0 to +10. In other words whereas counselling deals with clients with some degree of psychological distress and in need of a therapeutic intervention, coaching deals with personal growth of an individual who has not clinically presented and is regarded as 'well'. Coaching is a pragmatic approach to helping people manage their acquisition or improvement of skills (Clutterbuck, 1998)

Coaching can be in many forms such as life coaching, business, career, health and sports, where the coach specialises in their own field of expertise. Mentoring operates from a relationship perspective of sharing personal experience and knowledge of the field or situation. Coaching has an approach and language that differs from counselling, with the 'coach' working with the 'coached'. The role of the coach is to work with the coached to help them increase their self-awareness, achieve their personal targets and goals and increase their performance and motivation. They are not working therapeutically although they do share many of the skills used in counselling and psychotherapy (Kemp, 2008).

The coach acts as a mirror reflecting back the coached's thoughts, words and ideas to enable the coached to see things more clearly and, in doing so, to work out how to move forward. Coaches believe that the coached have all the knowledge they need; the coach is there to help them to tap into it.

Just like counsellors, the strength of alliance between coach and coached (therapeutic alliance in clinical terms) is important in achieving growth outcomes (Horvath, 2000, 2001, 2006; Horvath and Symonds, 1991). Thus the coach has a developmental partnership with the coached to help them to achieve their goals and each individual receiving an approach tailored for them.

Managing conflict

Managing conflict situations between people at work using mediation and facilitation skills is of increasing importance to a workplace counsellor and, with organisations needing to have in place alternative dispute resolutions such as informal methods, this will be an increasing area of work, especially for EAPs and internal workplace counsellors who have been trained in mediation. They can contribute especially where the conflict relates to the relationships between people rather than relating to a legal conflict. See Chapter 4 for more details on this important area.

Challenges of practicing counselling in organisations and the three cornered contract

This chapter has highlighted how counselling in organisations is quite different to traditional counselling and this is perhaps understood best by the concept of the 'three cornered contract', a concept originally coined by English (1975). In this scenario, whenever a counsellor sees an employee for counselling, there is one other 'person' present – the organisation, that is, three people in the room.

This presence could be felt by the employee who is experiencing bullying and harassment at work and could become concerned about what information is being fed back to their line manager, or it could be where the organisation has referred the employee for counselling with the expectation that a report should be written back about when they are able to return to work.

There could be ethical challenges, such as where the counsellor is seeing two clients – one feels harassed by his boss and the other frustrated with the incompetence of her team. The counsellor unwittingly takes both clients on – and then realises that they are talking about each other. What should happen here? A further ethical issue could be where the counsellor providing telephone counselling is told by their client that they are viewing pornography on the company computer as 'stress relief', which is against the organisation's policy. Should this information be disclosed?

Pickard (1997) makes the case that counsellors who practice in the workplace should receive additional training in organisational theories/practices and good ethical practice so that there is a greater understanding of the complexities of these influences and how they impact upon the process of counselling. In relation to organisational behaviour, Kinder reinforces this point and argues that workplace counsellors should 'pay attention to the wider system in operation and to take special care in drawing up clear contracts not just with clients but also with the organisation. Systemic and integrative approaches can be helpful here in dealing with all these dimensions' (2005: 23). Counsellors and EAP providers therefore need to pay attention to confidentiality arrangements and to set out clearly the boundaries between management referrals and self referrals, how informed consent should be sought for management referrals and the limits of confidentiality in relation to organisational policies such as for alcohol and drug misuse or in safety-critical industries.

From a perspective of individual training, a workplace counsellor needs to work through their own feelings about the organisation they are working within, otherwise this can get in the way of the counselling process. For instance, if they feel that the organisation is a 'big bad wolf', they may transmit this sense to their clients and set in motion a negative transference to the organisation. The three-cornered contract, signified by an equilateral triangle, becomes mis-shaped, with the organisation at a distance as the counsellor and employee become closer together (Figure 5.3).

This model has been developed by various authors (see Copeland, 2005) who have demonstrated how good quality clinical supervision arrangements can achieve a better balance between each party. Subsequent coaching supervision models have been developed which apply these models in the coaching context (Hawkins, 2011).

Future developments in workplace counselling and EAP

The UK EAP market is estimated at over £50 million per annum (EAPA, 2011). The market has changed considerably over the last five years, not only because of the changes in suppliers, but also the shift towards well-being and online services.

In Europe EAPs are gaining slow acceptance, the Employee Assistance European Forum was formed in 2002 to represent the industry across Europe and now has more than 60 members from 23 countries. However, the development has been slowed by the very concept of delivery. Mental health management may be dominated by social workers in one country, psychiatrists in another and psychotherapists

Equilateral triangle – ideal state

Organisation

Client   Counsellor

Collusion between the client and counsellor (with organisation pushed away)

Organisation

Client   Counsellor

Figure 5.3   Three-cornered contract

in another. The concept of the 'counsellor' as we know it does not exist in many countries, therefore the development of the EAP will vary across Europe and is unlikely to replicate the UK or US model.

The market in China remains more optimistic with a working population of 116 million and a growing acceptance of employee assistance with a reported market growth of EAP of over 300% per annum (Cheung, 2011).

Market developments in the UK appear to be based upon technology and health and well-being, particularly the convergence of the two. Increasingly EAP providers and internal counselling services are extending their services beyond the traditional counselling model to include much more emphasis on health and well-being, with a focus on improving the psychological health of employees. A central theme of well-being is the web-based well-being themed portal, providing a range of health information and fact sheets. Employees can sign up to receive health interest mailings based upon their preferences, and also targeted mail based upon the output from their health risk assessment (HRA). Employees completing their HRA can receive a personal risk-based health report aimed at changing their health behaviours. Participation data from the portal and aggregated health risks data can be provided to employers to enable them to target health promotional activities within the workplace.

Further technological developments are in the field of electronic-based counselling, with the emergence of counselling by email in a time delayed format. The client mails the counsellor from within a secure web portal and will typically receive a response from the counsellor within 24–48 hours. Live chat, Skype, webcam and MMS are all emergent deliveries for counselling and are likely to become more prevalent in the future. In addition; counselling within a virtual world environment through an avatar; where the client and therapist meet in a virtual room; are being explored. Such developments bring with them challenges around security and confidentiality, and indeed the experience in delivering such therapy.

The workplace counsellor needs to adjust not just to these new ways of delivering services, but their professional practice needs to adapt to the changing needs of organisations who are facing greater competition, austerity and will expect counsellors to be able to demonstrate that their interventions are effective.

Evaluation of outcomes

Users of EAP services are consistently satisfied with the service and report this in satisfaction questionnaires: 'Research studies consistently show that EAP's provide high levels of user satisfaction, significant clinical symptom relief for many cases, substantial improvements in work productivity for most cases and reduced absenteeism for some cases' (Attridge et al., 2009). Internal counselling services have been found to be effective, where an evaluation study on the Post Office showed a net saving of £102,000 over six months (Cooper et al., 1990). Evidence from elsewhere shows work improvement and absence reduction as much as 25%. (McLeod, 2001, 2008). McLeod concludes: 'All published studies of the economic costs and benefits of workplace counselling have reported that counselling/EAP provision at least covers its costs' (McLeod, 2001: 5). However, see McLeod and Henderson (2003) for a discussion and critique of the various methodological issues in conducting such research.

There are many claims made about the return on investment for EAPs, and these have produced some impressive figures with Return On Investment (ROI) anywhere between 3:1 and 10:1 (Dainas et al., cited in Jacobson and Attridge, 2010) Most of the studies are US based and therefore may have different assumptions for health costs, and therefore the applications of such models to the UK should only be done with considerable caution. However, when taking such global ROI calculations into account, it is highly unlikely that significantly high ROI values are reliable due to confounding variables and the almost certain double counting of effects and outcome. HR professionals should therefore apply considerable caution when global ROI calculations are made for the EAP contribution.

Given these factors it is probably more relevant to calculate the effect of EAPs and workplace counselling by taking a case by case approach and look at the effect of providing this early support on the individual's psychological well-being and resulting absence. There are a variety of different measures of outcome and CORE IMS is one such system. Although this includes measuring aspects such as service waiting time, at risk measures and number of planned/unplanned endings, the key output is to understand the progress of people in terms of outcomes through counselling. This can be obtained through a self-report questionnaire which is given at the start of therapy and then at the end. The scores are then compared with the 'distance travelled' in terms of psychological resilience obtained. With the online version (core-net) the scores are obtained for each session so the client's progress can be plotted throughout the therapy.

In 2012, Mellor-Clarke et al. (in press) looked at outcome data for more than 17,000 EAP counselling cases and compared them to data from NHS trust counselling data. The data showed that EAP clients had similar levels of clinical distress as NHS primary care trust patients but that the access time was six weeks quicker. Notably, EAPs were able to show broadly equivalent outcome data as measured by recovery or improvement rate. This highlights how employers who solely rely on the NHS could be extending their absence, for example, 63% of patients wait over six weeks for CBT (source – December 2009 Health Insurance survey of 152 primary care trusts). Therefore, provision of counselling services at work, such as via EAPs, provides early referral for treatment, which is vital for an early return to work.

Other than the financial benefits of having an EAP/workplace counselling service, organisations may have other reasons for putting in place services such as helping employees through change, providing legal duty of care, enhancing loyalty/ talent management, supporting employees who are subject to traumatic incidents and generally helping to reduce stress levels. It is therefore important for any evaluation to take into account the reason for purchasing the service. One senior customer commented that just one senior manager helped back to work more quickly through the workplace support would pay for the entire EAP service, while another viewed an EAP as vital, like an insurance policy, especially for crises such as where a suicide or sudden death took place in the organisation. HR professionals have emotion-laden roles and having access to a counselling service for their employees is important for reducing their own stress levels, so they do not have to provide this support in addition to all their other roles.

Future perspectives and strategic link to occupational health

As organisations focus more and more on performance and attendance the role of EAPs have grown, not only as an early intervention tool, but also in the management of mental ill health absence. The cost of mental ill health issues is stated as £26 billion per annum (Centre for Mental Health, 2007) accounting for around 40% of absence in the UK, therefore access to therapy that would help resolve such issues is important. Several EAP UK providers also provide occupational health, well-being and/or health insurance. The result of this in some instances is in positioning the EAP as part of a more holistic set of health management provisions, and it has been known for providers to embed EAP within other health products where it may appear to be nil cost to the employer. EAPs have also been embedded within income protection insurance as a preventative and early intervention tactic, designed to ultimately lower the cost of income protection claims. There are many who argue that this development is not true to the origin of the EAP, its strategic role and the tripartite relationship. To this extent US researchers have sought to demonstrate that such EAPs are not free and do have cost, the adage being that you value what you pay for.

In the management of workplace absence and mental ill health, occupational health (OH) and EAPs can work very closely together. Following referral to OH and initial assessment, the OH professional is perfectly placed to refer the employee immediately into the EAP. The EAP mental health professional may undertake assessment of the psychological health of the employee and can recommend psychological therapy. An EAP can also play an active part in the management of absence, both the direct and indirect causes. By providing early access to therapy through EAPs it can help to manage mental ill health issues causing absence, as well as associated mental ill health coexistent with other conditions, such as musculoskeletal conditions. It should be noted that there are different models in addressing absence management and some from OH would claim that it is better for them, rather than the EAP, to instigate counselling and psychological support given their role in also advising managers on how to help facilitate the employee back to the workplace. For further discussion about EAPs and the emerging themes see Kinder & Hughes (in press).

Summary

This chapter has outlined the fields of personal development and counselling in the world of work. It has highlighted the various theories about how careers develop and provided an explanation of how a practitioner can apply these approaches and use various tools to support individuals make informed choices about their future. Later in the chapter the field of counselling in the workplace was covered in terms of the practice of the workplace counsellor, the growth of EAPs and evaluation in terms of whether these services make a difference. We each passionately believe that this area of work is essential for HR practitioners and those working in related fields, not just to be aware of the skills and understanding required, but also to take an active interest in how employees can be supported during an ever increasing period of change.

The next chapter in this book moves towards development in the sense of promoting and improving an employee's performance at work, with a focus on career development and performance appraisal.

Explore further

- The following are useful websites and resources to learn more about this area:

Carroll, M. (1996) *Workplace Counselling*. London: Sage.

Carroll, M. and Walton, M. (1997) *Handbook of Counselling in Organisations*. London: Sage.

Cole, A. (2003) *Counselling in the Workplace*. London: Sage.

Kidd, J.M. (2006) *Understanding Career Counselling, Theory, Research and Practice*. London: Sage.

Kidd, J.M., Hirsh, W. and Jackson, C. (2004) 'Straight talking: the nature of effective career discussion at work', *Journal of Career Development*, 20 (4): 231–45.

Santos, P.J. (2004) 'Career dilemmas in career counseling groups: theoretical and practical issues', *Journal of Career Development*, 31 (1): 31–44.

Sarah, L.C.B., Arnold, J. and Cohen, L. (2009) 'How other people shape our careers: a typology drawn from career narratives', *Human Relations*, 62 (10): 1487–520.

Strawbridge, S., Woolfe, R. and Dryden, W. (2009) *Handbook of Counselling Psychology*. London: Sage.

www.itsgoodtotalk.org.uk/what-is-therapy/types-of-therapy (this outlines the different counselling therapeutic approaches)

EAPA's Buyers Guide (2011). Available free from www.eapa.org.uk

- Website addresses of various different providers involved in personal development:

www.careeranchorsonline.com
www.criterionpartnership.co.uk
www.hogrefe.co.uk
www.opp.eu.com
www.psychcorp.pearsonassessments.com
www.psychological-consultancy.com
www.savilleconsulting.com
www.strengthpartnership.co.uk
www.teamfocus.co.uk
www.uwplatt.edu/counselling/careers/values;

Discussion questions

1 Outline the differences between career advice, guidance and counselling.
2 How might you justify to a cynical finance director that it makes business sense to invest in an employee assistance programme?

1 What are the key areas from the first part of this chapter that a practitioner needs to target if they are to be effective in advising clients about career choice and personal development?
2 EAPs have been described as a 'strategic intervention' within an organisation. Critique this notion and outline how you would achieve this objective.

Examination questions

1 Describe and critique three of the key career development theories.
2 Outline and discuss how EAPs can be evaluated.

OP IN PRACTICE: A DAY IN THE LIFE OF ...

Professor Frank Bond, Professor of Occupational Psychology, and Head of Department, Goldsmiths, University of London

What areas of OP do you work within?	I primarily work in three areas: organisational development and change (including leadership development), work design, and counselling and personal development.
How did you become interested in this area?	My particular area of interest is how to assess and enhance a psychological process called psychological flexibility. This is a primary determinant of mental health and behavioral effectiveness, as hypothesised by one of the more recent, empirically based theories of psychopathology, Acceptance and Commitment Therapy (ACT). It refers to people's ability to focus on their current situation, and based upon the opportunities afforded by that situation, take appropriate action towards achieving their goals and values, even in the presence of challenging or unwanted psychological events (for example, thoughts, feelings, physiological sensations, images, and memories). Over 30 studies have shown that this psychological process predicts a wide-range of work-related outcomes, from mental health and job performance to absence rates.
	My interest in ACT and psychological flexibility stems from my interest in clinical psychology. Before training as an OP, I trained as a clinical psychologist, and I could almost immediately see how clinically based theories of emotional health and behavioural effectiveness (such as ACT) could be applied in the workplace, and doing that interested me. During

(Continued)

(Continued)

	my OP training, I saw that theories in the areas of mental health and personal development that OP were discussing were ones that clinical psychologists had already discarded (sometimes decades before). Thus, I saw that a lot of work could be done in this area of OP, and I have been trying to contribute to that work.
What has been the major academic development in this area?	I think that the major academic development in this area is a methodological one. Over the past 10 years, tightly controlled randomised controlled trials (RCTs) have become far more common, and our top journals now essentially require them. In addition, it is no longer possible to publish cross-sectional studies in most of the major journals. The enhanced use of RCTs and longitudinal designs give us a greater understanding of the theories and practices that we investigate, and this only serves to promote more effective practice.
To what extent does the practical application of your work inform your research?	I have always liked Kurt Lewin's mantra that there is nothing more practical than a good theory. Thus, I see both research/theory and practice as intrinsically linked. Indeed, my scientific philosophy centres around functional contextualism, which has the a priori scientific goals of both predicting and influencing behaviour. Thus, the practical implications of my research very much guide the questions that I ask, and the way I conduct my research.
What role do ethics have in your work?	Personally, I see ethics as part of a wider values-system that I have, and I try to apply those values in all that I do. I conceive of APA and BPS ethics guides as representing the most important and powerful of my values (for example, do not lie to your clients!); but, I also have others that help me to treat my co-workers with respect and consideration. I think of those as values, but I think that they could also be viewed as 'ethical' behaviour.
Can you give an example of a day in your working life?	I am an academic and head of my department of Psychology. Thus, I work in a university and spend a lot of my day interacting with colleagues and doing administration. I actually enjoy it, and it allows me to put into action a lot of my OP knowledge! I also conduct a good deal of research, which involves me spending a lot of time in organisations – mainly ones in the media and financial services sectors. In that role, I act a lot like any other consultant, but I am also very much acting as a researcher: designing methodologies and collecting and analysing data. In all, I find that my work provides me with a lot of variety, and I very much enjoy that.
How has your work changed in the last five years?	My leadership development approach has changed significantly. In line with research, it has moved away from lengthy group training approaches to a more coaching-focused approach, whereby I work with individuals on identifying and helping them to achieve their leadership-related goals. For companies, this is a bit more expensive approach to leadership development, but research does show that it is very effective.

| How do you see your work changing over the next five years? | I think that the ageing workforce will present a number of challenges and opportunities for Occupational Psychologists. Many people will want to work well into their 60s; others will be forced to, owing to increases in the pension age – all over the Western world. In addition, at least in the UK, there is no longer a mandatory retirement age. All of these changes will have an impact on OP; for example, in terms of training and development, ergonomics, counselling and personal development, and performance management. In addition, we do not yet know how our current middle-aged portfolio workers will approach their work, as they get into their 60s. |

OP IN PRACTICE: A DAY IN THE LIFE OF ...

Julianne Miles, Independent Practitioner, Director of Career Psychologists

What areas of OP do you work within?	My main focus is career counselling/coaching. I also run careers-related workshops, speak at careers-related events and am an occasional lecturer and career counsellor trainer.
	Within my area of adult career counselling, I specialise in working with mid-career professionals and managers, typically aged late 20s to early 50s. I have particular expertise in coaching women and MBAs. My main areas of focus are evaluating a potential career change, improving work-life balance and achieving a successful return to work after a break. I also work with individuals on increasing fulfilment in their current role through job crafting: developing their current role to better suit their strengths and interests.
How did you become interested in this area?	In my first career in corporate strategy and marketing, I saw a large number of people who were stressed and unhappy in their working lives, often struggling to reconcile the demands of intense work pressures with a desire for a fulfilling personal and family life. Once I had a family, I met many women who were finding it very difficult to return to the workplace in a satisfying and flexible role. Helping such individuals to find careers that were satisfying and also fitted with their lives was one of the key motivations for my career change. I can have a significant positive impact on people's lives which is highly rewarding.
What kinds of organisations are interested in your work and why?	The majority of my work is with individuals rather than organisations. I have worked with a UK business school, providing one-to-one career coaching services to the MBA students and workshops and lectures on career topics.

(Continued)

(Continued)

| How is your work informed by theory, literature and research? | My career counselling work is underpinned by evidence-based scientific research. I drew from career theories and counselling models in developing my career review framework: the classic work of Super, Holland, Egan, more recent reviews of the changing nature of careers (eg. John Arnold) and contemporary perspectives on careers such as narrative theory.

However, my influences are not limited to careers research. My broader psychological understanding of personality, motivation and cognitive psychology enables me to help my clients to understand the thoughts and feelings behind their behaviour at work and to address those that are holding them back from leading a fulfilling life. Positive psychology studies, solutions-focused and cognitive-behavioural coaching theory, leadership research and career change studies have all had a significant influence on my approach. |
| --- | --- |
| What role do ethics have in your day-to-day practice? | The greatest challenge in my day-to-day practice is maintaining professional boundaries of competence. Given the one-to-one nature of the client relationship, personal issues may come to the fore. I find it particularly important at the screening and contracting stages to distinguish my role as an Occupational Psychologist from that of a counselling psychologist or other type of therapist. The dominant issue for clients may actually be a problematic personal relationship or a debilitating anxiety problem. If I believe from initial conversations that personal or relationship counselling would be more appropriate, I will raise the possibility of a referral elsewhere.

Another area of boundaries is counsellor/coach versus advisor. As a psychologist, clients may put me in an expert role and look to be told 'what they should do'. I position myself as a guide who will empower my clients to make their own decisions rather than providing the answers myself. |
| Can you give an example of a day in your working life? | My main practice area is career counselling for mid-career individuals. People come to me with a career issue they are struggling to resolve: they may be confused about whether they are in the 'right' job, unhappy about their work-life balance, unsure how to progress or simply feeling 'stuck' and unhappy in their present role.

I run my career counselling practice from home. Most counselling sessions are face-to-face, although I work with a few clients by telephone or Skype where face-to-face meetings are impractical. Before starting to work with a client, we have a free-of-charge exploratory discussion. For a typical client looking for a full career review, I will guide them during 4–5 sessions through the stages of contracting, developing self-understanding, identifying and evaluating options and developing a clear action plan. |

	I usually spend 3–4 days a week on career counselling and the other days on a variety of other activities under the careers/work-life balance umbrella. A typical career counselling day involves 3 one-to-one client consultations of 1–2 hours each and an exploratory half-hour phone call with a potential new client. During the session, we focus on one or more agreed objectives, for example examining strengths or motivational blocks, using a combination of in-depth questioning and discussion, exercises and possibly psychometrics to increase self-understanding. Either side of a client meeting there is preparation and reflection/note-taking time. In the breaks between clients, I answer client emails and tackle business administration such as invoicing. I then work on one or more of the projects I am involved with at the time, such as preparing a lecture for MBA students on career models, creating materials for a workshop or writing a presentation for a return to work seminar.
How has your work changed in the last five years?	I have increasingly moved from a more broadly based Occupational Psychology portfolio to become a specialist in career counselling, initially through a career coach role at a UK business school and subsequently through founding and running my own career counselling business.
How do you see your work changing over the next five years?	I will continue to build up my career psychology business and develop the business offering. I have a strong interest in work-life balance and would like to develop increased individual and organisational services in this area.

References

ACAS (2011) 'The Equality Act – what's new for employers?'. Available at: http://acas.ecgroup.net/Publications?Adviceleaflets.aspx.

Adamson, S.J., Doherty, N. and Viney, C. (1998) 'The meaning of career revisited:implications for theory and practice', *British Journal of Management*, 9: 251–59.

Arnold, J. (1997) *Managing Careers into the 21st Century*. London: Chapman.

Arnold, J. (2004) 'The congruence problem in John Holland's theory of vocational decisions', *Journal of Occupational and Organisational Psychology*, 77: 95–113.

Arnold, J., Randal, R., Silvester, J., Patterson, F., Robertson, I. and Cooper, C. (2010) *Work Psychology, Understanding Human Behaviour in the Workplace*, 5th edn. Harlow: Pearson Education.

Arthur, A. (2005) 'When stress is mental illness: a study of anxiety and depression in employees who use occupational stress counselling schemes', *Stress and Health*, 21: 273–80.

Arthur, M.B. and Rousseau D.M. (1996) 'The boundaryless career as a new employment principle', in M.B. Arthur and D.M. Rousseau (eds), *The Boundaryless Career: A New Employment Principle for a New isation Organisational Era*. Oxford: Oxford University Press.

Attridge, M., Amaral, T. and Bjornson, T., Goplerud, E., Herlihy, P., McPherson, T., Paul, R., Routledge, S., Sharaar, D., Stepehenson D. and Teems, L. (2009) 'EAP Effectiveness and ROI'. *EASNA Research Notes*, 1 (3), October 2009.

BACP (2010) *Ethical Framework for Good Practice in Counselling and Psychotherapy*. Lutterworth: BACP.

Barnett, R.C and Shen, Y.C. (1997) 'Gender, high and low schedule control housework tasks and psychological distress:a study of dual earner couples', *Journal of Family Issues*, 18: 403–28.

BACP (2012) http://www.bacp.co:uk/admin/structure/files/pdf/9479_ethical%20 framework%20word%20june%202012.pdf.

Buon, T. (2004) 'Predicting the future', *Counselling at Work*.

Carroll, M. (1996) *Workplace Counselling*. London: Sage.

Centre for Mental Health (2007) Mental health at Work: Developing the Business Case.

Cheung, G. (2011) www.chinaeapforum.com.cn/en/address.asp

Clutterbuck, D. (1998) *Learning Alliances:Tapping into Talent* . London: Institute of Personnel & Development.

Cole, A. (2003) *Counselling in the Workplace*. London: Sage.

Cooper C.L., Sadri G., Allison T. and Reynolds, P. (1990) 'Stress counselling in the Post Office', *Counselling Psychology Review*, 3 (1): 3–11.

Copeland, S. (2005) *Counselling Supervision in Organisations: Profession and Ethical Dilemmas Explored*. London: Routledge.

EAPA UK (2011) *Employee Assistance Programmes: A Buyer's Guide*. EAPA.

EAPA UK (n.d.) www.eapa.org.uk/page--research.html

Egan, G. (2002) *The Skilled Helper: A Problem – Management and Opportunity – Development Approach to Helping*, 7th edn. Brooks/Cole.

Employee Benefits Magazine *Healthcare Research* 2011 *Standards Self-verification Process* (2011). Employee Assistance Programme.

English, F. (1975) 'The three-cornered contract', *Transactional Analysis Journal*, 5 (4): 383–4.

Erikson, E.H. (1957) 'Identity and the life-cycle'. *Psychological Issues*, 1: 1–171.

Erikson, E.H. (1980) *Identity and the Life Cycle.* New York: W.W. Norton.

Hall, D.T. (2002) *Career in and out of Organisations*. Glenview, IL: Scott, Foresman.

Hanisch, K.A. (1994) 'Job loss and unemployment research from 1994 to 1998; a review and recommendations for research and intervention', *Journal of Vocational Behaviour*, 55: 188–220.

Hawkins, P. (2011) 'Systemic coaching supervision', in: T. Bachkirova, P. Jackson and D. Clutterbuck (eds), *Supervision in Mentoring and Coaching: Theory and Practice*. Maidenhead: Open University Press.

Herriot, P. (2001) *The Employment Relationship: A Psychological Perspective*. London: Routledge.

Hirsch, P.M. and Shanley, M. (1996) 'The rhetoric of boundaryless – or how the newly empowered managerial class bough into its own marginalisation', in M.B. Arthur and D.M. Rousseau (eds), *The Boundary less Career: A New Employment Principle for a New Organisational Era*. Oxford: Oxford University Press.

Holland, J.L. (1997) *Making Vocational Choices*, 3rd edn. Odessa: Psychological Assessment Resources.

Horvath, A.O. (2000) 'The therapeutic relationship. From transference to alliance', *Journal of Clinical Psychology*, 56 (2): 163–73.

Horvath, A.O. (2001) 'The alliance', *Psychotherapy*, 38 (4): 365–72.

Horvath, A.O. (2006) 'The alliance in context: accomplishments, challenges and future directions', *Psychotherapy: Theory, Research, Practice, Training*, 43 (3): 258–63.

Horvath, A.O. and Symonds, D. (1991) 'Relation between working alliance and outcome in psychotherapy:a meta-analysis', *Journal of Counselling Psychology*, 38 (2): 139–49.

Hughes, R. and Kinder, A. (2007) *Guidelines for Counselling in the Workplace.* BACP: Lutterworth. Available free at www.bacpworkplace.org.uk.

Hughes, R., Kinder, A. and Cooper, C.L. (2012) *International Handbook of Workplace Trauma Support.* Chicester: Wiley-Blackwell.

Jacobson, J.M. and Attridge, M. (2010) 'Employee assistance programmes:an allied profession for work-life',in Sweet and J. Casey (eds), *Work and Family Encyclopaedia .* Chestnut Hill, MA: Sloan Work and Family Research Network.

Kemp, T.J. (2008) 'Coach self-management:the foundation of coaching effectiveness',in D.B. Drake, D. Brennan and K. Gortz (eds), *The Philosophy and Practice of Coaching: Insights and Issues for a New Era.* Chichester: Wiley-Blackwell.

Kidd, J.M. (2006) *Understanding Career Counselling, Theory, Research and Practice.* London: Sage.

Kinder (2005) 'Workplace counselling, a poor relation', *Counselling at Work,* Spring: 22–4.

Kinder, A. and Hughes. R. (eds) (in press) *EAP Guidelines.* UK Employee Assistance Professionals Association.

Kinder, A., Hughes, R. and Cooper, C.L. (2008) *Employee Well-being Support: A Workplace Resource.* Chichester: Wiley-Blackwell.

Levinson, D.J., Darrow, D.C., Klein, E.B., Levinson, M.H. and McKee, B. (1978) *The Seasons of a Man's Life.* New York: Knopf.

McLeod, J., (2001) Counselling in the Workplace: The Facts. A Systematic Study of the research Evidence. Rugby: British Association of Counselling and Psychotherapy.

McLeod, J. (2008) *Counselling in the Workplace: A Comprehensive Review of the Research Evidence,* 2nd edn. Lutterworth: BACP.

McLeod, J. and Henderson, M. (2003) 'Does workplace counselling work?', *British Journal of Psychiatry,* 182:103–4.

Mellor-Clarke, J., Twigg, E., Farrell, E. and Kinder, A. (in press) Benchmarking key service quality indicators in UK Employee Assistance Programme Counselling: A CORE System data profile. *Counselling Psychology Review.*

Murphy, G.C. and Athanasou, J.A (1999) 'The effect of unemployment on mental health' *Journal of Occupational and Organisational Psychology,* 72: 83–99.

Nicholson, N. (1990) 'The transition cycle: causes, outcomes, processes and forms', in S. Fischer and C.L. Cooper (eds), *On the Move; the Psychology of Change and Transition.* Chichester: Wiley.

Nicholson, N. and West, M. (1988) *Managerial Job Change: Men and Women in Transition.* Cambridge: Cambridge University Press.

Noon, M. and Blyton, P (2007) *The Realities of Work: Experiencing work and employment in contemporary society,* 3rd edn. Basingstoke: Palgrave MacMillan.

Office for National Statistics (ONS) (2002, 2010) *Labour Force Surveys.*

ONS (2008) *Labour Force Survey Employment Status.*

Overell, S. (2009) *Provocation Paper 3: The Meaning of Work.* Commissioned by the Work Foundation on behalf of The Good Work Commission.

Paul, K.I. and Moser, K. (2009) 'Unemployment impairs mental health: meta-analysis', *Journal of Vocational Behaviour,* 74: 264–82.

Pickard, E. (1997) 'Developing training for organisational counselling', in M. Carroll and M. Walton (eds), *Handbook of Counselling in Organisations.* London: Sage.

Rose, M. (1988) *Industrial Behaviour: Research and Control,* 2nd edn. Harmondsworth: Penguin.

Schein, E.H. (1993) *Career Anchors:Discovering your Real Values.* San Diego, CA: Pfeiffer.

Schwenk, E. (2006) 'The workplace counsellor's toolbox', *Counselling at Work,* 51: 20–3.

Sonnenstuhl, W.J. and Trice, H.M. (1990) *Strategies for Employee Assistance Programs: The Crucial Balance.* Ithaca, NY: Cornell University Press.

Spokane, A.R. (1985) 'A review of research on person-environment congruence in Holland's theory of careers', *Journal of Vocational Behaviour*, 31: 37–44.

Super, D. (1957) *The Psychology of Careers.* New York: Harper & Row.

Super, D. (1980) 'A lifespan, life-space, an approach to career development', *Journal of Vocational Behaviour*, 16: 282–98.

Tinsley, H.E.A. (2000) 'The congruence myth: an analysis of the efficacy of the person-environment fit model', *Journal of Vocational Behaviour*, 56, 147–79.

Totterdell, P., Wood, S. and Wall, T. (2006) 'An intraindividual test of the demands-control model:a weekly diary study of job strain in portfolio workers', *Journal of Occupational and Organisational Psychology*, 79: 63–84.

Warr, P. (2007) *Work, Happiness and Unhappiness.* Mahwah, NJ: Lawrence Erlbaum Associates.

6 Career development and appraisal

Juliette Alban-Metcalfe

Learning outcomes

This chapter will provide you with an understanding of the following:

- how career development and appraisal can contribute to important organisational outcomes;
- what an organisational career development system typically comprises;
- formal and informal career development opportunities;
- what constitutes an effective appraisal system for an organisation;
- how career development and appraisal often differ by level of employee;
- how bias operates in career development and appraisal;
- key considerations for career development in the new world within which organisations operate.

Introduction

Career development and appraisal can have untold benefits when they are designed and executed effectively, because they are critical to many crucial outcomes that leverage performance output. These include employee motivation, satisfaction, low turnover, appropriate usage and deployment of strengths, and employee engagement. Conversely, ineffective or biased career development and appraisal can have the opposite effect, including a disastrous impact on the bottom line. Occupational Psychologists have a critical role to play in helping organisations design these processes correctly.

What do we mean by career development?

Career development can be defined as the combination of: 'Psychological, sociological, educational, physical, economic, and chance factors that combine to influence the nature and significance of work in the total lifespan of any given individual' (NCDA, 2003: 2). We spend an average of at least one-third of our life at work, involved in activities that – whether or not we gain fulfilment from them – give 'meaning' to our lives. In other words, we judge the extent to which we are successful in our own eyes and in the eyes of others by whether or not we are able to achieve our work-related goals. Achieving, and being seen to achieve, are crucially important for our self-esteem and our overall level of happiness. For this reason alone, it is an important area for individuals and organisations to get right.

Organisational perspectives on career development

Background

Individual perspectives on career development (discussed in Chapter 5) and organisational perspectives are intimately related. To illustrate this with an example, there is evidence that the relative importance of 'career anchors' (Schein, 1978, 1993) has changed from one generation to the next (Schein, 1996). Understanding the implications of these changes is important for organisations to respond appropriately to how particular groups of employees might prefer to be treated (Brousseau et al., 1996), as new generations (X, Y and Z) populate the workforce.

Even within living memory, the nature of work and of employer-employee relationships have undergone significant change, and in the current economic climate, many employees no longer enjoy the kind of job security that was the norm. Among the more pervasive causative factors are: recession-related and other financial constraints (with implications for training budgets); identified skill shortages in certain key areas, such as IT; increased diversity (with the potential for employing staff with different skill sets); increased availability of information technology (with implications for more rapid and demanding communication, and reduced need for traditional office-based working); organisational restructuring and partnership working, including shared use of resources (with the potential for reduced costs at the expense of redundancy, and/or re-training); and globalisation, coupled with increased workforce mobility (with implications for a better person-job fit, and wider career opportunities).

Evidence from decades of research suggests that positive organisational outcomes (such as productivity and an improved bottom line) can be maximised by careful analysis of employees' talents and abilities, motives and needs, attitudes and values. Increasingly, it is becoming clear that one of the most powerful influences on organisational performance is 'employee engagement' (Alimo-Metcalfe and Alban-Metcalfe, 2008; MacLeod and Clarke, 2008), as discussed in Chapter 4. An integral part of an Occupational Psychologist's role is to increase and sustain employee engagement through effective advice and guidance on the following.

- How to match individual's values, motivations, talents, needs and attitudes, with organisational needs and values.
- How to achieve this match, through a combination of support and guidance (Kidd, 2006) and self-development (Bolles, 2009; Hopson and Scally, 1993; Hawkins, 1999).
- How to prepare individuals and organisations for future challenges and opportunities.
- How to create more positive 'meaning' for employees in what they do and how that contributes to overall organisational success.

There are a variety of ways in which organisations attempt to achieve these processes of career development successfully. For example, some employees have access to high potential development schemes – whereby individuals who are viewed as talented and desirable to keep within the organisation are provided with structured and well-funded opportunities for career development in line with their ambitions, and with organisational goals. That said, the majority of employees in an organisation are at a front line, junior first-line or middle management level – and organisations tend to be less inclined to spend significant amounts of money on their development than on more senior individuals who are regarded as more critical to the organisation's success. Therefore, there is a need for career development opportunities for employees to be available through a range of other routes.

Organisational career development opportunities

Within both small and large organisations, whether private or not-for-profit, a useful way of categorising career development opportunities is in terms of those that are 'corporately managed', 'self-managed', or a combination of both. Evidence from Gratton and Hailey (1999), Hirsch (2000, 2011), Kidd et al. (2004), Yarnall (2008) and others, suggests that there are some similarities, but many differences, in corporately managed and self-managed careers. The principal characteristics can be summarised as in Table 6.1.

Combined self-managed and corporate careers exhibit a combination of the characteristics outlined above. A further distinction is between the development opportunities open to those whose careers are corporately managed, compared to those that are self-managed. These can be summarised as shown in Table 6.2 and Box 6.1.

Table 6.1   Principal characteristics of corporately managed and self-managed careers

Corporately managed careers	Self-managed careers
Organisations plan ahead for the development of some of the employees' careers.	Organisations hire (and fire) staff dependent on their current and future short-term needs.
Organisations are proactive in facilitating career moves and associate skill development.	Only the (future) employee is proactive in their own development.
The staff selected for this development are usually senior managers and those in mid-career who have been seen to have potential.	Employees are selected as and when required.
Organisations invest significant amounts of money and resources in the development.	The cost of the investment, in terms of time and money, is borne entirely by the employee.
The process is part of 'succession planning', that is, a process whereby the organisation seeks to ensure that, as senior staff retire or move on, others are qualified to take their place.	Not applicable. Organisations may have strategic plans that foresee the hiring of employees with certain skill sets, but hiring is on an *ad hoc* basis.
The individuals selected commonly come from a 'talent pool', that is, a group of employees believed to possess the right kind of abilities, or to have the potential to develop them.	Not applicable. The only 'talent pool' that exists is external to the organisation.
Organisations are large enough, and are structured in such a way, that succession planning can be achieved.	Organisations of any size and structure can benefit from employees who have a self-managed career.
A given employee's career progression is likely to be achieved along pathways that may, to a large extent, be determined by the organisation.	Not applicable. Organisations do not see themselves as having any responsibilities in this area.
It has potential advantages for the organisation in that it gives it the ability to engage in strategic planning, in the confidence that the kind of staff that they will need will be there.	It has the potential advantage for the organisation to adopt a more flexible, and in some cases fluid, approach to staffing. The organisational assumption is that, if employees with particular skill-sets are required, they can be found.
It has the potential disadvantages of: 1 having a de-motivating effect on those staff who were not selected; 2 possibly requiring those selected to be geographically mobile, so as to participate in such programmes, or to take on secondments, when families are being raised and often when two careers are being managed within the same household; and 3 integrating/re-integrating such individuals into mainstream activities after completion of the programme.	It has the potential advantages that: 1 employing such staff is less likely to have a de-motivating effect on existing staff; 2 any career-related upheaval is assumed to be consequent on the future employee's own decisions; and 3 any integration actions required are no different from hiring any new member of staff. It has the potential disadvantages that: 1 the potential employees with the right kind of skill-set will not be affordable; or 2 the potential employees with the right kind of skill-set may not even exist.

Corporately managed careers	Self-managed careers
The expectation is that the employee will stay with the organisation over a more or less extended period of time, even throughout their entire working career.	There is the expectation that the employee will only continue to work for the organisation for a limited period of time.
Consistently with this expectation, a 'psychological contract' can be seen to exist between the organisation and the employee, which places certain obligations on each.	Accordingly, the only kind of 'psychological contract' likely to exist is one that respects the rights of the other to continue the period of employment only as long as it meets the needs of each of the parties.
Occupational Psychologists will: • advise organisations in relation to each of these activities; • contribute to the selection of staff (a) when first appointed to the organisation, and (b) when considered for 'accelerated' development; • contribute to the development of appropriate systems and processes; • support employees through guidance, training, and emotional support.	Occupational Psychologists active in this field will act on the basis of fees paid to them by the individual.
Occupational Psychologists have a reputation for quality, validity and rigour in provision in these areas.	

Table 6.2 Development opportunities for corporately managed and self-managed careers

Corporately managed careers	Self-managed careers
Organisations provide opportunities for obtaining feedback in areas such as: • specific job-related skills; • their general level of performance; • their leadership behaviour. Information gained in this way is used to provide targeted development activities. The feedback system is likely to be planned at a strategic level.	Organisations may provide feedback, based on performance on agreed tasks, but it is likely to be: • narrowly focused; • related to short-term goals and objectives; and • only provided during the contracted period of employment. Otherwise, any feedback received may either be absent, or, if given, it is likely to be *ad hoc*, and on a 'what is needed' basis. It may also be sought by the individual from willing feedback providers among their colleagues.
Organisations provide opportunities for career development in the form of training in areas such as: • project management; • managing performance; • specific job-related skills. The development opportunities are likely to be planned at a strategic level, and paid for by the organisation.	Organisations may provide opportunities for training in specific areas such as: • project management; • managing performance; • specific job-related skills. But only during the contracted period of employment.

(Continued)

Table 6.2 (Continued)

Corporately managed careers	Self-managed careers
Organisations provide opportunities for career development in the form of secondments and job-swaps, which can be: • within the organisation, or in another organisation; • within the same country or region, or abroad. The development opportunities are likely to be planned at a strategic level, and paid for by the organisation.	This kind of support will not be available, other than through periods of employment in different kinds of organisation. Gaining a broad range of experience will be at the discretion of, and be funded by, the individual themself.
Organisations provide opportunities for career development in the form of: • coaching and/or mentoring; • guest lectures, and Master Classes; • action learning sets; • formal network groups; • participation in leadership academies. The development opportunities are likely to be planned at a strategic level, and paid for by the organisation.	This kind of support will not be available, other than during periods of employment in different kinds of organisation. Access to such activities will have to be sought out by, and be funded by, the individual themself.
Each of these actions depends on the organisation's available funding and the role requirements. Organisations need, therefore, to have expert advice on how to tailor the development to individual and organisational requirements. This is where Occupational Psychologists can play an important part, aside from delivery of the activities.	Applicable only during periods when the individual is employed by the organisation.
In addition, greater clarity on Return on Investment is important for organisations in today's climate, where resources are generally fewer, and therefore where there is a drive to use external support in a more judicious way. Occupational Psychologists have a reputation for quality, validity and rigour in provision in this area.	Not applicable.
Even where career development opportunities are not entirely self-directed, they may be provided informally within an organisation. Line managers are often central to this, providing their employees with new and varied tasks, and with opportunities to become more 'visible' in the organisation, through participation in a particular project, or by taking on more responsibility. As career coaches or advisers to an organisation, Occupational Psychologists can play an important part in making this as effective as possible.	Not applicable.

The individual may have a limited choice in the range of actions open to them.	Within economic, social, and other, related, constraints, the individual is likely to have a wide range of actions open to them.
Occupational Psychologists will: • advise organisations in relation to each of these activities; • contribute to the development of appropriate systems and processes; • provide specific training and other development activities; • support employees through guidance and support.	Occupational Psychologists active in this field will act on the basis of fees paid to them by the individual.

Occupational Psychologists have a reputation for quality, validity and rigour in provision in each of the areas considered here.

Box 6.1

CASE STUDY: Effective career development impacting on the bottom line of a company

A range of career development opportunities are provided for staff in a large, global organisation that offers professional services in a wide range of areas that include human resource management. The philosophical basis of their approach to career development includes belief that:

• the career development of their staff is integral to their brand;
• the development of people skills and business understanding are their core business, and this can inform and be informed by the way they treat their own staff;
• both their staff and the organisation as a whole will benefit from a commitment to planned career progression;
• everyone in the organisation has some kind of talent.

The two principal entry routes to the company are young highly qualified graduates, and experienced specialists who have developed their career in other organisations. Competition for entry is great, as are the potential rewards, which for some include progression up to Partner level. Planning for career progression is shared jointly by the most senior member of each of the business units, who operates at a local level, and who works in association with a senior human resources specialist with the relevant expertise. Their joint aim is the development of talent at all levels in the organisation. The range of provision is wide, and includes:

• career counselling
• coaching for staff at every level;

(Continued)

(Continued)

- development programmes;
- participation in the organisation's voluntary work;
- planned experience of working with clients;
- secondments, some of which are international.

The process is managed so as to ensure a maximal return on investment.

The process of career development is seen as both iterative and progressive. It is iterative in the sense that, in each new role, the individual moves through a learning cycle of: acquiring new information, knowledge and skills → applying this in practice → evaluating their experience → acquiring new information, and so on.

Career development involves progression in that individuals utilise and build on their previous experience in a new context, and use their existing experience to increase knowledge and understanding, and to develop new skills, in each new role.

For a limited number of staff, a 'high potential development scheme' is in place, for which competition is keen. This is designed for individuals whose careers are to be accelerated, and who are offered additional developmental opportunities.

Effective performance appraisal

Performance appraisal describes an assessment (usually formal) of how a person has performed in their job, and includes discussion of what is expected next. However, it is important to distinguish between two different kinds of appraisal situation that commonly exist, as they differ in form and purpose. These are 'performance management' and 'developmental review'. There will now follow a discussion of both kinds.

Performance management

Performance management (PM) has been defined as: a process which contributes to the effective management of individuals and team in order to achieve high levels of organisational performance (Armstrong and Baron, 2012: 1). PM can be applied to whole organisations or to a single department, or team, as well as to a single individual. The overarching purpose is to reconcile the personal goals of all employees with organisational goals and, thereby, increase the productivity and profitability of the organisation (Zaffron, 2009).

The term PM also applies to individual members of staff. Here, it is useful to distinguish between the different types of PM process, which are: performance recording (in which individual performance is formally documented and feedback delivered, usually in the form of a written report); performance planning (a process by which goals and objectives are established); and performance coaching (in which a manager intervenes to give feedback and seeks to adjust performance). It is important to recognise that each of these interactions can be undertaken in a supportive or a non-supportive way (see developmental review below).

The design and implementation of a PM system at the individual level first requires a 'job analysis', followed by a 'job description' and, when a new appointment is to be made, a 'person specification'. Chapter 9 includes detailed descriptions of these processes. At a team, departmental or organisational level, the nature and purpose of what is to be achieved should also be made clear, along with clarity of roles and responsibilities, and the criteria for judging success.

A PM system, then, deals with *what* needs to be done to achieve individual or organisational success, and can be a very 'mechanistic' approach to appraisal. What PM, on its own, does not address, is *how* increased performance is to be achieved.

Developmental review

The purpose of undertaking a developmental review (DR) is to enable individuals to increase their performance by focusing both on their perceived strengths and areas for development, and on their needs and aspirations.

A successful DR review is one in which:

1 the *developmental* purpose of the review is made explicit;
2 the line managers initiative is, in effect, a conversation with her or his direct report that is genuinely two-way;
3 the initiative as to what to discuss rests primarily with the direct report/peer (though this does not preclude other issues being discussed);
4 preparation by both parties on pre-agreed agenda including needs and aspirations;
5 the line manager acts more as a coach, than as a mentor;
6 the conclusion of the review leads to the formulation of a personal development plan (PDP) devised by the individual, and supportive actions for the manager to take.

In many cases, organisations design and implement development centres (DCs), which are a sophisticated and resource-intensive form of DR. These comprise a series of exercises, usually over one or two days, in which a group of employees is assessed, through a battery of role-related exercises, tests and simulations. The similarities and differences between PM and DR approaches to performance appraisal are presented in Table 6.3.

Overview of approaches to performance appraisal

A major differentiator of how performance appraisal is approached is the level of employee in question. The particular skills required of someone in, say, a junior or middle management role will differ from those required in a senior position; and these will, in turn, differ from those in an executive role. The principal features of PM and DR are summarised in a simplistic form as follows:

Table 6.3 Individual performance appraisal

	Performance Management	**Developmental Review**
Principal focus	Monitoring performance	Personal and professional development
Purpose of meeting made explicit	Yes	Yes
Degree of formality of meeting	Tendency to be formal	More like a focused conversation
Introduction of subject matter to be discussed	Line manager	Both line manager and direct report
Line manager's role	Mentor – role of expert guide	Leader and coach – role of stimulating reflection
Feedback	Principally for the good of the organisation	Principally for the good of the individual
Output	Personal development plan to achieve organisational goals	Personal development plan to achieve personal goals
Recording of conclusions	Written, formal	Written, formal
Confidential	Yes, but may be shared with relevant senior staff	Yes, within parameters to be agreed
Use of the output	Rewards and/or promotion	Personal and professional developmental
Relationship with pay or other rewards	Likely	No
Principal benefit	The organisation	The individual

- Frontline level – for employees without formal managerial or leadership responsibility, performance appraisal is typically annual (or may take place less frequently in some organisations). The focus is usually on competencies (that is, *what* they do) related to specific job-related, team-related and/or customer-related tasks. Some discussion may take place about future aspirations.
- Junior levels of management – here, the range of factors for assessment will be more complex and might typically include: quality of informal communication; decision-making, with reference to limited criteria; information gathering; project planning; and organising people and resources. More discussion may take place about future aspirations. There should also to be discussion not just about *what* their role entails (competence), but also about their leadership style. That is, *how* they interact with others (Alimo-Metcalfe and Alban-Metcalfe, 2008).

- Middle to senior levels of management – the tasks to be assessed here will again be more complex. For example, communication is likely also to involve formal presentations, and require the written communication of complex ideas; decision making will be based on complex, sometimes conflicting data; analytical skills are required for assessing the value of information gathered; strategic and financial planning, plus some additional skills, such as business strategy skills, will be required; there will be the need for more sophisticated customer/client skills, along with 'bigger picture' thinking. Building on these 'generic' skills, those at the highest levels in an organisation will have to develop additional, more specific skills, such as, conceptual thinking and political skills. Among staff at these levels, *how* they interact with others assumes greater importance.

Occupational Psychologists have a critical role to play in establishing the appropriate criteria for performance appraisal tools and discussions. Much of this work is closely aligned with selection (explored in Chapter 9), as the key factors for effective role performance are established, using a similar methodology as in developing selection criteria. These include critical incident analysis and job shadowing. We are also often needed to remind organisations that it is not just tasks and professional skills that should be assessed in a performance appraisal situation; it is also important to ensure that behaviours be assessed formally. Thus, for example, a manager could be highly competent in organising people and resources, and implement their plans by deciding *what* people need to do, and (literally) telling them to get on with it. However, those managers that are able to harness employees' discretionary effort, motivation and commitment (all of which are very valuable to the organisation) will ensure that they pay attention to *how* they go about leading and managing.

Designing and selecting appropriate assessment criteria

The criteria on which to base a performance appraisal are the individual's ability to perform their role competently, their willingness to the engage in organisationally desirable behaviours, and in the case of those in a leadership role, the extent to which they engage with direct reports and peers, so as to achieve organisational goals. Information that can be used to specify the assessment criteria include competencies, and organisationally desirable behaviours (including citizenship behaviours, extra role behaviours and positive organisational behaviours). Each are described briefly below.

Competencies
Competencies are the actions that an individual needs to be able to perform in order to fulfil their role. Examples of competencies are the ability to:

- collect data;
- plan;
- organise;
- structure one's work.

Many competencies, such as to 'communicate effectively', are *generic* in nature. In other words, they are required of all staff. However, exactly what 'communicate effectively' means in practice may vary. Thus, different types and different levels of proficiency in communication, for example, formal written versus informal oral, or presentations to a large audience versus interpersonal communication, may be required of staff at different levels or in different roles in an organisation.

Other competencies are likely to be *specific*, either to individuals performing a certain role, or to staff at different levels in the organisation. Examples of specific competencies might include 'financial management', or 'strategic planning'. Most large, and many medium-sized, organisations have developed their own competency framework.

Competency frameworks perform a valuable role in both selection and career development, since they provide the basis on which job descriptions can be written, and against which performance can be assessed. One of the criticisms of many such frameworks, however, is that they fail to distinguish between 'competencies' *per se* and underlying 'personal qualities and values'. Personal qualities and values, such as being 'emotionally intelligent', or 'intellectually flexible', may be *necessary* for performing a certain role, but on their own they are *not sufficient*.

Furthermore, it is important to recognise that competencies relate to *what* an individual does, and that, for most roles, it is essential also to be able to analyse and to assess *how* they perform their role in a social context (Alimo-Metcalfe and Alban-Metcalfe, 2008). The latter is often ignored.

Organisationally desirable behaviours

In recent years, attention has focused on organisationally desirable behaviours, such as organisational citizenship behaviours (OCB), extra role behaviours (ERBs) and positive organisational behaviours (POB). OCB has been defined as:

> individual behavior that is discretionary, not directly or explicitly recognised by the formal reward system, and that in the aggregate promotes the effective functioning of the organisation. (Organ, 1988: 4)

The significance of OCBs is that they are discretionary behaviours, not part of the job description, and are performed by the employee as a result of personal choice. They constitute going above and beyond that which is in a job description and they can contribute positively to overall organisational effectiveness. Examples of OCBs include going well beyond the minimum requirements of a role, and not dealing with personal matters during work time (Law et al., 2005; Organ et al., 2006). OCBs are related to positive relations with others, and also to three aspects of well-being at work (autonomy, purpose in life and environmental mastery) (Alimo-Metcalfe and Alban-Metcalfe, 2012).

Extra role behaviours (ERB) have been defined as 'behavior that attempts to benefit the organisation and that goes beyond existing role expectations' (Organ et al., 2006: 33). Examples include: 'whistle-blowing', in which a member of staff makes public an action or actions taken by one or more members of their organisation that they consider to be in some way inconsistent with the organisation's principles and values, or simply immoral; and principled organisational dissent, which is similar to whistle-blowing, except that involves speaking out at meetings or other contexts within the organisation.

Positive organisational behaviours (POB) is 'the study and application of positively oriented human resource strengths and psychological capacities that can be measured, developed, and effectively managed for performance improvement in today's workplace' (Luthans, 2002: 59). An example of a POB would be helping a co-worker with a personal matter.

The use of 360-degree feedback: a contentious issue in career development

In its initial or 'traditional' form, organisational decisions about employees' career development were based on assessments made by their line manager (or other designated person). Such assessments can be seen, of their nature, to be partial, that is, based on only one perspective on the employee, and open to prejudicial or other bias. 360-degree feedback, also known as multi-rater feedback (MRF) or multi-source feedback (MSF), was introduced in order to address both of these issues, and has been in use in organisations for at least two decades. It involves an employee completing a self-assessment against a range of criteria, and then inviting their line manager, a selection of colleagues (peers in same team/department,

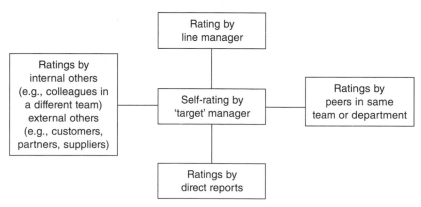

Figure 6.1 The 360 process

and direct reports) and others to complete the assessment using the same questions or criteria. In many 360-degree feedback systems, both internal and external others are also invited to complete the assessment. This can be important given that leadership behaviour has an impact that goes beyond the boundaries of a single team, department or organisation. The external rater could be from constituent groups that include: – customers; partners; and suppliers (Figure 6.1).

What is the value of 360-degree feedback?

The use of 360-degree feedback usually focuses on managerial or leadership ability. For reasons discussed in more detail later, it has been found to be a more valid way of collecting data than a wide range of other sources of performance data that include: qualitative comments, that have been solicited from key individuals; random observations of someone's behaviour; or casual conversations in the corridor.

A further, relevant factor when comparing 360-degree to traditional appraisal is the extent to which the perceptions of different types of rater are valid. The evidence available suggests that direct reports' assessments of their line manager can be, at least in the short and medium term, more accurate than an assessment centre (AC) in predicting performance, as assessed using objective performance criteria (see discussion of validity below).

Self-ratings versus ratings by others

The main reason why 360-degree feedback is so valued is because it is one of the best routes to understanding how self-aware you are. Self-awareness, which can be assessed in terms of the level of agreement between self-ratings and ratings by others, has been shown to be associated with higher levels of leadership performance (Fleenor et al., 2010). However, the same authors pointed out that this relationship does not hold true universally, and that contextual factors, including which 'other' ratings are used, and the choice of 360 tool, can have an impact here.

They also concluded that the relationship between 'self-other agreement' (SOA) and leadership performance is more complex than at first thought. This said, at an organisational level, there is evidence that high level of SOA among managers has the cumulative effect of increasing the job satisfaction and organisational commitment of staff (Halverson et al., 2005). The relationship between self-ratings and SOA congruence, and performance in ACs, is also far from simple, with a non-linear relationship appearing to emerge. Among the findings were: that those who rated themselves highest performed least well in ACs; and that others' ratings alone were not the best predictors, with peers tending to over-estimate the performance of poor performers (Atkins and Wood, 2002).

There is consistent evidence that self-ratings are largely inaccurate measures of how well a person is doing (Fleenor et al., 2010; Tsui and Ohlott, 1988). Indeed, it is been commented that 'Self-ratings alone, in general, are not considered to be accurate predictors of leadership outcomes because they are influenced by leniency bias ... [and that other] researchers have documented that self-ratings are unreliable, invalid, and inaccurate when compared to the ratings of others or objective criteria' (Fleenor et al., 2010: 1006).

It is for this reason organisations employ 360-degree feedback, so as to enable their staff, particularly those in a managerial or leadership role, to know how those who report to them, and those who work with them, feel about how they behave, and how effective they perceive them to be.

Design and practical use of 360-degree feedback systems

The stages in the design and practical use of a 360-degree feedback system are summarised in Figure 6.2.

At each stage, it is important that the *minimum* conditions or safeguards be in place.

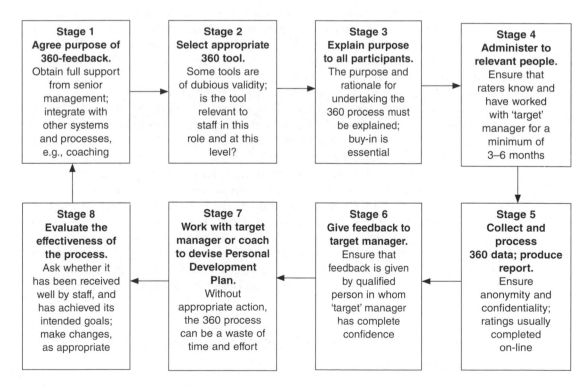

Figure 6.2   Design and use of the 360 process

Rating scales

The questions presented in a 360-degree feedback assessment are typically positively worded statements, with a multiple choice set of responses referred to as a 'Likert scale'. This allows the rater to indicate the extent to which they believe the target manager is characterised by a statement, such as, 'Has exceptional communication skills', along a six-point scale from 'Strongly agree' to 'Strongly disagree'.

Alternatively, the phraseology might be, 'Uses communication skills effectively', to which the rater is invited to respond in terms of frequency of behaviour. In this case, the rating scale might be 'Never does this' to 'Always does this'. The choice of phraseology will depend on the way in which the item is written.

The debate as to how many rating categories should be used also continues, with support for either 'forced-choice' scales (as on a four-point or six-point scale with no 'in-between' category), which it is argued obliges the rater to make a decision, rather than to 'sit on the fence' or three-point, five-point, seven-point (semantic differential), or even nine-point scales, with an 'in-between' point, which, it is argued, allows greater freedom. In any scale, however, it is important to include a 'Don't know' and a 'Not relevant' category.

One of the values of using rating scales is that the data can be used to calculate means and standard deviations, based on representative samples for different groups and subgroups. In this way, occupation-related, industry-related and other *norms* can be calculated, against which groups and subgroups of individuals can be judged. The data can also be used to develop *criteria* against which ratings of an individual's performance can be judged.

A fundamentally different way of collecting 360 data is to collect 'ipsative' data. The collection of such data involves asking the rater to make *relative* judgements about their own or someone else's personal characteristics or behaviour. In practice, the judgement to be made is in the form of, 'Characteristic A is more like me [or the person I am rating] than characteristic B'.

The validity of the 360-process can be increased by including qualitative comments. These can be very valuable in 'putting some flesh on the bone', and providing some context for interpreting the graphs and bar charts commonly used in reports. Potential dangers are: that the target manager might focus too much attention on the qualitative comments, at the expense of the more extensive quantitative data; and that, either because of their contents, or the style in which they are written or for some other reason, the comments made may be attributable to a particular individual rater, thereby removing her or his anonymity.

Evidence of the validity of the data provided in 360-degree feedback

For most of a person's career, information about how they are doing will only be provided by their line manager. This will be in the form of formal and informal performance feedback – during a formal review, or during a conversation they have on an informal basis. Many organisations do not even provide regular performance reviews for people, and so they may spend much of their career having no real idea of how well they are doing, other than the information they can glean from the outputs they or their team are producing.

As described above, performance feedback is often only given to an employee by their line manager. However, increasing research suggests that line managers may be inaccurate assessors of performance because:

- they are only one person's opinion;
- they do not see you acting naturally;
- they only see you in a limited range of situations;
- they do not attend to all aspects of your job – mostly just those that suit their purposes;
- they are subject to the effect of 'impression management'.

Researchers have concluded that other people with whom a target manager works can offer a different perspective, and are likely to be more accurate assessors of different aspects of the target manager's actions. The most common raters are described below.

Direct reports (sometimes referred to as 'subordinates')

These are members of your team or department, for whom you have the responsibility to direct, guide and support, and who are directly answerable to you for the quality of their performance. Ratings from direct reports are regarded as the most accurate assessments of all, particularly in relation to leadership ability (Hogan and Hogan, 2001). This is because they see you in a wide range of situations, and it is, therefore, difficult to 'pull the wool over their eyes'. Based on the argument that they are the ultimate focus of leadership, and the statement that 'A leader without followers is like a person going for a walk', direct reports are one of the most valuable sources of information about how you behave if you are truly to understand how effective you are as a leader. A famous longitudinal by study by McEvoy and Beatty (1989) examined how effective direct reports were in predicting the future effectiveness of their line manager, compared with assessment centre (AC) ratings. Using objective measures of the line manager's performance, they found that three and five years later, the direct reports were more accurate predictors than the AC. It was not until 10 years later that the AC data were a more accurate predictor.

While there are reasons for using direct report ratings to judge performance, their use, particularly in relation to *performance management*, is of questionable practical value. Among the reasons for this are: the process of collecting multi-source data might prove unmanageable; there is the danger that staff who are popular (for whatever reason) are likely to receive higher ratings than those who are not; and it would prove difficult to agree and to apply consistent criteria. Conversely, they are potentially one of the most valuable sources of data for *developmental purposes*.

Peers

The term 'peer' usually means colleagues who work in the same team or department as you. Ratings by colleagues who are in a different team or department are usually collected under the heading 'internal others'. Peer ratings tend to be more accurate than bosses because, as with direct reports, they see you in a wider range of contexts, and situations that are more naturalistic than when your boss is present. Therefore, they are more able to accurately rate performance generally. They are also more likely to be aware of the situational constraints of the job that could be affecting performance (Fletcher and Baldry, 1999).

The same practical issues as for direct reports would preclude their use for *performance management*, but they are also of value for *developmental purposes*.

Line manager

Most individuals have only one line manager, though, in some situations, two or more individuals may fit into this category. An example would be a hospital doctor who is answerable to the clinical director in relation to their clinical practice, but to someone else in relation to organisational issues. Taken in isolation, line manager ratings provides only a partial view of an individual's behaviour, and is situation-related (Alimo-Metcalfe, 1998). Line manager ratings have been shown to be affected by 'impression management tactics', resulting in a more favourable evaluation (Wayne and Ferris, 1990).

For practical purposes, the ratings given by a single line manager are the principal, and in most cases, the only basis for making performance management decisions. However, where monetary or other rewards, or promotions, are concerned, there is the need for the establishment of common organisation-wide or department-wide criteria, and for these to be applied equitably.

Other internal or external raters

Whereas internal others work for the same organisation as the target manager, albeit in a different team or department, external others work for a different organisation, for example, as a client or a supplier, or in a governance role. The value of both sources of ratings includes their interaction with the target manager is in quite a different context, a context in which the team, department or organisation is presenting itself to the outside world. By the same token, the criteria on which judgements are made are likely to be very different, thus raising the question of the extent to which it is meaningful to combine, say, customers and suppliers into a single score. Here, as with other rater groups, the best way to find out what they think about with how you behave and act is to ask them for specific areas of strength and developmental need.

The significance of collecting data separately from these different constituent groups lies in the *unique* perspective that each can offer. However, more recent statistical analyses have called into question the *extent* to which ratings from these different groups actually differ (Fleenor et al., 2010).

Personality assessment and career development

It is important to be aware of the widespread use of self-assessments of personality characteristics and preferences by candidates as part of a career development process. The underlying rationale is that the possession of certain characteristics is either an essential or desirable pre-requisite for a particular kind of role, or will enable the individual to perform and develop more effectively in that role. Alternatively, the personality instrument may be used to enable individuals and their colleagues to individually and collectively understand their behavioural preferences in how they approach a situation or task, and that they may differ from each other in these preferences.

The most commonly used personality diagnostic tools include: 'Firo B'; the 'Myers-Briggs type indicator (MBTI)'; and a number of instruments which assess dimensions that are regarded as assessing the 'Big 5' personality characteristics. The Big 5 headings are: agreeableness; conscientiousness; extroversion-introversion; neuroticism; and openness to experience. In some cases, such tools include a 'social desirability' or 'lie' scale, to try to identify which participants are trying to skew their responses so as to be a more attractive candidate for a position. These tools are discussed in more detail in Chapter 9.

Best practice guidelines

There are several guidelines for applying 360-degree feedback that need to be followed that will either 'make or break' its validity.

- Confidentiality of raters – in order to ensure open, honest and valid feedback, it is key to protect the anonymity of raters. One of the most effective ways to do this is to provide only 'grouped' feedback whereby, in each rater group, at least three people's responses have been aggregated to make the score.
- Target manager chooses their own raters – best practice is for the target manager to be allowed to choose their own raters. The criteria should be people who they believe know them well, and will be honest, but fair in their assessment, and have had enough contact with them in recent months to provide them with useful feedback. The alternative of having reviewers imposed is that the target manager may question the validity of their ratings (for example, he does not know me really; she has it in for me).
- Provision of a one-to-one feedback session with a trained person – 360-degree feedback may provide a target manager with potentially conflicting views of her- or himself, compared to what they previously believed. Therefore, it can be challenging to one's self-concept and, potentially, not something that a target manager can handle without support. Therefore, 360-degree feedback must be handled with great care, and one of the key guidelines for best practice is that the

target manager be provided with at least a 90-minute one-to-one feedback from a trained facilitator who can help them make sense of the report, and help them decide how they can act on any positive or negative feedback provided.

- Follow on conversations and developmental support – one of the main reasons why 360-degree feedback has been seen to fail in the past as a way of enhancing performance is because the provision of the feedback report was not followed by the formulation of a Personal Development Plan based on the report. This plan may include: coaching and/or mentoring; targeted workshops; action learning sets, or other developmental activities.
- Not for appraisal purposes – it is likely that when raters are asked to assess someone for performance management purposes, rather than it being purely developmental, they may (as noted above) change their rating of the target manager's behaviour. The 360-degree process can be used for appraisal purposes, but if it is this must be made explicit, right from the start. However, it is better suited to, and more effective in, supporting personally motivated developmental activity.

Box 6.2

OP IN PRACTICE

Designing an effective 360-degree intervention: Checklist

Stage 1

- Have you ensured the support of senior management?
- Does the 360-degree process fit in with existing systems of career development and appraisal?
- Will you be able to support those who complete the 360-tool?
- Have you trained those who will be giving the feedback?
- Has the project been properly costed?
- What criteria will be used to calculate the return on investment (ROI)?

Stage 2

- Do you have evidence of the reliability and validity of the 360-tool that you have chosen?
- Does it reflect the competencies required of staff at different levels and in different roles?
- Have you ensured that the competency statements use language suited to staff at different levels/in different roles?
- If it is to be used to assess leadership, does it assess both *what* leaders do, and *how* they perform their role, particularly when interacting with peers and direct reports?
- What kind of rating system do you want to use, and what are your reasons for this?
- Have you been able to collect data online, using an established computer system, so as to assure anonymity and confidentiality?
- Has the system for storing confidential data been made as secure as possible?

Stage 3

- Do all those who will be involved know the purpose of the 360-process?
- Have you ensured that the 'target' manager has been in post for at least three months, preferably six?
- Have you ensured that they are not currently suffering from undue personal or job-related stress?
- Have you ensured that they are not currently the subject of a disciplinary process?
- Are they confident about your assurances of the anonymity of the raters' responses, and the confidentiality of the written report and associated feedback?
- If qualitative comments are invited, are all raters aware of factors that might compromise their anonymity?
- Do the 'target' managers know how the data will be used (e.g., for performance management, or personal and professional development)?
- Is the 'target' manager aware of the extent to which her/his report will be shared (performance review), or remain totally confidential (development review)?
- Do the 'target' managers know how much support they can expect to receive in relation to meeting their needs and aspirations?
- Do line managers and/or the HR department know what kind of help they might be asked to give?
- Have you produced a FAQ document with answers to the most common questions?
- Is information about all aspects of the 360-process available on the intranet (if there is one)?
- Have you made arrangements for those who will go through the process to meet one another formally or informally, to discuss issues of concern?
- Have you ensured that all aspects of the process meet, at least, the minimum guide-lines set by the British Psychological Society, or your professional association?

Stage 4

- Have you informed 'target' managers of the need to obtain ratings from a wide range of relevant others?
- Have you given them any guidance on how to choose these raters, e.g., working with them in different roles, can be relied on to complete their ratings on time?

Stage 5

- Have you advised target managers of the need to have a minimum of two raters per category?
- Is the computer system set up such that each rater knows which questions to answer?
- Is the computer system set up such that reminders can be sent out automatically to those who have been slow to respond?

Stage 6

- Have you ensured that those giving feedback know the purpose of the feedback they give?

(Continued)

(Continued)

- Have you ensured that they have the appropriate qualifications for the task, e.g., training in giving feedback, including sensitivity to others' needs, and/or have a professional qualification in coaching and/or mentoring?
- Have you made alternative provision for providing feedback, if, for whatever reason, the selected coach/mentor is deemed unsuitable?

Stage 7

- Have you provided 'target' managers with training on how to write a Personal Development Plan?
- Have you provided those giving feedback on how to guide the writing of a Personal Development Plan?
- Have you made provision for follow-up activities, such as specific skills training, or Action Learning Sets?

Stage 8

- Have you set aside time and funding to evaluate the effectiveness of the intervention?
- To what extent have you been, or will you be, able to obtain the views of participants and others in a systematic way?
- Have the criteria for judging ROI been met?
- What lessons have been learnt?
- In what ways, if any, should the 360-process be modified in future?

The impact of bias in career development and appraisal

For decades, Occupational Psychologists have studied the reasons why, despite increasing diversity in our populations and workforces, this proportion of diversity is not reflected in organisations, particularly at more senior levels. Many theories have been put forward to explain this situation, and some have explained to a degree the reasons for this lack of diversity beyond the organisational experience – for example, some professions appealing more to men than women (Fouard, 2007). However, there is increasing evidence to suggest that bias in the ways that career development is provided, and the way that performance appraisal is conducted, are major contributors to diminishing the career prospects of people from under-represented groups in organisations (Elsesser and Lever, 2011).

Evidence of bias in career development for different demographic groups

Organisations want to have more diverse workforces because there is a strong business case to suggest that if they were more diverse and inclusive, they could benefit from greater profitability and avoidance of unnecessary costs (such as employment tribunals and turnover). These outcomes rely on the organisation providing career development opportunities to diverse people, not just attracting and recruiting them in the first place. Yet, there is increasing evidence to suggest that organisations unwittingly place barriers to career progression in the way of their employees, particularly those from currently under-represented groups (Alban-Metcalfe, 2004; Avery, 2011).

These barriers exist in a wide range of forms that can include the following:

- Selection and promotion criteria – many of the methods used to design these criteria are based on observation and/or questioning of current job incumbents. If these individuals or groups are demographically homogenous – in other words, if they are all or almost all white or male, for example – perceptions of success in the role will be based on a predominantly white, male perspective. The reason why this is important to be aware of is that research suggests that people from different demographic groups often have different perspectives of what is successful performance within a role, for example women (Rosener, 1990) and people from minority ethnic groups (Littrell and Nkomo, 2005). Therefore, people who are not white males are less likely to be successful in being selected and/or promoted into a role when white male perceptions are used to determine the assessment criteria, as alternative perspectives will not be rated high in interviews and/or other selection or promotion exercises. This is further discussed in Chapter 9.
- Lack of accessibility to formal development opportunities – a growing body of research suggests that people who are different from the predominant demographic group are less likely to be able to access training and development opportunities within their organisation (Jonsen et al., 2011; Stahl et al., 2010). There are a variety of reasons put forward to explain this, including less good quality relationships with their line manager, not being viewed as someone likely to succeed within the organisation – therefore, the organisation is less willing to spend money on their development. Another reason is linked to the previous bullet point – being assessed for development opportunities against criteria that are more related to a different demographic group.
- Lack of differentiation between individuals (related to line manager relationship) – Research from social and organisational psychology suggests that people are prone to what is popularly known as the 'halo and horns' effects when assessing someone they interact with. What this means in practice is that we tend to attribute positive characteristics to people who are similar to us in their appearance or demographic grouping and less positive characteristics to those who are different to us (Fleenor et al., 2010). In terms of the line manager relationship, it can play out in less high-quality relationships that can have a detrimental impact on the chances that they will give a direct report the opportunity to take on a more visible or high-profile assignment or role when they are different to them. This may be because subconsciously they do not have as much faith in that individual than in another direct report who is demographically similar to them.

- Lack of accessibility to informal career development opportunities (related to organisational culture) – studies have shown that people from different demographic groups than the predominant one can face barriers to career progression because they are less likely to be part of the 'in group' and therefore miss out on informal discussions that relate to interesting projects coming up, or the wider politics of the organisation (Alban-Metcalfe, 2004).
- Absence of career pathways that are attractive or that enable people to have an appropriate work-life balance – this can have a detrimental effect both on men and women, who do not want to spend their entire lives at work, and therefore avoid progressing within an industry, or leave an organisation to join another or set up as self-employed (Alban-Metcalfe, 2004).

Evidence of bias in performance management and appraisal for different demographic groups

Perhaps one of the most insidious barriers to career progression for people from different demographic groups than the majority is bias in performance management and appraisal. As is explained below, this situation means that even when a person is a good or outstanding performer in a role, they are unable to progress because their contribution is not formally (or informally) valued.

- Lack of performance feedback – a major factor that most people are not aware of is the suggestion that people who are demographically different from their line manager are less likely to be provided with regular, sufficient performance feedback. In other words, research findings suggest that people who are different from their line manager are not only less likely to be given as much feedback as others, but that the feedback they receive is more likely to be insufficient in terms of depth or quality to enable them to determine their development needs (Alban-Metcalfe, 2004).
- Inaccurate or biased performance feedback – related to the 'halo' and 'horns' effects described earlier in this section, line managers who are demographically similar to their direct report are more likely to notice when they do things well, and to attribute their success to stable factors such as competence, as opposed to unstable factors such as luck or chance. There is also evidence to suggest that when the direct report is demographically dissimilar to their line manager, they have to work much harder than those who are similar to be seen as successful, because they have to overcome the 'cognitive dissonance' that exists within their line manager's head. This describes a situation where the line manager has to first unconsciously get over the fact that they do not expect the individual to perform as well because they are 'different', and then move to recognise their success. This is a reason why people often talk about under-represented groups needing to be even better than majority group individuals to succeed.
- Other sources of bias include: having a personal liking or dislike for the person; primary or recency effect, whereby judgements are unduly influences by initial or most recent information; negativity bias, such as homophobia, or racial prejudice; differences in the extent to which individuals are able to use the whole of a rating

scale (central-tendency *versus* extreme response style); impact of the previous judgement made (contrast effect); time decay, such that relevant behaviours may have been forgotten; and rater's mood at the time making a judgement.

Specific advice given by Organisational Psychologists in how organisations can overcome bias in career development related to performance appraisal or selection systems is provided in Box 6.3.

Occupational Psychologists should also be aware of, and try to counter, the impact of other sources of difference, such as: access to formal and informal career opportunities; quality of line manager relationship; and reduced or biased feedback. One major way of addressing such situations is to try to ensure that everyone in the organisation, particularly those in formal leadership positions, are aware of unconscious bias. This can have a positive impact on reducing the occurrence of bias, thereby contributing to 'levelling the playing field' for under-represented groups.

Box 6.3

OP IN PRACTICE

Designing a bias-free selection or appraisal system

1. Ensure that the objectives are clear and are made explicit.
2. Develop a series of behavioural indicators.
3. Devise a system whereby different weightings can be assigned to more important and less important criteria.
4. Ensure that the assessment criteria are bias free – use a representative sample of current job holders or other subject matter experts to contribute to the design.
5. Select any psychometric tests carefully – bias can be introduced at this stage through use of psychometric tests that are based on a un-representative sample, and may be biased towards the majority group. Check the published data on the tests used to ensure they are free from bias.
6. Remove any unnecessary assessments – follow best practice in selection and assessment to ensure that only necessary criteria and assessments are applied to the process. Use Facet Theory to guide the phraseology of items. This involves ensuring that each criterion is presented in exactly the same way, e.g., refers to only one behaviour at a time, the behaviour is observable or readily inferable, all statements are written positively.
7. Train all assessors in avoidance of bias – through formal training with appropriately qualified experts.
8. Create a representative assessment panel – ensure assessors are diverse in both observation of exercises and any interview panels.
9. Ensure that assessors and others involved in the process have clear line of accountability.
10. Take particular care to monitor conversations during 'wash up' sessions – this can be a stage in which assessors relax a bit too much and start to introduce subjective and potentially irrelevant evidence into the selection decisions. It is important that there is a Chair of the panel present and there is carefully monitoring of decision factors and how they are made.

Career development and appraisal in the new world

This section will focus on some of the major factors that Occupational Psychologists need to be aware of as they approach career development and appraisal to ensure that the organisations they are supporting are fit for purpose for the present and future organisational environments.

Increased scrutiny of diversity and inclusion at all levels

One of the key points in the business case for greater diversity and inclusion among employees in organisations is increasing recognition of the value it creates in winning and keeping more customers. This diversity needs to be at the customer face at all levels in the organisation, and applies just as much to the public sector internationally, where increasing evidence suggests that the community can only be served well if there are people at every level who understand their needs and can interact with them successfully. The implications for Occupational Psychologists include ensuring that development systems allow talent to be recognised and rewarded, regardless of demographic background.

Increased scrutiny of the performance and behaviour of executives at the very top

The recent global financial problems encountered by major organisations, such as Enron, Lehman Brothers and Fannie Mae in the USA, have increased scrutiny on the behaviour of the boards of large organisations. In response to this, increasing numbers of organisations are now implementing board-level performance assessment, in which Occupational Psychologists have a key part in design and implementation (Alimo-Metcalfe, 2012).

Desire for talent development to be treated as 'business as usual'

There is an increasing recognition that organisations are not sustainable unless they have a strong talent pipeline continually developing talented employees, particularly leaders, to replace those who retire or move on. While many organisations have for some time had focused development programmes for those identified as 'high potential' individuals, there is increasing focus on the need for managers at every level continually to provide opportunities for all employees to develop formally and informally in order to provide people with the opportunity to realise their potential, and to increase performance.

Generations Y and Z

Organizations now have large numbers of individuals from 'Generation Y', char-actrised as those people born between 1980 and 1995, soon to be followed by those referred to as 'Generation Z', or the 'iGeneration', among other labels, who have grown up with the World Wide Web and the array of social media technologies connecting them to everyone, everywhere, at their finger-tips.

Many studies have pointed to Generation Y having a range of different demands to those of previous generations. These relate to their interest in self-development and improvement, expectations of financial success, increased results focus, desire for greater meaning in their work (feeling that its both interesting and important), focus on teamwork and expectations of fairness (ILM/Ashridge, 2011). While, obviously, less research has been published about Generation Z, some social commentators are sug-gesting that the period of global economic turmoil and high levels of unemployment have generated significant concerns regarding their employment prospects – long- and short-term (e.g. Tulgan, 2012). But the possibility to network globally and 'sell' onself online is a facility at which they will doubtless become extraordinarily adept. However, post-recession, they will be highly digitally savvy, and connected, and their need dur-ing the recession, to be entrepreneurial to secure employment, may well create signifi-cantly greater challenges for organisations to attract and retain their talent.

The implications for organisations are substantial, and include the need, from a career development perspective for: greater flexibility in how individuals work, includ-ing job-sharing, career breaks; more opportunities for 'homeworking/hotdesking, 'outplacement', either in the same or a different organisation; active encouragement of teamwork; and greater emphasis on organisational justice. In each of these areas, Occupational Psychologists and HR experts can enable organisations to rise to the challenge through: critical review of their recruitment, assessment and reward sys-tems; developing effective career development and appraisal processes, and criteria for advancement; and identifying route to greater staff fulfillment, in order to retain valued employees.

Summary

This chapter has demonstrated the wide range of ways in which Occupational Psychologists have a critical role to play in ensuring organisational success through shaping and delivering career development and appraisal. The evidence presented has shown that there are many complex factors to consider in ensuring that these processes are both effective and fair in meeting the needs of organisa-tions and their employees. At the same time, it is argued that many organisations still need to understand the ways in which inappropriate career development and appraisal can have a negative impact on their bottom line, and so Occupational Psychologists still have a job to do in illustrating the business case for their greater involvement in these areas (Boop et al., 2009; Jackson and Sirianni, 2009).

Throughout this chapter, the idea that organisations need to consider the health and well-being of their employees has been mentioned. Chapter 10 will explore the factors within an organisation that can impact on employees' health, and how these can be used to design work and the work environment more optimally for both health and performance.

Explore further

- General websites with useful resources related to career development and appraisal.These include:

    Chartered Institute for Personnel and Development (CIPD) – performance appraisal advice – http://www.cipd.co.uk/hr-resources/factsheets/performance-appraisal.aspx
    Chartered Management Institute – http://www.managers.org.uk
    Institute for Leadership and Management (ILM) – http://www.i-l-m.com/
    The Career Development Organisation (registered Charity) – http://www.crac.org.uk
    The 30% Club (committed to increasing gender diversity on Boards) – http://www.30percentclub.org.uk/

- Specific job and career websites related to career development to give you a sense of what this involves:

    Academic careers – http://www.jobs.ac.uk/careers-advice/managing-your-career
    Doctors–http://www.faculty.londondeanery.ac.uk/e-learning/careers-advice/a-framework-for-career-planning
    Engineers and technologists – http://www.theiet.org/membership/career/index.cfm
    Physiotherapists – http://www.csp.org.uk/professional-union/careers-development/career-development
    Professional dancers – http://www.thedcd.org.uk/
    Royal Navy – http://www.royalnavy.mod.uk/Community/Life-Management/Career-Development
    Teachers – http://www.education.gov.uk/get-into-teaching/faqs/life-as-a-teacher/career-prospects-and-development.aspx

- Alimo-Metcalfe, B. and Alban-Metcalfe, J. (2008) *Engaging Leadership: Creating Organisations that Maximise the Potential of Their People*. London: CIPD. Available at: http://www.cipd.co.uk/shapingthefuture/_leadershipreport.htm
- Davies, E.M. (2001) *Women on Boards*. London: Department for Business, Education and Skills. Available at: http://www.bis.gov.uk/assets/biscore/business-law/docs/w/11–745-women-on-boards.pdf
- Elicker, J.D., Levy, P.E. and Hall, R.J. (2006) 'The role of leader–member exchange in the performance appraisal process,' *Journal of Management*, 32 (4): 531–51.
- Hirsh, W. (2011) 'Positive career development for leaders', in J. Storey (ed.), *Leadership in Organisations: Current Issues and & Key Trends*, 2nd edn. London: Routledge. pp. 129–49.

- Livers, A.B. and Carver, K.A. (2002) *Leading in Black and White: Working Across the Racial Divide in Corporate America*. San Francisco, CA: Jossey-Bass.
- Marshall, V. and Wood, R.E. (2000) 'The dynamics of effective performance appraisal: an integrated model', *Asia Pacific Journal of Human Resources*, 38 (3): 62–90.
- Marshall Egan, T., Upton, M.G. and Lynham. S.A. (2006) 'Career development: load-bearing wall or window dressing? Exploring definitions, theories, and prospects for HRD-related theory building', *Human Resource Development Review*, 5 (4): 442–77.
- McDonald, K.S. and Hite, L.M. (2005) 'Reviving the relevance of career development in human resource development', *Human Resource Development Review*, 4 (4): 418–39.
- Niles, S.G. and Harris-Bowlsbey (2008) *Career Development Interventions in the 21st Century*, 3rd edn. Upper Saddle River, NJ: Prentice Hall.
- Parker, P. and Carroll, B. (2009) 'Leadership development: insights from a careers perspective', *Leadership*, 5 (2): 261–83.
- Sturges, J. (2011) 'The individualisation of the career and its implication for leadership and & management development', in J. Storey (ed.), *Leadership in Organisations: Current Issues and & Key Trends,* 2nd edn. London: Routledge. pp. 150–64.
- Taormina, R.J. and Gao, J.H. (2009) 'Identifying acceptable performance appraisa l criteria: an international perspective', *Asia Pacific Journal of Human Resources*, 47 (1): 102–25.
- UK Commission for Employment and Skills (2012) *Developing Business Developing Careers: How and Why Employers Are Supporting the Career Development of Their Employees*. London,: UKCES May. Available at: http://www.ukces.org.uk/assets/ukces/docs/publications/developing-business-developing-careers.pdf

Discussion questions

1 What factors would you consider when attempting to eliminate or reduce bias in performance appraisal?
2 How might you advise a company with little or no available budget, but wishes to provide meaningful career development opportunities for their employees?
3 On what basis would you present to a company the value you can add to their performance as an expert in career development and appraisal?

Sample essay questions

1 Imagine yourself in the role of a careers adviser. What advice would you give to an 18-22 year-old, who is about to embark on a career in management?
2 According to Charles Cooley (1902) we come to know what we are like from the way in which others treat us (the 'looking glass' self). If this is the case why do we need 360-degree/multi-rater feedback?

Sample examination questions

1   In the case of an individual who is joining the labour market for the first time, evaluate the potential advantages and disadvantages of a company managed and a self-managed career.
2   Justify a proposal to use of 360-degree/MRF by a company employing around 25,000 staff.

OP IN PRACTICE: DAY IN THE LIFE OF ...

Professor Beverly Alimo-Metcalfe, Professor of Leadership, Bradford University School of Management, Emeritus Professor, Leeds University, and Founding Director of Real World Group

What areas of OP do you work within?	• Leadership and culture change • Staff engagement and well-being • Personal and career development (particularly relating to gender and ethnic background bias in organisational practices) • Equality and diversity (particularly potential bias in leadership theory) • Team working • Governance (the role and effectiveness of Boards; leadership within the Board; the relationship between the effectiveness of Boards and the rest of the organisation) • Performance appraisal and 360–degree feedback, at individual, team, and organisational level. I'm particularly interested in how organisations create environments with high levels of employee engagement, in which people flourish. The nature of leadership in organisations is key to creating such a culture. I believe that career development should be embedded in the relationship between individuals and their line manager, and the quality of conversations and activities in which people engage with one another in their organisation.
How did you become interested in this area?	My initial interest in Performance Appraisal developed when I was a PhD student. It was evident that, even in leading UK companies, the process of performance appraisal was, at best, rudimentary. The need for this work was reinforced when I designed and directed an appraisal skills development programme for all academics and professionals at my then university (University of Leeds). My interest in Career Development stems from when I taught in a secondary school in a deprived area of Bradford. It was clear that the pupils had very low career expectations, and I sought to increase them, particularly by helping them to strengthen their self-concept and self-esteem and raising their career and life aspirations

This interest was stimulated further by the research I undertook at Sheffield University Social and Applied Psychology Unit, on the career development of male and female managers in the UK private sector. I had completed four degrees in psychology by this stage (BEd, MSc, MBA and PhD), and had never considered how gendered the psychological research literature was, or how important were the implications. In my PhD, which was about leadership behaviours in appraisal interviews, I referred to managers as 'he' throughout. It makes me shudder to realise my ignorance and how powerful were the forces of gender socialisation in my life.

When I attempted to draw attention to the importance of the lack of females in our sample, my concerns came as a surprise to both colleagues, and the matter was dismissed as irrelevant by them and by the professional managerial association who had commissioned the research (The British Institute of Management). This made me utterly determined to seek ways of increasing the female sample. In our eventual sample there were around 1,400 males and 993 females – which formed one of the largest sample of women managers ever studied.

As a result of these experiences, together with the research environment in which I worked, I became aware also of the sexism of research into the nature of 'career' and how different were the experiences of females and males working in organisations, and the difficulties of working in a sexist and masculine culture. This drove me to undertake writing and research around the gendered notion of career progression, focusing specifically on the numerous barriers encountered by women in relation to selection, appraisal and performance evaluation.

With respect to my research at Leeds University, I combined my passion for understanding the nature of leadership behaviours with a growing discomfort with US research on leadership which was based, yet again, on research from a totally male perspective. This became a three-year investigation of leadership, based on one of the largest samples – 4000+ managers and professionals in the NHS and local government – and probably the first to be deliberately inclusive by sex and ethnic background. The success of our research, which formed the basis of a new 360-feedback instrument, *The Transformational Leadership Questionnaire (TLQ)*, which was increasingly being adopted in leadership programmes, led to the formation of a University of Leeds spin-out company, now called Real World Group. I had also maintained a strong interest in development in the field of appraisal, and in particular the use of 360-feedback and developments in Assessment Centre methodologies and applications.

| **What kinds of organisations are interested in your work and why?** | Our work at Real World Group involves three areas of activity: conducting research; developing instruments to support individual, team, and organisational development; and consultancy. Most of our work has been with the public sector in the UK, but our work in the private sector is increasing, and we have developed strong links with large organisations abroad, and independent consultants, particularly in Australia, Singapore, China and the US. |

(Continued)

(Continued)

What have been the seminal research papers in this area?	Atwater, L.E. and Yammarino, E. (1992) 'Does self other agreement of leadership perceptions moderate the validity of leadership and performance predictions?, *Personnel Psychology*, 45 (1): 141–6. Fleenor, J.W., Smither, J.W. Atwater, L.E., Braddy, P.W. and Sturm, R.E. (2010) 'Self–other rating agreement in leadership: a review'. *The Leadership Quarterly*, 21: 1005–34. Gilligan, C. (1982) *In a Different Voice.* Harvard, MA: Harvard University Press. Greenhaus, J.H., Parasuraman, S. and Wormley, W.M. (1990) 'Effects of race on organisational experiences, job performance evaluations, and career outcomes', *The Academy of Management Journal*, 33 (1): 64–86. Greenhaus, J.H. and Parasuraman, S. (1993) 'Job performance attributions and career advancement prospects: an examination of gender and race effects', *Organisational Behavior and Human Decision Processes*, 55: 273–97. Marshall, J. (1984) *Women Managers: Travellers in a Male World.* Chichester: Wiley. McEvoy, G.M. and Beaty. R.W. (1989) 'Assessment centres and subordinate appraisals of managers: seven year examination of predictive validity', *Personnel Psychology*, 42 (1): 37–52. Nieva, V.F. and Gutek, B.A. (1980) 'Sex effects on evaluation', *Academy of Management Review*, 5: 267–276. Savickas, M.L., Nota, L., Rossier, J., Dauwalder, J.-P., Duarter, M.E., Guichard, J., Soresi, S., Van Esbroeck, R. and Van Vianen, A.E.M. (2009) 'Life designing: a paradigm for career construction in the 21st century', *Journal of Vocational Behavior*, 75: 239–50. Schein, E. (1993) *Career Anchors: Discovering Your Real Values.* San Diego, CA: Pfeiffer. Schein, E.H. (1996) 'Career anchors revisited: Implications for career development in the 21st century', *The Academy of Management Executive,* 10 (4): 80–8. Sturges, J., Conway, N., Guest, D. and Liefhooghe, A. (2005) 'Managing the career deal: the psychological contract as a framework for understanding career management, organisational commitment and work behaviour', *Journal of Organisational Behavior*, 26: 821–38.
What has been the major academic development in this area?	• Recognition of the challenges facing individuals and organisations in the context of a 'life designing' approach to career development. • Increased understanding of the nature and implications of work-life balance.

	• Talent Management – its critical importance to organisations in 'the war for talent'. • New models of leadership which emphasise leadership as a social process.
To what extent does the practical application of your work inform your research?	A great deal. The research we undertake is usually closely aligned to our particular areas of consultancy and instrument design. Although I am currently involved in two externally funded research projects, much of the research undertaken by myself and by my colleagues at Real World Group is designed to develop development tools and techniques for practical application.
What role do ethics have in your work?	Ethical principles are at the base of all the work we do at Real World Group, and are applied rigorously in every aspects of our work – research, consultancy and diagnostics. This is also true of my work as Professor of Leadership at the Bradford School of Management.
Can you give an example of a day in your working life?	There is no typical day. It may involve a conference presentation, or a workshop, or launching an organisational culture change intervention, or working closely with a Board on their feedback report from our Board Leadership 360, writing a research paper or attending one of the national advisory groups of which I am a member.
How has your work changed in the last five years?	In terms of work with leadership, I have seen an increased emphasis on the role of Boards in the areas of leadership and governance; greater sophistication in understanding of the nature of leadership as a social influence process; increased interest by professionals in their role in leadership in their teams and organisation; and increased research into the relationship between leadership and team working, staff well-being and attitudes to work. I have also seen much greater interest in employee engagement; increased research and consultancy in the area of equality and diversity; the use of Appreciative Inquiry more frequently as part of organisational transformation interventions; and the production of a wider range of 360 tools, for use at individual, team, and organisational level.
How do you see your work changing over the next five years?	I see more working across communities – public with private sector partnerships; an emphasis on building cultures of innovation and learning; and collaborative cross-cultural research and consultancy which will enrich our notions of leadership. I also see more more international work with strategic partners who have adopted our model of engaging leadership and want to use, or are using our instruments. In terms of 360 tools, I envisage greater sophistication in the development and use of 360 tools, particularly with reference to the impact of contextual factors; and empirical research to establish the validity of our 360 and other tools among managers and professionals in Australia, China, India, North America, and Pacific Rim countries.

References

Alban-Metcalfe, J. (2004) *Prospects: Diversity and the Career Progression of Managers in Local Government.* London: LRDL/IDeA.

Alimo-Metcalfe, B. (1998) '360 degree feedback and leadership development', *International Journal of Selection & Assessment*, 6: 35–44.

Alimo-Metcalfe, B. (2012) Engaging Boards. www.kingsfund.org.uk/publications.

Alimo-Metcalfe, B. and Alban-Metcalfe, J. (2008) *Engaging Leadership: Creating Organisations that Maximise the Potential of Their People.* London: Chartered Institute for Personnel Development.

Alimo-Metcalfe, B. and Alban-Metcalfe, J. (2012) *Leadership During Tough Times: Understanding into Action.* Leeds: Lædan Press.

Atkins, P.W. and Wood, R.E. (2002) 'Self-versus others' ratings as predictors of assessment center ratings: validation evidence from 360-degree feedback programs', *Personnel Psychology*, 55: 871–904.

Armstrong, M. and Baron, A. (2012) *Performance Management.* London: Chartered Institute of Personnel & Development.

Avery, D.R. (2011) 'Support for diversity in organisations:a theoretical exploration of its origins and offshoots', *Organisational Psychology Review*, 1: 239–56.

Bolles, R.N. (2009) *What Color is your Parachute?* Berkeley, CA: Ten Speed Press; Updated Annually.

Boop, M.A., Bing, D.A. and Forte-Trammell, S. (2009) *Agile Career Development: Lessons and Approaches From IBM.* IBM Press.

Brousseau, R., Driver, M., Eneroth, K. and Larrson, R. (1996) 'Career pandemonium: realigning organisations and individuals', *Academy of Management Executive*, 10: 52–66.

Elsesser, K.M. and Lever, J. (2011) 'Does gender bias against female leaders persist? Quantitative and qualitative data from a large-scale survey', *Human Relations*, 64: 1–4.

Fleenor, J.W., Smither, J.W., Atwater, L.E., Braddy, P.W. and Strum, R.E. (2010) 'Self-other rating agreement in leadership:a review', *Leadership Quarterly*, 21: 1005–34.

Fletcher, C. and Baldry, C. (1999) 'Multi-source feedback systems:a research perspective', in C.L. Cooper and I. Roberston (eds), *International Review of Industrial and Organisational Psychology*, 14: 149–193.

Fouad, N.A. (2007) 'Work and vocational psychology: theory, research, and applications', *Annual Review of Psychology*, 58: 543–64.

Gratton, L. and Hailey, V.H. (1999) 'The rhetoric and reality of 'new careers', in L. Gratton, V.H. Hailey, P. Stiles (eds), *Strategic Human Resource Management.* Oxford: Oxford University Press.

Halverson, S.K., Tonidandel, S., Barlow, C.B. and Dipboye, R.L. (2005) 'Self-other agreement on 360-degree leadership evaluation', in S. Reddy (ed.), *Multi-Source Performance Assessment: Perspectives and Insights.* Hyderabad: ICFAI University Press. pp. 125–44.

Hawkins, P. (1999) *The Art of Building Windmills: Career Tactics for the 21st Century.* Liverpool: Graduates into Employment Unit: University of Liverpool.

Hirsh, W. (2000) *Succession Planning Demystified.* IES Report No. 372. Brighton: Institute for Employment Studies.

Hirsh, W. (2011) 'Positive career development for leaders', in J. Storey (ed.), *Leadership in Organisations: Current Issues and Key Trends.* London: Routledge. pp. 129–49.

Hogan, R. and Hogan, J. (2001) 'Assessing leadership:a view from the dark side', *International Journal of Selection & Assessment*, 9: 40–51.

Hopson, B. and Scally, M. (1993) *Build Your Own Rainbow.* Leeds: Lifekskills Associates.

Institute of Leadership & Management/Ashridge Business School (2011) *Great Expectations: Managing henevection.* London: Institue of leadership & Management.

Jackson, D.W. and Sirianni, N.J. (2009) *Building the Bottom Line by Developing the Front Line: Career Development for Service Employees.* Harvard, MA: Business Horizon.

Jonsen, K., Maznevski, M.L. and Schneider, S.C. (2011) 'Diversity and its not so diverse literature:an international perspective', *International Journal of Cross Cultural Management*, 11: 35–62.

Kidd, J.M. (2006) *Understanding Career Counselling.* London: Sage.

Kidd, J.M., Hirsh, W. and Jackson, C. (2004) 'Straight talking: the nature of effective career discussion at work', *Journal of Career Development*, 30: 231–45.

Law, S.K., Wong, C. and Chen, X.Z. (2005) 'The construct of organisational citizenship behavior: should we analyse after we have conceptualised?', in D.L. Turnipseed (ed.), *Handbook of Organisational Citizen Citizenship Behavior.* New York; Nova Science Publications.

Littrell, R.F. and Nkomo, S.M. (2005) 'Gender and race differences in leader behaviour in South Africa', *Women in Management Review*, 20: 562–80.

Luthans, F. (2002) 'The need for and meaning of positive organisational behaviour', *Journal of Organisational Behavior.* 23: 695–706.

MacLeod, D. and Clarke, N. (2008) *Engagement for Success: Enhancing Performance through Employee Engagement.* Available at: www.bis.gov.uk

McEvoy, G.M. and Beatty, R.W. (1989) 'Assessment centres and subordinate appraisals of managers: a seven-year examination of predictive validity', *Personnel Psychology*, 42: 37–52.

NCDA (National Career Development Association) (2003) 'Career development: a policy statement of the National Career Development Association Board of Directors (adopted 16 March 1993; revised 2003). Available at: http://www.ncda.org/pdf/Policy.pdf (accessed 24 September 2012).

Organ, D.W. (1988) *Organisational citizen Citizenship Behaviour: The Good Soldier Syndrome.* Lexington, VA: Lexington Books.

Organ, D.W., Podsakoff, P.M. and MacKenzie, S.P. (2006) *Organisational citizen Citizenship Behaviour: It Nature, Antecedents and Consequences.* London: Sage.

Rosener, J. (1990) 'Ways women lead', *Harvard Business Review*, 68: 119–225.

Schein, E.H. (1978) *Career Dynamics: Matching Individual and isation Organisational Needs.* Reading, MA: Addison-Wesley.

Schein, E.H. (1993) *Career Anchors: Discovering your Real Values.* San Diego, CA: Pfeiffer.

Schein, E.H. (1996) 'Career anchors revisited: implications for career development in the 21st century', *Academy of Management Executive*, 10: 80–88.

Stahl, G.K., Maznevski, M.L., Voigt, A. and Johsen, K. (2010) 'Unraveling the effects of cultural diversity in teams:a meta-analysis of research on multicultural work groups', *Journal of International Business Studies*, 41: 690–709.

Tsui, A.S. and Ohlott, P. (1988) 'Multiple assessment of managerial effectiveness: interrater agreement and consensus in effectiveness models', *Personnel Psychology*, 41: 799–803.

Tulgan, B. (2012) 'High-maintenance Generation Z heads to work'. *USA Today*, 26 June. Available at: http://usatoday30.usatoday.com/news/opinion/forum/story/2012-06-27/generation-z-work-millenials-social-media-graduates/55845098/1(accessed 19 November 2012).

Wayne, S.J. and Ferris, G.R. (1990) 'Influence tactics, affect, and exchange quality in supervisor-subordinate interactions: a laboratory experiment and field study', *Journal of Applied Psychology*, 75: 487–99.

Yarnall, J. (2008) *Strategic Career Management – Developing your Talent*. Oxford: Butterworth-Heinemann.

Zaffron, L. (2009) *Performance Management: The Three Laws of Performance: Rewriting the Future of your Organisation and your Life*. Boston, MA: Harvard University Press.

7 Design of environments and work: health, safety and well-being

Fehmidah Munir and Hilary McDermott

Learning outcomes

By the end of the chapter you will have:

- increased your knowledge of existing theory and practice on design of environments and work regarding health and safety;
- developed an understanding of application of psychological knowledge to a range of occupational and organisational issues, problems and settings;
- gained an understanding of the concept of risk and risk management;
- gained an understanding of human factors and how they are a key ingredient of effective workplace health and safety management;
- understood how human behaviour can impact on workplace health, safety and well-being;
- developed an understanding of implementing and evaluating interventions in a range of occupational and organisational settings.

Introduction

This chapter provides an insight into the design of work environments and how the principles of Occupational Psychology can be used to inform the design of work and the work environment to match the capabilities of human performance. With a focus on occupational health, safety and well-being, the chapter offers an overview of relevant legislation and an outline of important considerations that impact on employees' health. It introduces important concepts such as risk, hazard and human factors, and provides practical examples of how these concepts can influence the potential for an accident. The chapter offers two distinct approaches to health and well-being, one based on engineering controls and the other from a psychosocial viewpoint.

Occupational health and safety management: the legal context

Health and safety at work within the UK is primarily controlled by both national and European legislation. The principal piece of UK legislation is the Health and Safety at Work Act 1974. Since the introduction of the Act in 1974, a number of supplementary Regulations have also been passed which cover a wide range of issues relevant to the workplace. The use of legislation and regulatory requirements as a means for controlling and improving health and safety at work has grown considerably in the UK over the past 40 years. The history of such legislation can be traced back to the Industrial Revolution. The associated growth in machinery and manufacturing at that time not only changed the nature of working practices in the UK but it also led to a dramatic increase in the UK workforce. Women and children were employed in the factories where working conditions were often harsh, combining long hours with poor conditions (heat and dust) and dangerous machinery. The combination of fatigue, heat and unguarded moving machinery meant there were high mortality and morbidity rates.

Public attention of the poor working conditions led to the introduction of factory safety laws in the 19th century that aimed to bring the factories under control and protect workers, particularly women and children. These early pieces of legislation were reactive in nature, whereby each piece of health and safety law dealt with a different problem as and when it became recognised. By the middle of the 20th century, safety legislation in the UK was considered to be largely ineffective in protecting workers against injury and ill health, and in 1970 a committee on Safety and Health at Work was set up under the chairmanship of Lord Robens. The report of the committee led by Lord Robens (Great Britain Committee on Safety and Health at Work, 1972) suggested that health and safety legislation in the UK needed a radical overhaul. When passed in 1974, the Health and Safety at Work Act placed a duty on every employer to ensure, so far as is reasonably practicable, the health, safety and welfare at work of all his or her employees. In addition, there was also a duty on employers to consider risks to members of the public.

Since the passing of the Health and Safety at Work Act, much of the UK health and safety law has derived from European directives. The statutory instruments known as the 'the big six' or the 'six pack' came into force in the UK in 1992 under the Health and Safety at Work Act, and these safety regulations implemented key European directives on workplace health and safety. The Regulations comprising the 'big six' are:

• Management of Health and Safety at Work Regulations 1992 (amended 1999);
• Workplace (Health, Safety and Welfare) Regulations 1992;
• Provision and Use of Work Equipment Regulations 1992 (amended 1998);
• Manual Handling Operations Regulations 1992;

- Display Screen Equipment Regulations 1992;
- Personal Protective Equipment at Work Regulations 1992.

The Management of Health and Safety at Work Regulations provided a general framework for managing work-related health and safety, whereas the other five offer specific requirements in relation to specific hazards (such as manual handling). All six regulations, however, have the common requirements to assess the risk to all employees and others, to take steps to reduce such risks and to provide regular information and training in relation to identified health and safety risks. The role of legislation therefore includes supporting a culture of effective management systems. A further piece of legislation that is important when considering the design of work and work environments is the Equality Act 2010. This was discussed more fully in Chapter 4.

An employee with a disability or health condition is therefore protected at work by both the Health and Safety at Work Act 1974 and the Equality Act 2010. Employers are required to make reasonable adjustments to the work environment or the work itself to allow employees to undertake their tasks safely.

Health and safety: important concepts

In order to fully understand and engage with the rest of this chapter, it is necessary to introduce some important key concepts related to occupational health and safety and to define these concepts for you.

Safety – the condition of being protected from or unlikely to cause danger, risk or injury. (*Oxford English Dictionary* [OED], 1989)

Health – is a state of complete physical, mental and social well-being, and not merely the absence of disease or infirmity. (WHO, 1946: 100)

Accident – an unfortunate incident that happens unexpectedly and unintentionally, typically resulting in damage or injury. (OED, 1989)

Hazard – anything that may cause harm. (Health & Safety Executive [HSE], 2006, 3)

Risk – is the chance (big or small) of harm being done, as well as how serious that harm could be. (HSE, 2006: 3)

Job design and occupational health and safety

Unintentional injuries and adverse effects on health can arise as a result of an individual's interaction with their work; and in such a context, work refers to the task and the working environment in which the task is completed. An early model of human-workplace interaction was proposed by Smith and Sainfort (1989) (Figure 7.1) and this model addresses those aspects which we define as 'human factors'. Human factors can be defined as 'the environmental, organisational and job factors, and human and individual characteristics which influence behaviour at work in a way which can affect health and safety' (HSE, 2009, p5.). In other words, they refer to three interrelated aspects: the job, the individual and the organisation, and it has been recognised for some time that a careful consideration of these interrelated aspects can reduce the number of accidents, injuries and cases of occupational ill health. Smith and Sainfort's model introduces five components of human-workplace interaction: the person; task activities; the environment; technology; tools and machinery; and the work organisation and supervision. Task factors and technology, tools and machinery fall under the human factors label 'task factors'. The 'person' refers to the human and individual characteristics and the 'environment and work organisation and supervision' can be mapped onto organisational factors. Each of these elements are discussed in more depth in Figure 7.1.

Figure 7.1   A model of occupational safety and health performance

Source: Adapted from Smith and Sainfort (1989).

- The person – individual characteristics (both physical characteristics and psychological characteristics) will affect how a person undertakes a task and how they interact with and respond to the work environment around them. Physical characteristics might include height, weight, physical strength and dexterity, while psychological characteristics include cognitive functioning and motivation levels. Competency and skill levels are also important factors. If the task demands are beyond an individual's ability due to either physical limitations, psychological limitations or skill level there will be potential for an accident.

- Task factors – refer to the specific tasks an individual is required to undertake as part of their work. The pace of work, the physical demands of such work and the type of activities undertaken (repetitive work) all fall under the umbrella of 'task factors'. If the physical demands of a particular task are too great, then human error may occur. Likewise, if the rate of work is too fast, this will also influence the probability of an accident.

- Technology, tools and machinery – are the items used to complete work-related tasks. These items can vary from being very simple to use (such as a calculator or notebook) to extremely complex (such as technologically advanced or computerised machinery) and the use of each will demand specific perceptual, cognitive and motor skills from the human operator. The design of these tools should take into consideration the abilities and limitations of human perceptual, cognitive and motor skills. Any mismatches between human ability and the design of technology tools and machinery may increase the potential for human error which in turn can lead to a subsequent accident.

- The Environment – the work environment has the potential to expose workers to a huge range of hazards, including material hazards such as chemicals and toxic agents and specific hazardous environmental conditions such as excessive noise, excessive temperatures and inadequate lighting. Poor environmental conditions can affect a worker's ability to see, hear or concentrate and this can lead to exposure to risk. For example, loud noise can prevent effective communication regarding the presence of a hazard or the transmission of instructions. Likewise, excessively high temperatures can induce fatigue and poor lighting can diminish the ability to see clearly. All such factors can increase the likelihood of an accident arising.

- Work organisation and supervision – organisational and managerial factors, such as safety culture and supervision policies, can affect an employee's behaviour at work and, as such, can influence exposure to hazards and subsequent accident risk. Safety culture has been defined as 'the product of individual and group values, attitudes, perceptions, competencies and patterns of behaviour that determine the commitment to, and the style and proficiency of, an organisation's health and safety management' (Nieva and Sorra, 2003, p18.). If the management policies do not pay sufficient regard to health and safety, such an attitude is likely to permeate throughout the organisation.

Conversely, an organisational climate with a strong management position on safety will result in employees with an equally committed regard for their own and others' safety.

Box 7.1

OP IN PRACTICE

Mind your backs: safe systems for ambulance staff

Nature of the problem

The healthcare sector is an example of a high-risk industry for musculoskeletal disorders, particularly back pain. Ambulance staff are most at risk of musculoskeletal injuries as a result of patient handling. Studies have identified that patient loading is a major risk factor for such injuries, with poor design of lifting equipment being a major cause. Jones and Hignett decided to evaluate three ambulance loading systems (easi-loader, ramp/winch and tail lift) to identify a preferred system on the basis of safety and usability.

The method

Three data collection methods were employed: field data, questionnaire and postural analysis.

In total, 378 hours of observational field data were collected over a period of several months, whereby different loading systems were observed in operation at different times of the day/night. In addition to this, interview data were collected from the ambulance staff regarding the stretcher systems in use. Observational data were analysed using hierarchical task analysis and link analysis. Data were then triangulated and summarised as a taxonomy of key design problems.

A questionnaire on the design of the loading systems was circulated electronically nationwide to ambulance staff and manufacturers. The questionnaire asked participants to rank design problems in order of their perceived importance.

Laboratory experiments were undertaken to collect postural analysis data.

Results and implications

Operator and patient safety: The study identified that patient and operator safety were regarded as the most important operational factor. The tail lift stretcher was found to perform best for this factor. Design safety problems associated with the ramp/winch included finger traps and discomfort for the patient. The easi-loader stretcher was identified as presenting the most problems for patient and operator safety, whereby operational difficulties and equipment failure were reported.

Manual handling: Risks were identified with all systems and included the weight of the stretcher (tail lift), non-use of the winch (ramp/winch) and mechanical/electrical faults.

Time factor: The easi-loader was the fastest system to operate with the ramp/winch being the slowest. This is an important factor considering the time crucial nature of patient transportation.

In conclusion, the field and experimental studies identified the tail lift as the overall preferred ambulance loading system. The tail lift reduces the risks in relation to manual handling activities and was found to be sufficiently versatile to load stretchers, carry chairs, wheelchairs and walk-in patients. Additional design improvements were suggested including simplifying operational designs.

Jones, A., and Hignett, S. (2007). 'Safe access/egress systems for emergency ambulances', *Emergency Medicine*, **24**: 200–205.

Issues of job design in the psychosocial context

A key role for organisational management is to design jobs in such a way that it enables employees to complete work safely and efficiently. Organisations may also design jobs to inspire job motivation, satisfaction and commitment. Overall, designing jobs is not an easy task and a job that is poorly designed can ultimately cause work stress and ill health. So what is job design? Slack et al. (2004) describe the different approaches to job design according to five performance objectives:

- Quality – an employee's ability to produce high-quality products and services with minimal error.
- Speed – how quickly an emergency task can be achieved will depend on the way that emergency services are organised.
- Dependability – tasks that require dependable delivery of services need to be designed to take into account all aspects of the job – from working arrangements to uniforms.
- Flexibility – being flexible in producing high volume service during certain seasonal periods, such as Christmas.
- Cost – the number of customers served per hour.

Two further objectives were identified by Slack et al. that influence job design:

- Health and safety issues – jobs need to be designed so that the health and well-being of the employee who does the job is not endangered.
- Quality of working life – issues such as employee stress level and attitude, job variety and job security need to be taken into account when designing jobs.

Further consideration of these factors is provided late in this chapter where human factors are considered from a more psychosocial aspect in relation to the design of the work environment and its impact on employee stress and well-being.

Concept of organisational behaviour

An organisation is made up of individuals who interact with each other and work toward common goals. They can be organised into groups and subgroups in order to achieve these goals. However, these individuals have different skills, abilities and responsibilities and may behave in ways which can influence organisations and the outcome of common goals. There are many definitions of organisational behaviour that range in perspective from the individual and the group in organisations, to management practice, and even to occupational stress and employee well-being. Therefore, organisational behaviour can be viewed from three different levels.

- Individual – where theories about individual behaviour can help to explain the behaviour of organisations. This includes looking at personalities, motivation, attitudes, values and learning.
- Group – looking at the way individuals interact within a group or team, and includes looking at decisions, leadership, power, conflict and politics.
- Organisational – where the structure and design of the organisation influence organisational behaviour. This includes looking at organisational culture, change and development.

As organisations today have to continually adapt in order to remain competitive and effective, there is enormous interest in how working conditions affect both worker productivity and health. For example, high-performance organisations may be effective in meeting customer demands, but conversely may have high stress levels among their employees due to poor environmental work design.

Organisational behaviour and stress

What is stress?

Stress occurs when environmental demands exceed the adaptive capabilities of the individual resulting in physiological or psychological changes (McCoy and Evans, 2005). According to Selye (1936) stress is the last general level in an individual being's reactions to every imaginable kind of strain, challenge and demand. Physiological stress reactions consist of a pattern of physical changes in the body that are activated when exposed to stressors. These stress reactions are a common occurrence that allows us to function on a daily basis (Levi, 2005). For example, normal stress reactions are what keep you on your toes while playing sport and sharpens your concentration when you are studying for an examination. However, it is when an individual's physiological reactions to stress

Table 7.1 Some signs and symptoms of stress

Physical symptoms	Emotional symptoms	Cognitive symptoms	Behavioural symptoms
• Aches and pains • Migraines • Sleep problems • Weight problems • High blood pressure • High cholesterol • Heart disease • Diarrhoea or constipation • Digestive problems • Nausea, dizziness • Allergies • Frequent colds	• Moodiness • Depression • Dissatisfaction • Anxiety • Frustration • Irritability or short temper • Feeling overwhelmed • Sense of loneliness and isolation	• Memory loss • Poor concentration • Constant worrying	• Using alcohol, cigarettes or drugs to relax • Relationship problems • Aggressiveness • Eating more or less • Sleeping too much or too little • Nervous habits (e.g. nail biting)

become frequently great (acute) and/or prolonged (chronic) that they can result in physical and/or mental tension, illnesses such as heart disease and ultimately premature death.

Table 7.1 presents some of the common signs and symptoms of stress. The more signs and symptoms an individual experiences, the more at risk they are of stress overload (although symptoms of stress can also be caused by other psychological and medical problems).

What is the difference between strain and stress?

Strain refers to:

A great or excessive pressure or demand on one's body, mind or resources. For example to be exposed to mental tension.

Stress refers to:

An individual's physiological and/or psychological reactions to excessive strain, challenge or demand.

The experience of stress can be viewed from a number of different models of stress. One of the earliest models of stress was developed by Cannon (1932). According to Cannon, the stress reaction can be stimulated by a wide variety of psychosocial stimuli that are either physiologically or emotionally threatening and disrupt the body's homeostasis. These *external* threats produce the 'fight or flight' response, increasing activity rate and arousal. These physiological changes enable the individual either to escape from the source of stress or fight. Selye (1985) also recognised that the stress response can result from a variety of different kinds of stressors. However, he focused on the *internal* aspects of stress and defined stress as 'nonspecific'. Developed in 1936, Selye's general adaptation syndrome (GAS) describes three stages in the stress process that an individual subjected to prolonged stress goes through.

- Alarm reaction – describes an increase in activity and occurs when the individual is exposed to a stressful situation. This stage is equivalent to the fight or flight response and includes the various emotional and physiological responses when confronted with a stressor.
- Resistance – is a stage of continued state of arousal which involves coping and attempts to reverse the effects of the alarm stage. If the stressful situation is prolonged, the high level of hormones during this phase may upset homeostasis potentially leading to ill health.
- Exhaustion – occurs after prolonged resistance. This is reached when the individual has been repeatedly exposed to the stressful situation and the body's energy reserves are finally exhausted and breakdown occurs.

Both Cannon's and Selye's early models of stress were presented as an automatic response to an external stressor. More recent models allow for active interaction between the individual and external stressors. Lazarus and Folkman (1984) proposed a cognitive theory of stress which addresses this interaction. According to Lazarus (1995), stress is best viewed as a relationship between an individual and his or her specific environment and not on the physiological responses. Although Lazarus acknowledged physical stressors, he argued that stress only occurs when an individual makes an appraisal in which the demands (for example, work demands) exceed his or her resources (for example, ability to cope). Lazarus defined two types of appraisal:

- Primary appraisal – the individual appraises the event as stressful/challenging, positive and controllable or irrelevant. If the event is appraised as stressful, the event is then evaluated as either a harm/loss, a threat or a challenge. A harm/loss is perceived as an injury or damage that has already taken place. A threat is considered as something that could produce harm or loss. A challenge is considered as potential for growth, mastery or some form of gain.
- Secondary appraisal – occurs after assessment of the event as a threat or a challenge. Secondary appraisals address what one can do about the situation. During secondary appraisal the individual now assesses his or her coping resources and options.

According to this 'transactional' model of stress, the way an individual appraises an event plays an important role in determining, not only the magnitude of the stress response, but also the kind of coping strategies that the individual may engage in to deal with the stress (Lazarus and Folkman, 1984). The following section discusses coping strategies in more detail.

Moderators of stress

Lazarus (1999) proposed that if a situation is not appraised as taxing or exceeding one's coping resources, then it is not likely to be experienced as stress. Differences in the conceptualisation of coping have led to a number of ways of classifying coping strategies. Lazarus and Folkman defined coping as 'constantly changing cognitive and behavioral efforts to manage specific external or internal demands' (1984: 141). Folkman and Lazarus (1980) made a distinction between problem-focused and emotion-focused coping strategies. Problem-focused strategies embrace a wide range of problem-orientated strategies that are often directed at defining the problem, generating alternative solutions, weighing them up and then acting upon them. Emotion-focused strategies are more likely to occur when an event has been appraised as stressful and where nothing can be done to modify its harm, threat or challenging environmental condition. Other researchers and experts have also identified coping strategies. For example, engagement versus disengagement coping (Carver et al., 1989) and proactive coping (Aspinwall and Taylor, 1997).

There are a number of other factors that affect coping such as personality (habitual traits). Vollrath (2001) reports that personality influences the frequency of exposure to stressors, the type of stressors experienced and the appraisals made. In a review by Carver and Connor-Smith (2010), those who are high in neuroticism are more likely to have more interpersonal stress exposure, tendencies to appraise events as highly threatening and have low coping resources (Penley and Tomaka, 2002). In contrast, extroverts and those with high conscientiousness consider perceiving events to be challenges rather than as threats and make positive appraisals of coping resources (Penley and Tomaka, 2002; Vollrath, 2001).

Stress, coping and personality type have been linked to health outcomes. Good coping strategies are associated with higher emotional well-being, functional status and adaptive health behaviours (Lazarus, 1999). Personality types such as neuroticism have been linked to stress-related maladaptive responses leading to psychological outcomes such as clinical anxiety and depression in those with high neurotiscim (Malouff et al., 2005). Conscientiousness has a consistent protective effect that is associated with lower risk for internalising or externalising problems (Malouff et al., 2005) and greater subjective well-being (Steel et al., 2008). Extroversion is also associated with greater well-being (Steel et al., 2008) and better physical health (Carver and Connor-Smith, 2010). In contrast, neuroticism is associated with poorer health and slower cardiovascular recovery from stress (Chida and Hamer, 2008).

Box 7.2

CASE STUDY: Understanding stress

Dean is a 59 year old male who lives on his own in a small cul de sac. He works night shifts in a factory. Dean likes order and on a day to day basis manages well. He does however get very upset by unplanned changes in his routine and unexpected demands on his time. Three months ago, a large family moved into the vacant house next door. The family have not kept their garden tidy and occasionally park their car outside Dean's house which has upset him. They have also been noisy on occasions while Dean has been trying to sleep. Dean has not spoken to his new neighbours directly but has written a letter to them complaining about these matters. The neighbours have not responded back but there is now friction between the two households. Since the neighbours have moved in, Dean has been experiencing sleep difficulties and headaches and he has been drinking alcohol more than usual.

- Why might Dean have reacted to his neighbours in this manner?
- What can be done to resolve the situation?
- How might a resolution improve Dean's health?
- What effect might this have on Dean's ability to work?

Overall, poor health outcomes associated with stress are complex and a result of maladaptive responses to stress and a complex set of physiological reactions (Shirom et al., 2009). There is also inter-individual variability in stress response. These are related not only to coping resources and coping effectiveness, but also socio-demographic factors (for example, gender, age, education), personality factors, social support and the actual or perceived level of control an individual has over their circumstances or environment such as the work environment.

Work stress

In simple terms, work stress can be defined as 'the adverse reaction people have to excessive pressures or other types of demand placed on them at work' (HSE, 2011b). The effect of working conditions on the employee can be considered from two broad aspects: issues of job design, such as job demands and level of job control; and design of the physical work environment.

Job design, psychosocial issues and stress

Potential issues with job design are where work conditions are created that result in, for example, too much work or too little work; tight deadlines; highly repetitive work; necessity to work fast; job insecurity and the prospect of redundancy; lack of decision making and use of judgement in the job; confusing work role; poor relationship with management and others; and lack of management support (Cooper and Marshall, 1976; Cox, 1993). Working conditions can also affect work-life balance not only in terms of long working hours, but the spillover of negative work experiences into home life (Cooper and Marshall, 1976). Exposure to stressful conditions at work can adversely affect employee physical health and emotional well-being. However, it is important to remember that workplace stressors do not function in isolation from each other, and that their interactive effects on health and well-being may be cumulative (O'Driscoll and Brough, 2010). Some of the most important factors are examined in more detail below.

- Work demands – there are broadly three types of work demands that can influence health and well-being: physical (loading heavy goods into trucks); cognitive (making more telephone calls); and emotional demands (being in charge of looking after terminally ill patients). Work demands refers to either having work that cannot be completed in the time available (that is, too much work and not enough time) (Kahn, 1980) or when employees do not have the necessary skills or resources to complete the task regardless of how much time they have (French and Caplan, 1973). Work demands can give rise to a number of symptoms of stress, including negative health behaviours (and coping strategies) such as drinking and smoking (Kjeerheim et al., 1997); psychological outcomes such as depression and anxiety and burnout (Hakanen et al., 2008), work-related behaviours such as poor job performance, dissatisfaction with work and absenteeism from work (Jex and Crossley, 2005; Oeji et al., 2006) and, finally, physical symptoms and health outcomes such as hypertension and cardiovascular heart disease (Karasek and Theorell, 1990) and musculoskeletal disorders (Halford and Cohen, 2003). Much of the work on the effects of work demands has been carried out around the job demand-control (DC) model by Karasek (1979), which was later expanded to the job demand-control-support (DCS) model (Johnson and Hall, 1988) (see below).

- Job role – there are three types of role stressors: role overload; role ambiguity; and role conflict. Role overload is similar to the notion of work demands and refers to the number of different roles an employee has to fulfil at the same time (O'Driscoll and Brough, 2010). Role ambiguity refers to the lack of clarity or information over what an employee's job entails in terms of its role or functions (Beehr, 1976). Role conflict is defined as when incompatible or conflicting job demands are made, causing confusion as to what the job entails. For example, when an employee is asked to carry out work that is not part of the job description. Role ambiguity and role conflict have been linked to work stress and psychological strain (O'Driscoll and Beehr, 1994). Role conflict has also been linked to job dissatisfaction and higher anxiety levels (Arnold, 2005). Conflict between work and family roles has also received much attention and evidence suggests that work-to-family conflict as well as family-to-work conflict can have an effect on psychological distress and poor physical health (Frone, 2003). Aspects of job role are discussed further below, as part of Hackman and Oldham's (1976, 1980) job characteristics model (JCM).

- Working hours – work schedules are an important part of job design and include what time an employee starts, the hours they work per day or per week, and the pattern of work hours (for example, shift work, flexible hours and overtime). Both shift work (such as rotating shifts, compressed workweeks and irregular hours) and long working hours have been linked to a number of negative health and well-being outcomes (Martens et al., 1999; Sparks et al., (2001). They have also been connected to cardiovascular heart disease (White and Beswick, 2003) and cancer (Hansen, 2001).
- Job control – refers to the freedom an employee has in deciding how to meet the demands of the job or how to perform the tasks (Karasek and Theorell, 1990). It can also refer to having control over other aspects of the job, such as when to start and finish work and having input into the functioning of the workplace. Employees with little or no control over work are reported to experience high levels of psychological strain (Spector, 2009). This is because lack of control creates feelings of incompetence leading to a reduction in emotional well-being. Research also suggests that having control over one's work can help minimise psychological distress experienced as a result of work stressors such as role ambiguity (Beehr, 1976). Therefore, control plays an important role in the job stress process, and the importance of having control over one's work is outlined in both in Hackman and Oldham's (1980) JCM and Karasek's DC model (see below).
- Social support – workplace social support refers to 'overall levels of helpful social interaction available on the job from both co-workers and supervisors' (Karasek and Theorell, 1990: 69). Different sources of support (for example, colleagues and family) and types of support (for example, emotional and informational) have been linked to reducing the impact of workplace stressors but, in some cases, it can also strengthen the relationship between the stressor and the strain instead of weakening it (Beehr and Glazer, 2005). The role of social support is discussed further below as part of the DCS model.

There are a number of job design/job stress theories that help us to understand how work can have a psychosocial impact on the individual and how this can directly or indirectly influence health outcomes. Some of these models are briefly discussed below.

Job characteristics model

Hackman and Oldham's (1976, 1980) JCM explains that there are different effects on worker behaviour from various aspects of jobs. It is based on the idea that the job

Box 7.3

OP IN PRACTICE

Is being a good organisational citizen causing you stress?

Nature of the problem

Individual initiative, a type of organisational citizenship behaviour, relates to employees who voluntarily engage in task-related behaviours that are beyond what is minimally required of them, e.g. coming into work early or staying late, volunteering for projects in addition to normal task duties at a marked level of intensity. However, it has been suggested that such initiatives might lead to role overload, job stress and work-family conflict. The researchers examined whether individual initiative has more negative implications for women in terms of work-family conflict.

The method

Two surveys were mailed to 622 graduates of a university in the United States. Participants were asked to complete one survey and to give the other to their spouse / partner if appropriate. 170 completed surveys were returned. The survey measured individual initiative, role overload, job stress and work-family conflict. Data were analysed using hierarchical regression analysis.

Results and implications

As predicted, individual initiative was associated with role overload and work-family conflict. Among both men and women individual initiative and work-family conflict were associated, however this relationship was much stronger for women.

The results of this study show that 'going the extra mile' is associated with stress, over-load and work-family conflict. This suggests that engaging in citizenship behaviours night have negative implications for employees and may discourage them from going beyond the call of duty.

Bolino, M.C. and Turnley, W.H. (2005) 'The personal costs of citizenship behaviour: the relationship between individual initiative and role overlaod, job stress, and work-family conflict', *Journal of Applied Psychology*, 90: 740–8.

task itself coupled with individual characteristics is key to outcomes such as employee motivation, satisfaction and performance. Hackman and Oldham defined five core job characteristics that were critical for job design and these outcomes. They are: skill variety; task identity; task significance; autonomy; and feedback (Hackman et al., 1975). For example, Hackman et al. argued that boring and repetitive jobs suppress motivation to perform well, whereas a challenging job enhances motivation. Skill variety, autonomy and decision authority are three ways of adding challenge to a job. Job enrichment (for example, improving work processes and environments) and job rotation are the two means of adding variety and challenge. Hackman et al. identified three psychological states that an individual derived from these job characteristics: the experienced *meaningfulness of the job*; the experienced *personal responsibility*; and the *knowledge* received on work performance. Each of these psychological states coupled with certain job characteristics lead to one or more of the outcomes descried above. The JCM has been highly influential in studies of job redesign interventions and research into the model itself has supported the validity of the JCM. However, few studies have examined the psychological states, focusing instead on the direct impact of the job characteristics on the outcomes (see Mackay, 2007, for a discussion). The JCM (or JCT as it is referred to) is also discussed in Chapter 4.

Job demand–control theory

Perhaps one of the most well-known theoretical models to explain the relationship between work demands and poor emotional and physical health is Karasek's (1979) DC model. This theory puts forward four different types of jobs related to the level of job demands and job control, and the possible health and well-being outcomes associated with these (Karasek and Theorell, 1990). Figure 7.2 summarises the types of jobs that might result from different combinations of job demands and job control.

The model suggests the following:

- high job demands with low control – these types of jobs are linked to both psychological and physical strain (high-strain jobs);
- high demands with high control – these are seen as 'active' jobs and are linked to well-being, learning and personal growth;
- low demands and high control – these types of jobs are linked to low levels of job strain;

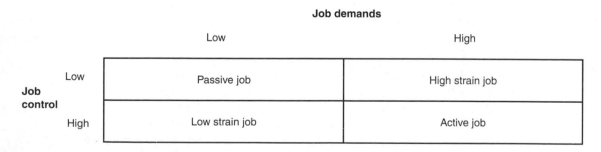

Figure 7.2 Job demand-control model
Source: After Karasek (1979).

- low demands and low control – these are seen as 'passive' jobs and are potentially linked to high levels of job strain.

Some of the evidence for these different job types and their associated health and well-being outcomes have already been mentioned above. For further discussion on whether the model is a good predictor of work stress, see De Lange et al. (2003). A third work factor, social support, was added to the model by Johnson and Hall (1988). They suggested that, like job control, social support may 'buffer' the effects of high demands – that is, high demands, low control and high support – on health and well-being. Social support is therefore viewed as an important resource for alleviating strain. Both job control and support are recognised as psychosocial work characteristics that can lead to either job strain (when faced with low control or low support), or well-being. In this sense, these characteristics are considered to be moderators (that is, alter the effects of stressors on strains) of the stress-strain relationship. Personal characteristics, such as personality, level of confidence (self-efficacy) and certain coping styles, have also been linked as moderators to the stress-strain relationship. Some of these individual characteristics and how they interact with stress have been outlined above.

Effort–reward imbalance model

The DC model is not the only model to help us understand work-related stress. Siegrist's (1996) effort-reward imbalance (ERI) model has two dimensions, effort and reward. The ERI model suggests that work-related stress can occur when an employee's perceptions of the rewards of working do not match their perceptions of the effort involved. This imbalance between effort and reward can lead to poor emotional well-being and other health problems. An advantage of this model over the job strain model (job DC theory) is its broader scope for assessing both constructs. *Effort* is evaluated by two components: *extrinsic* workload (for example, increase in workload) and *intrinsic* effort or *need for control*, which is regarded as a stable personality characteristic. Need for control is assessed by using six dimensions of coping behaviour, which are combined to form two factors: *immersion* and *vig*or. A review by van Vegchel et al. (2005) showed that the extrinsic part of the ERI model has considerable empirical support. However, certain personality characteristics such as overcommitment require more research in order to fully assess the strength and predictability of this model.

Person–environment fit theory

The person-environment (PE) fit theory also describes how work-related stress can occur when there is poor compatibility between the person and his or her environment (Caplan, 1987). This is discussed in more detail in Box 7.4 in relation to physical work environment.

Box 7.4

CASE STUDY: Activity

Jamila is a hospital-based nurse who works on a post-operative ward for the rehabilitation of the elderly. Jamila works full-time and rotates between 12-hour day and night shifts. Recently Jamila has found her work quite difficult. There has been an organisational re-structure and her responsibilities have increased as a result. Recurrent staff shortages and budget constraints have meant additional duties have had to be shared among the remaining staff team. For example, previously Jamila was responsible for between 4–6 patients, whereas now she has 8 patients and on night shift she has additional responsi-bilities for other wards. Her additional duties include auditing of care plans and medica-tion errors, falls and near misses. She has received no training on how to undertake these. Jamila feels that these additional administrative duties undermine her nursing skills and she is finding it difficult to manage both roles. On top of this, managing patients' expectations and conversing with distressed family members is taking its toll on Jamila. Despite raising these issues with the ward manager, no alterations have been made to her responsibilities and no additional support or training has been offered.

• How would each of the models of job stress – job characteristics, job demand-control and effort-reward imbalance – describe Jamila's current work situation?

Design of the physical work environment

The design of physical work environments takes into consideration elements that enable organisations to operate optimally but also comfortably and safely. These include designing ambient conditions (for example, lighting, acoustics, ventilation and thermal comfort) and spatial organisation (for example, level of enclosed space and density of work stations in an office). The effects of environmental design on health and performance of workers can be positive and optimise per-formance by supporting the needs and requirements of workers by, for example, stimulating thinking and group communication (McCoy and Evans, 2005). However, when the physical environment is designed in such a way that it inter-feres with tasks taken toward achievement (for example, densely packed worksta-tions, poor lighting), it compromises not only performance and organisational success (Becker and Steele, 1995), but also stress and well-being.

There are a number of theoretical models of work stress that consider the physical work environment as a factor. A key theoretical model is the concept of PE fit, which is defined as the level of compatibility between the person and his or her environment (Caplan, 1987). PE fit is a multi-dimensional concept and various types of PE fit have been defined including person-organisation fit and person-job fit. However, to understand the importance of the physical work environment on employee stress, PE can be defined as the match between differ-ent environmental demands and the skills and abilities of the person (Edwards and Harrison, 1993). This approach is from an environmental psychology and ergonomics perspective. For example, the extent to which a worker's ergonomically designed workstation environment, or demand, complements the worker's individual physical and psychological characteristics, or abilities (Miles and Perrewé, 2011). In this context, a misfit between the person and the environment leads to psychological, physiological and behavior strains (Caplan, 1987), limit motivation and performance and impede social interaction (McCoy and Evans, 2005). For instance, the following outcomes have been reported for employees working in noisy conditions: impaired performance of complex tasks (Broadbent, 1971); symptoms of physiological stress (Lercher et al., 1993); lower job motivation (Evans and Stecker, 2004); and reduced job satisfaction (Sundrom et al., 1994).

Environmental comfort is another theoretical model that states workspace either supports the tasks and activities that are being performed there (comfort condition), or it fails to support them and in fact slows them down (uncomfortable condition) and causes stress' (Vischer, 2007: 181). Vischer (2005) describes three hierarchical comfort categories within this model:

- Physical comfort – includes basic needs such as safety and hygiene and which are met through building and other regulations.
- Functional comfort – defined as 'ergonomic support for user's performance of work-related tasks and activities' (Vischer, 2007: 179). It includes ergonomic furniture for office users and visual comfort such as adequate lighting to perform tasks.
- Psychological comfort – includes feeling in control over workspace, having a sense of belonging and ownership and having control over one's privacy (Kupritz, 2000; Steele, 1986; Vischer; 2007).

McCoy and Evans (2005) suggest that lack of control over one's physical work environment has negative consequences for motivation and well-being, which can ultimately lead to symptoms of stress and depression. They suggest that environmental stressors should not be examined in isolation but in conjunction with the psychosocial work environment as the nature of work tasks, level of autonomy and work load demands are likely to be moderators of the effect of physical working conditions on stress (Evans et al., 1994). For further discussion on whether the PE fit model and its moderators are a good predictor of work stress, see Kristoff-Brown et al. (2005) for a review.

Designing workplaces to promote good health and well-being

The risk management approach

Both physical risks and psychosocial risks to health, safety and well-being require risk management. Over the past 40 years, the major shift in UK legislation has been away from prescriptive regulations, which dictate specific approaches to health and safety in the work environment, towards a more proactive and empowering approach involving the management of health and safety through the control of safety and health hazards. Risk management in occupational health therefore offers a systematic, proactive, evidence-based problem solving approach to eliminating hazards within the work environment. It marks a step away from a focus on hard technical failures towards a managerial responsibility for health and safety involving hazard identification, risk reduction and management.

The Management of Health and Safety at Work Regulations 1999 stipulate specific preventative measures for the effective management of health and safety at work. Every UK workplace is required to carry out a risk assessment in order to identify, assess and manage all major work-related risks. A risk assessment is therefore a careful consideration of the major risks to individuals which may arise through the course of work activities. Employers do not have to eliminate all risks from the work environment, but there is a requirement to protect individuals *as far as is reasonably practicable*. This means identifying potential hazards within the workplace (anything with the potential to cause harm) and implementing measures to control the risks presented by such hazards. The HSE have published guidance on risk assessment and this offers a five-step practical approach (HSE, 2011a) outlined in Box 7.5.

Box 7.5

How to: five steps to risk assessment

1 Identify the hazards

E.g. check obvious hazards, check accident and ill-health records to identify other hazards

2 Decide who might be harmed and how

E.g. identify groups of people by certain job type

3 Evaluate the risks and decide on precaution

E.g. examine current hazard or risk control, decide on other precautions and how to implement them

4 Record findings and implement them

E.g. write down results from risk assessment and action plan

5 Review risk assessment and update if necessary

E.g. review action plan and ensure completion; assess emerging risks

(HSE, 2011a)

Box 7.6

Activity

Think about a workplace with which you are familiar. This maybe where you have worked part-time or where a member of your family currently works. Try and identify at least three hazards (*a hazard is anything that may cause harm*) within that particular work environment. Consider who might be a risk of injury or ill health as a result of each hazard and think about any control measures that are in place to protect individuals from such harm. Are there any other control measures that you think might be necessary?

The five-step approach is a straightforward way of taking the necessary steps as required by law. This is not the only way to undertake a risk assessment though; in some cases more complex quantitative procedures are adopted, particularly in work situations where hazards are more serious, such as within the nuclear industry. However, for the majority of UK work environments, this five-step approach provides a convenient and practical guide to risk assessment and management.

A working example of guidance and a risk assessment is reproduced in the Appendix. This is not the complete document but is an extract and it is reproduced here by kind permission of E-on (UK).

Managing and reducing psychosocial risks at work

Many workplace surveys report a high prevalence of stress at work that is significantly affecting not only employee health and well-being, but also work productivity, sickness absence and turnover. A number of strategies have been adopted by organisations to help to reduce stress levels and employees cope with tensions of stress. These strategies take the form of stress preventions and intervention and can be defined in terms of primary, secondary and tertiary level interventions. Primary interventions are those that target job redesigns such as giving employees more autonomy in their job and participation in decision making. It also includes making structural changes in organisational processes and policies. This type of strategy is considered to be beneficial to all employees as it is targeted at the organisational level. It is also considered to be the most preventative and therefore, the most effective (Cartwright and Cooper, 2005). Secondary and tertiary interventions are aimed at the individual levels with secondary strategies involving stress management programmes to help employees extend their personal resources so that they can cope more effectively with the stress experienced. These strategies are usually targeted at high-risk groups. Tertiary interventions are targeted at employees who have already developed stress-related health problems, and strategies here include counselling and employee assistance programmes, and rehabilitation for those who have returned to work following sick leave due to work stress. These levels of interventions are discussed in more detail below.

Implementing primary interventions

Primary interventions are aimed at changing work practices. By using methods such as employee survey data and organisational data on productivity and sickness absence, organisations can identify the problems affecting group(s) of employees and then implement changes that benefit all employees at the group or organisational level. There are two broad types of primary intervention: those that are aimed at socio-technical changes; and those aimed at psychosocial intervention (Parkes and Sparkes, 1998). Socio-technical changes involve objective changes to the work, such as reducing work tasks and changing or improving work equipment. Psychosocial changes are aimed at changing aspects of work that employees perceive to be an issue, such as perceived level of job control and perceptions of role ambiguity and social support. Making changes to the design, organisation and management of work can be a lengthy but rewarding process and both managers and employees are involved in the intervention design. If managed correctly, primary interventions do not have to be expensive or disruptive to the organisation (Randall and Nielsen, 2010). Primary interventions can take a while to work and to be effective because it takes a while for employees to adjust to the new working practices. However, Semmer (2003) reports that such interventions are effective in the medium to long term because they deal with the problems that put employees' health at risk. There are many examples of primary-level interventions. One such example is the psychosocial risk management approach by Cox and colleagues (Cox, 1993; Cox, Griffiths and Rial-González, 2000; Cox, Griffiths, Barlow, et al., 2000). Based on the five step risk management approach highlighted above, Cox and colleagues typically outline seven steps in their psychosocial risk management approach (Cox, Griffiths and Rial-González, 2000):

1 identification of hazards;
2 assessment of related risk;
3 design of interventions that are reasonable and practical;
4 implementation of control strategies;
5 monitoring and evaluation of effectiveness of control strategies;

6 feedback and reassessment of risk;
7 review of information needs, and training needs of employees.

There are a number of international examples of the psychosocial risk management approach such as the one above. This is because for many countries the psychosocial risk management represents a legal requirement (see European Framework for Psychosocial Risk Management [PRIMA-EF]).

Implementing secondary interventions

Secondary interventions focus on training employees to respond differently to difficult work situations by training them to think and/or behave differently (Randall and Nielsen, 2010). The most popular type of secondary intervention is stress management training (SMT), which varies considerably in terms of the activities that can be offered to employees to help them manage stress effectively. These might include the following:

- Cognitive behavioural therapy training – based on Beck's (1995) cognitive therapy, the main aim of this technique is to enable employees to become aware of their stress-related emotions and/or negative thoughts (for example, anger, guilt, helplessness) and to reduce stress by changing the way an employee perceives sources of stress.
- Relaxation and meditation techniques – these are quite popular in SMT and are designed to help employees cope better with the consequences of stress by encouraging deep muscle relaxation (by using stretching or breathing techniques). Biofeedback methods are often used in conjunction with relaxation methods – these involve measurement of physiological reactions to stress, such as heart rate, blood pressure and galvanic skin responses (that is, sweating) to inform individuals of their effectiveness to reduce stress (Giga et al., 2003).
- Exercise – research suggests that exercise plays an important role in improving health and stress resilience. Exercise releases endorphins which relieve symptoms of depression, anger and aggression (Brill and Cooper, 1993). It also helps to release energy and strengthens the body to withstand high levels of stress.
- Job-related skills training – includes courses in assertiveness, time management and training to carry out core components of the job (Randall and Nielsen, 2010), and appear to appear to be relatively effective strategies (Richardson and Rothstein, 2008).
- Multimodal approaches – includes a combination of approaches rather than one single approach to manage stress.

Implementing tertiary interventions

Interventions at the tertiary level typically involve the provision of counselling or referral to specialist support services and treatment in the form of employee assistance programmes (EAPs). EAPs can offer a number of different services such as the provision of confidential assessment, counselling and therapeutic services for employees experiencing a wide range of personal, emotional and psychological problems. Some EAPs also offer advice and information on a range of issues that go beyond work-related stress, such as domestic, legal and financial matters. Other tertiary interventions may include workplace health promotion. For further reading on EAPs, see Chapter 5.

The effectiveness of interventions

A number of systematic reviews (a systematic method of identifying and critically assessing a number of studies on the same problem) and meta-analytic studies (a systematic method that uses statistical techniques for combining results from different studies to obtain a quantitative estimate of the overall effect of a particular intervention) have been conducted to evaluate the effectiveness of some of the interventions outlined above. In a meta-analysis of primary and secondary interventions, Richardson and Rothstein (2008) examined interventions that fitted one of the following categories: cognitive-behavioural, relaxation, organisational, multimodal or alternative. Within the studies they examined, they found that relaxation interventions were most frequently used, and organisational interventions were scarce. When reviewing the effect sizes of the interventions, they found that cognitive-behavioural programmes consistently produced larger effects than other types of interventions. However, if other treatment components were added the effect was reduced. A similar finding was reported by Seymour and Grove (2005) in their systematic review on workplace interventions for those with common mental health problems.

In the same review by Seymour and Grove (2005), limited evidence for the effectiveness of exercise either as prevention or cure for stress-related mental health problems in the workplace was found. However, in a meta-analysis for workplace physical activity interventions, Conn et al. (2009) reported a moderate effect size between physical activity interventions and job stress. Nonetheless, effects on most variables were substantially varied because diverse studies (for example, type of physical activity) were included. Support for workplace health promotion programmes as being effective comes from a systematic review by Kuoppala et al. (2008) who report that, overall, there is moderate evidence that workplace health promotion (for example, exercise and promoting healthy lifestyle) decreases sickness absences (an indicator of work stress) and increases mental well-being.

Box 7.7

OP IN PRACTICE

Intervention for work-related stress

The brief:

A national manufacturing company has noticed an increase in a number of employees seeking treatment for musculoskeletal pain; and the number of employees taking short term (1 or 2 days) sickness absence has almost doubled in some work teams in the past six months. The company have recently completed their annual psychosocial risk assessment, following the best practice guidelines as outlined by the Health and Safety Executive. In addition, they have also carried out their own survey to identify further risks. The findings are summarised below.

Four hazards identified from risk assessment:

- High work load
- Stringent timing control (e.g. how quickly employees worked on production line)
- Little task variety
- Poor line manager support

Findings from survey data:

Questionnaires sent to 600 workers and 554 completed questionnaires were received by the occupational health and safety unit.
    Average age of sample = 52 years, range = 16 to 62.
    Gender = 35% female.
    The participants reported the following:

- Higher levels of mental strain
- Higher levels of job-related-anxiety
- Lower levels of job satisfaction
- Higher levels of health complaints (e.g. back pain, hypertension etc.).

    As mentioned above, the company also had high sickness absence and high number of employees seeking treatment for musculoskeletal pain.

- Based on the findings above, what type of intervention(s) would be suitable for managing hazards, stress and health problems within this company?
- How would you go about implementing these?
- How would you design a study to measure whether your intervention(s) have been effective or not?

There are few systematic reviews or meta-analytic studies examining organisational-level interventions. This is because organisational interventions are quite complex to design and, in certain situations, difficult to implement a control group. In a systematic review by Egan et al. (2008), four organisational-level implementations of interventions were reviewed: employee participation; changing job tasks; shift changes; and compressed working weeks. In many of the studies, the researchers found poor reporting of how the interventions were implemented, making it difficult to evaluate their effectiveness. Much better techniques are required in reporting these types of interventions before any firm conclusions can be drawn as to their effectiveness.

Summary

This chapter introduced some of the key concepts in the design of the work environment and the effect this may have on safety, health and well-being. It is evident that the design of the work environment and work itself for health, safety and well-being is complex and influenced by a number of factors, such as the tools, technology and machinery used, the work tasks, human-workplace interaction and group behaviour and dynamics. These are further complicated by human error and individual differences such as personality, perceptions and proneness to stress. Making workplaces safe by minimising the risks of work to health and well-being is not only underpinned by legislation, but also good practice by organisations who offer a range of primary, secondary and tertiary interventions. In times of economic hardship, when organisations are faced with downsizing or restructuring, it is even more important that organisations are aware of the risk of uncertainty to employee safety, health and well-being. This chapter offers a starting point to students' understanding of the concepts and the complexities surrounding work, safety, health and well-being.

The book now continues the focus on interventions, moving from the perspective of health and well-being, to an exploration of the psychological concepts of change and organisational development.

Explore further

- De Lange, A.H., Taris, T.W., Kompier, M.A.J., Houtman, I.L.D. and Bongers, P. M. (2003) '"The very best of the millennium": longitudinal research and the demand-control-(support) model', *Journal of Occupational Health Psychology*, 8 (4): 282–305.
- DeJoy, D.D.M. (2005) 'Behavior change versus culture change: divergent approaches to managing workplace safety', *Safety Science*, 43: 105–29.

- Hult, C. (2005) 'Organisational commitment and person environment fit in six western countries', *Organisation Studies*, 26 (2): 249–70.
- Lazarus, R.S. and Folkman, S. (1984) *Stress, Appraisal, and Coping*. New York: Springer.
- Leka, S. and Houdmont, J. (2010) *Occupational Health Psychology*. Chichester: Wiley-Blackwell.
- Miles, A.K. and Perrewé, P.L. (2011) 'The relationship between person-environment fit, control, and strain: the the role of ergonomic work design and training', *Journal of Applied Social Psychology*, 41 (4): 729–72.
- Norman, J. (2002) *The Design of Everyday Things*. New York: Basic Books.
- Stranks, J. (2005) *Health and Safety Law*, 5th edn. Harlow: Pearson Education.
- Verhofstadt, E., De Witte, H. and Omey, E. (2009) 'Demand, control and its relationship with job mobility among young workers', *Economic and Industrial Democracy*, 30 (2): 266–93.
- Health and Safety Executive – http://www.hse.gov.uk
- Health and Safety Executive (Stress Management Standards) – http://www.hse.gov.uk/stress/standards/index.htm

Discussion questions

1 Has a specific situation or event caused you stress? What specific result or action have you taken because of the stressful event (either emotionally or physically)?
2 What are the long-term consequences if a stressful situation is not dealt with? List all possible consequences that are evidence-based.

Sample essay questions

1 Critically evaluate aspects of job design that can contribute to work stress.
2 Critically discuss the evidence for secondary interventions in reducing work-related ill-health.

Sample examination questions

1 Outline the key legislations that is important when considering the design of work and work environments.
2 Using a case study approach, describe in detail how an organisation can carry out the five risk assessment steps as outlined by the Health and Safety Executive.

OP IN PRACTICE: A DAY IN THE LIFE OF ...

Professor Ivan Robertson, Director of Robertson Cooper Ltd and Professor of Organisational Psychology, Leeds University Business School

What areas of OP do you work within?	My own work focuses on psychological well-being, leadership and performance in organisations. The starting point for most of the work I get involved in is the fact that high levels of psychological well-being in a workforce are associated with high levels of performance for the individuals and their organisations – psychological well-being is also important in everyone's overall health and happiness.
How did you become interested in this area?	In the first 25 years or so of my career I was particularly interested in personality and individual differences – and that was the topic of my doctoral research. My interest in those areas led me towards research in personnel selection and assessment. I wanted to understand the individual difference factors that were associated with success in specific jobs and occupational areas.
	All of my research was focused on finding ways of matching people to jobs more effectively – and hence ensuring better levels of performance. I began to get interested in the impact that assessment and selection decisions had on candidates. In doing this work I began to see the very significant impact that assessment and selection processes were having, not just on people's career progression but also on their health and well-being. I got more and more interested in understanding how people could be both successful – and psychologically healthy at work. Instead of being focused only on performance I started to focus on combining high performance with high well-being.
	In 1999 Professor Cary Cooper and I co-founded a company (Robertson Cooper Ltd) that specialises in helping organisations to perform at their best while staying healthy.
What have been the seminal research papers in this area?	The demands, control, support models of occupational stress (Karasek, 1979 and Karasek and Theorell, 1990) laid the groundwork for all of the later research attempting to understand the workplace factors that are important for positive psychological well-being. The work of positive psychologists (for example, Fredrickson's broaden and build theory; Fredrickson, 2001) has helped to change the landscape and reinforced a growing emphasis on positive psychological well-being as a platform for flourishing individuals and organisations – as opposed to merely the absence of stress. Empirical research demonstrating the important role that psychological well-being plays in individual health and happiness (for example, Kuper and Marmot, 2003; Lyubomirsky, King and Diener, 2005) and in organisational success (for example, Harter, Schmidt and Keyes, 2003). My latest book with Cary Cooper (Robertson and Cooper, 2011) provides a summary of research and practice in this area.
What has been the major academic development in this area?	The most significant research findings in this area relate to the establishment of the key workplace factors that influence the psychological well-being of people at work. These findings have been formalised, for example, in the Health and Safety Executive's Management Standards. The research underlying the development of these areas has provided the platform for a range of reports giving advice and guidance on well-being at work (for example, The UK government's Foresight report, Foresight, 2009). It also provides the basis for the ASSET model (Johnson, 2009), which my colleagues and I use extensively in our work with clients.

To what extent does the practical application of your work inform your research?	The practical application of my work often provides data and ideas for research. For example (with colleagues) I have recently published a research article that focuses on the extent to which psychological well-being enhances the role that employee engagement plays in productivity. All of the data for this came from surveys that were done directly to meet client needs. One of the things that I believe in very strongly is that it is healthy for the profession to minimise the barriers between research, practice and teaching in Occupational Psychology.
What role do ethics have in your work?	Ethical issues are so central to the work of Occupational Psychologists that they are embedded in our everyday work. Maintaining the confidentiality of individual data, trying to ensure that organisations tackle human behaviour issues in an ethical and professional way, recognising the boundaries and limitations of one's own professional competence – and many other ethically loaded issues – are part and parcel of the everyday work of a practising Occupational Psychologist.
Can you give an example of a day in your working life?	A typical day will usually involve a mixture of activities and tasks, reflecting my hybrid role as a researcher, teacher and practitioner. Although I usually earmark at least one day a week for research or teaching activities, it is rare for any single day to be spent exclusively on one part of my role or another. The exception to this is when I need to allocate a day to writing or preparing a presentation. This could involve a whole day spent working on a report for a client, writing part of a research article for a journal, working on a book chapter, or preparing a lecture for the university or a presentation for a conference of some kind.
How has your work changed in the last five years?	I think that the main changes have been the increased interest across all sectors of the economy in all of the issues that relate to well-being at work. It seems to be an area that is beginning to capture the attention of everyone who is interested in the workplace.
How do you see your work changing over the next five years?	For me personally, I'm hoping to work a little less and play a little more – but I guess that's not what the question is really about! I expect to see more research emerging that will demonstrate the benefits of improved psychological well-being at work – and I also expect to see more tools, approaches and interventions developed that draw on this research and help people and organisations to be more successful and psychologically healthy.

OP IN PRACTICE: A DAY IN THE LIFE OF	
Emma Donaldson-Feilder, Independent Practitioner, Director of Affinity Health at Work	
What areas of OP do you work within?	Health, well-being and engagement in the workplace, which naturally leads to management and leadership, job design, organisational development, team working, coaching and individual development, learning and development, employee relations and motivation.

(Continued)

(Continued)

How did you become interested in this area?	Having spent 12 years working in a range of organisations prior to becoming an OP, I saw the impact of work on people (including me). I could see, and experienced first hand, what a difference these factors made to individuals' health, well-being and engagement – and thereby to their performance at work. When I changed career to become an OP, I was clear that I wanted to focus on health, well-being and related topics, and I have followed that path ever since.
What kinds of organisations are interested in your work and why?	Our work at Affinity Health at Work is relevant to all kinds of organisations. That said, it is probably mainly the larger organisations that have the resources to do proactive work around health and well-being.
How is your work informed by theory, literature and research?	My aim is that everything I do should be underpinned by theory, literature and research – as well as the evidence I have gathered through my own experience. I have always said that I conduct research in order to ensure that my practice is truly evidence-based, but I am a practitioner in order to ensure that the research I do is very practically focused and relevant in practice.
What role do ethics have in your day-to-day practice?	Ethics are essential to my practice. I feel a high standard of integrity is one of our key differentiators. This would include issues such as maintaining confidentiality, transparency, doing what you say you are going to do, getting informed consent where appropriate, consultation and participation of individuals on issues that concern them, and integrity in all dealings with clients, individuals, organisations, colleagues … everybody. It would also mean engaging in reflective practice.
Can you give an example of a day in your working life?	I work from an office in my home, but I am often out and about at clients' offices or other locations. If at home I will be: – Writing a report – for example, on a survey conducted for a client organisation – Developing practical toolkits and guidance – for example, based on the research we have conducted at Affinity Health at Work – Conducting telephone interviews – for example, to understand what organisations are doing on health and well-being and track progress over time, in order to develop a report or practical guidance – Reviewing and editing reports developed by others – Putting together proposals for research or consultancy – Writing papers, articles, book chapters – Participating in conference calls with clients or for the various working groups and committees of which I am part – Planning and scheduling – And, of course, dealing with hundreds of emails and other administration (including running the finances for a Ltd Co, including VAT returns, end of year accounts, etc., etc.)

	If I'm out and about I will be: – Attending meetings with clients and potential clients – Conducting coaching sessions – Conducting supervision sessions – particularly for coaching psychologists, but also for other OP work – Conducting interviews and focus groups – Running training and workshops – Facilitating team-building or other group sessions – Lecturing and presenting – Meeting with colleagues to discuss new or existing pieces of work – research, consultancy, writing and so on – Attending Continuing Professional Development
How has your work changed in the last five years?	My initial work involved lots of learning and development interventions. I have moved away from this into conducting research and providing consultancy, together with a certain amount of presenting, lecturing and writing.
How do you see your work changing over the next five years?	I hope to increase the amount of coaching and coach supervision I do. I would also like to move more into providing advice on Government policy around workplace health, well-being and engagement.

References

Arnold, J. (2005) *Work Psychology: Understanding Human Behaviour in the Workplace,* 4th edn. Harlow: Person Education.

Aspinwall, L.G. and Taylor, S.E. (1997) 'A stitch in time: self-regulation and proactive coping', *Psychological Bulletin*, 121: 417–36.

Beck, J.S. (1995) *Cognitive Therapies: Basics and Beyond.* New York: Guilford.

Becker, F. and Steele, F. (1995) *Workplace by Design.* San Francisco, CA: Jossey-Bass.

Beehr, T.A. (1976) 'Perceived situational moderators of the relationship between subjective role ambiguity and role strain', *Journal of Applied Psychology*, 61: 35–40.

Beehr, T.A. and Glazer, S. (2005) 'Organisational role stress', in J. Barling, E.K. Kelloway and M.R. Frone (eds), *Handbook of Work Stress.* London: Sage. pp. 7–33.

Brill, P.A. and Cooper, K.H. (1993) 'Physical exercise and mental health', *National Forum*, 73 (1): 39–49.

Broadbent, D.E. (1971) *Decision and Stress.* London: Academic Press.

Cannon, W.B. (1932) *The Wisdom of the Body.* New York: W.W. Norton & Co.

Caplan, R.D. (1987) 'Person-environment fit theory and organisations: commensurate dimensions, time perspectives, and mechanisms', *Journal of Vocational Behavior*, 31: 248–67.

Cartwright, S. and Cooper. C. (2005) 'Individually targeted interventions', in J. Barling, E.K. Kelloway and M.R. Frone (eds), *Handbook of Work Stress.* London: Sage. pp. 607–22.

Carver, C.S. and Connor-Smith, J. (2010) 'Personality and coping', *Annual Review of Psychology*, 61: 679–704.

Carver, C.S., Scheier, M.F. and Weintraub, J.K. (1989) 'Assessing coping strategies: a theoretically based approach', *Journal Personality and Social Psychology* , 56: 267–83.

Chida, Y. and Hamer, M. (2008) 'Chronic psychosocial factors and acute physiological responses to laboratory induced stress in healthy populations: a quantitative review of 30 years of investigations', *Psychological Bulletin*, 134: 829–85.

Conn, V.S., Hafdahl, A.R., Cooper, P.S., Brown, L.M. and Lusk, S.L. (2009) 'Meta-analysis of workplace physical activity interventions', *American Journal of Preventive Medicine*, 37: 330–9.

Cooper, C.L. and Marshall, J. (1976) 'Occupational sources of stress: a review of the literature relating to coronary heart disease and mental ill-health', *Journal of Occupational Psychology*, 49: 11–28.

Cox, T. (1993) *Stress Research and Stress Management: Putting Theory to Work.* Sudbury: Health and Safety Executive.

Cox, T., Griffiths, A., Barlow, C., Randall, R., Thomson, L. and Rial-González, E. (2000) *Organisational Interventions for Work Stress: A Risk Management Approach.* Sudbury: HSE Books.

Cox, T., Griffiths, A. and Rial-González, E. (2000) *Research on Work-Related Stress.* European Agency for Safety and Health at Work. Luxembourg: Office for Official Publications of European Communities.

De Lange, A.H., Taris, T.W., Kompier, M.A.J., Houtman, I.L.D. and Bongers, P.M. (2003) '"The very best of the millennium": longitudinal research and the demand-control-(support) model', *Journal of Occupational Health Psychology*, 8 (4): 282–305.

Edwards, J.R. and Harrison, R. V. (1993) 'Job demands and worker health: three-dimensional re-examination of the relationship between person–environment fit and strain', *Journal of Applied Psychology*, 78: 628–48.

Egan, M., Bambra, C., Petticrew, M. and Whitehead, M. (2008) 'Reviewing evidence on complex social interventions: appraising implementation in systematic reviews of the health effects of organisational-level workplace interventions', *Journal of Epidemiology and Community Health*, 63: 4–11.

Evans, G.W. and Stecker, R. (2004) 'Motivational consequences of environmental stress', *Journal of Environmental Psychology* , 24: 143–65.

Evans, G.W., Johansson, G. and Carrere, S. (1994) 'Psychosocial factors and the physical environment: inter-relations in the workplace', in C. Cooper and I. Roberston (eds), *International Review of Industrial and Organisational Psychology*, Vol. 9. New York: Wiley.

French, J.R.P. and Caplan, R.D. (1973) 'Organisational stress and individual strain', in A.J. Marrow (ed.), *The Failure of Success.* New York: AMACOM.

Folkman, S. and Lazarus, R.S. (1980) 'An analysis of coping in a middle-aged community sample', *Journal of Health and Social Behavior*, 21: 219–39.

Frone, M.R. (2003) 'Work-family balance', in J.C. Quick and L.E. Tretrick (eds), *Handbook of Occupational Health Psychology.* Washington, DC: American Psychological Association. pp. 143–62.

Giga, S.L., Faragher, B. and Cooper, C.L. (2003) 'Identification of good practice in stress prevention/management', in J. Jordan, E. Gurr, S.I. Giga, B. Faragher and C.L. Cooper (eds), *Beacons of Excellence in Stress Prevention. Health and Safety Contract Research Report No. 133.* Sudbury: HSE Books.

Great Britain Committee on Safety and Health at Work (1972) *Report of the Committee 1970–1972. Selected Written Evidence. Chaired by Lord Robens. No. 5034.* London: HMSO.

Hackman, J.R. and Oldham, G.R. (1976) 'Motivation through the design of work: test of a theory', *Organisational Behavior and Human Performance*, 16: 250–79.

Hackman, J.R. and Oldham, G.R. (1980) *Work Redesign.* Reading, MA: Addison-Wesley.

Hackman, J.R., Oldham, G.R., Janson, R. and Purdy, K. (1975) 'A new strategy for job enrichment', *California Management Review*, 17: 57–71.

Halford, V. and Cohen, H.H. (2003) 'Technology use and psychosocial factors in the self-reporting of musculoskeletal disorder symptoms in call center workers', *Journal of Safety Research*, 34: 167–73.

Hakanen J.J., Schaufeli, W.B. and Ahola, K. (2008) 'The job demands- resources model: a three-year cross-lagged study of burnout, depression, commitment, and work engagement', *Work & Stress*, 22: 224–41.

Hansen, J. (2001) 'Increased breast cancer risk among women who work predominantly at night', *Epidemiology*, 36: 101–10.

Health and Safety Executive (HSE) (2006) *Essentials of Health and Safety at Work*, 4th edn. Sudbury: HSE Books.

Health and Safety Executive (2009) *Reducing Error and Influencing Behaviour.* Sudbury: HSE Books.

Health and Safety Executive (2011a) 'Five steps to risk assessment', leaflet INDG1163 (rev1). Sudbury: HSE Books.

Health and Safety Executive (2011b) 'What is stress?'. Available at http://www.hse.gov.uk/stress/furtheradvice/whatisstress.html (accessed 15 October 2011).

Jex, S.M. and Crossley, C.D. (2005) 'Organisational consequences', in J. Barling, E.K. Kelloway and M.R. Frone (eds), *Handbook of Work Stress.* London: Sage. pp. 575–601.

Johnson, J.V. and Hall, E.M. (1988) 'Job strain, workplace social support and cardiovascular disease: a cross-sectional study of a random sample of the Swedish working population', *American Journal of Public Health*, 78: 1336–42.

Kahn, R. (1980) 'Conflict, ambiguity, and overload: three elements in job stress', in D. Katz, R. Kahn and J. Adams (eds), *The Study of Organisations.* San Fransisco, CA: Jossey-Bass. pp. 418–28.

Karasek, R. (1979) 'Job demands, job decision latitude and mental strain: implications for job design', *Administrative Science Quarterly*, 24: 285–306.

Karasek, R. and Theorell, T. (1990) *Healthy Work: Stress, Productivity and the Reconstruction of Working Life.* New York: Basic Books.

Kjeerheim, K., Haldorsen T., Andersen A., Mykletun, R. and Aasland, O.G. (1997) Work-related stress, coping resources and heavy drinking in the restaurant business. *Work Stress*, 11: 6–16.

Kristoff-Brown, A.L., Zimmerman, R.D. and Johnson, E.C. (2005) 'Consequences of individuals' fit at work: a meta-analysis of person–job, person–organisation, person–group, and person–supervisor fit', *Personnel Psychology*, 58: 281–342.

Kuoppala, J., Lamminpää, A. and Husman, P. (2008) 'Work health promotion, job well-being, and sickness absences- a systematic review and meta-analysis', *Journal of Occupational & Environmental Medicine*, 11: 1216–27.

Kupritz, V.W. (2000) 'Privacy management at work: a conceptual model', *Journal of Architectural Planning Research*, 17: (1): 47–63.

Lazarus, R.S. (1995) 'Psychological stress in the workplace', in R. Crandall and P.L. Perrewé (eds), *Occupational Stress: A Handbook.* New York: Taylor & Francis. pp. 3–14.

Lazarus, R.S. (1999) *Stress and Emotion.* New York: Springer.

Lazarus, R.S. and Folkman, S. (1984) 'The coping process: an alternative to traditional formulations', in R.S. Lazarus and S. Folkman (eds), *Stress, Appraisal, and Coping.* New York: Springer. pp. 141–78.

Lercher, P., Hörtnagl, J. and Kofler, W.W. (1993). Work noise annoyance and blood pressure: combined effects with stressful working conditions. *International Archives of Environmental and Occupational Health*, 65: 22–8.

Levi, L. (2005) 'Spice of life or kiss of death?', in C.L. Cooper (ed.), *Handbook of Stress Medicine and Health*, 2nd edn. London: CRC Press.

Mackay, A. (2007) 'Approaches to motivation', in A. Mackay (ed.), *Motivation, Ability, and Confidence Building in People.* Oxford: Butterworth-Heineman. pp. 36–68.

Malouff, J.M., Thorsteinsson, E.B Schutte, N.S. (2005) 'The relationship between the five-factor model of personality and symptoms of clinical disorders: a meta-analysis', *Journal of Psychopathology and Behavioural Assessment*, 27: 101–14.

Martens, M.F.J., Nijhuis, F.G.N., Van Boxtel, M.P.J. and Knottnerus, J.A. (1999) 'Flexible work schedules and mental and physical health. A study of a working population with non-traditional working hours', *Journal of Organisational Behavior*, 20: 35–46.

McCoy, M. and Evans, G.W. (2005) 'Physical work environment', in J. Barling, E.K. Kelloway and M.R. Frone (eds), *Handbook of Work Stress.* Thousand Oaks, CA: Sage. pp. 219.

Miles, A.K. and Perrewé, P.L. (2011) 'The relationship between person-environment fit, control, and strain: the role of ergonomic work design and training', *Journal of Applied Social Psychology*, 41 (4): 729–72.

Nieva, V.F. and Sorra, J. (2003) 'Safety culture assessment: a tool for improving patient safety in healthcare organisations', *Quality and Safety in Health Care*, 12 (2): 17–13.

O'Driscoll, M.P. and Beehr, T.A. (1994) 'Supervisor behaviors, role stressors and uncertainty as predictors of personal outcomes for subordinates', *Journal of Organisational Behavior*, 15 (2): 141–55.

O'Driscoll, M.P. and Brough, P. (2010) 'Work organisation and health', in S. Leka and H. Houdmont (eds), *Occupational Health Psychology.* Chichester: Wiley-Blackwell. pp. 57–87.

Oeji, P., Dhondt, S. and Wiezer N. (2006) 'Conditions for low stress-risk jobs: Europe's case', *European Journal of Social Quality*, 6: 81–108.

Oxford English Dictionary (OED) (1989) Oxford: Clarendon press.

Parkes, K.R. and Sparkes, T.J. (1998) *Organisational Interventions to Reduce Work Stress: Are They Effective? A Review of the Literature.* Sudbury: HSE Books.

Penley, J.A. and Tomaka, J. (2002) 'Associations among the big five, emotional responses, and coping with acute stress', *Personality and Individual Difference*, 32: 1215–28.

Randall, R. and Nielsen K. (2010) 'Interventions to promote well-being at work', in S. Leka and J. Houdmont (eds), *Occupational Health Psychology.* Chichester: Wiley-Blackwell. pp. 88-123.

Richardson, K.M. and Rothstein, H.R. (2008) 'Effects of occupational stress management programs. A meta-analysis', *Journal of Occupational Health Psychology*, 13: 69–93.

Selye, H. (1936) A Syndrome Produced by Diverse Nocuous Agents. *Nature*, 138: 32–32.

Selye, H. (1985) The nature of stress. *Basal Facts*, 7: 3-11.

Semmer, N. (2003) 'Job stress interventions and organisation of work', in L. Tetrick and J.C. Quick (eds), *Handbook of Occupational Health Psychology*. Washington, DC: American Psychological Association. pp. 325–53.

Seymour, L. and. and Grove B. (2005) 'Workplace interventions for people with common mental health problems: evidence review and recommendations', a report for the British Occupational Health Research Foundation (BOHRF). Available at: http://www.bohrf.org.uk/downloads/cmh_rev.pd (accessed 1 November 2011).

Shirom, A., Armon, G., Berliner, S., Shapria, I. and Melamed, S. (2009) 'The effects of job strain on risk factors for cardiovascular disease', in C.L. Cooper , J. Campbell and M.J. Schabracq (eds), *International Handbook of Work and Health Psychology*, 3rd edn. Chichester: Wiley-Blackwell. pp. 49–75.

Siegrist, J. (1996) 'Adverse health effects of high effort – low reward conditions at work', *Journal of Occupational Health Psychology*, 1: 27–43.

Slack, N., Chambers, S. and Johnston, R. (2004) 'Job design and work organisation', in N. Slack, S. Chambers, and R. Johnston (eds), *Operations Management*, 4th edn. Harlow: Financial Times/Prentice Hall. pp. 233–59.

Smith, M.J. and Sainfort, P.C. (1989) 'A balance theory of job design and for stress reduction', *International Journal of Industrial Ergonomics*, 4: 67–79.

Sparks, K., Cooper, C.L., Fried, Y. and Shirom, A. (2001) 'The effects of work hours on health: a meta-analytic review', *Journal of Occupational and Organisational Psychology*, 70: 391–408.

Spector, P.E. (2009) 'The role of job control in employee health and well-being', in C. Cooper and I. Roberston (eds), *International Review of Industrial and Organisational Psychology*, Vol. 9. New York: Wiley. pp. 173–196.

Steel, P., Schmidt, J. and Shultzm, J. (2008) 'Refining the relationship between personality and subjective well-being', *Psychological Bulletin*, 134: 138–61.

Steele, F. (1986) *Making and Managing High Quality Workplaces: An isation Organisational Ecology*. New York: Teachers College Press.

Sundrom, E., Town, J., Rice, R., Osborn, D. and Brill, M. (1994) 'Office noise, satisfaction, and performance', *Environment and Behavior*, 14: 543–59.

van Vegchel, N., de Jonge, J., Bosma, H. and Schaufeli, W. (2005) 'Reviewing the effort–reward imbalance model: drawing up the balance of 45 empirical studies', *Social Science & Medicine*, 60: 1117–31.

Vischer, J.C. (2005) *Space Meets Status: Designing Workplace Performance*. Oxford: Taylor & Francis/Routledge.

Vischer, J.C. (2007) 'The effects of the physical environment on job performance: towards a theoretical model of workspace stress', *Stress and Health*, 23: 175–84.

Vollrath M. (2001) 'Personality and stress', *Scandinavian Journal of Psychology*, 42: 335–47.

White, J. and Beswick, J. (2003) *Working Long Hours (WPS/02/10)*. Sheffield: Health and Safety Laboratory.

WHO (World Health Organisation) (1946) 'Preamble to the Constitution of the World Health Organisation as adopted by the International Health Conference, New York, 19 June–22 July 1946; signed on 22 July 1946 by the representatives of 61 States (Official Records of the World Health Organisation, no. 2, p. 100) and entered into force on 7 April 1948.

Appendix

Table 7.A1   Example of a risk assessment

RISK ASSESSMENT TITLE		Court attendance					REFERENCE NUMBER
			Risk rating				Further controls if required
Hazard	Who might be harmed and how?	Existing controls	P	E	C	R	
DSE	Agents and FTL suffering muscular-skeletal disorders, eye strain and headaches All Court packs are emailed for completion and printing	Online DSE assessment and training undertaken by all Agents and FTL and all control measures fully implemented Agents are required to take regular comfort breaks when working on DSE	R	R	Se	L	None
Vehicle	Agents, FTL, members of the public involved in RTI's Poorly maintained or damaged vehicles	All fleet vehicles are serviced and MOT'd according to the manufacturers guidelines Basic vehicle checks (for example, fluid levels, lights, tyre check) carried out daily All FTL's complete check of agent's vehicle during work review Guidance and advice provided in the FDR H&S handbook GSA / PSA Training provided to Agents and FTL's	R	R	V	M	Agent's 'Monday timesheet' to be modified to include confirmation that the vehicle checks have been carried out that week Rollout of revised GSA/PSA training to all court officers
Driving	Agents, FTL's, members of the public involved in RTI's	Online Driver risk assessment process completed by all who drive on company business Driver Licence mandate completed which allows FTL's to check status of Agent's licence	R	R	V	M	Monitor weekly Tracker reports to ensure comfort breaks taken when driving long distances or for long period of time

RISK ASSESSMENT TITLE		Court attendance					REFERENCE NUMBER
Hazard	**Who might be harmed and how?**	**Existing controls**	**Risk rating**				**Further controls if required**
			P	**E**	**C**	**R**	
		FTL's observe driving behaviour during work reviews/Court visits General guidance and advice provided in the FDR H&S Handbook					Regular update of TomTom to enable better planning of journeys
Unsafe/ unfamiliar areas	Agents and FTL's	Agents predominantly work in area they are familiar with; Courts are normally secure buildings with good security GSA / PSA Training provided to provide Agents and FTL's with knowledge on things to consider and precautions to take when entering unsafe areas Always park the vehicle in an easily accessible location with a clear means of escape Agents familiarise themselves with the layout of each Court Clear instruction not to enter any area or premises the Agent considers, following on-site risk assessment, to be too unsafe	U	I	S	L/M	If an Agent is required to work in an area they are not familiar with, they must contact the Court Officer Manager or local Court Officer of that area for a briefing on any issues, risks or concerns they need to be aware of Court information data currently being pulled together Provide lockable case/storage for warrant paperwork, which should have wheels as car parks can be some distance from Court

Table 7.A2   Example of how to work out the risk rating

Step 1 – Estimate the likelihood that the consequences will occur once the individual is exposed to the hazard and select the most appropriate probability category from the Exposure Bar Line.

Almost certain	The most likely and expected result if the hazard - event takes place
Quite possible	Quite possible would not be unusual even 50/50 chance
Unusual but possible	Unusual but possible sequence or coincidence
Remotely possible	Remotely possible coincidence
Conceivable but unlikely	Has never happened after many years of exposure but is conceivably possible
Practically impossible	Practically impossible; has never happened before

Step 2 – Estimate how often an individual interacts with a hazard and select the most appropriate exposure category from the Exposure Bar Line.

Very Rare	Not known to have occurred
Rare	Occurs rarely, but has been known to occur
Infrequent	Occurs between once per month and once per year
Frequent	Occurs approximately once per day
Continuous	Occurs many times per day

Step 3 – Identify the most likely outcome of a potential accident, including injuries, property damage and/or environmental damage, and select the most appropriate consequence category from the Consequences Bar Line.

Consequence	Human	Economic
Catastrophe	Multiple fatalities	Total loss
Disaster	Fatality	Extensive financial loss (greater than £5m)
Very serious	Severe injury / permanent disability	Significant financial loss £1m–£5m)

Serious	Major injury such as broken bones	Significant financial loss (£500K–£1m)
Substantial	Lost time / medical treatment	Notable financial loss (£5K–£50K)
Minor	Minor / first aid treatment	Negligible financial loss (up to £5K)

Step 4 – On the risk rating nomagram [below], draw a line through the 'probability' on the left and the 'exposure' to the hazard, and stop at the 'tie line'.

Step 5 – Then draw a line from that point on the tie line, and through the consequences level. This should give you the risk level from the separate table. Record the risk level on the risk assessment form. Repeat for all identified hazards.

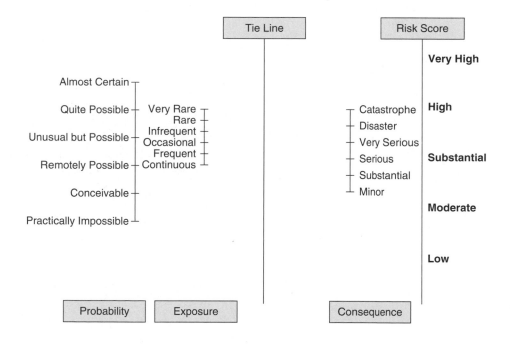

Step 6 – From the risk calculator, the following table is used to determine the priority of treatment of risks.

Score	Action
High or very high	Do something about these risks immediately
Substantial or moderate	Do something about these risks as soon as possible
Low	These risks may not need immediate attention and may be considered acceptable

NOTE: The risk assessment calculator is intended as a guide to identify level of risk. The risk scores calculated should be interpreted with caution. It should only be used as a basis for consistency of reasoned judgment.

8 Organisational development and change

Nigel Guenole and David Biggs

Learning outcomes

By the end of this chapter you will understand the following concepts:

- what makes an organisation effective;
- a systems perspective on organisations;
- types of organisational structure;
- the tendency of all organisational systems toward entropy;
- fundamental issues in organisational development and change;
- how things get done within organisational structures;
- models of organisational change;
- selection and training in support of the renewal of open systems;
- the role of Occupational Psychologists in organisational development.

Introduction

While there are many definitions of organisational development and change in academic and practitioner literatures, the definition we will adopt in this chapter is from Martins: 'Organisational development and change is the study and practice of creating or responding to differences in the states of individuals, groups, organisations, and collectives over time. Implicit in this definition is that change involves difference, as the target of change goes from one state or condition to another – for example, an individual changing from one role to another, a group changing from one decision process to another, or an organisation going from one structural arrangement to another' (2011: 692). To understand the need for organisational development and change it is necessary to understand what an effective organisation looks like, the challenges faced by people who try to keep them effective, and how these people address the challenges. We cover each of these aspects of organisational development and change in detail in this chapter.

Fundamental issues in organisational development and change

Martins (2011) suggested that there are two fundamental issues that permeate organisational development and practice. The first is the issue of whether change within organisations is best characterised as discrete episodes (for example, a planned move from one organisational structure to another) or whether it is continuous (for example, through constant staffing changes), while the second is whether or not managers in organisations have the ability to initiate change and influence its course. As we will see, the answers academics and practitioners provide to these questions have important implications for the recommendations Occupational Psychologists can provide to managers in organisations. While there is no overarching theory of organisational development that encompasses all of the positions of the different theorists and practitioners on these two fundamental issues, the *punctuated equilibrium model* (Gersick, 1988, 1989, 1991) developed from evolutional theory steers a convenient course between the extreme positions of both sides.

Change from a punctuated equilibrium perspective is, in general, characterised by slow discrete change episodes, for example, the implementation of a new performance appraisal system. From time to time, however, and usually in response to critical environmental realities, seismic shifts occur in organisations (Senior and Swailes, 2010). For example, new legislation affecting an entire industry sector may place constraints on an organisation's operating procedures. During tectonic change, managers have the ability to influence what is happening proactively. During periods of rapid environmental change, managers are generally limited to reacting to events rather than shaping their course. From the punctuated equilibrium perspective then, there are clearly times at which Occupational Psychologists, along with managers in organisations, have the ability to initiate and influence the course of change in organisations. To do so effectively, managers need to know about the change process itself, as well as strategies for the implementation of change.

A systems perspective on organisations

By referring to an organisation as a system, the idea is that an organisation is a set of interacting elements that transforms inputs from the environment into outputs for external consumption. The concept of an organisation as a system is demonstrated in Leavitt's (1965) framework of organisational effectiveness as shown in Figure 8.1. In this system, inputs from the environment are transformed by the organisation, which is comprised of the organisation's people, its structure, technology, the tasks it performs and its culture. All of these organisation's subsystems impact each other, and the goods and services they produce are consumed within the wider environment. Importantly, this representation of an organisation is an open system, because the system interacts with its environment. Most organisations have an external environment whether it is customers, shareholders, financial markets and so on. The two most relevant variations of systems theory for our purposes are socio-technical systems theory and open systems planning theory.

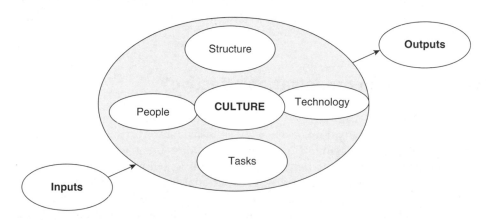

Figure 8.1   Leavitt's (1965) framework of organisational effectiveness

Socio-technical systems theory

Socio-technical systems (STS) theory proposes that each organisation is comprised of a technical system and a social system, and both must be optimised if the organisation is to function effectively. STS emerged out of a Tavistock Institute study of the British coal-mining industry. Trist (1981) wrote that the industry was not as productive as expected based on technological developments. The discovery of one mine that was functioning effectively revealed a stark contrast with the typically poor working conditions of the ineffective mines. The effective mine showed 'a set of relatively autonomous groups inter-changing roles and shifts and regulating their affairs with a minimum of supervision. Cooperation between task groups was everywhere in evidence; personal commitment was obvious, absenteeism low, accidents infrequent, productivity high' (Trist, 1981: 8). Trist suggested that this early work led to STS theory, which in contrast to the trend of increasing bureaucracy in organisational systems at the time, was characterised by design features that made work more meaningful, such as the creation of autonomous work groups functioning in a work system rather than emphasising close monitoring of employees in particular jobs.

Open systems planning

French and Bell (1995) trace open systems planning theory (OST) to work by Clark, Crone and Jayaram in the 1950s that sought to optimise the interface between organisations and their environments. French and Bell suggest that the central tenets of OST are that, for an organisation to be effective, it needs to closely study the expectations of its stakeholders, develop both likely and ideal possible future scenarios and, finally, decide action plans to achieve ideal states. They also note that a good rule of thumb for identifying the boundary between an organisation and its environment is that more interactive exchange occurs across the putative boundary than within it.

What makes an organisation effective?

Robbins and Judge (2012) suggest that indicators of organisational effectiveness include high productivity, low absence levels, satisfactory turnover, low levels of counter-productive behaviour (for example, looking busy when you are not), strong evidence of citizenship behaviour (for example, helping colleagues who are busy) and high engagement. Recently, occupational health psychologists, such as Quick and Tetrick (2002), have added well-being outcomes, such as good safety records, low grievances and an absence of violence, to these productivity related outcomes. In particular, the work of Bond and his colleagues (for example, Bond and Bunce, 2001; Bond et al., 2008) has focused extensively on organisational devel-opment and change interventions that address the health of organisations under the umbrella of organisational effectiveness.

However, the identification of measures of organisational effectiveness is dif-ficult and is typically dependent on who is consulted, there is no universal agreement on how the performance of organisations ought to be measured (DeVinney et al., 2010), or even what level of performance ought to be measured (for example, at the level of the individual, the level of the team or the level of the organisation). This is referred to as the criterion problem, or the performance paradox.

Some indication of what past scholars have considered indicators of effectiveness, however, can be ascertained by looking at the categorisation systems for performance outcomes used in meta-analyses. Meta-analyses can be thought of as quantitative summaries of independent primary studies (as described in Chapter 3). Typical cate-gories for outcome variables targeted by organisational development and change interventions from a meta-analysis by Roberts and Robertson (1992) are presented in Table 8.1.

Box 8.1

CASE STUDY: Big Pharma

In January 2012 *The Guardian* newspaper reported that pharmaceuticals companies have been working to make medicines more affordable to people in developing countries (Sarah Boseley's Global Health Blog: 'GSK's Andrew Witty on the future of pharma collaboration to help poor countries'). Quoting GSK pharmaceuticals chief executive Andrew Witty:

'There are sensible areas where we can work together for the public good, for society's good. We can still compete like crazy in other areas, but there are areas where we can work sensibly together and, guess what, there are also changes to the business model which allow us to be successful in areas which have historically been very difficult. So, e.g. you might have opening up intellectual property today – we and others are opening up more compound libraries for more research into difficult disease areas. We can be more flexible in the business model than the industry has been historically. It doesn't mean the industry can't compete but we can do things a bit differently.'

Exercise: Conduct a brief 30 minute investigation into the current state of the pharmaceuticals industry using information available in the media and internet search engines. Discuss with your colleagues whether this new approach in the pharmaceuticals industry will enhance or inhibit organisational effectiveness.

From the perspective of open systems theory, are these developments necessary in order for large pharmaceuticals firms to remain effective?

Perhaps the best advice for Occupational Psychologists grappling with the difficult issue of defining organisational effectiveness is to recognise that performance is likely to be multi-dimensional, and that performance can be

Table 8.1   Categories of outcome variables targeted by OD interventions

Quality of organisational arrangements
Quality of social factors
Quality of technology
Quality of the physical setting of work
Quality of individual behaviour
Organisational performance (e.g. profitability, turnover and absenteeism)
Individual development (e.g. health, personal development)

conceptualised across multiple levels (that is, individual, team or organisational level). Most important of all, the dimensions of performance that are considered important will very likely vary depending on who it is in the organisation you ask, so understanding the perspective of your clients is critical.

It is also important to note that all organisational development interventions attempt to *improve* organisational standing on these variables. This is consistent with the values of organisational development and change, which French and Bell (1999) noted were from the outset humanistic, democratic and optimistic, albeit with a greater focus today on productivity. The forces of time and change will inevitably render the existing organisational strategy, structure and processes ineffective, regardless of the criteria ultimately adopted for gauging effectiveness and of the level at which effectiveness is measured. Planned change efforts will therefore need to be undertaken to restore, maintain and enhance organisational effectiveness.

Different types of organisational structures

Organisational structures typically emerge out of the need to group individuals together to get work done (Senior and Swailes, 2010). For a long time, organisational structure has been thought to be related to organisational effectiveness (Capon et al., 1990; Dalton et al., 1980). In order to understand the different types of structures that organisations might take on and why certain structures might be preferable to others, it is important to understand the different dimensions on which organisational structures vary, as these can have implications for the development and change in organisations. Robbins and Judge (2012) noted that most organisational structures can be characterised by their standing on a series of six structural dimensions, and these are questions anyone establishing or restructuring needs to address. We draw on their definitions of these dimensions here.

Specialisation

How specialised or broad should the job be that each person does in the organisation? Narrow jobs are highly specialised (such as a data entry clerk), while jobs that involve a broad range of tasks are not very specialised (such as a secretary). This is an important consideration because a high degree of work specialisation can be counter-productive to employee health and productivity when work becomes too specialised (Hackman and Oldham, 1976).

Departmentalisation

The next dimension of organisational structure and design, is departmentalisation, and refers to how employees will be grouped. Employees working on similar tasks may be arranged into the same department such as marketing or procurement. This is known as functional departmentalisation, and brings advantages because employees spend time with colleagues that do similar work. Alternatively, organisations might consider organising their operations into divisions based on products (for instance, in a car manufacturer this could be divided by the model of car), geography (UK or international) and processes. Again, this is a key consideration in change interventions in terms of how well information will flow between groups and teams of workers.

Span of control

The next dimension for consideration in organisational design is to decide the ratio of managers to employees that an organisation will adopt. A structure in which few employees report to each manager is considered a narrow span of control, while a structure where many employees report to each manager reflects a wider span of control. This decision is critical, because of the impact a span of control can have on how quickly organisations can respond to changing environments. Sometimes employees can bypass layers of management, however, this may not be the correct thing to do politically.

Formalisation

If the tasks that the workers perform in an organisation are all strictly documented, this is known as high formalisation. High formalisation is more likely to be appropriate in organisational roles where there is either a certain or best way to accomplish a particular job, for instance, those working in HM Revenue & Customs or call centre staff. However, high levels of formalisation are likely to be less appropriate if an organisation requires its staff to be innovative or creative and discuss issues outside of their allotted department.

Chain of command

This dimension refers to the line of authority that begins with the leader of the organisation and proceeds through the ranks of seniority to the most junior employees. A long chain of command would indicate a very hierarchically organised structure, for instance as seen in the army or the police force. While it was once the case that each worker only had one manager to whom they were responsible, this may not be the case today, as in matrix structures employees often have more than one manager to whom they are accountable. Indeed, in consultancy firms roles are sometimes even reversed, so that an individual on a project may become the manager of their line-manager (Biggs, 2010).

Centralisation

If decisions on important issues are primarily made by a core group of senior stakeholders within an organisation, then the decision making within the organisation is considered highly centralised. Otherwise, if the decision making is more participative and involves diverse input, the level of centralisation in the organisation is considered low. High centralisation therefore would be an organisation where power is held at the top of the organisation and decision making would be top-down. As with other dimensions of organisational design, centralisation has important consequences for an organisation's ability to respond to changing operating environments.

Interestingly, organisational structure and design differ (Senior and Swailes, 2010). Structure usually occurs almost haphazardly to get the work done. Organisational design, however, is the deliberate attempt to organise the organisational structure in a rational manner. Usually this is completed by the senior management team and the way it is depicted is often like an organisational chart with a hierarchy, with them at the top controlling the employees below (Senior and Swailes, 2010).

The different configurations on the dimensions of organisational design, and the archetypal structures that the different configurations create, can be considered more *mechanistic* or more *organic* (Burns and Stalker, 1961). High levels of both formalisation and centralisation characterise mechanistic organisational structures, and low levels of formalisation and centralisation characterise organic organisational structures (Rahim et al., 2012).

Box 8.2

GROUP EXERCISE

Understanding organisational structures 1

Think about each of the following organisations and discuss in a group where you think they stand on the six dimensions of organisational structure. Answers are included on the online site.

- Your local corner shop
- British Army
- Prison Service
- Google
- McDonalds
- John Lewis

What implications do the organisational structures of these organisations have for what they do and what they can achieve?

Different configurations of these six dimensions of organisational design can also lead to different archetypal organisational structures, such as simple organisations and matrix structures:

- A simple structure is also known as a flat structure, and is characterised by having no departmentalisation, high centralisation, a wide span of control and low formalisation. These characteristics make the structure ideal for a small business due to the degree of responsiveness and accountability it creates. However, as an organisation grows the structure is highly impractical.
- A matrix structure exists where organisational roles have multiple reporting lines that cover two forms of departmentalisation. For example, an organisation might have roles where employees report to a functional manager in the marketing department, but also to a manager responsible for the development of a particular product. This allows matrix structures to capitalise on the advantages of different types of departmentalisation. However, care must be taken to ensure that the role ambiguity that matrix structures can create is managed effectively, as role ambiguity can have negative effects on performance and health. Organisations adopting team structures group individuals into interdependent social systems to perform tasks for which they have shared responsibility.

Since the 1980s new forms of organisational structures have also emerged:

- Team structures occur when organisations form work groups with full responsibility for organisational operations, and are often incorporated into bureaucracies to counter the negative effects of too much structure.
- Adhocracies are small core organisations that outsource many major business functions, giving increased flexibility and responsiveness.
- Boundaryless organisations are structures that let information flow freely within and between inter- and intra-organisational boundaries.

Box 8.3

EXERCISE

Understanding organisational structures 2

Military organisations face unique challenges when it comes to organisational design. First, the chain of command is a critical mechanism for maintaining accountability. Secondly, military personnel may often operate in environments where they do not have easy access to senior personnel.

Discuss ways in which a military organisation can preserve the structure so crucial to its effectiveness while at the same time permitting the flexibility needed to deal with constantly changing environments, where structured processes and procedures may be ineffective and unattainable.

Box 8.4

EXERCISE

Understanding organisational structures 3

Thinking once again about the six organisations in Box 8.2, do you think each of the following organisations would be better described as mechanistic or organic? Again answers are provided on the online site.

- Your local corner shop
- British Army
- Prison Service
- Google
- McDonalds
- John Lewis

Deciding on an organisational structure

The structure an organisation adopts is often evolved haphazardly, but should be determined by factors such as the predictability of its operating environment, its operational strategy, its technology and size (Visscher and Visscher-Voerman, 2010). Often in organisational design, Occupational Psychologists can think about an organisation with the senior management team from a blank piece of paper. Implementing the new structure, however, could be difficult unless politics and power are considered (Biggs, 2010). There are few certain recommendations that can be made about structures for different operating environments, strategies, technologies and sizes.

Environment

The operating environment will determine how an organisation competes. According to Dess and Beard (1984), environments vary along three dimensions: complexity, referring to the number of competing stakeholders that need to be considered; dynamism, referring to the rate of change in the organisation's operating environment; and munificence, referring to the favourability of the organisation's operating environment for continued growth. Visscher and Visscher-Voerman (2010) argued that structures should be decided on the ease with which they can handle their inherent uncertainty. Other things being equal, the more dynamic, complex and less munificent an operating environment is, the more organic organisational structure should be to handle its demands.

Strategy

This may be defined as the policies and procedures in an organisation that gives a continued competitive advantage. The two most common taxonomies of business strategies are Porter's (1980) competitive strategies and Miles and Snow's (1978) archytypes. Porter proposed that organisations could either compete by *differentiation*, developing valuable and entirely new products or services; *cost leadership*, becoming the lowest cost producer; or they could pursue a strategy of *focus* and serve a niche in the market. Miller (1986) elaborated on these strategies and suggested that differentiation can reflect genuine innovation or market led differentiation. Miles and Snow (1978) used archytypes in their taxonomy, describing organisations as either prospectors, analysers, defenders or reactors. DeSarbo et al. summarise the Miles and Snow framework as follows: 'Prospectors are technologically innovative and seek out new markets; Analysers tend to prefer a 'second-but-better' strategy; defenders are engineering-oriented and focus on maintaining a secure niche in relatively stable market segments; and Reactors lack a stable strategy and are highly responsive to short-term environmental exigencies' (2005: 47).

Box 8.5

EXERCISE

Identifying organisations with different strategies

Can you think of at least one organisation that adopts each of the different business strategies of Porter and Miles and Snow? Is it easier to classify organisations using the Porter model or the Miles and Snow typology?

Size

Blau's (1970) theory of structural differentiation is the most researched model of the relationship between organisational size and organisational structure. Blau defined larger organisations as those that have more employees. He said that differentiation referred to factors describing the complexity of the organisational structure (for example, the number of organisational levels and number of departments), and administration refers to support services needed to run the organisation. Blau's theory proposed that larger organisations would tend to be more differentiated, but that organisational size and structural differentiation should be inversely related to administration due to administrative economies of scale achievable when organisations grow. This is easy to see when comparing the simple structure typically adopted by small business owners and the bureaucratic and matrix structures often adopted by multinationals. Based on empirical longitudinal studies, Cullen et al. (1986) noted, however, that the theory does a better job of explaining the current state of an organisation than the processes that characterise changes in structure over time due to growth or declining size.

Technology

David et al. (1989) wrote that the definition of technology in organisations is elusive, but that it generally refers to the degree of routineness of work tasks, where routineness is comprised of the following dimensions: task predictability or worker familiarity with day-to-day tasks; problem analysability or the degree to which objective solutions exist to departures from typical work experience; and interdependence or how much workers rely on each other to complete work tasks. David et al. noted that it is generally accepted that when technology is routine, higher levels of performance will result from mechanistic organisational structures, while where performance is non-routine, higher organisational performance will result from organisational structures that are organic. Furthermore, at the group level, they showed that performance is better predicted by the degree of alignment between the technology and structure than by either technology or structure alone.

Environment, strategy, technology and size are essential aspects to consider in organisational design. The process of implementing this has been given attention by Visscher and Visscher-Voerman (2010). They summarised the process of organisational design as a phase type model. This ADIE (analysis, design, implementation, evaluation) model contains four steps:

1   analysis of the design problem;
2   design of a solution;
3   implementation of the solution;
4   evaluation of the effectiveness of the solution given the original problem.

Visscher and Visscher-Voerman (2010) went further to state that the approach taken in this process can be very different. This depends largely on the organisation or consultancy involved. They ascertained three approaches (rational, dialogical and pragmatic) that management could take in organisational design.

In the rational design approach, the design is seen as the construction of structural characteristics of the organisation. This concerns analysing the current design in terms of its division of labour, allocation of tasks and the mechanisms to manage them. The design process is a rational problem solving approach that follows the ADIE model. The analysis phase is possibly one of the most crucial in the rational design approach. A lot of effort goes into ascertaining the current organisation so that an effective solution can be devised, moving the organisation forward. The best solution is probably the one that completes as much as it can in terms of the original problem. Implementation then tends to be separated from the analysis and design phases. This may be typically done with the senior management team as opposed to a consultancy. The final evaluation phase ascertains the extent to which the solution met the pre-established objectives (Visscher and Visscher-Voerman, 2010).

In the dialogical approach, the design is similar to the rational approach but differs in that the political system of the organisation is prioritised over and above rational designs. The consent of the key individuals for the design and solutions put forward is seen as essential (Visscher and Visscher-Voerman, 2010). This may lead to the final design being more in line with the political features of the organisation rather than its efficiency as in the rational approach. Nevertheless, the commitment of the key figures involved in the organisational design is considered to be of greater benefit than the efficiency of the design itself. This would aid in the implementation of the design as it takes into account the politics of the organisation.

The pragmatic approach differs again from the rational and the dialogical views. In both the rational and dialogical approaches the aim is to be reductionist and simplify down the complex nature of the organisation. With the pragmatic approach this complexity is embraced and absorbed rather than simplified down. This approach tends to adopt the ADIE model all at the same time. Thus, an analysis is done through interviews, this leads to a design of a solution that is implemented and then evaluated to see if it works in the organisation. Designing and analysis are seen as interwoven events. The objective of this approach is to change the organisation rather than to set a blueprint for change from the outset. Thus, this approach is very much hands-on in terms of the implementation (Visscher and Visscher-Voerman, 2010).

Factors that affect what happens within organisational structures

Within the organisational structure that is designed, or the existing structure, there are processes through which inputs become transferred into outputs. Topics related to organisational processes that have received considerable attention, and indeed can be considered subject areas in their own-right, include: leadership; decision making and empowerment; teamwork; power and politics; and organisational culture. In the following section, these topics are addressed.

Leadership and management

Leadership and management are two distinctive concepts but ones that complement each other and are necessary for the functioning of organisations. Leadership experts since Bennis (1966) have noted that both management and leadership are important for organisational success. Kotter (1990) stated that leadership is about anticipating change and providing a vision for the future; whereas management is about planning and control. Zalesnik (1977) agreed, stating that managers are implementers of the ideas of others; they are engaged in directing people and resources in the achievement of organisational objectives, resolving differences and reaching consensuses as required to achieve this end. Leaders, conversely, are visionary; their focus is on the way the world would ideally be, rather than some-one else's conception of how it should be, and they are prepared to embrace risk in bringing their vision to reality. This view of the defining features of leadership is consistent with Katz and Khan's (1966) view, which represents the increase in influence over simply complying with organisational policies and procedures.

Some researchers in the last century believed leadership was a quality attributed to people whose success was primarily due to situational factors outside their control. They referred to a tendency of people to attribute the success of leaders to the leaders themselves, which they called 'the romance of leadership' (Meindl et al., 1985). However, the balance of evidence today is consistent with the idea that leadership is critical to organisational success. Studies of chief executive officer effectiveness across decades involving hundreds of companies from a wide range of industries (Day and Lord, 1988) point to the positive impact of strong leadership on organisational performance. Research today also converges on the conclusion that in addition to being important for organisational development, leadership is largely learned from one's experiences (De Vries et al., 2010).

Research into leadership is characterised by the period it originated from, which is important to consider, as many earlier theories of leadership re-emerge in today's workplace (that is, behavioural theories have re-emerged whereby simulations stimulate actual behaviours in assessment centres, which are then measured). Before concluding on leadership, it is essential to examine the main research areas that scholars have identified. These may be listed as trait or characteristic theories, behavioural theories, contingency theories and transformational leadership.

Trait or characteristic theories

Very early studies in leadership examined the leader themselves and their traits. The great Victorian historian Thomas Carlyle commented that history was carved by the biography of great men. This 'great man' hypothesis gave rise to the trait theory of leadership (Judge et al., 2002). Terman (1904) proposed that all members of society were both leaders and followers that would implement or imitate respectively. Scientists during this period looked at an incredible array of leadership traits such as height, personality and intelligence. Other traits examined included age, height, weight, physique, appearance, fluency of speech, intelligence, scholarship and so forth (Stogdill, 1948). Reviews of this work by Stogdill (1948) suggested that these studies did not have much luck identifying traits that reliably differentiated leaders from non-leaders.

With improvements in trait-based measures of personality, later studies found differences between leaders and non-leaders. Judge et al. (2002) used a qualitative approach initially followed by a meta-analysis of quantitative results. They found correlations with leadership for four of the big five traits including: extraversion, neuroticism, conscientiousness and openness to experience. Only agreeableness did not have a significant relation to leadership. Out of all the factors, extraversion was the most consistent correlate of leadership across their meta-analysis.

This is probably not surprising as this trait comprises factors such as social boldness and willingness to take calculated risks. The research by Judge et al. indicated support for the leader trait perspective; however, whether this is linked with success as a leader in terms of performance has not been fully explored in the literature. Certainly, by leaving out the behavioural aspects, this literature does not allow for a holistic view of the leader (Derue et al., 2011).

Behavioural theories

The lack of success with the great man hypothesis led researchers on leadership to focus on what leaders actually did, that is, leadership behaviour (Derue et al., 2011). This was promoted on the view that leaders were not necessarily born (as in the trait approach) but could be cultivated through distinctive patterns of behaviour.

Fleishman, Stogdill and colleagues embarked upon the Ohio State studies in the 1950s that measured dimensions of leadership behaviour (Fleishman and Harris, 1998). They found that there were two main behaviours that arose, namely initiating structure and consideration. Initiation of structure has a focus on providing clear direction, whereas consideration is a leadership style based around interpersonal relationships. Interestingly, more recent research reflects these two aspects of leadership behaviour. Biggs (2010) examined two firms in terms of their job analyses to create a competency framework for consultants, used by students to evaluate themselves for development into a consultancy career. One of these competencies was leadership defined as: 'The extent to which an individual takes on the responsibility for providing focus to a team and develops members of that team' (Biggs, 2010: 321). Both aspects of providing direction and subordinate development are thus essential in a leader.

Other research in this area came from McGregor's (1960) theory that there are two types of human theories X and Y. Theory X is that people are lazy and unwilling to work, whereas theory Y states the opposite, that humans want to work and govern this in a constructive way. Kurt Lewin studied this early in the 1960s using children that were led by three types of leaders: autocratic (who relied on coercion); democratic (who relied on consensus); and laissez-faire (who relied on allowing people to make up their own minds). If theory X is correct then people need autocratic leaders to tell them what to do. If theory Y is correct then people just need direction and consensus to work well. Out of these leader categories, research has persistently shown that democratic managers get the most out of their team (Luthar, 1996).

Further research has expanded on these theories. Likert (1967) expanded the notion of autocratic and democratic leadership style adding four dimensions of leadership. These included: exploitative authoritative, where fear and threats are used to direct; benevolent authoritative, where reward is used to direct effort; consultative, where rewards are used appropriately and employees have a moderate amount of influence; and participative, where the group participates and is involved in goal setting and reward. Derue et al., (2011) also examined behavioural and trait-based theories in leadership. Although behavioural theories did have a greater impact than traits (gender, intelligence and personality) on leader effectiveness, group performance, follower job satisfaction and satisfaction with leader. They suggested that both behaviours and traits need to be taken into account with leadership development.

Contingency theories

By the early 1960s, the behavioural styles theory seemed not to explain all of the results emerging in practice. This led to research examining the situational circumstances that leaders faced (Derue et al., 2011). Elaborate models of situational leadership, focusing on the leadership behaviours required in a range of situations, were developed to explain the unanticipated variability in results. The main theories coming out of this work include: leadership continuum, Fiedler's model, normative model and leader-membership exchange theory.

The leadership continuum theory was perhaps the first contingency theory proposed by Tannenbaum and Schmidt (1973). They put forward a model based on the autocratic versus democratic leader but added situational factors as a force. Basically, three forces operated: the force of the leader, the force of the subordinate workers and the force in the situation. Thus, in an organisation where an autocratic style is preferred, even though a manager may be naturally more democratic in style, it is likely that the force of the situation may adjust the leader's behaviours towards being more autocratic.

Fiedler (1967) also put forward an influential model of contingency theory stating that three factors influenced a leader's behaviour. These factors were: task structure, where work is organised by procedures and regulations; position power, the degree to which a leader can yield power either to punish or reward employees; and finally leader member relations, where a liked and respected leader will have the advantage.

On the last aspect of Fiedler's factors, the leader-member exchange (LMX) theory developed by Dansereau et al. (1975) expands this concept. This theory sees leadership as a process that occurs between individuals where leaders develop better relationships with followers. As a measure, it has developed considerably since its inception, looking at both the leaders and the subordinates' perspectives (O'Donnell et al., 2012). However, it is somewhat limited as it only examines the dyadic relationship between leader and subordinate and does not look at other relationships that may exist in the workplace (Biggs et al., in press).

Although there are other contingency theories on leadership, the ones detailed above are the principle theories in the literature. Nevertheless, they have shown limited effectiveness in predicting leadership behaviour and 'empirical support for existing contingency approaches has been weak' (Derue et al., 2011: 42). One of their main problems is the confusion of leader with manager. In the behavioural theories this was quite a precise distinction but in the contingency theories this has become blurred.

Transformational leadership

Derue et al., (2011) state that transformational leadership is important to recognise as a contemporary trend in the research. The model is sometimes referred to as a full-range leadership theory, and it encompasses three different styles: transactional leadership, transformational leadership and laissez-faire leadership. Transformational leaders engender commitment to the group through a variety of means including, and among other methods, articulating a compelling vision of where it is that you are going and understanding the individual needs of group members (Bass, 1990). It should be clear that transformational leadership encompasses and expands the domain covered by initiating structure in the behavioural studies mentioned earlier. Transactional leaders get things done by using traditional exchange relationships, for example, pay and bonuses. The final style in the full range leadership theory is laissez-faire leadership, or the abdication of the responsibility to lead. This has been found to lead to ineffective leadership more than perhaps any of the other methods mentioned so far.

Box 8.6

EXERCISE

Transformational leadership

After reading the section on transformational leadership, and using your knowledge of famous leaders from all walks of life, list two examples each of leaders who are transactional, transformational and laissez-faire in style. What is it about each of the leaders that makes you assign them to one category or another?

Recent leadership theories

Several important 'new wave' theories of leadership have emerged that also warrant attention. One such theory of leadership is *authentic leadership*. Authentic leadership is considered to be the root of all positive leadership, and emerged from a distinction researchers observed between true transformational leaders and leaders who were pseudo-transformational. Pseudo-transformational leaders are seen as having the hallmarks of good leaders but lacking the moral direction, transparency and balanced processing and decision making of true transformational, that is, authentic leaders (Avolio et al., 2009). The challenge for authentic leadership researchers is to develop good psychometric measures and show that it is something truly different to transformational leadership. In the wake of the 2007 financial crisis, ethical leadership has arisen as a research topic (Stouten et al., 2012). Ethical leaders act in the best interest of followers; they principally do not enact harm upon their followers by respecting the rights of all parties (Stouten et al., 2012). Certainly this is an area of current research. Other areas include examining emotional intelligence and even spiritual intelligence within leaders.

Decision making and psychological empowerment

Occupational Psychologists' understanding of the importance of empowerment at work emerged out of the job enrichment literature, when psychologists studied ways to overcome the negative health effects of making work too specialised. A key distinction in the empowerment literature is whether empowerment is thought of as being primarily structural or psychological. Structural empowerment refers to organisational designs (structures, procedures and policies) that support the ability of workers to have an influence over their work and the direction of the wider organisation. While structural empowerment has been defined in many different ways, empowerment-like concepts are at the heart of a number of theories of work design. A work design model, the *demands characteristics model* (Karasek, 1979), explained fully in Chapter 7, proposes that an individual's experience of stress is a function of the demands of the role and the control that they have to decide how they go about doing their jobs. Karasek said very demanding roles would not lead to stress so long as workers have high control over how they do the job. High control in Karasek's model can be likened to the notion of structural empowerment. Further, the idea of empowerment at the team level is also implicit in the conception of socio-technical systems theory (see earlier section on organisations as systems).

According to Spreitzer (1996), psychological empowerment has four dimensions: the level of control over how a worker does their job; self-efficacy or the worker's level of confidence in their ability to perform their job well; the worker's experience of the meaning in their work or the fit between the role and their values; and impact or the worker's understanding of the level of importance of their job. Empirical research suggests a link between psychological, worker motivation and subsequent performance (Chen and Klimoski, 2003), and recent meta-analytic evidence (Seibert et al., 2011) also highlights the importance of psychological empowerment for overall organisational effectiveness.

If an Occupational Psychologist helps to empower workers they are in effect giving more freedom regarding what workers do and when and how they do it. Despite the positive effects that result from empowering employees, an unavoidable consequence of empowerment then is that organisations with empowered workers are open to risks, because human decision makers under pressures of uncertainty are known to rely on decision-making shortcuts or heuristics that can lead to undesirable outcomes (Khaneman, 2011). Both the concept of empowerment and its potential consequences are important in considering organisational development and change.

Teamwork

Kurt Lewin considered group work to be the management of individuals in social contexts, as opposed to their management as individuals (Zander, 1979). This definition sounds as though it might as easily be applied to teams. While some differentiate between groups and teams, for example, by saying that groups tend to come together to exchange information to facilitate subsequent individual performance while teams have collective responsibility for performance, here we will use the terms interchangeably (Johnson and Johnson, 2009). Groups are fundamental in organisations and are an important phenomenon in organisational development and change. Different researchers have viewed groups as having different functions. Depending on your perspective, groups can be considered a cause of social behaviour, a consequence of social behaviour or the context in which social behaviour occurs. They are impacted by the physical context in which they exist, for example: other things being equal, crowding increases levels of stress; the social nature of the group's environment, for example, whether it is cooperative or competitive; and the paths and stages through which they have developed.

Box 8.7

GROUP EXERCISE

Are groups always a good idea?

While it might seem like teamwork is always a good idea, there are times when they might not be the best option. For example, when all of the knowledge required to perform a particular task resides in the mind of a single individual, it might be better to let that individual get on with the job. In pairs, brainstorm any other conditions under which you think groups might not be a good idea.

The Hawthorne Studies – a decade long study of work group practices in the early 20th century – had a strong effect on the study of groups and teams. These were carried out between 1927 and 1932, initially to see the effect of reduced lighting to conduct relay-assembly tests and bank-wiring tests (Gillespie, 1991). However, the Hawthorne legacy is that researchers interested in the workers unwittingly produced better results in the employees – an experimenter effect. Sundstrom et al. (2000) noted that these examined teams of workers in a wiring room at the Hawthorne plant at Western Electrical and illustrated the strong effect that norms can have on worker behaviour, providing the impetus for much of the research on groups and teams that would follow, along with the methods that the research would adopt. Sundstrom et al. (2000) noted several key points relevant to groups and teams that it is important to recap here. First, there are many different types of teams: management teams, service teams and production groups to name a few. Second, the criteria used to evaluate team effectiveness are extremely varied. Some are generic global measures of effectiveness as rated by managers, while others are more specific facets of performance such as productivity. Outcomes indicating the psychological health of the team have also been popular (for example, cohesion and integration). Finally, the closest psychologists have come to identifying a general environmental predictor of team effectiveness is team reward structures. The case study in Box 8.8 demonstrates how this may work in practice, whereby team based bonuses were implemented in this UK Birmingham gauge manufacturer.

> **Box 8.8**
>
> **CASE STUDY: Modifying behaviour in a Birmingham gauge manufacturer**
>
> Previously, a Birmingham gauge manufacturer had concentrated on the lower end of the gauge manufacturing market, where price was more critical than quality. Due to increasing foreign competition, the company decided to expand into more lucrative markets where the emphasis is on quality rather than price. The company had previously used piece rate payments to encourage productivity, but this had the expected effect of encouraging quantity rather than quality. The piece rate system was replaced by team pay and quality incentives.
>
> The team focus was critical as teams, rather than individuals, were involved in building the product from start to finish, and so the reward system emphasised team and task identity. Quality was weighted as being more important than quantity to ensure that products were right first time. The project was a success and ensured the longevity of the company by enabling it to exploit new quality and higher value markets.
>
> Extract from original published as Biggs, D.M. (2004) 'Modifying behaviour in a Birmingham gauge manufacturer'. *People and Organisations at Work*, Summer Edition, British Psychological Society, Leicester. ISSN 1746–4188.

Power and politics

Power may be defined as the force at one's disposal to influence others. A manager thus can make a subordinate complete a task related to their job. Politics is different to power as it often involves covert mechanisms to increase an individual's power over others (French and Raven, 1959).

Early definitions of organisational politics centred on behaviour that was self-interested and without official organisational approval (for example, workers getting what they want without going through formal channels by using personal relationships), and it was also generally considered in a negative light (Ferris et al., 1989). Today it is recognised that it is very difficult to have an organisation in which politics of some form is not played out (Ferris and Kacmar, 1992). It is thought that there can even be positive outputs from politics within organisations. For example, workplace politics can be important for securing critical resources for a work group; rumours in organisations could serve to get information about important organisational issues to decision-makers in organisations more quickly.

Ferris et al. (1989) proposed a model of organisational politics where they argued that it is workers' observation of the aforementioned self-interested behaviour and the consequences of their knowledge that was most important in explaining organisational outcomes. That is to say, it is the perceptions of office politics that really matters. This model is illustrated in Figure 8.2.

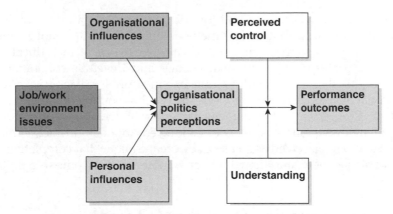

Figure 8.2   Perceptions of office politics (Ferris and Kacmar, 1992)

In Ferris et al.'s model of the perceptions of office politics, the quality of the immediate work environment is negatively related to perceptions of office politics (that is, a better work environment is perceived as free of politics). Organisational design characteristics (through the level of organisational ambiguity they create), and personal demographics directly influence one's perception of an organisational environment as being politicised. The perceived level of politics impacts outcomes, such as job involvement, work stress and efforts to avoid the work environment. The strength of the link between perceived politics and these dependent variables varied according to the worker's beliefs about their level of control over the political process and their understanding of the process. Political skill in individuals has certainly arisen as a research interest in recent years.

Organisational culture

Organisations measure dimensions of organisational climate (for example, tradition) and culture (for example, empowerment) because of the expected relationships with individual and team level performance. French and Bell (1995) suggested that organisational climate refers to the ways that people react to policies and procedures; and climate is relatively easy to change, at least as compared to organisational culture. Organisational culture they said, in contrast, refers to the shared values, beliefs and attitudes that guide what we see as right and wrong, and it is very difficult to change. While early climate and culture researchers typically used measures that focused on aspects of the work environment, such as how much autonomy a person had over their job, later research began to focus on the employees' affective reactions to these policies. While earlier research focused on linking individual level ratings of climate and culture dimensions (for example, job autonomy), in employee surveys with individual level outcomes, such as job performance, more recent research links individual level cognitive and affective responses to survey questions to both business unit and organisational level out-comes using sophisticated statistical methodologies. It is important to note that employee surveys measuring climate and culture are one of the critical ways in which the outcomes of organisational change and development initiatives are assessed. An initial survey provides a time one measure for diagnosis, after which organisational development interventions such as those outlined in this chapter are undertaken. Progress in achieving desired goals of the interventions are then assessed in follow-up surveys, usually conducted annually. In fact, climate and culture surveys are perceived as so useful by organisations that completing them is an inescapable fact of organisational life for workers at large companies today.

The need for organisational development interventions

One important tenet of both open systems planning and socio-technical systems theories is that, left alone, systems, and therefore organisations, have a tendency to decay. This tendency is often described as the process of entropy (Dover and Lawrence, 2010). While there are numerous reasons an organisation might tend towards entropy, one of the most common reasons for an organisation to deterio-rate over time is a change in its operating environment. Indeed, you might see this yourself if you follow current events such as the on-going financial crisis which began with the fall of Lehman Brothers in September 2008. Whether due to envi-ronmental change or internal change, because of this natural tendency towards entropy, the people responsible for managing organisations need to undertake planned change to both maintain and also enhance the effectiveness of the organ-isations they run (Dover and Lawrence, 2010). This is the purpose of organisa-tional development and change.

While the need for organisational development and change is clear, how best to understand the change process itself is not (Senior and Swailes, 2010). This has led to a divergence between academics developing theoretical models that practitioners have difficulty applying, and practitioners developing implementation models that academics believe are lacking in rigor. In this chapter, we will attempt to bridge this gap by adding the theoretical aspects and how practitioners have then attempted to address this through processes such as PRINCE2 and MSP (Biggs, 2010).

Different change process theorists have argued that organisational development and change has different causes and stages. According to Van de Ven and Poole (1995) there are four categories of theories about change. Each proposes a range of both generative mechanisms for change and sequences of stages of change.

1 The first model was a life cycle model of change that suggested organisations proceed through a sequence of changes that are linear and irreversible; the causal forces of such change being natural forces. Change under this model they suggested could be considered organic.

2   The second model of change was evolutionary. Change proceeded through a series of stages that was recurrent, cumulative and probabilistic. Change was necessitated under this model by the necessity of survival under conditions of competitiveness and resource scarcity.
3   The third model was dialectic change, where change proceeded through a re-occurring sequence of confrontation and resolution over conflicting values. Change was driven here by competition between opposing interests.
4   The fourth model category was teleological, where change proceeded through repeating stages of goal setting, implementation and adaptation to reach an ultimate end goal. The generating mechanism here was consensus and cooperation to reach an ideal state.

The complexity of change process theories led Porras and Robertson (1992) to suggest that consultants need elaboration of theoretical models to incorporate practical steps that they can use in actual implementation of development and change processes.

Theoretical models of organisational change and their importance

If Occupational Psychologists understand the way changes occur in human systems, they are more likely to be able to influence their course. Perhaps the most widely known and influential model of organisational change that offers such an understanding was provided by Kurt Lewin (1951). Lewin suggested the current state of any aspect of organisations is an equilibrium resulting from the interaction of opposing forces. He said that the forces maintaining an organisational equilibrium can be identified using a process he called force field analysis. Behavioural change then involves moving between equilibriums, as can be seen in Figure 8.3.

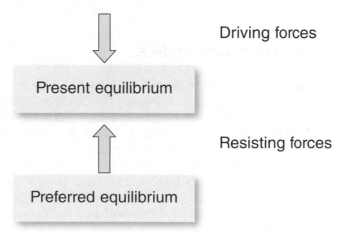

Figure 8.3   Lewin's force field model

Any change that occurs in a human system was said by Lewin (1951) to be comprised of three conceptual stages, which Schein (1987) would later elaborate by describing the psychological process in each stage.

In the first stage of the process, Lewin said that an unfreezing of the existing behaviour occurs. Schein expanded on the unfreezing phase, saying that in this stage of change people experience discomfort with the current situation, and this discomfort provides the motivation for behavioural change to occur. Lewin referred to the next stage as the moving phase. Schein (1987) describes this stage as one where people see their existing behaviour differently due to new information from social comparisons. In the third stage, which Lewin referred to as refreezing, Schein suggested that people incorporate the new information into their self-concepts. Amendments to this model have been proposed; for example, Weick and Quinn (1999) suggested that where change is continuous, change is less a process of unfreezing than it is one of shaping the direction of change already underway. Nevertheless, Lewin's model of the change process has been more influential than any other.

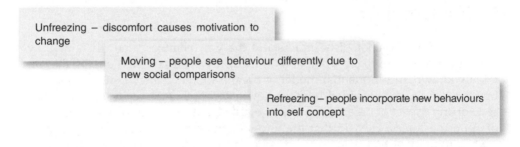

Figure 8.4   Lewin's model of the change process

Change implementation models

Lewin's (1951) model of the human change process has been very fruitful for understanding change Ven and Van de, Poole's (1995) classification of theories according to generative mechanisms and sequences adds to our theoretical understanding of change. Generally speaking, however, process theory, or the study of how and why organisational development and change occurs, has been the preserve of academics, whose work has been criticised by practitioners at times for what they see as its lack of relevance. In this section, we will address (1) how the change process leads to increased organisational effectiveness and (2) what it is that Occupational Psychologists can change in the organisations to increase effectiveness.

How the change process leads to increased organisational effectiveness

Porras (1987) and Porras and Robertson (1992) described a model of how organisational interventions impact organisations, and the model was supported by a meta-analysis from Robertson et al. (1993). This model, illustrated in Figure 8.5, shows that organisational development and change interventions impact one or other of four interdependent organisational subsystems. These interdependent systems include social factors, organising arrangements, technology and the physical setting. Because these subsystems are interdependent, any direct effects of organisational interventions on one or other of the organisational systems impacts the other subsystems. These changes to the social factors, arrangements, technology and physical setting that result from organisational change efforts then

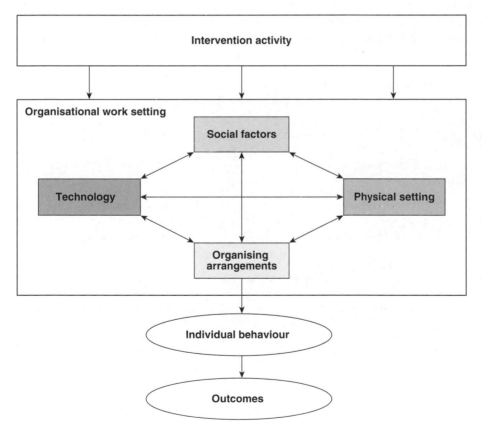

Figure 8.5 How interventions impact effectiveness
Source: Porras and Robertson (1992).

impact individual behaviour; and the changes in individuals' behaviour produce changes in outcomes, such as individual development and organisational performance. This model, in addition to having meta-analytic support, is consistent with the view that interventions, if they are to be successful, must influence how people behave on the job (Robertson et al., 1993).

Hard and soft systems model of change

Another way of examining the practicalities of organisational change has been put forward by Senior and Swailes (2010) who focus on the complexities of change. Using the Paton and McCalman (2000) TROPICS (timescales, resources, objectives, problem, interest in problem, control, source of problem) test, organisational change can be considered hard or soft (see Figure 8.6). Soft systems model of change have already been considered in Lewin's theory of organisational development (OD). These changes are characterised by having time scales ill-defined, resources uncertain, and so on (as outlined in Figure 8.4). Hard systems models of

The TROPICS factors

HARD	SOFT
Time scales clearly defined	Time scales ill-defined
Resources needed for change identified	Resources needed for change uncertain
Objectives clearly defined	Objectives unclear
Perception of problem shared by all	Problem unidentified
Interest in problem limited	Interest in problem is widespread
Control maintained by managing group	Control is shared by people external to the managing group
Source of problem within the organisation	Source of problem outside organisation

Figure 8.6   The TROPICS test
Source: Paton and McCalman (2000).

change are much better defined, since the scales are known, resources delivering the change are identified and the objectives are clearly stated.

Senior and Swailes (2010) demonstrate how a hard systems model of change can be conducted. For example, the hard systems model approach is very similar to project management systems such as PRINCE2, redesigned in 2009 by the Office of Government Commerce (Biggs, 2010). Much effort goes into the initiation of the project which is then encapsulated into a project initiation document that sets out the criteria to run the project in the implementation phase. PRINCE2 is used across the public and private sectors to run projects to great effect, but what about soft systems or OD?

Senior and Swailes (2010) demonstrate how OD may run in practice demonstrating a soft systems approach. In commercial and public sector organisations, programme management tends to be used to govern change where there are unclear objectives, timescales and control. A programme is run on a similar basis as a project but, rather than having a clear project initiation document defining the

---

Box 8.9

CASE STUDY: Clothing retailer uses MSP and PRINCE2 for simultaneous soft and hard systems change

A well known High Street retailer was becoming increasingly under threat from several external sources which included grocery stores, internet and newer high street retailers. The company was also seen as old fashioned; and it appeared to appeal only to a small section of the population.

To become more 'hip', more customer focused and more with the times, the organisation had to do something fast, but it had no idea what to do. The only thing certain was that change was needed. A programme was set up to deliver this change through three phases; however, at the outset these phases were only loosely planned.

The first phase of the programme implemented projects that were clear in their objectives, timescale and resources (hard systems change); these included projects such as improving the selection of staff and implementing systems for training were delivered by Human Resources. Other projects, such as a feasibility project of developing a grocery arm of the business, were also completed. Once this phase of the programme had been delivered, it then went on to actually change its HR processes (an outcome of this phase) and also to implement a grocery arm of the business in the next phase of the programme (as this was found to be feasible in the initial phase).

This case study demonstrates how both soft systems (the programme) and hard systems change (the projects) can run simultaneously and be managed in a complementary way.

way forward, the programme is run on a business case basis and has a far more dynamic and changeable structure. In a similar way to PRINCE2 the Office of Government Commerce has created a system to manage this, called managing successful programmes or MSP (Biggs, 2010). This system did get a revision in 2007 but has basically remained the same, governing many programmes of change. Programme management can be used where there are a number of shared issues in an organisation, where the outcome is not clear but can be resolved across a variety of projects (Lycett et al., 2004).

What do Occupational Psychologists change to improve effectiveness?

Several writers have offered useful classification systems for thinking about the types of change interventions that Occupational Psychologists might employ. Friedlander and Brown (1974), for example, proposed that there were two broad categories of organisational development and change interventions: *human processes* and *techno-structural* interventions. *Human processes* interventions included: participative decision making; goal setting/management by objectives; realistic job previews; team building; and survey feedback. *Techno-structural* interventions included job re-design; job enrichment; job enlargement; flexible working arrangements.

Neuman et al. (1989), who adopted this classification framework in their assessment of the impact of the various interventions on work attitudes, suggested techno-structural interventions tend to focus on Hackman and Oldham's (1976) job characteristics model (JCM). The JCM model is one of the most important work design models in Occupational Psychology, and states that if jobs have certain characteristics, they will induce motivational states in workers, which will subsequently lead to increased performance. The model is explained fully in Chapter 7.

Consistent with this view of what organisations change, French and Bell (1995) suggest that OD interventions typically target strategy, organisational structure, processes and/or culture. In essence, organisation improvements occur through the practice of action research. Action research may be defined as applying scientific method to practical problems. Indeed, often the unique selling point of an Occupational Psychologist is the application of research methods in an applied way. In organisational development, systematic means of gathering data are applied. This may range from interviews through to questionnaires and organisational analysis. This data then forms part of the prescribed solution that is subsequently implemented.

Appreciative inquiry is another method used by organisations and as a management consultancy tool to direct the change process. In essence, rather than listing what is wrong with the organisation and what needs to be fixed, appreciative inquiry focuses on what the organisation does well, appreciating its positives through inquiry. Questions are asked about what is going right and where are the organisation's successes (Cooperrider et al., 2003). By focusing on achievements, even on an individual basis, factors that led to those successes can be teased out, identified and repeated.

Although there are many different taxonomies of interventions that organisations change, Austin and Bartunek (2003) point out that they have in common that large group efforts are often the focus of organisational development and change interventions. This is because of a recognition, consistent with the participative ethos of organisational development and change, that the best way to get a large group of people to function in a new way is to involve them in the decision making process. Nevertheless, they also noted that today organisational development and change specialists recognise that people do not always want to participate in the change process.

Summary

In this chapter, we have covered the theoretical aspects of change but also how change may happen at a practical level. Often change may start as a programme where the final outcome, the people and the business benefit are not understood. Martins (2011) defined change as going from one state to another but how this manifests itself is difficult to determine. The work of Bond and his colleagues (Bond and Bunce, 2001; Bond et al., 2008) focused on organisational development and change interventions that improve organisational effectiveness. Improving the organisation to release business benefit is really the ultimate goal of change.

When an organisation is considered a system, it is easier to see how it may operate as a set of interacting elements that transforms inputs from the environment into outputs for external consumption. Systems thinking in organisational development has aided research to model and address issues in this area.

Organisational design is the deliberate attempt to make the organisation more effective by organising the structure in a rational manner (Senior and Swailes, 2010). Robbins and Judge (2012) noted that most organisational structures can be characterised by six dimensions: specialisation; departmentalisation; span of control; formalisation; chain of command; and centralisation. Formalisation and centralisation are evident in mechanistic organisational structures, whereas organisations without this are more organic in structure. The process of implementing organisational design has been summarised as the analysis, design, implementation, evaluation (ADIE) model (Visscher and Visscher-Voerman, 2010). A pragmatic approach to organisational design may be better than more reductionist types, as the political structure of the organisation and all its intricacies can be considered.

Topics related to organisational processes include: leadership; decision making and empowerment; teamwork; power and politics; and organisational culture. Leadership in organisational change is essential with several authors making reference to change agents who are ultimately responsible for the development of the organisation (Derue, et al., 2011). Managers and leaders are different. Most theoretical positions acknowledge this and tend to either work on the born manager (great man theories) or that individuals can learn appropriate repertoires of behaviour (behavioural theories). In the contingency theories the role of manager and leader do become rather merged but they add a situational component to previous theories, although some question whether that is relevant. More recent theories include transformational leadership and other leadership theories that have been linked to authenticity, ethics and even spirituality.

Empowerment is equally important, especially structural empowerment where the concept is woven into the very fabric of the organisation. This motivates individuals to work productively but also aids their general well-being as shown by Karasek (1979). Teamwork within organisations is vital. Measuring teamwork is fraught with difficulty. Nevertheless, research has shown that team-based bonuses and rewards motive teams to work effectively together. Power and politics were considered earlier on in the chapter within organisational design but warrant attention in their own right. The concepts are often used interchangeably in the literature but they should not be. Power is the force of being able to get someone to do your will. Politics is the covert mechanisms which can be used to increase power. In organisational change it is essential to identify both power and politics and if necessary change the eventual solution and implementation to suit all those involved. This is set in an organisational culture which also needs to be addressed in the change solution.

There exist some differences between academic and practitioner though on implementing change interventions, which have been addressed in the chapter. According to Van de Ven and Poole (1995) there are four categories of theories about change: life cycle model of change, evolutionary, dialectic change and teleological. These models are important to consider but other authors have added more practical solutions to change. Lewin (1951) proposed the force field analysis where forces driving the change were pitted against those that resisted the change. This is useful in deciding the change that needs to take place. Other authors have detailed the complexity of change in describing how it may lead to greater organisational effectiveness (Robertson et al., 1993).

The work by Barbara Senior and colleagues was considered in terms of describing change as either hard or soft systems. This relates back to the systems approach to change but in essence describes change as either certain (hard systems) or uncertain (soft systems) on Paton and McCalman's (2000) timescales, resources, objectives, problem, interest in problem, control, source of problem factors. This approach is really an attempt to integrate academic and practitioner knowledge on organisational change. Biggs (2010) explains this further by stating that in industry, hard systems change is governed by projects such as in PRINCE2 and soft system change by programmes such as MSP. The complexities of both of these systems are beyond the scope of this text; nevertheless, some insight in how they can be deployed was given.

Finally in the chapter, a few of the intervention techniques employed by Occupational Psychologists and consultants were reviewed. Hackman and Oldham's (1976) job characteristics model is highly influential even today in examining situational variables at work. Although criticised in terms of not effectively considering the individual involved, it is a remarkable piece of work and still used today to explain organisational change interventions. Action research was also considered, being the application of scientific method to practical problems. Indeed, years ago this was seen as the fundamental difference between an Occupational Psychologist and management consultant in that Occupational Psychologists had a strong awareness of research design and statistics (even though many students do not like the subject). Appreciative inquiry was also considered, whereby positives in an organisation are identified and worked on.

Explore further

- The following books are more in-depth examinations of organisational change:

Gallos, J.V. (2006) *Organisational Development*. San Francisco, CA: Wiley.
Hughes, M. (2006) *Change Management: A Critical Perspective*. London: Chartered Institute of Personnel and Development.
Senior, B. and Swailes, S. (2010) *Organisational Change*. Harlow: Pearson Education.

- For more information on examining organisations in terms of consultancy based approaches to change and also using PRINCE2 and MSP in an applied setting the following text is recommended:

Biggs, D.M. (2010) *Management Consulting: A Guide for Students*. Andover: Cengage Learning. (Chapters 4, 8 and 9.)

- Other related journal articles worth reading (all SAGE titles) include:

Ardichvili, A. and Manderscheid, S.V. (2008) 'Emerging practices in leadership development: an introduction', *Advances in Developing Human Resources*, 10 (5): 619–31.

Gilley, A., McMillan, H.S. and Gilley, J.W. (2009) 'Organisational change and characteristics of leadership effectiveness', *Journal of Leadership & Organisational Studies*, 16 (1): 38–47.

Huffman, B.J. and McCarty Kilian, C. (2012) 'The flight of the phoenix: interpersonal aspects of project management', *Journal of Management Education*, 36 (4): 568–600.

Levin, M. (2012) 'Academic integrity in action research', *Action Research*, 10 (2): 133–49.

• The Management Consultancies Association (MCA) host an award ceremony that is highly prized in the consulting field. A number of these enterprises involve organisational change. Students can investigate some of these fascinating projects directly from the MCA website that range from public to private sector work.

http://www.mca.org.uk/awards/2012/winners

• IBM in this web-link give a fascinating look at the differences between programme and project management.

http://www.ibm.com/developerworks/rational/library/4751.html

Discussion questions

1 Discuss ways in which a bureaucratic organisation might go about improving psychology empowerment
2 How might an open systems theory approach to organisational development help a large UK bank remain effective in the current economic climate?
3 Which of the factors that determine organisational structure (environment, strategy, size and technology) do you think a leader can most easily influence?

Sample essay question

1 What implications does an OD professional's view about the nature of change have for what they will expect of organisational leaders?

Sample examination question

1 What are the differences between hard models and soft models for change? Evaluate the usefulness of making such a distinction.

OP IN PRACTICE: DAY IN THE LIFE OF ...

Sarah Lewis, Managing Director at Appreciating Change	
What areas of OP do you work within?	My interest is in organisational change and development.
How did you become interested in this area?	Shortly after university I became a social worker, with children in care. Over the years I worked around the care system and it became clear that children were part of a system, and that you had to understand their behaviour in that context. My last few years in that career were spent working at a residential family centre where we attempted to influence the family system to make it safer for the children. At the same time I was involved in senior management and began to appreciate the whole organisation as an interconnected system, which spurred my interest in OD and Change.
What kinds of organisations are interested in your work and why?	Potentially all organisations since they all face the challenge of adapting to a changing world. In practice though organisations that like to work with me are those that have at least the beginnings of an appreciation of their organisation as a living human system; who understand the value of social capital in their organisation even if they couldn't define it.
How is your work informed by theory, literature and research?	Extensively. I believe that as someone who works with people to 'improve things' I am involved in a moral endeavour and must be able to justify every intervention I make. I draw particularly on social psychology, group psychology and increasingly positive psychology. In addition I studied philosophy and sociology at college and I draw on a social constructionist understanding of the world. I am very interested in working with the idea that how we talk about the world affects how we then act into the world; so I am very interested in ideas of sense and meaning making among people.

In addition to my specialist areas of interest, more 'central' psychology theory and research such as personality theory, locus of control, equity theory and so on underpin my choice of speech or action in a particular moment of intervention. |
| **What role do ethics have in your day-to-day practice?** | A clear ethical stance and understanding is very important to me in the work that I do. What I do is not a value free exercise; it is not neutral and un-impactful: I intend to have an effect and I intend for that effect to be benevolent. This means I need to know what I am evaluating my actions against, for example I must have a sense of the ethical bounds of my work. In general terms I would say that, as psychologists, we have powerful knowledge and tools at our disposal. |

(Continued)

(Continued)

	What we say and do affects people's emotional state, sense of self and identity, and their levels of motivation. In organisational terms we interfere with dynamics and relationships that people have to continue to work within after we have moved on to the next assignment. This responsibility needs to be constrained and informed by a clear ethical framework.
Can you give an example of a day in your working life?	Today I was in a meeting with some people working to plan an event at a very tricky time in the organisation's unfolding history. Great care must be taken to accommodate 'the whole system' in the room, not just the people but the many different stories of 'how it is'. Tomorrow I am working with a group of thirty people drawn from across an organisation of about 800 to focus, with an appreciative inquiry process, on building bridges between different functions to enhance organisational learning and sharing. This event is taking place within a context of the recent 'employee survey results' and, is one of a series of such events that need to be discrete yet connected and focused on the same key issues, without being duplications of each other. Last week I gave an internal presentation to an organisation as part of their annual 'learning week' for staff, and next week I'm meeting a business advisor to work on ever more ideas for marketing my services. This is not an untypical spread of activities over a few days: negotiating interventions, delivering interventions, spreading the word, and working on the business.
How has your work changed in the last five years?	I work less as an associate to others and so am more able to deliver assignments in accordance with my psychological and organisational development principles. For example, I am always able to work with an understanding of the organisation as a social and relational entity, and from a positive or appreciative perspective.
	Increasingly I am working with larger organisational groups, and with more senior leadership teams which is all very exciting. As my understanding of the impact of working with 'whole systems' grows, I am frustrated at the lessened impact of what I do when I am unable to negotiate this with an organisation.
How do you see your work changing over the next five years?	I would hope to do more of what I do currently with more challenging assignments. For example, I am very interested to get involved in the use of technology and social media to support Appreciative Inquiry informed events and processes for large geographically dispersed groups and organisations.

References

Austin, J. and Bartunek, J. (2003) Theories and practices of Organization Development. In W. Borman, D. Ilgen and R. Klimoski (eds.), Handbook of Psychology: Vol. 12, Industrial and Organizational Psychology. New York: John Wiley & Sons: 309–32.

Avolio, B., Walumba, F. and Weber, T. (2009) Leadership: Current theories, research, and future directions. *Annual Review of Psychology*, 60, 421–49.

Bass, B.M. (1990) 'From transactional to transformational leadership: learning to share the vision', *Organisational Dynamics*, 18 (3): 19–31.

Bennis, W. (1966) *Changing Organisations*. New York: McGraw-Hill.

Biggs, D.M. (2010) *Management Consulting: A Guide for Students*. London: Cengage Learning.

Biggs, D., Swailes, S. and Baker, S. (in press) The worker relations scale: a 3-component model for measuring relations at work.

Blau, P.M. (1970) 'A formal theory of differentiation in organisations', *American Sociological Review*, 35: 201–18.

Bond, F.W. and Bunce, D. (2001) 'Job control mediates change in a work reorganisation intervention for stress reduction', *Journal of Occupational Health Psychology*, 6: 290–302.

Bond, F.W., Flaxman, P. and Bunce, D. (2008) 'The influence of psychological flexibility on work redesign: mediated moderation of a work reorganisation intervention', *Journal of Applied Psychology*, 93: 645–54.

Burns, T. and Stalker, G.M. (1961) *The Management of Innovation*. Tavistock: London.

Capon, N., Farley, J.U. and Hoenig, S. (1990) 'Determinants of financial performance: a meta-analysis', *Management Science*, 36: 1143–59. (Special issue on strategy.)

Chen G. and Klimoski, R.J. (2003) 'The impact of expectations on newcomer performance in teams as mediated by work characteristics, social exchanges, and empowerment', *Academy of Management Journal*, 46 (5): 591–607.

Cooperrider, D.L., Whitney, D. and Stavros, J.M. (2003) *Appreciative Inquiry Handbook*. Bedford Heights, OH: Lakeshore Publishers.

Cullen, J.B., Anderson, K.S. and Baker, D.D. (1986) 'Blau's theory of structural differentiation revisited: a theory of structural change or scale?', *The Academy of Management Journal*, 29: 203–29.

Dalton, D.R., Todor, W.D., Spendolini, M.J., Fielding, G.J. and Porter, M. (1980) 'Organisational structure and performance: a critical review', *Academy of Management Review*, 5: 49–64.

Dansereau, F., Graen, G. and Haga, W.J. (1975) 'A vertical dyad linkage approach to leadership within formal organisations: a longitudinal investigation of the role making process', *Organisational Behavior & Human Performance*, 13 (1): 46–78.

David, F.R., Pearce, II, J.A. and Randolph, W.A. (1989) 'Linking technology and structure to enhance group performance', *Journal of Applied Psychology*, 74 (2): 233–41.

Day, D.V. and Lord, R.G. (1988) Executive leadership and organizational performance: suggestions for a new theory and methodology. Journal of Management, 14(3), 453–64.

Derue, D.S., Nahrgang, J.D., Wellman, N. and Humphrey, S.E. (2011) 'Trait and behavioral theories of leadership: an integration and meta-analytic test of their relative validity', *Personnel psychology*, 64 (1): 7–52.

DeSarbo, W.S., Di Benedetto, C.A., Song, M. and Sinha, I. (2005) 'Revisiting the miles and snow strategic framework: uncovering interrelationships between strategic types, capabilities, and firm performance', *Strategic Management Journal*, 26: 47–74.

Dess, G. and Beard, D. (1984) 'Dimensions of organisational task environments', *Administrative Science Quarterly*, 29: 52–73.

DeVinney, T., Yip, G. and Johnson, G. (2010) 'Using frontier analysis to evaluate company performance', *British Journal of Management*, 21 (4): 921–38.

De Vries, R.E., Bakker-Pieper, A. and Oostenveld, W. (2010) 'Leadership = communication? The relations of leaders' communication styles with leadership styles, knowledge sharing and leadership outcomes', *Journal of Business & Psychology*, 25 (3): 367–80.

Dover, G. and Lawrence, T.B. (2010) 'Technology, institutions, and entropy: understanding the critical and creative role of maintenance work', *Research in the Sociology of Organisations*, 29: 259–64.

Ferris, G.R. and Kacmar, K.M. (1992) 'Perceptions of organisational politics', *Journal of Management*, 18: 93–116.

Ferris, G.R, Russ G.S. and Fandt P.M., (1989) Politics in organizations. In Impression Management in the Organization, Giacolone, R.A, Rosenfeld, P. (eds). Lawrence Erlbaum: Hillsdale, NJ: 143–70.

Fleishman, E.A. and Harris, F.E. (1998) 'Patterns of leadership behavior related to employee grievances and turnover: some post hoc reflections', *Personnel Psychology*, 51 (4): 825–34.

Fiedler, F. (1967) *Theory of Leadership Effectiveness*. New York: McGraw-Hill.

French, W.L. and Bell, C.H. (1995) *Organisation Development: Behavioral Science Interventions for Organisation Improvement*. Upper Saddle Rover, NJ: Prentice Hall.

French, J.R.P., Raven, B. (1995) The bases of social power. In D. Cartwright and A. Zander. Group dynamics. New York: Harper & Row

Friedlander, F. and Brown, L.D. (1974) Organization development. *Annual Review of Psychology*, 25, 313–41.

Gersick, C.J.G. (1988) 'Time and transition in work teams: toward a new model of group development', *The Academy of Management Journal*, 31 (1): 9–41.

Gersick, C.J.G. (1989) 'Marking time: predictable transitions in task groups', *The Academy of Management Journal*, 32 (2): 274–309.

Gersick, C.J.G. (1991) 'Revolutionary change theories: a multilevel exploration of the punctuated equilibrium paradigm', *The Academy of Management Review*, 16 (1): 10–36.

Gillespie, R. (1991) *Manufacturing Knowledge: A History of the Hawthorne Experiments*. New York: Cambridge University Press.

Hackman, J.R. and Oldham, G.R. (1976) 'Motivation through the design of work: test of a theory', *Organisational Behavior and Human Performance*, 16: 250–79.

Johnson, D.W. and Johnson, F.P. (2009) *Joining Together Group Theory and Group Skills*. Upper Saddle River, NJ: Pearson.

Judge, T.A., Bono, J.E., Ilies, R. and Gerhardt, M. (2002) 'Personality and leadership: a qualitative and quantitative review', *Journal of Applied Psychology*, 87: 765–80.

Kahneman, D. (2011) *Thinking, Fast and Slow*. New York: Farrar, Straus and Giroux.

Karasek, R. (1979) 'Job demands, job decision latitude and mental strain: implications for job redesign', *Administrative Science Quarterly*, 24: 285–307.

Katz, D. and Kahn, R.L. (1966) *The Social Psychology of Organisations*. Chichester: Wiley.

Kotter, J.P. 1990, 'What Leaders Really Do'. Harvard Business Review, May-June, pp. 37–60.

Leavitt, H.J. (1965) 'Applied Organizational Change in Industry: Structural, Technological, and Humanistic Approaches,' Chapter 25, in J. March (Ed.), Handbook of Organizations, Rand McNally, Chicago, 1965, 1144–70.

Lewin, K. (1951) *Field Theory in Social Science*. New York: Harper.

Likert, R. (1967) The human organization: Its management and value, New York: McGraw-Hill

Luthar, H.K. (1996) 'Gender differences in evaluation of performance and leadership ability: autocratic vs. democratic managers', *Sex Roles*, 35 (5–6): 337–61.

Lycett , M., Rassau, A. and Danson, J. (2004) 'Programme management: a critical review', *International Journal of Project Management*, 22 (4): 289–99.

Martins, L.L. (2011) 'Organisational change and development', in S. Zedeck (ed.), *APA Handbook of Industrial and Organisational Psychology*, Vol. 3 . Washington, DC: American Psychological Association. pp. 691–728.

McGregor, D. (1960) The Human Side of Enterprise. Howard Baumgartel. Administrative Science Quarterly, 5, 3, 464–67.

Meindl, J.R., Ehrlich, S.B., and Dukerich, J.M. (1985) The romance of leadership. Administrative Science Quarterly, 30, 78–102.

Miles, R.E. and Snow, C.C. (1978) *Organisational Strategy, Structure, and Process*. New York: McGraw-Hill.

Miller, D. (1986) 'Configurations of strategy and structure: towards a synthesis', *Strategic Management Journal*, 7: 233–49.

O'Donnell, M., Yukl, G. and Taber, T. (2012) 'Leader behavior and LMX: a constructive replication', *Journal of Managerial Psychology*, 27 (2): 143–54.

Paton, R.A. and McCalman, J. (2000) *Change Management. A Guide to Effective Implementation*, London, Sage.

Porras, I. (1987) *Stream Analysis: A Powerful Way to Diagnose and Manage Organisational Change*. Reading. MA: Addison-Wesley.

Porras, I. and Robertson, P., (1992) 'Organisation development: theory, practice, and research', in M.D. Dunnette and L.M. Hough (eds), *Handbook of Industrial and Organisational Psychology*, 2nd edn, vol. 3. Palo Alto, CA: Gonsulting Psychologists Press. pp. 719–822.

Porter, M. (1980) *Competitive Strategy*. New York: Free Press.

Rahim, A., Biggs, D. and Schley D.G. (2012) 'Organisational design', Chapter in A. Rahim (ed.), *Management: Theory, Research, and Practice*. San Diego, CA: Cognello Academic Publishing.

Robbins, S. and Judge, T. (2012) *Organisational Behavior* . Prentice Hall.

Roberts, D.R. and Robertson, P.J. (1992) 'Positive-findings bias, and measuring methodological rigor, in evaluations of organisational development', *Journal of Applied Psychology*, 77: 918–25.

Robertson, P.J., Roberts, D.R. and Porras, J.I. (1993) 'Dynamics of planned organisational change: assessing empirical support for a theoretical model', *Academy of Management Journal*, 36 (3): 619–34.

Quick, J.C. and Tetrick, L.E. (2002) *Handbook of Occupational Health Psychology*. Washington, DC: APA.

Schein, E.H. (1987) *Process Consultation: Volume II Lessons for Managers and Consultants*. Reading, MA: Addison-Wesley.

Seibert, S. E., Wang, G., Courtright, S. (2011) Antecedents and Consequences of Psychological and Team Empowerment in Organizations: A Meta-analytic Review. Journal of Applied Psychology, vol 96, 2011.

Senior, B. and Swailes, S. (2010) *Organisational Change*. Harlow: Pearson Education.

Spreitzer, G.M. (1996) 'Social structural characteristics of psychological empowerment', *Academy of Management Journal*, 39 (2): 483–504.

Stogdill, R.M. (1948) 'Personal factors associated with leadership; a survey of the literature', *Journal of Psychology*, 25: 35–71.

Stouten, J., van Dijke, M. and De Cremer, D. (2012) 'Ethical leadership: an overview and future perspectives', *Journal of Personnel Psychology*, 11 (1): 1–6.

Sundstrom, E., McIntyre, M., Halfhill, T. and Richards, H. (2000) 'Work groups: from the Hawthorne studies to work teams of the 1990s and beyond', *Group Dynamics*, 4 (1): 44–67.

Tannenbaum, R. and Schmidt, W.H. (1973) 'How to choose a leadership pattern', *Harvard Business Review*, 51 (3): 162–80.

Terman, L.M. (1904) A preliminary study in the psychology and pedagogy of leadership. Pedagogical Seminary, 11, 413–51.

Trist, E. (1981) 'The evolution of socio-technical systems: a conceptual framework and an action research program', occasional paper no. 2. Ontario Quality of Working Life Center.

Van de Ven, A.H and Poole, M.S. (1995) Explaining development andchange in organizations. Academy of Management Review, 20, 510–40.

Visscher, K. and Visscher-Voerman, J.I. (2010) 'Organisational design approaches in management consulting', *Management Decision*, 48: 713–31.

Weick, K.E. and Quinn, R.E. (1999) 'Organisational change and development', *Annual Review of Psychology*, 50: 361–86.

Zalesnik, A. (1977) 'Managers and leaders: are they different?', *Harvard Business Review*, 67–74.

Zander, A. (1979) 'The psychology of group processes', *Annual Review of Psychology*, 30 (1): 417–42.

9 Selection and assessment

Anna Koczwara and Vicki Ashworth

Learning outcomes

This chapter aims to:

- provide an overview of selection and assessment processes and its impact on individuals and organisations;
- describe how selection systems exist within organisations;
- explain the role of job analysis and the methods for conducting it as part of a selection assessment process;
- understand the role of reliability and validity in choosing assessment methods;
- describe a range of commonly used assessment methods and their relative strengths and weaknesses;
- illustrate the stages required to design an organisational selection process;
- identify the key diversity and fairness concerns inherent within selection and assessment;
- consider selection and assessment from the candidate perspective;
- discuss how principles from selection can be transferred to assessment in other contexts;
- explore emerging themes in selection and assessment and their future implications.

Introduction

Selection and assessment (S&A) is the area of Occupational Psychology that focuses on the organisational need to have people in positions who either have the characteristics required for effective job performance or the capacities for learning and development. This may occur through selection into a role or through assessing the changes in a person's characteristics as a result of learning, training or development. In fact, the area of selection and assessment is arguably one of the areas where Occupational Psychologists have had the most significant impact over the last century in terms of both research and practice. We will use evidence from research and expert insights to illustrate the application of S&A principles to the workplace. Case studies will also be presented.

Practitioners and researchers contribute to selection and assessment by developing, implementing and evaluating assessment methods that help to ensure that what organisations use are robust, reliable and valid (Zibarras and Woods, 2010). Attempts to improve selection and assessment procedures reflect the underlying belief that individuals differ from one another in terms of attributes such as abilities, knowledge, skills, motivations, behaviours and personality traits. Considering then that no two people are the same and that certain characteristics increase the chance of being successful in certain roles, the aim of assessment is to identify the applicant who is the best fit for the role or who has the capacities for relevant training/development.

In Chapter 1 the history of Occupational Psychology was explored, including that of selection and assessment. Today a wide variety of assessment methods are regularly used by organisations, particularly in selection. In fact, organisations typically report spending more on selection than on any other aspect of human resource management (Schmitt and Chan, 1998).

With such extensive use, the effectiveness of S&A methods is a critical area for Occupational Psychologists to consider. This will in part depend on the organisational context in which they are being employed, but will also depend on what skills, abilities or competencies need to be measured. However, the validity of such assessments depends not only on what measurement methods are chosen and the quality of them, but also on the combination in which they are used.

It is widely recognised that the adoption of assessment methods with high predictive validity increases overall employee performance; which in turn can increase organisational outputs in terms of profit and productivity (Hunter et al., 1990). A good selection process is also beneficial to candidates since they are selected to a role for which they are suitable while providing them with an insight into what that role will entail. As such, selection research has increasingly focused on selection as a two-way process – not only focusing on how an employer chooses an employee but also how a candidate reacts to the processes and the impact this has on their decision to work there.

Selection systems in organisations

Best practice selection is an iterative process, where the selection system evolves over the course of time. Specifically, evaluation data from candidate reactions, validation studies and utility assessments (all discussed later in the chapter) can help inform improvements, such as updating the selection criteria, assessing the effectiveness of the methods used and improving how the process is implemented (Patterson and Lane, 2007). Designing selection systems within organisations should not be viewed as a 'one off' activity, but rather as a cyclical process, where evaluation and responding to changing environmental needs feeds into re-design to enhance effectiveness and efficiency.

Figure 9.1 summarises the key stages in a selection system, the foundation of which comprises a thorough job analysis, which in turn guides the choice of suitable assessment methods. Empirical validation studies are then used to monitor the reliability and validity of the process over time. These coupled with analysis of candidate reactions to the process and utility assessments can all feed into identifying areas for further review and re-design. More information about each of these stages is provided as the chapter progresses.

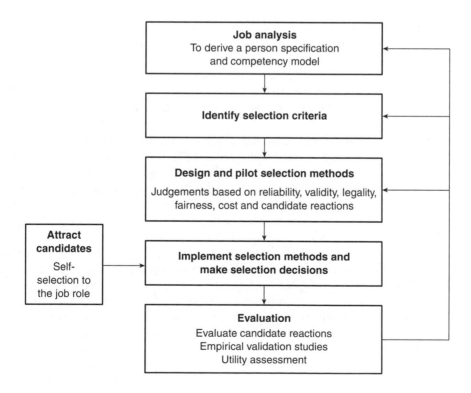

Figure 9.1   Key stages in the selection process

Source: Aadapted from Patterson and Lane (2007).

It is important to remember that selection, assessment and validation techniques will not be the same for all organisations. For example, smaller organisations may not have the resources to follow each of the key best practice stages outlined above. Effective selection is, of course, still of great concern to smaller organisations, since each employee constitutes a greater percentage of the workforce than in large organisations, therefore making mistakes more costly (Atkinson and Meager, 1994). In particular, validation can prove to be more problematic for smaller organisations since it is often difficult to examine how well an assessment method predicts performance due to small numbers recruited in a single year. Small organisations may therefore look to benchmark their selection systems against leading organisations in their field (Robertson and Smith, 2001). Where it is not possible to examine predictions of performance, ensuring the content of assessments is appropriate (that is, content validity) may be acceptable (Wyatt et al., 2010).

Selection as a predictor of job performance

Assessment methods used in selection aim to predict an applicant's suitability to the role and subsequent job performance. This is known as the 'predictivist paradigm' and assumes that 'true variance' in a candidate's behaviour can be identified by the assessment method (Anderson, 2001). However, predicting job performance is more complex than it appears. This is caused by the multidimensional nature of performance itself and the difficulties in measuring this accurately.

Performance has been conceptualised as either *typical* performance, or what an individual 'will do', or *maximal* performance, which describes what an individual 'can do' or their 'potential'. In practical terms, the assessment of maximal performance is often most useful when trying to identify suitable candidates for early career positions where they will need to develop themselves. For more senior roles where there is less need for career development and potential opportunity, a typical performance approach is favoured.

Research has shown that different types of assessment are better at predicting either typical or maximal performance. Specifically, cognitive ability/intelligence is a better predictor of maximal performance, whereas personality is a better predictor of typical performance (Marcus et al., 2007). So depending upon the aims, different assessment methods will be more appropriate; for example, in executive assessments for very senior roles, Occupational Psychologists often employ personality measures, followed up with an interview to explore the reported personality profile. This enables a better understanding of how these senior executives typically approach work and whether this is likely to be a good fit to the role.

Selection as a two-way social process

Traditionally, the sole purpose of selection processes was to fit people to the job (Derous and De Witte, 2001). However, the concept of the selection process being a *two-way process* began to develop in the late 1980s. Early research by Wanous (1980) described a two-stage matching process that occurs between the applicant and the organisation. The first match is where the organisation matches its job requirements with the individual's qualifications and the second match involves the applicant matching his or her needs with the role requirements, and the organisation's culture and values. Research by Herriot (2004) describes the selection process as a series of social interactions, during which the applicant matches their own social identities (for example, beliefs about themselves and their values) to their current perceptions of the organisation in order to make decisions about whether to stay or leave a selection process.

Research suggests that candidate perceptions of a selection process are important in the two-way social process. Candidate perceptions include the perceived fairness of the assessment methods and whether they feel that they were treated appropriately. Research has shown that candidates who have negative experiences of a selection process are less likely to re-apply for the role (Gilliland, 1993), and may openly criticise it to others, potentially limiting future applications (Truxillo et al., 2002). Moreover, candidates who felt that the process was unfair or biased may file legal complaints against the organisation (Macan et al., 1994). This, coupled with the reported 'war for talent' (in which organisations compete to attract highly skilled applicants), illustrates why candidate attraction and perceptions are now also viewed by many as integral to high quality assessment processes.

An important candidate attraction tool can be realistic job previews (RJPs), so that candidates know what to expect if they are successfully appointed and to encourage candidates to believe that this is a role they would want. RJPs a formal and intentional recruiting approach designed to communicate both the desirable and undesirable aspects of a job before an applicant has accepted a job offer. Ultimately, the purpose of the RJP is to successfully recruit and retain candidates, enhance job satisfaction and understanding, and reduce new employee turnover (Phillips, 1998). Case study 3 (Box 9.3) describes how the introduction of RJPs assisted in reducing turnover in a large financial organisation. The RJP can also clarify the psychological contract (described in Chapter 4) between an employee and the organisation, which in turn should reduce any inconsistencies between the description of the job role, and the actual experience of the candidate (Phillips, 1998).

One example of an organisation incorporating RJPs is KPMG's graduate recruitment process. A recent review by Snowdon (2011) describes how their one-hour immersive computer-delivered test assesses applicants on attributes including empathy, curiosity, judgement, creativity and decision making, by providing a timed working simulation that mimics the reality of company life. One of the main drivers for KPMG in introducing this assessment was that some of their new joiners had no clear sense of what their jobs would involve and became disillusioned soon after they arrived. Thus, the aim was to provide applicants with a realistic glimpse of the role to help shape accurate expectations of what it would entail.

The role of job analysis in selection and assessment

Job analysis is a systematic process for collecting and analysing any type of job-related information by any method for any purpose (Ash, 1988). It has been described by some as the basis for virtually all human resource activities necessary for the successful functioning of organisations (Morgeson and Campion, 1997; Oswald, 2003). Typical job analysis information comprises the responsibilities, tasks, working conditions, organisational position and knowledge, skills and abilities (KSAs) relevant to a given role (Robertson and Smith, 2001). Job analysis is most commonly used to set the foundations for an organisation's selection process, and the defensibility of selection processes against legal challenge is increased (Gutman, 2000).

Traditionally. job analyses were more work-oriented, focusing on the job itself. For example, detailing the purpose of the role the work objectives responsibilities and equipment/technology used. This assumes that the job in question is stable, that it exists and that the job tasks are measureable through either third-party observation, or self-reporting techniques. However, these assumptions are less relevant today owing to various rapid changes experienced by modern organisations, such as the rise of self-managing teams new technologv outsourcing and diversifying workforces (Burke and Cooper, 2006). These pressures on organisations have increased the need for a flexible, cross-functional workforce and have facilitated the creation of many roles for which a more flexible approach to job analysis is necessary. As such, person-orientated job analyses have become more commonplace, where the focus is on the knowledge, skills, abilities and behaviours required to perform the job successfully (Sandberg, 2000).

Methods of job analysis

Although no standard approach to job analysis exists, it is generally agreed that the process can comprise up to six stages as shown in Box 9.1.

As the 'job data collection' stage suggests, there are multiple ways to gather and analyse job information. Therefore, a best practice approach would be to gather job information from multiple sources using multiple methodologies. This multi-method approach increases the credibility and validity of the results by enabling identification of job relevant information not available from a single method. This prevents potential bias (Gatewood and Field, 2001), and helps identify similarity and overlap between the different outputs (Brumback et al., 1974). The most prominent job analysis methods are discussed below.

Box 9.1

How to: Conduct a job analysis

Stage	Description
1 Identify how JA information is to be used	This determines the type of job information required and the most suitable data collection methods.
2 Review relevant background information	Review relevant documents such as organisational charts, job descriptions and existing evaluation criteria. This assists in understanding how the role relates to other positions in the organisation.
3 Select representative positions to analyse	Identify all job positions to be analysed and select a representative sample. This is a time saving measure, useful when a number of similar jobs, e.g. assembly line workers, are to be analysed.
4 Job data collection	The actual analysis of the job can be conducted using a variety of methods, including observation, interviews and questionnaires.
5 Job data review and analysis	Data collected is then reviewed with former or current incumbents and their managers/supervisors. This ensures that the data is correct and encourages buy-in to the results.
6 Reporting	Reports are developed as required. Typically a job description and job specification are produced.

Source: Adapted from Jenkins and Curtin (2006).

Observation

This consists of observing and noting the physical activities of employees as they carry out the job in question; it provides first-hand information regarding the job responsibilities and tasks. However, this approach is time consuming, and does not provide information on the cognitive role requirements, nor can it be easily applied to newly created roles.

Interview

This approach is perhaps the most commonly used and typically involves asking job holders and their managers/supervisors questions regarding the responsibilities, tasks, working conditions, organisational position and KSAs relevant to the role in an individual or group setting. Interviews are advantageous as they allow for direct input from relevant individuals, and can also enable a future-focused approach. However, it is a time-consuming process and depends on the skill of the interviewer. Also, some interviewees may distort the information, for example, by exaggerating their roles if they are distrustful of the interviewer's motives.

Questionnaire

Questionnaires can be distributed to elicit relevant job-related information. There are two types of questionnaire: generic and bespoke.

1 Generic questionnaires, such as the position analysis questionnaire (PAQ) and the management position description questionnaire (MPDQ), are commercially available tools that cover areas such as physical activities, relationships with others and job context. While generally applicable to most roles and relatively easy to administer, the generic questionnaires can lack the level of detail required to provide a comprehensive analysis.
2 The bespoke questionnaire approach involves the development of a 'purpose built' job analysis questionnaire (JAQ) based on information gathered from background documents and stakeholder interviews (see Jenkins and Curtin [2006] for a review of the process). Bespoke JAQs are advantageous in that they are comprehensive, more relevant than generic tools, and encourage stakeholder ownership; however they are very labour intensive and expensive to prepare.

Critical incident technique

The critical incident technique (CIT; Flanagan, 1954) is a widely used qualitative job analysis method, which is used to obtain specific behavioural descriptions of relevant work activities. Critical incidents (CI) are crucial situational demands in a given role and the behaviours that discriminate between successful and unsuccessful job performance in these situations; they are usually developed through interviews with stakeholders. CIT presents a flexible, inexpensive method of obtaining rich information regarding a job from an employee's perspective. Moreover, CIs can also be a valuable resource in developing situational interviews (Janz et al., 1986), assessment centre tasks and situational judgement tasks (McDaniel and Nguyen, 2001). However, the process relies heavily on the respondent providing accurate information regarding events. In addition, common events are likely to be missed as these are less memorable, so it is best to complement CIT with other approaches.

Strategic job analysis

The strategic job analysis (SJA) concept (Palmer and Valet, 2001; Schneider and Konz, 1989) was developed as a future-focused approach. SJA comprises job analytic methods, which aid in the prediction of how jobs are likely to adapt and change, by aligning existing and future jobs with the strategic orientation of the organisation. A common SJA method is to hold workshops with various subject matter experts (SMEs) and discuss potential future changes.

Competencies and competency models

Competency models (also introduced in Chapter 6) refer to the collections of characteristics, behaviours and KSAs a jobholder requires in order to perform their role competently (Green, 1999; Rodriguez et al., 2002). A *competency* can be considered as the specific characteristics and behaviour patterns a job holder is required to demonstrate in order to be effective in their role.

In recent years, competency modelling has been used by organisations as an alternative to job analysis, however, there has been debate among organisations and academics regarding the differences between competency modelling and traditional job analysis. According to Campion et al. (2011), there exist a number of practical differences between traditional job analysis and competency modelling. In addition, Sanchez and Levine (2009) outline six key theoretical distinctions between the two. Both perspectives are demonstrated in Table 9.1.

Despite the differences between traditional job analysis and competency modelling, Sanchez and Levine (1999, 2009) believe that the two are best used to supplement, rather than replace, each other; and that job analysis can be used to enrich the practice of competency modelling.

Table 9.1   Traditional job analysis versus competency modelling

	Traditional job analysis	Competency modelling
Practical Differences (adapted from Campion et al., 2011)	Senior management pay less attention	Senior Management pay more attention
	Less user friendly	More user friendly
	Not tended to be used in talent management	Used in talent management (distinguishing between average and top performers)
	Not linked to organisational goals and strategies	Linked to organisational goals and strategies and actively aligned to HR procedures
	Does not tend to include progression information	Often includes information about change/ progression to next level
	Usually a bottom up (starts with employees) process	Usually a top down (starts with senior management) process
Theoretical differences (adapted from Sanchez and Levine, 2009)	To describe behaviour	To influence behaviour
	Sees the job as an external object to be described	Sees the job as a role to be enacted
	Focus is the job itself	Focus is the organisation
	Oriented in the past	Oriented in the future
	Looking at typical performance	Looking at maximal performance
	Measures latent trait	Measures clinical judgement

Deriving person specifications and job descriptions

Job analysis data can be used in a variety of ways. The two most common products of the job analysis process are the *job description*, which outlines the responsibilities, tasks, working conditions and organisational position of the job in question, and the *person specification*, which describes the skills, knowledge and qualities needed to perform a particular job.

The person specification translates the requirements outlined in the job description into tangible features that applicants must demonstrate in order to be considered for the role. Typically, person specifications describe the role and its key responsibilities, essential and desirable qualifications, experience, work related competencies and behavioural competencies.

To identify the relative importance of various attributes identified for a given job, Morgeson and Campion (2000) suggest using a validation survey. This is a list of the tasks, responsibilities, KSAs previously identified with rating scales attached. This is distributed to a variety of informed stakeholders, who are asked to rate the importance of each identified KSA. The results of the survey are used to derive the person specification, particularly in terms of what criteria are essential and what are desirable. As a final stage in the validation process, all relevant data would then be reviewed by an independent panel of experts in job analysis and competency modelling to establish the content validity of the person specification.

Box 9.2

CASE STUDY 1: Job analysis for UK Foundation Year One (FY1) doctors

In 2010 Work Psychology Group were tasked with improving the selection of Foundation Year One (FY1) doctors in the UK. Foundation Training for doctors forms a two year bridge between undergraduate medical school and specialist training, for example as a surgeon or a general practitioner. Being a Foundation Doctor is compulsory for all newly qualified medical practitioners in the UK.

A systematic, multi-method job analysis was conducted to define the professional attributes (as opposed to clinical knowledge and skills) that are expected by incumbents in the first year of this training programme – that is, to determine the role of a (FY1) doctor.

The multi-methods job analysis approach contributed toward the credibility and validity of the process by triangulating data from three different job analysis methods:

- *Literature review:* A thorough review of all existing policy documentation and relevant publications.

- *Interviews:* 51 semi-structured interviews carried out with a variety of key stake-holders, including incumbents and supervisors. Interviewees were asked for examples of specific incidents from the FY1 job that characterised effective or non-effective performance to identify the key skills and attributes needed to perform as a FY1 doctor.
- *Observation:* Researchers observed thirteen FY1 doctors over a total of twenty-nine hours. They recorded the tasks, responsibilities, behaviours, attributes of the FY1 doctors in order to gain a greater insight and understanding into their tasks and responsibilities, as well as the professional attributes required to perform the role successfully.

The outcomes of the job analysis were analysed using template analysis (King, 2004) to identify the key themes within the data. The template underwent a number of iterations and quality checks.

This resulted in nine professional attributes being defined, namely: (1) Commitment to Professionalism, (2) Coping with Pressure, (3) Effective Communication, (4) Learning and Professional Development, (5) Organisation and Planning, (6) Patient Focus, (7) Problem Solving and Decision Making, (8) Self-Awareness and Insight and (9) Working Effectively as Part of a Team. These were set out in a 'Professional Attribute Framework', which lists behavioural descriptors representative of each attribute.

A survey was then conducted to validate the outcomes of the job analysis with 230 individuals from a variety of organisations associated with UK medical education and training. The results from the validation survey indicated that all nine Professional Attributes were rated as important for a FY1 doctor and important to evaluate at selection.

- Can you identify any other job analysis methods that could have been used in this case study and what the potential advantages and disadvantages of using these?
- What information would you provide to interviewees when inviting them to take part in a job analysis interview?

(Medical Schools Council, 2011)

Assessment methods

Standards for choosing assessment methods

Once the required KSAs for a given role have been identified and the assessment criteria established, the next step is to determine appropriate assessment methods. There are various assessment methods available and as Occupational Psychologists we must consider reliability, validity and utility when choosing these.

Reliability

The purpose of assessing reliability is to quantify the amount of error in measurement. Hence, it is useful to examine whether an assessment method provides adequate, accurate measurement. Reliability is evident in two components: the extent to which the assessment produces scores that are stable over time; and the extent to which the items in the assessment are consistent. There are a number of ways in which reliability can be considered in an assessment context including the following:

Test re-test reliability – administer the assessment to groups of individuals at two time points, ensuring that the test conditions are similar on both occasions. A strong positive correlation between the scores on the assessment on both occasions assures high reliability.

Parallel forms – in order to prevent practice effects or over-exposure to test materials in large scale assessments, two or more assessments of equivalent content and difficulty are administered. High reliability is characterised by a strong positive correlation between applicants' scores on the parallel forms.

Internal consistency – when items in an assessment are measuring the same construct. Internal consistency can be calculated in several ways:

1 Split-half reliability involves splitting the items within an assessment in half. Scores on the two half tests are then correlated to check whether they are consistent.
2 Cronbach's alpha or coefficient alpha overcomes the problem present in the split-half technique by taking into account the correlation of each individual item with the overall score obtained from the assessment. These item-total correlations are used to calculate an overall reliability. Values greater than 0.7 are desirable for internal consistency in assessment (Kline, 1999).
3 Inter-rater reliability provides an indication of the degree to which two or more assessors agree in their ratings on a given method, providing evidence that the assessment reflects the competence of the applicant rather than the partial judgements of the assessor.

Validity

The validity of an assessment method indicates the extent to which it measures the attribute it claims to measure. This is vital in ensuring that practitioners have confidence in the assessments they use and the decisions they make based on these methods. Assessment validation can come in many forms:

Face validity – based on a qualitative judgement and aims to establish whether test items appear to be relevant for their purpose or 'look right' to applicants. It is often one of the best predictors of candidate perceptions of a process (Hausknecht et al., 2004).

Content validity – another qualitative appraisal of the assessment validity but, unlike face validity, it is carried out by subject matter experts rather than the applicants. An assessment is content valid when it encompasses a representative basis of the construct being measured.

Construct validity – establishing whether the assessment is measuring the constructs (for example, attribute/skill/proficiency) that it claims to be measuring. In practice, this is often achieved by correlating a well-established measure of the construct the assessment claims to measure with the assessment under investigation to look for highly correlated scores.

Two aspects of construct validity are *convergent* and *divergent validity*. Convergent validity is demonstrated when results for an assessment method are consistent with results from scales measuring similar constructs, and divergent validity is demonstrated when results for an assessment method are inconsistent with scales measuring unrelated constructs.

Criterion validity – establishes whether the assessment method predicts important criteria. To establish criterion validity, assessment scores must be correlated with scores from criterion measures; there are two forms:

1 Concurrent validity – demonstrated by correlating assessment scores with criterion (for example, job performance) scores measured at the same time, so for example if job incumbents are asked to sit the assessment and the results compared to their current appraisal ratings.
2 Predictive validity – demonstrated by collecting assessment scores first, followed by criterion scores at some point in the future (a time lag of usually three months to one year). This is seen to be more robust as it can predict likely future performance.

If assessment scores are collected as part of a selection process, the challenge here is range restriction: only high scoring applicants are selected, thus the performance of low scoring candidates cannot be measured for the criterion as they have been rejected from the selection process.

Incremental validity – the gain in validity resulting from adding new predictors to an existing selection system. This form of validity can help determine whether or not a particular method provides a significant improvement in addition to the use of another approach. For example, does the addition of a cognitive ability test to an interview improve the ability to identify the best candidates compared to using the interview alone?

Utility

HR interventions such as personnel selection processes can be expensive to design and implement. HR managers often have to produce evidence showing the effectiveness of a selection process (Morrow et al., 1997). A variety of methods for doing this exist, however, the most established is the *utility analysis*, which calculates the benefit of selection process by appraising a combination of factors related to quality, quantity and costs (Macan and Foster, 2004).

By conducting utility analyses, the value of the selection process can be measured and actions can be taken depending on its effectiveness. Case study 3 (Box 9.6) outlines how a large financial organisation aimed to improve the cost effectiveness and efficiency of its high volume end-to-end recruitment process through review, re-development and validation. However, utility analysis should not simply be viewed as calculating the costs of the selection/assessment process. These are important, but must be balanced against the long term costs of appointing applicants with capability problems who will need further support and training or may decide to leave the role, thus requiring a further assessment process.

Selection assessment methods

There are a great many selection and assessment methods available, and the choice of which to use will depend on a number of factors, including suitability, cost and available timeframe. However, whichever method is chosen, you must ensure that the candidate is assessed against the competencies identified as part of a job analysis.

CVs, application forms and biodata

These are often the first form of contact between applicants and organisations and can therefore influence the outcomes of the selection process considerably. CVs consist of 'hard' verifiable items such as educational qualifications and 'soft' items such as applicant's hobbies/experiences. However, the unstandardised nature of CVs is questionable (Searle, 2003) with the decision of what to include is left up to the applicant.

Application forms are often standardised and consist of questions relating to an individual's qualifications, past experience or competencies identified as important during job analysis. Although the content covered may be similar to that in a CV, the organisation has more control over what information is presented and therefore the same information can be collected from multiple candidates in a standardised way. However, recruiters may not always act in a consistent way and thus their subjective biases when reviewing application form questions can impact decisions (McKinney et al., 2003).

A limitation of using standardised application forms is the developing industry of websites and organisations which provide model answers to questions and provide guidance for presenting CVs. As a result, some organisations have developed other ways to sift applicants in the first instance. For example, the process for selecting trainee general practitioners no longer includes application form questions but rather two machine markable tests that are completed in controlled conditions.

Biodata consists of any scoreable information about the applicant's background that can be related to job success. Items on biodata scales can be either subjective, for example, to what extent an applicant agrees/disagrees with a particular statement, or objective, such as level of qualifications the applicant may hold. Schmidt and Hunter's (1998) meta-analysis of assessment methods reported the criterion validity for biodata to be low-medium (0.35).

References

References are widely used to obtain information on applicants. However, despite this high level of usage the validity evidence is relatively low, for example,

Schmidt and Hunter's (1998) meta-analysis of assessment methods reported the criterion validity for reference checks to be 0.26. One reason for the poor validity may be that they are not reliable in terms of providing a true representation of the candidate.

Unstructured and structured interviews

Interviews are popular and appear in many forms. They vary from an unstructured format, which consists of an informal set-up between interviewer and potential employee, to the structured interview which encompasses a more regimented question-answer session.

Structured interviews in particular can be a valid means of selecting employees. In a structured interview process, interview questions are derived from a thorough job analysis; questions are consistent across interviewers and interviewees; and interviewers use a consistent set of criteria/competencies or behaviourally anchored rating scale to evaluate interview responses (Huffcutt et al., 2001). Research shows that unstructured interviews have lower levels of reliability due to subjectivity and their vulnerability to bias (Cook, 2004). Schmidt and Hunter's (1998) meta-analysis reports criterion validity values of 0.38 for unstructured interviews and 0.51 for structured interviews, which is favourable to other methods including cognitive ability tests.

Interviews can be differentiated further between *behavioural* (Janz, 1989) and *situational* interviews (Maurer et al., 1999). Behavioural interviews involve asking interviewees to describe past behaviours that are job relevant and are the basis for competency-based interviews. This interview approach assumes that past behaviour will predict future behaviour. An example question to assess client relationship skills is:

> ' Tell me about a time you developed good working relationships with a client? '

Situational interviews present hypothetical job-related scenarios and interviewees are asked how they would respond. Situational interviewing is based on goal setting theory and the premise that intention to behave predicts future behaviour. An example situational question to assess client relationship skills is:

> ' Imagine you have been working to design a new training programme for a client. When you are half-way through the project, the manager you were delivering the project for at the client organisation unexpectedly leaves and you now need to deliver the work for a new person. How would you approach this situation and how would you ensure the new client is satisfied with what you deliver? '

Box 9.3
OP IN PRACTICE

How to: conduct best practice interviews

Prior to the interview	*Establish interviewers*	• All interviewers should be trained in basic principles of best practice interviewing and the selection process in question. This could be face-to-face training, or an e-learning module. Training should involve calibration to ensure standardisation between interviewers and familiarisation with potential errors and biases such as fatigue, and primacy and recency effects. • The number of interviewers per interview should be decided. Panel interviews with two or more interviewers have greater validity than interviews conducted by a single interviewer.
	Confirm selection criteria and person specification	• A competency based interview should be based around previously defined selection criteria, ideally from a person specification derived from a job analysis. • Each selection criteria, or competency, should be accompanied by positive and negative behavioural indicators or a behaviourally anchored rating scale.
	Familiarisation of material	• Interviewers should be familiar with all documentation prior to interviewing.
	Agreement of interview format and content	• To enhance standardisation, all candidates should be asked the same question(s) where possible and all interviews should be of the same length. This allows all candidates to be compared on a like-for-like basis. • All questions should be prepared and agreed in advance. • If there is more than one interviewer, it should be agreed beforehand what roles each interviewer will take and the exact format of the interview.
During the interview	*Interview technique*	When conducting an interview there are a number of best practice principles to consider: • *Put the applicant at ease*; a minute or two of small talk is appropriate to build rapport • *Avoid short answer questions*, i.e. that can be answered with yes or no • *Avoid leading questions*, e.g. you do want this job don't you? • *Avoid totally open ended questions*, e.g. tell me about yourself • *Ask one clear question at a time*; avoid multi-question statements, e.g. have you experience in data inputting and what programmes have you used?

			• *Avoid interrupting the applicant*; spend more time listening than speaking • *Use appropriate probes where necessary to elicit more information*, e.g. what factors did you consider? What was the outcome? • *Use effective non-verbal communication*, e.g. nodding of the head to indicate listening
		Scoring and evaluation	Best practice suggests that a standardised process should be followed when scoring and evaluating an applicant. One established method is known as ORCE (Observe, Record, Classify and Evaluate). • *Observe* – objectively observe the applicants' performance and avoid common biases such as 'halo and horns' and 'attribution biases' • *Record* – it is not always necessary for an interviewer to record everything an applicant says, but do record sufficient information to make an objective assessment about the applicant • *Classify* – interviewers should classify the evidence against a predetermined rating criteria such as a positive and negative indicators or a behaviourally anchored rating scale • *Evaluate* – after classification, interviewers should evaluate the evidence against the person specification or a predetermined rating scale
Following the interview		*Feedback*	• Feedback should be provided to all candidates on how they performed, following the interview. • This should take place within two weeks of the interview so that it can be of benefit to the applicant.

A key drawback with situational interviews is that they do not take into account different levels of experience and how this may influence responses. They therefore are not appropriate in all contexts, such as graduate recruitment (Moscoso, 2000).

Simulations and work sample tests

Work sample tests and simulations present the candidate with work-based scenarios, varying in how much they represent the real work situation. They are a more contextualised, albeit more costly, approach compared to other assessments for evaluating how knowledge and experience acquired have translated into skilled performance (Lievens and Patterson, 2011).

Simulations can vary in the extent to which there is high or low fidelity to real work situations. This considers the extent to which the simulation replicates the task and whether applicants can respond exactly as if they were actually in the job situation (Motowidlo et al., 1990). High fidelity simulations present job-related situations to candidates and require behavioral responses from those candidates. Low fidelity simulations present candidates with written or video-based descriptions of job-related scenarios and ask them to indicate how they would react by choosing an alternative from a list of predetermined responses (Lievens and Patterson, 2011).

Examples of high fidelity simulations include assessment centres (ACs) as a whole, and many of the exercises incorporated within them. These may include: work-tray exercises where applicants work through a fictitious email 'in-box' of someone in the role they are applying for; simulations where they interact with actors playing the role of, for example, a customer or colleague; and group exercises where applicants partake in a joint meeting or discussion. In general, applicants respond favourably to work samples and simulations as they provide an opportunity to demonstrate their abilities and skills in a relevant context (Weekley and Ployhart, 2006). One of the most commonly used types of low fidelity simulations in assessment are situational judgement tests (SJT). Both SJTs and ACs are described in more detail below.

Psychometric tests

Psychometric tests are structured tests, taken in exam-like conditions, which aim to objectively measure a person's ability, or aspects of their personality.

Ability and aptitude measures

Tests of ability and aptitude measure overall reasoning or specific elements of ability/aptitude, such as verbal, numerical, abstract or mechanical abilities. Different tests are often designed to target different groups – for example, graduates, professionals or administrative levels. When deciding to use such a test it is important to ensure the test is appropriate for the level of applicants, that is, it not too difficult or too easy. Using a test that is not of the appropriate difficulty level will reduce its ability to discriminate effectively between applicants, as scores are likely to be clustered together rather than covering the full range of the test. Similarly it is important to select a measure which assesses competencies relevant for the role. For example, for an analyst role which involves working with numerical data, a numerical reasoning test would be reasonable; for a computer programmer, a test of diagrammatic reasoning, which looks at ability to understand logical processes, may be appropriate.

Aptitude or ability tests have been shown to be the single best predictor ($r = 0.55$) of job performance (Schmidt and Hunter, 1998). In a large-scale review of many meta-analytical studies, Ones et al. (2005) produced compelling evidence that cognitive ability tests do predict job performance across a variety of roles.

While ability and aptitude tests display good predictive power, research has indicated that applicant reactions can be less than positive (Roznowski et al., 2000).

Although such tests are easy to administer and cost effective, particularly in large-scale recruitment, it is widely cited that they demonstrate adverse impact against ethnic minorities (Roth et al., 2003). However, a meta-analysis has shown a narrowing of difference in cognitive ability performance between black and white groups over successive decades of the late 20th century, supporting a cultural/developmental theory of ethnic group differences in test performance (Woods et al., 2011).

Taking the evidence into account, it is not always appropriate to use ability/aptitude test for all selection purposes and certainly not in isolation, but rather in combination with other methods.

Personality measures

The past decade has seen an increasing interest and research in using personality measures in the selection context (Morgeson et al., 2007). Personality assessment aims to measure where a person lies on personality dimensions. Inferences can then be drawn about an individual's likely behaviours and reactions to particular situations. Understanding how personality influences behaviour and performance at work is critical to matching the right people to the right jobs.

There are a number of models that try and explain personality in the context of selection. One of the most dominant is the idea of 'traits'. Trait theory assumes personality traits such as extraversion or conscientiousness are stable over time and situations, and that they are distinctive (thus differentiating individuals from one other). One of the most popular trait approaches is the five-dimension personality model, nicknamed the 'Big Five', proposed by Goldberg (1981), but also commonly referred to as the 'Five-Factor Model' (McCrae and Costa, 1985). The factors are:

1 Openness to experience – the tendency to be imaginative, independent and interested in variety versus practical, conforming and interested in routine.
2 Conscientiousness – the tendency to be organised, careful and disciplined versus disorganised, careless and impulsive.
3 Extraversion – the tendency to be sociable, fun-loving and affectionate versus retiring, sombre and reserved.
4 Agreeableness – the tendency to be softhearted, trusting and helpful versus ruthless, suspicious and uncooperative.
5 Neuroticism – the tendency to be calm, secure and self-satisfied versus anxious, insecure and self-pitying.

Ones et al. (2007) concluded that the Big Five predicts important organisational behaviours such as performance, leadership, motivation and work attitudes. Further research shows that conscientiousness can be a valid predictor of job performance (Judge et al., 1999) and explains variance in performance beyond that explained by cognitive ability. Burke et al. (2006) found high scores on extraversion and self-efficacy to be positively related to being involved in work.

The use of personality assessment in selection can offer various benefits. Allowing a candidate to provide their own perspective can reveal possible areas to probe during an interview. Personality assessments have also been found to reduce adverse impact (that is, selection of a disproportionate number of members from one social, cultural, gender group over another). Baron and Miles (2002) found that group differences can be reduced if personality measures are added to the ability tests.

However, when using personality in selection, practitioners should take into account a number of considerations. Personality measures are prone to response distortion where applicants answer questions in a socially desirable way or present themselves in an improved manner (Rosse et al., 1998). However, many personality scales now have 'built-in' countermeasures such as dedicated social desirability scales (de Jong et al., 2010). Like ability tests, personality measures should not be used in isolation, and are often used more extensively for development purposes, rather than for selection.

Situational judgement tests

SJTs are tests designed to assess individuals' judgement regarding situations encountered in the workplace. Candidates are presented with a set of hypothetical work-based scenarios and asked to make judgements about possible responses. A variety of response formats, such as ranking or multiple choice, can be used. Since candidates' responses are evaluated against a predetermined scoring key the outputs of the test are standardised; each candidate's responses are assessed in exactly the same way and it is therefore possible to make comparisons between candidates. An example SJT is provided in Box 9.4.

Box 9.4

Example situational judgement test item

Mr Johnson is admitted with a minor groin abscess requiring surgical drainage although he is otherwise well and has full mental capacity. Four hours prior to surgery Mr Johnson informs a nurse that he wishes to self discharge as he says he is

---

due in court. Mr Johnson's next of kin are aware that he has been admitted for surgery and that he is due in court. The nurse asks you to speak to him.

Rank in order the following actions in response to this situation (1= Most appropriate; 5= Least appropriate).

A Allow Mr Johnson to leave but advise him to see his General Practitioner if there are further problems
B Prevent Mr Johnson from leaving by phoning security
C Explain to Mr Johnson the risks of leaving without treatment
D Telephone Mr Johnson's next of kin to ask them to try and persuade him not to leave
E Allow Mr Johnson to leave but ask him to return to the hospital as soon as possible

Patterson and Ashworth (2011)

SJT scenarios are normally based on extensive analysis of the job role, to ensure that test content reflects the most important situations that a candidate may face. They tend to be concerned with testing attitudes and ethical values (not generally tapped into by other measures) rather than knowledge, although they are often used in combination with knowledge tests to give a better overall picture of an applicant.

SJTs have been used extensively in many occupational groups and are becoming an increasingly popular selection method in large-scale selection processes and are used, for example, by the police, Department of Work and Pensions, as well as in many public and private sector graduate recruitment processes and training schemes.

Evidence has shown that as a selection method, SJTs demonstrate good reliability and validity (McDaniel et al., 2001). The research literature indicates that SJTs are able to predict job performance and training criteria across a range of occupations (Chan and Schmitt., 2002; Patterson et al., 2009). A number of studies have shown that SJTs demonstrate incremental validity beyond structured interviews, tests of IQ and personality questionnaires (Koczwara et al., 2012; McDaniel et al., 2007).

Differences in mean scores on SJTs between different ethnic groups are smaller than for tests of cognitive ability (Mototwidlo and Tippins, 1993), thus showing less adverse impact. Applicant perceptions relating to SJTs are generally positive, perhaps due to the relevance of the scenarios to the target role.

Assessment centres

Assessment centres (ACs), which are a method/approach rather than a physical place, have become a highly popular selection method in organisational settings.

The objective of an AC is to combine a range of assessment methods so that a full indication of an applicant's competence is achieved (Woodruffe, 1993). ACs typically involve multiple assessments of applicants across a range of exercises with multiple assessors; and as such they are often viewed as a reliable and valid approach (Ones and Viswesvaran, 2003). The strength of ACs lies in the richness of the assessment system and the detailed data produced. However, ACs often show what is known as the 'exercise effect' (competencies correlate more highly with each other than the same competency across exercises; Robie et al., 2000) and as such have limited construct validity. In addition, since assessors are used to observe, record and evaluate candidates' performance, assessors are vital to the success of ACs (Chen, 2006).

In order for an AC to be effective it must be carefully designed and use the most applicable methods for identifying those candidates most suited for the role in question. To this end, ACs typically comprise of four distinct stages (see BPS Best Practice Assessment Centre Guidelines; 2010).

1   *Pre-planning* that involves identification of why an AC is needed, gaining support from stakeholders, outlining the objectives of the AC, and initiating an AC policy.
2   *Development* of the process includes conducting a job analysis and using the results to devise appropriate simulations, which are integrated to measure the range of defined competencies. This is a crucial stage of the process which involves key stakeholders in the development of an AC matrix by selecting the most suitable methods for assessing the key competencies identified in the job analysis (some methods may be able to assess multiple competencies). Development of AC exercises usually involves a number of key stages, including trialling and review, and the development of the scoring framework and assessor guidance. Scoring of the exercises may take the form of behaviourally anchored rating scales or competency and global ratings using the key competencies and associated behavioural indicators.
3   Once the AC is designed and logistical factors addressed, it can be *implemented* in stage 3 (ideally ACs are piloted before hand, however this may be difficult due to time and cost constraints).
4   *Post-implementation* involves making decisions on the outcome of the centre (usually by having a meeting of stakeholders and assessors or 'wash-up'), providing feedback to the candidates, and setting up procedures to monitor the outcomes of the centre which will then feed back in to the development of future ACs.

In fact, both 'unqualified assessors' and 'inadequate training' are thought to negatively influence the validity of ACs (Chen, 2006: 254).

Principles for designing assessment methodologies

Box 9.5

CASE STUDY 2: Developing a situational judgement test for selecting foundation doctors

Having completed training at medical school, approximately 8,000 students apply annually for a junior doctor post in the NHS as part of Foundation Training, including applicants who were trained outside the UK. Here, medical students enter the world of employment and carry substantial responsibility for the healthcare of patients. This is a key career transition for doctors where they develop the competencies to become a practicing clinician. Following the job analysis conducted for Foundation Doctors (see case study 1), a Work Psychology Group was commissioned to develop and evaluate an SJT to replace the competency based application form.

Construction of the test consisted of a series of stages, following best practice test design:

- o By consulting with stakeholders and medical students, we established the test specification, including the criterion to be assessed, the item types and response formats, the test length and how it was to be administered.
- o We held seven item writing workshops to develop SJT items. These were held with subject matter experts and all items were reviewed by a core team of SJT experts to ensure all items met SJT item writing principles.
- o We held focus groups with Foundation Doctors to ensure items were fair and realistic.
- o A concordance panel was then run; this involves subject matter experts taking the test to identify consensus about the correct answers and to finalise the scoring key. Any items with low consensus were rejected.
- o All items were piloted with medical school students. The analysis indicated that the SJT was a reliable and valid method for use in selection to the Foundation Programme. Tests for group differences were also conducted.
- o Finalised items were entered into a live item bank. This item bank will require yearly review to ensure existing items are still relevant and fit for purpose.
- o A continued yearly item development process will take place; all new items will be piloted alongside the live test each year.

- • What issues might you need to consider when designing item content for an applicant pool that includes people who have been trained in different countries?
- • Which stages of the test construction process are particularly important from a face validity perspective?
- • When may an SJT be an appropriate inclusion to a selection process?

(Medical Schools Council, 2011)

Box 9.6

CASE STUDY 3: Development and validation of a high volume recruitment process

In order to provide a more cost effective end-to-end recruitment process with use of on-line sifting and more efficient use of face-to-face assessments, a large financial organisation sought to review, validate and improve their recruitment process for high volume and clerical roles.

Service and operations roles make up around 50% of the organisation's head count and thus it was imperative that a reliable and valid recruitment process was in place. With up to 200,000 applicants a year, a methodology was required that was able to successfully select the right people for the job, but in a way that was manageable for the organisation and cost efficient.

The process began with a project to revise the capabilities required for each role type ('cluster') and to establish line managers' requirements for the assessment process. The project involved interviews with line managers and role holders and observations of role holders performing their jobs.

Following this phase, realistic job previews (RJPs) were developed for all role clusters. It had been apparent that a lack of clarity about job requirements was a reason for some of the short term tenure within the roles, and hence each RJP provided details of the typical activities undertaken in role and the characteristics of people who are likely and unlikely to enjoy the role.

The modified recruitment process also included:

- An online Suitability Screen (aka Work Styles Assessment) which covered motivational, attitudinal and preference attributes for each of the eight role clusters, rather than a 'one size fits all' personality assessment that had been used previously.
- A telephone assessment focussing on key predictors of success, such as capability to engage with customers.
- A Line Manager Assessment which included situational interview questions and work sample exercises.

Benefits include reduced time-to-hire due to a more resource efficient process, and cost savings due to the earlier stages reducing number of applicants for the later stages of the assessment. Candidate feedback is positive suggesting broad support and an independent third party review suggests that the end-to-end process is one of the most cost effective of its kind.

Revalidation exercises indicate that the recruitment process is providing better quality candidates at line manager assessment, resulting in a decrease in short term tenure and a reduction in overall dropout rate during the recruitment process. Further work is scheduled to investigate the use of high fidelity online simulations to further enhance the RJP element of the process.

> ## Questions
>
> - What sources of information would you consider when designing the content for these assessments?
> - What factors would you need to consider if looking to improve the efficiency and effectiveness of a selection process as described in this case study?
> - What validation and evaluation exercises would be beneficial for a selection process, such as the one described in this case study, to determine whether the re-development had met its aims?

Diversity and fairness issues in selection

Legal requirements regarding equal opportunities in the UK and impact when developing global processes

In the UK, employment law, such as the Equality Act 2010 (see Chapter 4) addresses discrimination based on a number of demographics including gender, ethnicity, age and disability. For example, advertisements are generally prohibited from stating preferences for applicants from specific age groups. However, if the requirement is essential for adhering to a job requirement and reasonable adjustments cannot be made (for example, a female personal instructor for a female-only gym), then, selecting on the basis of that characteristic is appropriate.

Not only does discrimination legislation impose duties on employers and organisations not to discriminate, the legislation also imposes a duty to make reasonable adjustments to the way organisations work. In selection and assessment this often refers to providing reasonable adjustment for those defined as having a disability. A disability is defined as a physical or mental impairment that has a substantial and long term adverse effect on the person's ability to carry out normal day-to-day activities. Reasonable adjustments may include additional time during assessments or providing assessment materials in different sizes or formats.

Globalisation of organisations means that selection processes are conducted in a diverse range of legal contexts, each dealing with fairness in selection differently. Although Europe and the USA do have certain rules in common, when developing global processes, any differences in employment law will need to be considered carefully.

Adverse impact, differential validity and review of different selection methodologies for adverse impact

In assessment, adverse impact occurs when there is a disproportionate success rate on the test for certain groups. This indicates that a particular group may be systematically disadvantaged as a result of the assessment method. The four-fifths rule of thumb is a statistical convention used to judge the severity of adverse impact. This states that the proportions of one group 'passing' a selection stage should not be less than four-fifths or 80% of another. If the proportion is less than 80%, then adverse impact is confirmed (Collins and Morris, 2008).

Unfair selection decisions may be made if adverse impact is found to result in discrimination. However, the existence of adverse impact does not solely constitute discrimination *if* performance in the assessment is found to replicate performance in the workplace (Cook, 1996). Validity plays a crucial part in determining whether a method is unfair. If the assessment is proven to be valid then selecting the highest scoring candidates will also mean the highest performing employees are selected. This therefore can provide legal defensibility. However, if the assessment predicts performance differently for different demographic groups then this is problematic. This is known as differential validity and implies that estimation of a candidate's job performance can differ depending on the demographic group they belong to. Thus, if differential validity is demonstrated, the assessment is considered to be an unfair selection method (Ployhart and Holtz, 2008).

Hough et al. (2001) reviewed adverse impact evidence for a variety of assessment methods (Table 9.2), collating data on the differences in assessment scores between different demographic groups; for example, men, women, ethnic minorities, older and younger workers:

Table 9.2   Potential adverse impact of different assessment methods

Assessment Method	Potential Adverse Impact	Demographic
Cognitive Ability Tests	High	*Ethnicity* – White groups score higher than Black groups on various ability tests – White groups score higher than Hispanic groups in US data – White groups score lower than East Asian groups on measures of g

	Moderate	Gender – Men and women score equally on general ability tests – Women score higher on verbal tests – Men score higher on spatial and numerical tests
	Moderate	Age – Older candidates tend to score lower on measures of g
Personality Measures	Moderate	Gender – Women score higher on Agreeableness, and traits relating to Affiliation and Dependability
	Low	Ethnicity – Small or negligible differences on the Big Five across ethnic groups
Assessment Centres	Moderate	Ethnicity – Black groups score lower than Caucasian groups
	Moderate	Age – Older candidates score lower than younger candidates
Work Sample Tests	Moderate	Ethnicity – Black candidates score lower than Caucasian candidates – Ethnic differences are smaller in work samples than other assessment methods and so are preferable in reducing adverse impact
	Moderate	Gender – Men score lower than women
Interviews	Moderate	Ethnicity – Caucasian groups scored slightly higher compared to Black groups – Caucasian groups scored slightly higher than Hispanic groups in US data
	Low	Gender – Evidence less clear/differences likely to be negligible overall and likely to be moderated by perceptual factors such as interviewer biases (Moscoso, 2000)
Biodata	Low	– Small differences in scores across ethnicities, gender and age – If scores based on educational background, adverse impact against some ethnic groups may increase

Direct and indirect discrimination and equal opportunities

Discrimination occurs when a person is treated differently and less favourably to people in another group. UK employment law recognises two types of discrimination: direct and indirect discrimination. *Direct discrimination* in a selection setting would have occurred, for example, if a woman was deliberately not selected for a promotion because the selectors believe that she may take substantial time off for maternity. *Indirect discrimination* would have occurred, for example, if a height limit of five feet ten inches were imposed as a condition for people applying for a particular occupation, as this would exclude a higher proportion of individuals from some ethnic groups compared to others, and the height limit could not be justified by the needs of the job. Indirect discrimination does not suggest that the assessor or recruiters are prejudiced; instead, it is an unseen form of discrimination. It is considered unlawful if there is no evidence to show it is a reasonable method of assessment (Dainty and Lingard, 2006). Hence, assessment methods are considered to be fair if they are job relevant and if there is evidence of validity.

One way to address a perceived imbalance as a result of discrimination is through positive action. This seeks to tackle an imbalance in employment opportunities among targeted groups which have previously been disadvantaged, or been subject to discriminatory policies and practices, or under-represented in the workforce (Stratigaki, 2005). It does *not* imply:

- selecting a certain number of people from an under-represented group, irrespective of merit;
- selecting purely on the basis of race or gender to correct an imbalance unless it can be shown that being of a particular sex or race is a genuine occupational qualification.

It is, however, lawful to welcome applications from under-represented groups, and to provide special training opportunities for them once they have been selected, but selection itself must be based purely on job-related factors (Kirton and Greene, 2002).

Candidate/applicant experiences of selection and assessment

There is a growing recognition that selection and assessment should be seen as a two-way process through which the applicant also makes an informed choice about whether to take up a role and forms opinions about the organisation. For these reasons, Occupational Psychologists have become increasingly interested in the candidate or applicant experiences of selection and assessment.

Selection as attraction

Research suggests that recruitment practices can define an organisation's image and reputation (Turban and Cable, 2003) and that a robust and fair recruitment process imparts a positive organisational climate (Anderson, 2001). Selection processes can also provide 'clues' to applicants in terms of what it will be like to work within that environment (Phillips and Gully, 2002), for example through realistic job previews.

Organisations that use fair selection processes are likely to increase their ability to attract the best applicants and recruit successfully (Schmitt and Chan, 1999). An organisation's selection practices may become known among particular target audiences, occupational groups and professional communities from which they recruit, and this could either attract or deter future applicants, thus potentially effecting the applicant pool. Furthermore, the extent to which a selection process discourages good applicants or reduces job acceptance rates will have a negative impact upon the overall utility of the selection process (Murphy, 1986).

Candidate perceptions – theories of procedural and distributive justice

How a candidate perceives the selection process has important implications for the organisation. Candidate perceptions can be examined using the concepts of *procedural* and *distributive justice*. These theories are derived from organisational justice; a concept developed from Adams' (1965) equity theory (as explored in Chapter 4). Procedural justice refers to the perceived fairness of the selection and assessment procedures *that lead to* decision outcomes. Distributive justice can be conceptualised as fairness associated with *outcome decisions* (Gilliland, 1993).

Gilliland (1993) devised a 10-rule framework (Table 9.3) for procedural justice to conceptualise applicants' perceptions of the fairness of selection systems.

Table 9.3 Ten-rule framework of procedural justice (Gilliland, 1993)

	Procedural Rule	Description
1	Job Relatedness	Assessment is specific to the role applicants are applying for and measures relevant content
2	Opportunity to Perform	The chance for applicants to demonstrate their knowledge, skills and abilities
3	Reconsideration Opportunity	Opportunity for applicants with mitigating circumstances to re-apply, challenge or modify the decision-making evaluation process

(Continued)

Table 9.3 (Continued)

	Procedural Rule	Description
4	Consistency	Selection process being consistent across people and over time (standardisation)
5	Explanation Feedback	The provision of timely and informative feedback of assessment outcomes
6	Selection Information	Readily available information prior to selection assessment and provision of justification for a decision
7	Honesty	Importance of truthfulness and avoidance of concealing information that may be useful to applicants
8	Interpersonal Treatment/Effectiveness	The extent to which all applicants are treated in a respectful manner
9	Two-way Communication	The opportunity for applicants to offer input and have their views considered during the selection process
10	Propriety of Questions	Ensuring appropriate and relevant questions are asked to applicants

Procedural justice is important in determining fairness perceptions but does not necessarily provide the full picture. Distributive justice theory can fill some of those gaps. Distributive justice suggests that candidates will evaluate distribution of outcomes with respect to an equity rule, that is, did they receive an outcome they felt they deserved? Perceptions of distributive justice can be fostered when outcomes are perceived to be equally applied. Gilliland (1993) also provided a three-rule framework (Table 9.4) to explain distributive justice.

Table 9.4 Three-rule framework of distributive justice (Gilliland, 1993)

	Distributive Rule	Description
1	Equity	Individuals should receive rewards that are consistent with the input they contribute
2	Equality	Individuals should have an equal chance of receiving the outcome, regardless of differentiating characteristics, e.g. knowledge or ability
3	Special Needs	Rewards should be distributed on the basis of individual needs and preferential treatment offered where applicable

Evaluations of inequity may produce negative emotions thus motivating individuals to alter their behaviour and/or attitude (Patterson and Zibarras, 2011; Patterson et al., 2011; Truxillo et al., 2004), for example viewing the organisation less positively or being reluctant to reapply for positions within the organisation.

Box 9.6

How To ... use appropriate assessment materials

Confidentiality	• Assessment materials should be treated confidentially and release into the public domain avoided. • Data should be stored under controlled access and only released to those with legitimate authority and who are qualified to use and interpret them.
Psychometric data	• Results of psychometric assessments (e.g. ability or personality measures) should be incorporated into reports which explain their context and offer appropriate interpretation (Van Vianen et al., 2004).
Record and evaluation documents	• Use of recording sheets, classification and evaluation sheets and algorithms for decision-making is recommended where appropriate. • Recording detailed information about the candidates' performance and decisions made is beneficial because it provides clear justifications for unsuccessful applications and assures legal defensibility.

Box 9.7

How To ... provide effective and informative applicant feedback

• Feedback should be made available to applicants regarding their performance, although the level of detail provided will depend upon the volume of applicants being assessed and whether the applicants are internal or external to the organisation.

• Feedback should inform applicants of where they displayed good performance (to help instil confidence) and identify areas of improvement.

• Note that giving poor feedback is worse than giving no feedback at all (Kluger and DeNisi, 1996).

(Continued)

(Continued)

- Aguinis (2009) developed the following guidance on providing effective feedback to applicants:

Timeliness	Feedback delivered close to the assessment
Specificity	Specific behaviours or aspects of performance are reported
Verifiability	Focus on accurate, verifiable evidence, not rumour or inference
Consistency	The tone of feedback should not be subject to huge variation
Privacy	Presented at an appropriate time and place to avoid embarrassment
Consequences	Potential outcomes of behaviour/responses are communicated to conceptualise feedback
Description First	Clear descriptions of performance precede evaluations
Confidence in Applicant	Emphasise that any negative feedback is targeted at performance not the person
Advice	Identify and explain areas of improvement

Contemporary issues in selection and assessment

Emerging issues in selection and assessment

Person-organisation fit

Person-organisation fit focuses on selection from the organisation and applicant perspective, that is, the 'fit' must be right for both parties (Kristof, 1996). The 'fit paradigm' makes a number of assumptions:

- organisations and jobs change, and so does the relationship between them; therefore it is impossible to predict the future;
- organisations need employees who will 'grow' with them;
- focus in selection is on finding a relationship that is mutually beneficial;
- employers seek to recruit the 'whole person'.

This perspective has become increasingly prevalent in both academia and practice (for a review see Arthur et al., 2006) and some say it may become the sole consideration of KSAs for selecting employees (Bowen et al., 1991).

Originally, only single dimensions of person-organisation fit were used when analysing selection processes, nevertheless, this was described as insufficient. This criticism led to the identification of multiple person-organisation fit dimensions that simultaneously and directly influenced employee satisfaction and commitment (see Edwards and Billsberry [2010] for more details).

Technological developments

Research and practice in selection and assessment are continually evolving. One area that is currently at the forefront is continuing technological developments, including the impact of this on global selection; the assessment of applicants across multiple locations or nationalities within the same process.

Computer-based testing

While there are practical advantages for putting assessments online, as assessment methods become increasingly sophisticated, there are also a number of issues. For example, some applicants may approve of online application forms, perceiving them to be faster and easier to complete. Yet, others may experience technical difficulties, perpetuating negative applicant reactions (Bauer et al., 2004). Online testing also raises questions about dishonesty and cheating. In response, test suppliers have attempted to design systems to confirm the identity of test takers to remove these problems. These include producing parallel formats to retest candidates under supervision to verify scores or examining the equivalence of formats (that is, assessing whether an applicant's score on a paper-and-pencil test is equivalent to a test administered online).

Another element to computer based testing is the emergence of adaptive testing. This is when the candidate answers an item correctly, then the computer selects a slightly, and, difficult item more if the candidate provides an incorrect answer, then the computer selects a slightly easier one. Given that information about tests items is widely available, the concept of a unique test for every candidate (such as with adaptive testing) is appealing in tackling cheating and practice effects (Van der Linden and Glas, 2000).

Moreover, it is not just the assessment methods but also the candidates themselves that are becoming tech-savvy. The demand to transfer paper-and-pencil assessments onto an online platform is challenging as this is not necessarily an area of expertise for psychologists. The future could see the assessment and selection market being driven by such technical consultants rather than psychologists. Thus, psychologists and selection practitioners need to continue with on-going professional development in order to overcome such challenges.

Video-based CVs

Increased use of technology in screening procedures has resulted in the emergence of 'video-resumes': video-recorded messages in which applicants present themselves to employers (Doyle, 2010). Job seekers are increasingly using video sharing and related Internet sites to present themselves to potential employers as an alternative to paper-based CVs. This multimedia approach allows applicants to demonstrate skills and abilities that are often difficult to capture with paper-based CVs. In particular, this may be an opportunity for those whose writing skills are limited. Video CVs are an emerging recruitment method; however, further research is required to understand potential threats and benefits to applicants and organisations.

Multi-media SJTs

Video technology may be considered for selection procedures if the organisation wishes to visually replicate what may occur in the workplace. One such selection procedure that has taken advantage of this is SJTs (Lievens and Sackett, 2006). There are lots of advantages to using video-based SJTs: they can depict richer and more detailed behavioural incidents increasing their fidelity; they require little to no reading benefitting candidates who would otherwise perform poorly on written tests; watching a video may be more natural for many poeple; they may provide a more realistic job preview; they have high face validity.

Richman-Hirsch et al. (2000) found that students reacted more favourably to a multimedia format of a conflict resolution skill SJT compared with a computerised and a written format of the same test. The students found the multimedia SJT more face valid, more enjoyable and more modern than the other two versions. However, there are some downsides, for example multimedia SJTs are often costly to develop and may inadvertently add irrelevant contextual information, consequentially introducing more error into the measurement of SJTs (Weekley and Jones, 1997).

Global selection

As more and more organisations are engaging in international recruitment, practitioners and researchers are focusing on the impact this has on selection and assessment procedures. Internet-based recruitment processes are often considered to be a way of improving international recruitment in global organisations. However, it is uncertain whether cultural differences and familiarity with technology has an impact upon the way in which applicants present themselves when only an Internet-based selection procedure is provided (Booth, 1998). Applicants who are unfamiliarity or have limited access to computer technology are likely to be placed at a disadvantage.

There is demand for further research to be conducted in terms of investigating the influence of technology on selection processes (Petrides et al., 2010); the ways in which this mediates both the applicant's perspective and the organisation's perspective, and particularly how this might vary cross-culturally given the trend for organisational growth in terms of global expansion.

Summary

Selection and assessment practices are used extensively in organisations, and the development of valid and reliable selection processes that take into account the perspectives of both the organisation and the candidate play a major role in occupational psychology research and practice.

Best practice selection is an iterative process, where the selection system evolves over the course of time. Typically the first stage in any selection process involves a thorough job analysis which provides systematic information regarding responsibilities and the KSAs required to perform a role competently. These are often then developed into a competency model. Data from these two practices are then used to develop a job description and person specification.

There is a wealth of tools available for use in assessments which can enable applicants to demonstrate behaviour through either high and low fidelity simulations of job requirements or describe previous performance. Suitable assessment tools should be selected based on the requirements outlined in the job description and person specification. It is important for these methods to be reliable, valid, fairly administered and for multiple methods to be used to ensure the best possible representation of the candidate. This will reduce the likelihood of legal challenge, and unfavorable candidate perceptions of the process and of the organisation. Wherever possible, evaluation following a selection process should take part with results feeding into improvements for future use.

Assessment methods are not exclusive to selection; they are also used in a variety of other contexts such as development and training. However, it is important to remember that irrespective of the context within which they are used, best practice principles should always be considered.

The next chapter will focus on performance in the role (as opposed to performance in order to secure the role), with an exploration of theory and practice around training.

Explore further

- Guidance on best practice in selection can be drawn from several sources. With regards to psychometric testing, the BPS Psychometric Testing Centre provides guidelines and information:

http://www.psychtesting.org.uk/the-ptc/guidelinesandinformation.cfm

- There are also guidelines for assessment centres from the International Taskforce.

http://www.assessmentcenters.org/pdf/AssessmentCenterGuidelines_2009.pdf

- Selection/assessment processes can typically generate a large volume of applicant data. The BPS Best Practice Guidelines (2010) and the Data Protection Act (1998) provide recommendations with respect to applicants' rights and access to information within the UK

http://www.bps.org.uk/sites/default/files/documents/generic_professional_practice_
  guidelines.pdf
http://www.ico.gov.uk/for_organisations/data_protection.aspx

- Journals can provide a wealth of information on current selection issues and future direction. Two of the most well known and respected journals in this field are:

International Journal of Selection & Assessment - Blackwell Publishing Ltd.
Personnel Psychology - Wiley Periodicals, Inc.

- Various books and online resources are available that may make useful further reading:

The Oxford Handbook of Personnel Assessment and Selection (Oxford Library of Psychology) (2012). Neal Schmitt.
www.pdri.com/images/uploads/Selection_Assessment_Methods.pdf

Sage online resources

- Kleinmann, M., Ingold, P., Lievens, F., Jansen, A., Melchers, K. and König, C. (2011) 'A different look at why selection procedures work: the role of candidates' ability to identify criteria', *Organisational Psychology Review*, 1 (2): 128–46.
- Vecchione, M., Alessandri, G. and Barbaranelli, C. (2012) 'Paper and pencil and web-based testing. The measurement invariance of the big five personality tests in applied settings', *Assessment*, 19 (2): 243–46.

Discussion questions

1 You are approached by a HR manager who is concerned that anecdotally their new graduate assessment process is being perceived negatively by candidates. What advice would you give them, including how to investigate it further and what factors they should consider?
2 You are approached by a telecommunications company who are expanding the number of customer service operators they employ. As they currently do not have a competency model for the role, they ask you to put together a proposal for this work. What steps would you want to include?
3 Your consultancy firm delivers the graduate recruitment selection process for a government department. They are interested in enhancing the process by using a Situational Judgement Test and ask you how they could go about doing this. What would you advise?

Sample essay questions

1 Critically appraise three assessment methods considering both research evidence and practical applications.
2 What potential risks to fairness are inherent in assessment processes and how can you mitigate against these?

Sample examination questions

1 Discuss how selection and assessment practices impact upon organisations and their applicants.
2 Evaluate the role of technology in assessment processes.

OP IN PRACTICE ... DAY IN THE LIFE OF ...

Professor Fiona Patterson, Cambridge University and Director, Work Psychology Group

What areas of OP do you work within?	My core research and practice area is selection and assessment, but this is often as part of a broader organisational development and change programme. Over the past ten years a major client group for me has been the UK National Health Service (NHS), which is the second largest organisation in the world and recruitment is a high stakes, high volume activity. My work there has focused on selection and assessment but this has all been part of a larger transformation agenda, which brings my work more into the realms of organisational development and change. For example, in designing and validating selection practices in the NHS, there are several layers of stakeholders who have an interest in the selection methods used. Thus, selection decisions must encompass views from supervisors (e.g., consultant physicians), trade unions (e.g., the British Medical Association), the regulators (e.g., General Medical Council), professional bodies (e.g., Medical Royal Colleges), employers associations (e.g., NHS employers), government (e.g., Department of Health), patients and so on. These parties may not agree on how selection should best be delivered. So the need to gain stakeholder buy-in and acceptance is an important issue which I've termed the 'political validity' of selection as this is an important consideration in high stakes settings.
How did you become interested in this area?	Mainly through my PhD research which was in selection, psychometrics and innovation. I was working at Ford as an internal psychologist at a time when the organisation wanted to invest in how to develop more creative and innovative engineers. I was asked to design new selection tools to enhance creativity and innovation and that led to a long term interest as there weren't any robust tools available at the time. My PhD focuses on developing a new selection tool for innovation.

(Continued)

(Continued)

What have been the seminal research papers in your research area?	I would say that Flanagan's (1954) paper on Critical Incident Technique is seminal. It's such a powerful tool in conducting job analyses and for generating content in test development for situational judgement tests, for example. In fact, a key paper for our research group was our initial job analysis study conducted with UK general practitioners using critical incident technique as one of the methods in our study. We published the results in the British Journal of General Practice (Patterson et al., 2000) – the feedback we got on this paper was that it was highly innovative because we interviewed patients' about their expectations for selection doctor (whereas it was usually doctors making the decisions alone).
What has been the major academic development in this area?	I think a major development in selection and assessment has been some statistical breakthroughs to allow more sophisticated analysis with large data sets using, for example, meta-analytic studies. This has had such a major impact in organisational practice since validity generalisation gives a kind of league table regarding which methods work best, for example knowing that structured interviews are better than unstructured ones. That said, one can only get so far with meta-analyses, we also need to examine causal relationships, and structural equation modelling has transformed the social sciences in testing causal relationships between indicators. For example, we now know that SJTs work far better than personality tests in selection in predicting subsequent job performance. Using these kinds of analyses, on the back of about ten years of validation research, we have been able to demonstrate the real business value of the work we do in medical selection. We have shown that for every £1 spent on good selection and assessment, the NHS gets back £8 in reduced training costs. This is the kind of information that clients need to know.
To what extent does the practical application of your work inform your research?	Most of the work I have done is informed by practice. I don't see an academic-practitoner divide – that's a red herring to me. For example, my PhD came out of a practical problem in an organisation competing with Japanese manufacturers and needing to increase levels of innovation. Much of the selection and assessment research I do within the NHS comes out of practical problems – such as how to select in valid and reliable ways. In my research role we explore the issues using the very latest research and then transfer this knowledge to the client to create practical, sustainable solutions.

What role do ethics have in your work?	On the research side, everything I do requires ethical approval via stringent ethics committees, whether that is at the University level or NHS level and so on. We also have our own professional standards when we work within the corporate sector for example. As a team at Work Psychology Group [WPG], it is central to everything we do; our values are about professionalism and integrity. We also encourage people to become chartered as I strongly believe that this validates your practice as an independent professional. The important aspect of ethics at work is *who* is the client; in large change programmes it's often also very important to protect the rights of individuals.
Can you give an example of a day in your working life?	Well, I spend half my time as an academic, and half my time in consulting practice, but to be honest, there is no typical day. It might start off by discussing with the management team what is on the agenda for the day/week and then working out how the team will be involved – so there's performance management issues to grapple with in running a team of psychologists. I spend a great deal of time reviewing and signing off reports and proposals internally, so I'm very close to the day-to-day running of WPG. I would say 40–50% of my time is spent speaking to clients, either on the phone or face-to-face. I also really enjoy the time I take to write papers – perhaps one of the most enjoyable aspects of my job is reflecting on what I've done and writing it up for peer scrutiny. I also spend significant time giving keynote talks and running seminars, both in my capacity at the University and also attending conferences and speaking at various meetings.
How has your work changed in the last five years?	Although I know a great deal about selection, assessment and psychometrics, my work has moved more towards organisational development and strategy – for example, although I've been typically involved in selection research, such as conducting validation studies, these are always linked to the overall strategy of an organisation which influences their development and change. Having this type of strategic view, I am more focused on demonstrating added value. In the past it might have been more about the design and then evaluation, but now I deal much more with the senior level people and these are who determine OD strategy.

I suppose also in terms of my own profile I started out in the corporate sector for over ten years (manufacturing and retail) and then I did my PhD and moved into academia. Since, I've co-founded a consulting practice where we now have over 12 psychologists, which is great fun as I've got a fantastic team and they are a high achievers. Owning a business has improved my research and consulting practice because you have to see things from the line management perspective more clearly – being an employer I have far more understanding of what organisations might want from Occupational Psychologists. |

(Continued)

(Continued)

| How do you see your work changing over the next five years? | I've recently been giving advice on government policy internationally in departments of health and education. The world is changing rapidly in South East Asia and this is a fertile ground for new learning regarding a transformation and strategic agenda. Given my experience and expertise I will be doing more of this over the next five years, influencing corporate and government policy and learning about international differences in the process. |

OP IN PRACTICE ... DAY IN THE LIFE OF ...

Dr Maire Kerrin, Director, Work Psychology Group

What areas of OP do you work within?	I work in selection and assessment and innovation. From a practitioner point of view, in selection we [Work Psychology Group] are involved in the design, development, testing and validation of selection methods in both public and private sectors. We take forward all parts of the process, starting with the job analysis, through to design and on to the evaluation. As a company we don't sell off-the-shelf products, everything we do is bespoke for the particular client we are working with. We have expertise in assessment centre and situational judgement test (SJT) design, particularly in high stakes settings.
How did you become interested in this area?	When I finished my MSc I actually couldn't think of anything worse than ending up working in selection and assessment! My perception was that it was all about selling off-the-shelf psychometric tests. So I started my career in training and development moving through to organisational development and change where I began to recognise that selection and assessment is just one part of broader organisational change. Being involved in developing bespoke selection methods calls for creativity and innovation in the design process, which is very different from selling off-the-shelf products.
What kinds of organisations are interested in your work and why?	Over the years Work Psychology Group has built up expertise in healthcare and medical selection, so a proportion of our work has been with the public sector. However, we also conduct quite a significant amount of work for the private sector, for example in finance, manufacturing and retail. In terms of the healthcare sector, our clients like our work because it is rigorous and research-based. In medical selection, it is large scale high stakes selection, so there is a more intense demand to demonstrate the validity and fairness of the methods. The private sector also want to know the measures are robust and evidence based, but it's more about selling it into the business, making sure that it's palatable in terms of price and developing something based on the business needs.

How is your work informed by theory, literature and research?	As a business we have taken a strategic approach ensuring that all our consultancy work is evidence based. In fact a large part of our client work is published in the psychology, management and medical education literature. The healthcare work that we have done requires evidence of validity, reliability and fairness. Publishing our research in peer reviewed journals means that we can demonstrate this and that we are credible. We have individual links to universities such as City University and Cambridge University where we currently teach and we are also linked with a network of academics from other universities such as Nottingham, Leicester and Sheffield. Personally we all maintain our CPD [continued professional development] through teaching, which means that we keep up to date on new developments in the field. We often take on projects that are not necessarily profitable but are pilots that drive our research and development as a business.
What do you think have been the major developments in this area?	One of the key things in selection and assessment has been the ability to put assessments online. While this is not a new concept, it is a challenge to make sure that we successfully transfer what we do in paper and pencil, like SJTs, to an online platform. As online platforms are not necessarily our area of expertise, there is a concern that technical consultants could end up driving the offering rather than psychologists. It's important to stay on top of this and make sure we are working alongside the right people. From a theoretical point of view, I think the rise of the use of SJTs has also been a major development alongside the use of more sophisticated face-to-face assessments.
What role do ethics have in your day-to-day practice?	Ethics – this is part of the values within our organisation around trust, professionalism and integrity. We return to these values regularly to review what they mean to us in our day-to-day practice. In terms of ethical practice – it links to the culture in our organisation and there are the formal aspects like applying for ethics through committees, but as psychologists, we all have to have our own internal radar on ethical practice, and that's when it helps to have colleagues to bounce ideas around.
Can you give an example of a day in your working life?	This really varies from day to day. It could be that in the morning I am office based where I have a team meeting, then perhaps a meeting with the accountant, or our finance manager. In the afternoon I might be with a client in the manufacturing sector where I'm giving one-to-one feedback to senior managers.

(Continued)

(Continued)

Following that, I could be back in the office writing a tender or a proposal for an organisation. There really is no typical day – my role in the organisation is such that I have some internal-focused activities and also some outward-focused activities. Within our organisation there is a cyclical nature to our business where certain times of years are particularly busy. For example, in September to November and then January to March we have significant repeat work with clients who have recruitment and selection rounds at these times of years, so we are very busy organising and running these activities. But overall, it's really different from day to day, which makes for a very interesting and challenging job!

References

Adams (1965) 'Inequity in social exchange', in L. Berkowitz (ed.), *Advances in Experimental Social Psychology*, vol. 2. New York: Academic Press.

Aguinis, H. (2009) *Performance Management*. Upper Saddle River, NJ: Pearson/Prentice Hall.

Anderson, N. (2001) 'Towards a theory of socialisation impact: selection as pre-entry socialisation', *International Journal of Selection and Assessment*, 9 (1–2): 84–91.

Arthur, W. Jr, Bell, S.T., Villado, A.J. and Doverspike, D. (2006) 'The use of person organisation fit in employment decision making: an assessment of its criterion related validity', *Journal of Applied Psychology*, 91: 786–801.

Ash, R.A. (1988) 'Job analysis in the world of work', in S. Gael (ed.), *The Job Analysis Handbook for Business*. New York: Wiley. pp. 3–13.

Atkinson, J. and Meager, N. (1994) 'Running to stand still: the small firm in the labour market', in J. Atkinson and D. Storey (eds), *Employment, the Small Firm and the Labour Market*. London: Routledge.

Baron, H. and Miles, A. (2002) 'Ethnic differences on personality questionnaires'. Paper presented at the British Psychological Society Occupational Psychology Conference, Blackpool.

Bauer, T.N., Truxillo, D.M., Paronto, M.E., Weekley, J.A. and Campion, M.A. (2004) 'Applicant reactions to different selection technology: face-to-face, interactive voice response, and computer-assisted telephone screening interviews', *International Journal of Selection and Assessment*, 11 (2–3): 135–48.

Booth, J.F. (1998) 'The user interface in computer- based selection and assessment: applied and theoretical problematics of an evolving technology', *International Journal of Selection and Assessment*, 6 (2): 61–81.

Bowen, D.E., Ledford, G.E., Jr and Nathan, B.R. (1991) 'Hiring for the organization, not the job', *Academy of Management Executive*, 5 (4): 35–52.

BPS Best Practice Assessment Centre Guidelines (2010) Available at: http://www.psychtesting.org.uk/the-ptc/guidelinesandinformation.cfm (accessed 6 January 2012).

BPS Best Practice Guidelines (2010) Available at: http://www.bps.org.uk/sites/default/files/documents/generic_professional_practice_guidelines.pdf (accessed 7 October 2011).

Brumback, G.B, Romashko, T., Hahn, C.P. and Fleishman, E.A. (1974) *Model Procedures for Job Analysis, Test Development, and Validation*. Washington, DC: American Institutes for Research.

Burke, R.J. and Cooper, C.L. (2006) 'The new world of work and organisations: implications for human resource management', *Human Resource Management Review*, 16: 83–5.

Burke, R.J., Matthiesen, S.B. and Pallesen, S. (2006) 'Personality correlates of workaholism', *Personality and Individual Differences*, 40 (6): 1223–33.

Campion, M.A., Fink, A.A., Ruggeberg, B.J., Carr, L., Phillips, G.M. and Odman, R.B. (2011) 'Doing competencies well: best practices in competency modelling', *Personnel Psychology*, 64: 225–62.

Chan, D. and Schmitt, N. (2002) 'Situational judgment and job performance', *Human Performance*, 15: 233–54.

Chen, H.C. (2006) 'Assessment center: a critical mechanism for assessing HRD effectiveness and accountability', *Advances in Developing Human Resources*, 8 (2): 247–64.

Collins, M.W. and Morris, S.B. (2008) 'Testing for adverse impact when sample size is small', *Journal of Applied Psychology*, 93 (2): 463–71.

Cook, M. (1996) *Personnel Selection and Productivity*. Chichester: Wiley.

Cook, M. (2004) *Personnel Selection: Adding Value Through People*, 4th edn. Chichester: Wiley.

Dainty, A.R.J. and Lingard, H. (2006) 'Indirect discrimination in construction organisations and the impact on women's careers', *Journal of Management in Engineering*, 22: 108–18.

Data Protection Act (1998) Available at: http://www.legislation.gov.uk/ukpga/1998/29/section/7

de Jong, M., Pieters, R. and Fox, J. (2010) 'Reducing social desirability bias through item randomised response: an application to measure underreported desires', *Journal of Marketing Research*, 47 (1): 14–27.

Derous, E. and De Witte, K. (2001) 'Looking at selection from a social process perspective: towards a social process model on personnel selection', *European Journal of Work and Organisational Psychology*, 10: 319–42.

Doyle, A. (2010) Video resume – video resumes for job seekers. Available at: http://jobsearch.about.com/od/resumes/g/videoresume.htm (accessed 19 February 2010).

Edwards, J.A. and Billsberry, J. (2010) 'Testing a multidimensional theory of person-environment fit', *Journal of Managerial Issues*, 22 (4): 476–93.

Flanagan, J.C. (1954) 'The critical incident technique', *Psychological Bulletin*, 51: 327–58.

Gatewood R.D. and Field, H.S. (2001) *Human Resource Selection*. New York: Harcourt.

Gilliland, S.W. (1993) 'The perceived fairness of selection systems: an organisational justice perspective', *The Academy of Management Review*, 18 (4): 694–734.

Goldberg, L.R. (1981) 'Unconfounding situational attributes from uncertain, neutral and ambiguous ones: a psychometric analysis of descriptions of oneself and various types of others', *Journal of Personality and Social Psychology*, 41: 517–52.

Green, P.C. (1999) *Building Robust Competencies: Linking Human Resource Systems to isation Organisational Strategies*. San Francisco, CA: Jossey-Bass.

Gutman, A. (2000) 'Recent supreme court ADA rulings: mixed messages from the court', *The Industrial-Organisational Psychologist*, 37: 31–41.

Hausknecht, J.P., Day, D.V. and Thomas, S.C. (2004) 'Applicant reactions to selection procedures: an updated model and meta-analysis', *Personnel Psychology*, 57: 639–83.

Herriot, P. (2004) 'Social identities and applicant reactions', *International Journal of Selection & Assessment*, 12 (1–2): 75–83.

Hough, L.M., Oswald, F.L. and Ployhart, R.E. (2001) 'Determinants, detection and amelioration of adverse impact in personnel selection procedures: issues, evidence and lessons learned', *International Journal of Selection and Assessment*, 9: 152–94.

Huffcutt, A.I., Weekley, J.A., Weisner, W.H., DeGroot, T.G. and Jones, C. (2001) 'Comparison of situational and behavioural description interview questions for higher level positions', *Personnel Psychology*, 54: 619–54.

Hunter, J.E., Schmidt, F.L. and Judiesch, M.K. (1990) 'Individual differences in output variability as a function of job complexity', *Journal of Applied Psychology*, 75: 28–42.

Janz, T. (1989) 'The patterned behavior description interview: the best prophet of the future is the past', in R.W. Eder and G.R. Ferris (eds), *The Employment Interview: Theory, Research and Practice*. Thousand Oaks: Sage. pp. 158–68.

Janz, T., Hellervik, L. and Gilmore, D.C. (1986) *Behavior Description Interviewing*. Boston, MA: Allyn & Bacon.

Jenkins, S.M. and Curtin, P. (2006) 'Adapting job analysis methodology to improve evaluation practice', *American Journal of Evaluation*, 27 (4): 485–94.

Judge, T.A., Higgins, C.A., Thoresen, C.J. and Barrick, M.R. (1999) 'The big five personality traits, general mental ability, and career success across the life span', *Personnel Psychology*, 52 (3): 621–52.

Kirton, G. and Greene, A. (2002) 'The dynamics of positive action in UK trade unions: the case of women and black members', *Industrial Relations Journal*, 33 (2): 157–73.

Kline, P. (1999) *The Handbook of Psychological Testing*, 2nd edn. London: Routledge.

Kluger, A.N. and DeNisi, A. 1996). The effects of feedback interventions on performance: a historical review, a meta-analysis, a preliminary feedback intervention theory. *Psychological Bulletin*, 119: 254–84.

Koczwara, A., Patterson, F., Zibarras, L., Kerrin, M., Irish, B. and Wilkinson, M. (2012) 'Evaluating cognitive ability, knowledge tests and situational judgement tests for postgraduate selection', *Medical Education*, 46 (4): 399–408.

Kristof, A.L. (1996) 'Person-organisation fit: an integrative review of its conceptualisations, measurement and implications', *Personnel Psychology*, 49: 1–49.

Lievens, F. and Patterson, F. (2011) 'The validity and incremental validity of knowledge tests, low-fidelity simulations, and high-fidelity simulations for predicting job performance in advanced-level high-stakes selection', *Journal of Applied Psychology*, 96 (5): 927–40.

Lievens, F. and Sackett, P.R. (2006) 'Video-based vs. written situational judgment tests: a comparison in terms of predictive validity', *Journal of Applied Psychology*, 91: 1181–8.

Macan, T.H. and Foster, J. (2004) 'Managers' reactions to utility analysis and perceptions of what influences their decisions', *Journal of Business and Psychology*, 19: 241–53.

Macan, T.H., Avedon, M.J., Paese, M. and Smith, D.E. (1994) 'The effects of applicants' reactions to cognitive ability tests and an assessment centre', *Personnel Psychology*, 47: 715–38.

Marcus, B., Goffin, R.D., Johnston, N.G. and Rothstein, M.G. (2007) 'Personality and cognitive ability as predictors of typical and maximum managerial performance', *Human Performance*, 20 (3): 275–85.

Maurer, S.D., Sue-Chan, C. and Latham, G.P. (1999) 'The situational interview', in R.W. Eder and M.M. Harris (eds), *The Employment Interview Handbook*. Thousand Oaks, CA: Sage. pp. 159–77.

McCrae, R.R. and Costa, P.T., Jr (1985) 'Comparison of EPI and psychoticism scales with measures of the five-factor model of personality', *Personality and Individual Differences*, 6: 587–97.

McDaniel, M.A. and Nguyen, N.T. (2001) 'Situational judgment tests: a review of practice and constructs assessed', *International Journal of Selection and Assessment*, 9: 103–113.

McDaniel, M.A., Hartman, N.S., Whetzel, W. and Grubb, L. (2007) 'Situational judgement tests, response instructions, and validity: a meta-analysis', *Personnel Psychology*, 60 (1): 63–91.

McDaniel, M.A., Morgeson, F.P., Finnegan, E.B., Campion, M.A. and Braveman, E.P. (2001) 'Use of situational judgment tests to predict job performance: a clarification of the literature', *Journal of Applied Psychoogy*, 8 (4): 730–40.

McKinney, A.P., Carlson, K.D., Mecham, R.L., III, D'Angelo, N.C. and Connerley, M. (2003) 'Recruiters use of GPA in initial screening decisions: higher GPA's don't always make the cut', *Personnel Psychology*, 56: 823–45.

Medical Schools Council (2011) *Improving Selection to the Foundation Programme, Final Report*. London: Medical School Council.

Morgeson, F.P. and Campion, P. (1997) 'Social and cognitive sources of potential inaccuracy in job analysis', *Journal of Applied Psychology*, 5: 627–55.

Morgeson, F.P., Campion, M.A. (2000) 'Accuracy in job analysis: toward an inference-based model', *Journal Organizational Behaviour*, 21: 819–827.

Morgeson, F.P., Campion, M.A., Dipboye, R.L., Hollenbeck, J.R., Murphy, K. and Schmitt, N. (2007) 'Are we getting fooled again? Coming to terms with limitations in the use of personality tests for personnel selection', *Personnel Psychology*, 60: 1029–49.

Morrow, C.C., Jarrett, M.Q. and Rupinski, M.T. (1997) 'An investigation of the effect and economic utility of corporate-wide training', *Personnel Psychology*, 50: 91–119.

Moscoso, S. (2000) 'Selection interview: a review of validity evidence, adverse impact and applicant reactions', *International Journal of Selection and Assessment*, 8: 237–47.

Motowildo, S.J., Dunnette, M.D. and Carter, G.W. (1990) 'An alternative selection procedure: the low-fidelity simulation', *Journal of Applied Psychology*, 75 (6): 640–7.

Mototwidlo, S.J . and Tippins, N. (1993) 'Further studies of the low-fidelity simulation in the form of a situational inventory', *Journal of Occupational and Organisational Psychology*, 66: 337–44.

Murphy, K.R. (1986) 'When your top choice turns you down: effect of rejected offers on the utility of selection tests', *Psychological Bulletin*, 99 (1): 133–8.

Ones, D.S. and Viswesvaran, C. (2003) 'Job-specific applicant pools and national norms for personality scales: implications for range restriction corrections in validation research', *Journal of Applied Psychology*, 88 (3): 570–7.

Ones, D.S., Dilchert, S., Viswesvaran, C. and Judge, T.A. (2007) 'In support of personality assessment in organizational settings', *Personnel Psychology*, 60: 995–1027.

Ones, D.S., Viswesvaran, C. and Dilchert, S. (2005) 'Cognitive ability in personnel selection decisions', in A. Evers, O. Vockuijl and N. Anderson (eds), *Handbook of Selection*. Oxford: Blackwell. pp. 143–73.

Oswald, F.L. (2003 'Job analysis: methods research and applications for human resource management in the new millennium', *Personnel Psychology*, 56 (3): 800–2.

Palmer, H. and Valet, W. (2001) 'Job analysis: targeting needed skills', *Employment Relations Today*, 28 (3): 85–91.

Patterson, F. and Ashworth, V. (2011) 'Situational judgement tests: the future of medical selection?'. Available at: http://careers.bmj.com/careers/advice/view-article.html?id=20005183 (accessed 6 January 2012).

Patterson, F. and Lane, P. (2007) 'Assessment for recruitment', in N. Jackson, F. Jamieson and A. Khan (eds), *Assessment in Medical Education and Training*. Oxford: Radcliffe. pp. 62–74.

Patterson, F. and Zibarras, L.D. (2011) 'Exploring the perceived construct of job discrimination in selection', *International Journal of Selection and Assessment*, 19 (3): 251–7.

Patterson, F., Baron, H., Carr, V., Plint, S. and Lane, P. (2009) 'Evaluation of three short-listing methodologies for selection into postgraduate training in general practice', *Medical Education*, 43: 50–7.

Patterson, F., Ferguson, E., Lane, P.W., Farrell, K., Martlew, J. and Wells, A. (2000) 'Competency model for general practice: implications for selection, training and development', *British Journal of General Practice*, 50: 188–93.

Patterson , F., Zibarras, L., Carr, V., Irish, B. and Gregory (2011) 'Evaluating candidate reactions to selection practices using organisational justice theory', *Medical Education*, 45 (3): 289–97.

Petrides, K.V., Weisntein, Y., Chou, J., Furnham, A. and Swami, V. (2010) 'An investigation into assessment centre validity, fairness and selection drivers', *Australian Journal of Psychology*, 62 (4): 227–35.

Phillips, J.M. (1998) 'Effects of realistic job previews on multiple organisational outcomes: a meta-analysis', *Academy of Management Journal*, 41 (6): 673–90.

Phillips, J.M. and Gully, S.M. (2002) 'Fairness reactions to personnel selection techniques in Singapore and the United States', *The International Journal of Human Resource Management*, 13 (8): 1186–205.

Ployhart, R.E. and Holtz, B.C. (2008) 'The diversity-validity dilemma: strategies for reducing racioethnic and sex subgroup differences and adverse impact in selection', *Personnel Psychology*, 61 (1): 153–72.

Richman-Hirsch, W.L., Olson-Buchanan, J.B. and Drasgow, F. (2000) 'Examining the impact of administration medium on examinee perceptions and attitudes', *Journal of Applied Psychology*, 85: 880–7.

Robertson, I.T. and Smith, M. (2001) 'Personnel selection', *Journal of Occupational and Organisational Psychology*, 74: 441–72.

Robie, C., Osburn, H., Morris, M., Etchegaray, J. and Adams, K. (2000) 'Effects of the rating process on the construct validity of assessment center dimension evaluations', *Human Performance*, 13 (4): 355–70.

Rodriguez, D., Patel, R., Bright, A., Gregory, D. and Gowing, M.K. (2002) 'Developing competency models to promote integrated human resource practices', *Human Resource Management*, 41: 309–24.

Rosse, J.G., Stecher, M.D., Miller, J.L. and Levin, R.A. (1998) 'Impact of response distortion on preemployment personality testing and hiring decisions', *Journal of Applied Psychology*, 83 (4): 634–44.

Roth, P.L., Huffcutt, A.I. and Bobko, P. (2003) 'Ethnic group differences in measures of job performance: a new meta-analysis', *Journal of Applied Psychology*, 88 (4): 694–706.

Roznowski, M., Dickter, D.N., Hong, S., Sawin, L.L. and Shute, V.J. (2000) 'Validity of measures of cognitive processes and general ability for learning and performance on highly complex ise computerised tutors: is the G factor of intelligence even more general?', *Journal of Applied Psychology*, 85: 940–55.

Sanchez, J.I. and Levine, E.L. (1999) 'Is job analysis dead, misunderstood, or both? New forms of work analysis and design', in A. Kraut and A. Korman (eds), *Evolving Practices in Human Resource Management The SIOP Practice Series*. San Francisco, CA: Jossey-Bass. pp. 43–68.

Sanchez, J.I. and Levine, E.L. (2009) 'What is (or should be) the difference between competency modelling and traditional job analysis?', *Human Resource Management Review*, 19: 53–63.

Sandberg, J (2000) 'Understanding human competence at work: an interpretative approach', *Academy of Management Journal*, 43: 9–25.

Schmidt, F.L. and Hunter, J.E. (1998) 'The validity and utility of selection methods in personnel psychology: practical and theoretical implications of 85 years of research findings', *Psychological Bulletin*, 124 (2): 262–74.

Schmitt, N. and Chan, D. (1998) *Personnel Selection. A Theoretical Approach: Foundations for Organisational Science*. London: Sage.

Schmitt, N. and Chan, D. (1999) 'The status of research on applicant reactions to selection tests and its implications for managers', *International Journal of Management Reviews*, 1 (1): 45–62.

Schneider, B. and Konz, A. (1989) 'Strategic job analysis', *Human Resource Management*, 28 (1): 51–63.

Searle, R.H. (2003) *Selection and Assessment: A Critical Text*. Milton Keynes: Open University/ Palgrave McMillian.

Snowdon, G. (2011) 'A crash course in consultancy'. Available at: http://www.guardian. co.uk/money/2011/oct/28/career-consultancy-recruitment-training (accessed 17 September 2012).

Stratigaki, M. (2005) 'Gender mainstreaming vs positive action: an ongoing conflict in EU gender equality policy', *European Journal of Women's Studies,* 12 (2): 165–86.

Truxillo, D.M., Bauer, T.N., Campion, M.A. and Paronto, M.E. (2002) 'Selection fairness information and applicant reactions: a longitudinal field study', *Journal of Applied Psychology*, 87: 1020–31.

Truxillo, D.M., Steiner, D.D. and Gilliland, S.W. (2004) 'The importance of organisational justice in personnel selection: defining when selection fairness really matters', *International Journal of Selection and Assessment*, 12: 39–53.

Turban, D.B. and Cable, D.M. (2003) 'Firm reputation and applicant pool characteristics', *Journal of Organisational Behaviour*, 24 (6): 733–51.

Van der Linden, W.J. and Glas, C.A.W. (eds) (2000) *Computerised Adaptive Testing: Theory and Practice*. St Paul, MN: Assessment Systems Corporation.

Van Vianen, A.E.M., Taris, R., Scholten, E. and Schinkel, S. (2004) 'Perceived fairness in personnel selection: determinants and outcomes in different stages of the assessment procedure', *International Journal of Selection and Assessment*, 12: 149–59.

Wanous, J.P. (1980) *Organisational Entry: Recruitment, Selection, and Socialisation of Newcomers*. Reading, MA: Addison-Wesley.

Weekley, J.A. and Jones, C. (1997) 'Video based situational testing', *Personnel Psychology*, 50: 5–50.

Weekley, J.A. and Ployhart, R.E. (2006) *Situational Judgment Tests: Theory, Measurement and Application*. San Francisco, CA: Jossey Bass.

Woodruffe, C. (1993) 'What is meant by a competency?', *Leadership & Organizational Development Journal*, 14 (1): 29–36.

Woods, S.A., Hardy, C. and Guillaume, Y.R.F. (2011) *'Cognitive ability testing and adverse impact in selection: meta-analytic evidence of reductions in black-white differences in ability test scores over time'*, paper presented at DOP Annual Conference, Stratford-Upon-Avon, UK.

Wyatt, M.R.R., Pathak, S.B. and Zibarras, L.D. (2010) 'Advancing selection in an SME. Is best practice methodology applicable?', *International Small Business Journal*, 28: 258–73.

Zibarras, L.D. and Woods, S.A. (2010) 'A survey of UK selection practices across different organisation sizes and industry sectors', *Journal of Occupational and Organisational Psychology*, 83: 499–511.

10 Training

Kamal Birdi and Tracey Reid

Learning outcomes

On completion of this chapter readers will be able to:

- understand the difference between training, education and development in the workplace;
- explain the main stages of the training cycle;
- describe the importance of conducting organisational, task and person needs analyses as a basis for initiating and developing training interventions;
- understand the importance of stating clear aims and objectives for training;
- discuss the advantages and disadvantages of different individual and team training methods;
- describe different models and strategies for training evaluation;
- explain the different types of factors that can influence the effectiveness of training.

We will first discuss the meaning of learning at work and emerging trends, then describe the training cycle as an overarching framework for training development, followed by detailed exploration of needs analysis, design and delivery and evaluation of training activities. The final section will highlight research findings on factors influencing training effectiveness.

Introduction

The training of employees in new knowledge and skills is a crucial lever for organisations to ensure that their workforce is capable and flexible enough to meet the ever-increasing challenges facing them in the 21st century. The CIPD Learning and Talent Development Survey 2011 reported that UK organisations spent an average of £350 per employee per year, and allowed an average of five days a year, on training and development activities (CIPD, 2011). The American Society of Training and Development estimated that US organisations spent US$125.88 billion on employee learning and development in 2009 alone (ASTD, 2010). Given these significant investments in training activities, it is vital that these initiatives are as effective as possible in enhancing learning and work performance. This chapter will therefore outline and discuss the principles of putting together training activities with impact.

Learning and related concepts at work

Learning can be defined as experience giving rise to a relatively permanent change in knowledge, skills or attitude (Birdi et al., 1997). These changes may lead to changes in subsequent work behaviour, but it is not a given. Learning at work can be facilitated through training, educational or developmental activities and it is worth clarifying the distinctions between these concepts.

- Training activities – for example, attending a presentation skills workshop, tend to have a narrow focus, with specific objectives and are reasonably well-structured. The aim is to get all trainees to the same level of performance and the emphasis is very much on what you can do.
- Educational activities – for example, undertaking an MBA, tend to have broader focus but are still reasonably well-structured. The aim is to capitalise on individual differences and the emphasis is on what you know.
- Developmental activities – for example, entering a mentoring relationship, have a longer-term perspective with objectives not necessarily tied to a specific job but more relevant to the general career progress of an individual. The degree of structure varies and can include training or educational activities. However, developmental activities do also include an element of reflection where a person can consider what their life and career goals are, evaluate their current capabilities against those needed to achieve their goals and plan a learning strategy to enhance the required capabilities. Typically in the workplace, this can take place in the form of an annual performance development review.

Of course, learning activities can overlap in their training, educational or developmental functions. The focus of this chapter is on training activities but many of the lessons can be applied to the other two types of learning interventions.

Setting the workplace learning scene

As the 21st century progresses, there are a number of emergent trends and issues in relation to workplace learning that should be noted.

The 'skill intensity' of employment is increasing (see Chapter 1). Manual labour tasks are being undertaken more and more by technological solutions, meaning that people are being required to make greater use of their cognitive and interpersonal skills in the workplace instead. The rise of service industry jobs (for example, call centres) and knowledge work sectors is evidence of this.

There is a greater emphasis on 'self-managed' learning. Organisations have taken the perspective that individuals are responsible for their own learning and have become less prescriptive in their training activities. Instead, employees are expected to take more responsibility for shaping their learning portfolio, with facilitation from the organisation or Government funding. Typically, this has been seen in organisations through the embedding of annual development reviews where learning goals are proposed by employees and discussed with their line managers (see Chapter 6). The focus of these discussions has therefore widened to include general employability, as well as learning related to specific job-related needs.

There still tends to be an unequal distribution of training activities in the working population. Smaller amounts of training are typically undertaken by those: with fewer educational qualifications; at lower job levels; older people; longer tenure employees; part-time employees; and employees in smaller establishments. One should therefore be aware that there are still many 'traditional' non-learners and efforts need to be undertaken to ensure they are not excluded from valuable training and development activities.

Technology is being increasingly used with the workplace learning domain. From the use of interactive CD-ROMs in the 1980s to the use of the Internet, virtual learning and mobile technologies, the flexibility in time, format and space of learning has exponentially increased from the old days of straightforward classroom instruction. 'Blended' learning, using a mixture of technological and non-technological approaches, is being seen as a means of building on the strengths of both approaches.

Corporate universities are on the rise. There has always been a tension between the specific, contextual learning needs of organisations and the generalisability of educational provision offered by traditional colleges and universities. As a means of resolving this tension, a number of organisations have set up their own 'universities' with accredited qualifications. McDonald's Hamburger University, Motorola and Boeing are examples of some of the many organisations setting up these initiatives.

There is a greater pressure to align business/strategic needs with learning needs (Noe and Tews, 2012). Human resources are being treated the same as any other resource and hence any investment in people needs to be shown to generate concomitant organisational benefits. The need for effective and efficient training interventions is therefore paramount and we shall now discuss how to address this.

The training cycle

The training cycle describes the main stages of needs analysis, design and delivery of training and evaluation. Figure 10.1 illustrates how these stages can be linked

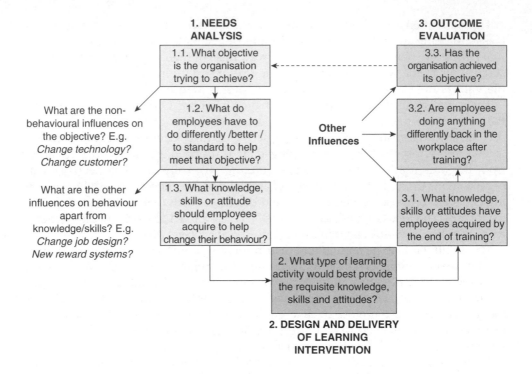

Figure 10.1   A Strategic Approach to Training

together to provide a systematic approach to developing learning interventions in organisations. We will briefly describe the model overall and then the following sections will cover each of the three phases in more detail.

Let us take a hypothetical example. BuildOrg is a construction company that you have just started working for as a member of their training and development team. BuildOrg is an international organisation, with specialities in the areas of building offices, flats and shopping centres. You have been tasked with developing strategically important training initiatives for the following year. Where do you start?

We should commence with Stage 1, needs analysis, where we define why training is needed (if at all), what tasks training is needed in and who needs training (Boydell and Leary, 1996). Following the path defined in Figure 10.1, we start with the initial strategic question of 'What is the organisation trying to achieve?' In the case of BuildOrg, discussions with senior management have revealed that a significant concern for their company is that many customers are complaining that the doors on their buildings are not working properly. This has led to many warranty claims and knock-on impacts on other projects, which means BuildOrg revenue has decreased by 10%. Consequently, BuildOrg have decided that 'reducing customer complaints on doors to 0% for the following year' is a strategic priority and therefore something we should focus on. We then have to move down to the next set of needs analysis questions (1.2) to identify if it is worker behaviour issues we need to address ('What do employees have to do differently/better/to standard to help meet that objective?') or other issues ('What are the non-behavioural influences on the objective?) in order to achieve the strategic objective. We might find out in our investigations that the cause of malfunctioning doors is not due to inadequate fitting by workers but instead due to use of poor quality materials. In that case, the solution to the problem would be to invest in better quality materials (a non-behavioural issue) and hence a (behavioural) solution would not be required. However, if our observations indicated that materials and technology were fine and that poor fitting of doors was the cause of the problem, then we know we need a behavioural intervention.

We then move down to our next set of needs analysis questions (1.3) to try and understand why the desired behaviour or performance of individuals is not up to requirements. Here, we want to understand whether the poor door fitting is a learning issue (that is, workers do not have the necessary knowledge or skills) or caused by other factors such as low motivation. In the latter instance, it may be that pressure from managers to complete jobs speedily has meant workers know how to fit doors but cut corners to get the job done on time. If that is the case then the appropriate intervention may be to issue guidelines to supervisors to ensure quality is maintained over speed, implement quality of performance as a performance appraisal criterion or recruit more workers to just fit doors. However, if the issue is a lack of knowledge or skills of door-fitting, then a learning solution would be the most appropriate intervention. It is worth noting that attitudes, motivation and self-confidence can all be improved through training (Kraiger et al., 1993) if this is indicated as an important area requiring improvement. At this part of the process, where a learning deficit is pinpointed as a crucial lever for change, work needs to be done to understand precisely what tasks need to be conducted better in the job and what knowledge, skills or attitudes need to be developed through job/task analysis techniques (see later for more details). In BuildOrg, we can conclude at the end of the needs analysis that, in order to reduce door complaints to none next year, construction workers need to be fitting doors properly on the job, and in order to do this they need to possess the most up-to-date knowledge and skills about how to fit doors.

Stage 2 then concerns the design and delivery of the learning intervention. The output from the needs analysis is used here initially to define the aims (general scope) and objectives (specific desired learning outcomes) of the intervention. We then weigh up which activities would most effectively develop the required learning outcomes. For example, we may use a lecture to introduce trainees to the different types of doors available (a knowledge outcome) but use practical exercises to develop the skill outcome of fitting particular types of locks to doors. In this phase we would also evaluate our resources to undertake these activities, develop learning activities, train trainers and move towards a pilot before starting to run the programme. Within BuildOrg, we might decide to go for a three-day door-fitting course for all relevant construction personnel in which a mixture of lecturing, watching videos and guided practice on fitting a range of doors is used.

The final phase of the training cycle is shown on the right hand side of Figure 10.1 and concerns the evaluation side of things. Evaluation here covers the extent to which the learning, work behavioural and organisational targets outlined in the needs analysis are actually being met as a result of taking part in the learning intervention. The first question we need to address is the extent to which the knowledge, skills and attitudes we intended to convey through the training are actually being acquired (3.1). This is typically assessed through tests, practical exercises and questionnaires administered at the end of training. However, it is not enough to ensure that learning has taken place, we also need to follow trainees back into the workplace to check whether their work behaviour has changed (3.2). This transition is known as the 'transfer of training' and on many occasions this can be problematic (Noe, 2010). In BuildOrg, we might conduct random worksite observation visits to check that doors are being installed properly a month after trainees attend the course. Finally, we need to check that customer complaints about poor door fitting, our original strategic objective, has consequently fallen to the desired levels (3.3). Hopefully it has, and we can then move on to our next strategic objective for needs analysis.

In Figure 10.1, we also point out for steps 3.1 to 3.3 that 'other influences' may impact on the learning, work behaviour and organisational outcomes we are aiming to change. These other influences may be caused by individual differences in trainees, variations in training method design, the type of task being learned, or the work environment itself (Aguinis and Kraiger, 2009; Arthur et al., 2003; Burke et al., 2011; Powell and Yalcin, 2010). The end of this chapter will outline these potential influences on training effectiveness in more detail.

Figure 10.1 has broken down the training cycle into a series of sub-questions. This is one of many instructional systems development (ISDs) models which represent training as a series of subsystems, and are themselves part of the greater organisational system. Figure 10.2 shows an ISD developed by Patrick et al. (1986), which provides a detailed, systematic route through the key phases.

There are a number of advantages to ISDs:

- They systematically outline the steps to take when putting together a learning intervention.
- They can serve as a common map for coordinating activities, especially in large-scale organisations where different groups may undertake different stages.
- They can be used as an evaluation framework of the training development process itself to check that major functions are being followed.

However, such approaches can be bureaucratic and inflexible, and ISD models specify 'what to do' rather than 'how to do'. The following sections will outline strategies for how to conduct the major phases.

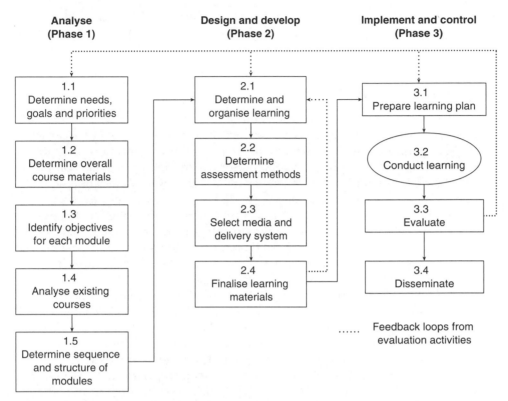

Figure 10.2   The Learning Systems Development Model (Patrick et al., 1986)

Training needs analysis

As outlined in our earlier example, training needs analysis (TNA) refers to the process necessary to establish why training is needed, what training is needed in and who needs training (Chiu et al., 1999; Gould et al., 2004). This phase is crucial for if it is not done properly the following problems may occur.

- Training may be wrongly used as a solution to a performance problem when in fact something else is the contributor.
- Training programmes may have the wrong content, objectives or methods.
- Trainees are sent to programmes for which they do not have enough of the basic skills, knowledge or experience and so may struggle with the content.
- Training will not deliver the expected learning, behaviour change or financial results that the company expects and so money and time spent on training will be wasted.

McGehee and Thayer (1961) outlined the three main aspects of needs analysis 50 years ago and these still hold well now. These are outlined below.

Organisational analysis

This first stage is about defining why training is (or is not) needed for helping the organisation meet its strategic objectives. Strategic importance can be garnered by gathering information on the *current status* of the organisation in terms of achievement of strategic goals/targets/performance metrics or major problems that are being faced. Such information is gathered through examination of objective performance records (for example, productivity, quality, absence levels and so on), by getting feedback from others (through benchmarking, customer surveys) or from self-analysis (for example, executive teams reviewing their vision and strategy). Current performance can therefore be assessed against past performance, other organisations or units, or against desired levels to identify shortfalls that need to be addressed. Another driver for training initiatives is to look to *anticipated future changes* in, for example, the market/client base, technology, legislation, organisational structuring and other initiatives. Such changes may require employees to work in different ways and hence need to learn new knowledge and skills. Training needs exist if there are barriers to achieving objectives; the barriers are due to inadequate levels of employee behaviours and the behaviours can be enhanced through the acquisition of appropriate skills, knowledge or attitudes. Goldstein (1993) recommends securing senior organisational support early on and having the involvement of cross-functional teams with a close awareness of the training topic in order to have a successful TNA phase.

Task analysis

Next, we need to determine precisely what job tasks we should focus on, their performance standards and which knowledge, skills, attitudes and abilities are required to carry out those tasks. These will help define the instructional objectives for our learning intervention. Box 10.1 outlines the four key steps to conducting a task analysis for TNA purposes.

Person analysis

The final type of needs analysis concerns how to choose the appropriate recipients of the training. Person analysis therefore determines who needs training and what kind of instruction they need. Organisations commonly make the mistake of sending people on training courses for which they are under-prepared or where the training material is irrelevant for their jobs. Methods for selecting the right trainees include using interviews, questionnaires or structured assessment tools like proficiency tests or performance appraisals. These approaches should demonstrate

Box 10.1

How to ... conduct a task analysis during training needs analysis

A. Development of task statements:

First, we identify what tasks are performed in the job and to what standard. The goal is to write a series of sentences that convey *what* the worker does, *how* the worker does it, to *whom* or *what*, and *why* the worker does it. For example, from a General Labourer's job on a building site, one task might be 'Removes old plaster from walls in a safe and efficient manner in order to prepare for replastering or redecoration'. A number of methods (e.g. observations, interviews) can be used to collect this information and the most common are summarised in Table 10.1 with their concomitant advantages and disadvantages.

B. Development of task clusters:

Task statements are then grouped into homogenous clusters to make them more usable and manageable. A good approach is to ask Subject Matter Experts (SMEs) to sort out the task statements into meaningful categories that reflect important dimensions of work. Following the General Labourer example, we may say one cluster of tasks relates to decorating walls. The task clusters should then be prioritised in order of importance for the job role or requirements we are focusing on.

C. Knowledge, Skill, Ability (KSA) analysis:

The next step is to define the underpinning KSAs required to perform the tasks (Goldstein and Ford, 2002). *Knowledge* can be defined as a body of information that, if applied, makes adequate job performance possible. *Skill* is the capability to perform job operations with ease (usually psychomotor capacities). *Ability* refers to other capabilities needed to perform the job function (e.g. physical strength, memory capacity). Again, Subject Matter Experts can be asked to do this though questions such as 'What does a person need to know in order to [decorate walls]?' or 'What are the characteristics of good and poor employees on [decorating walls]?' The KSAs can also be clustered into meaningful categories.

D. Development of training program from the KSA-Task Links:

In this stage we can now define the aims and objectives of the training and start designing the training activities which will best enhance the specific KSAs we are interested in.

the gap between the current levels of each person's KSAs and the desired level. The size of that gap and the number of people affected define the amount of effort needed in terms of training. For a small gap in competence or a small number

Table 10.1   Methods of collecting task analysis information

Method	Advantages	Disadvantages
Observation through personal or technological means (e.g. video)	• Generates data relevant to natural work environment • Minimises work interruption	• Needs skilled observer • May affect employee behaviour • Issues of when and for how long observation takes place
Questionnaires through paper-based or internet means	• Cheap • Collect data from many people • Data easily summarised in numbers, charts, figures	• Takes time to put together • Danger of low response rate • Lack detail
Interviews with stakeholders	• Good at uncovering details • Can explore new issues • Can modify questions depending on interviewee	• Take time to do • Hard to analyse • Need skilled interviewer
Focus groups with a mix of stakeholders	• Useful with complex issues which need different perspectives • Can modify questions to explore issues	• Takes time to organise • People may be reluctant to speak out in front of others • Only one person can speak at a time
Documentation (e.g. manuals, records)	• Good source of information on procedure and tasks • Objective	• Can be out of date material • Could be too hard to understand if not familiar already with the nature of the work • Could be limited accessibility

of individuals, a few one-to-one coaching sessions with more experienced employees would be enough. If many employees demonstrate a large gap, then a substantive training programme would be introduced.

By the end of the needs analysis phase, we should therefore have answered the following questions.

- What objectives the organisation wants to achieve and how the attainment of objectives can be measured (organisational analysis).
- What standards of work behaviour are required by employees (task analysis).
- What employees should know (knowledge) to carry out work behaviour (task analysis).
- What employees should be able to do (skills) to carry out work behaviour (task analysis).
- How employees should feel (attitudinal factors) with respect to the work behaviour (task analysis).
- Who needs training (person analysis).

Training aims and objectives

Once we have finished our needs analysis phase, we can put together the aims and objectives for the learning intervention as a means of directing our efforts towards meaningful ends.

Aims involve general statements of intent for the training activity and can be summarised in a sentence or two. For example, in BuildOrg, we might be running a one-day safety training workshop and we would state the general aim of this workshop as 'To improve understanding and use of good health and safety practices on building sites.'

Box 10.2

CASE STUDY 1: Motivating Learners (CIPD, 2006)

Internet-only Bank Egg employs 2,500 people across three sites within the UK. The company's philosophy towards learning and development is one that allows employees to operate within self-imposed limits, which can be enhanced and extended through appropriate training interventions. As their Chief People Officer (CPO) explains: *'We want to equip people with the means to develop, motivate them to stay and to envisage the future they desire and make it real. People use discretionary effort because of their emotional attachment to Egg. In that way they get what they want and Egg gets what it wants'*. Hence, in understanding their employees' motivation and learning preferences this facilitates the perfect match between the organisational needs and what the employee wants to learn. Egg's HR Intranet has a set of operating practice tools available within which employees can fully use their talents. However, these operating tools are not a specific process to be followed but an ongoing relationship the individual employee has with Egg, in which their CPO believes *'complex and unpredictable organisation design and results will emerge'*.

In addition, by completing a 'know your people' course, Egg equips its people managers with the necessary skills and understanding of how to recognise people's motivations, development needs and career aspirations, thereby helping their employees in what they take on. A further course, 'committed conversations', is designed to develop managers' competence in conducting conversations that allow people to choose their learning path. This development fits the individual and meets the needs of immediate outcomes and long-term career growth. Egg believes that their greatest success will come when Egg's needs and the talent of each employee are fully satisfied.

1 What are the other benefits to the organisation from offering individual learning and development preference programmes?
2 How might management support an increase in uptake of training and career development activities?

Objectives are much more precise. They specify what a person will know or be able to do by the end of training. It is important to have clear objectives since they indicate the scope and content of training to both participants and facilitators and narrow learning to purely relevant information. They also help as a measure of mastery since you can check whether the learning objectives have been achieved after participants have finished the course. Mager (1984) states that behavioural objectives should have the following features:

- performance – state what a learner is expected to be able to do by the end of training;
- conditions – describes the important conditions (if any) under which performance is to occur;
- criterion – wherever possible, describes the criterion of acceptable performance by describing how well the learner must perform to be considered acceptable.

In our BuildOrg example of safety training, we would state our objectives as follows:

By the end of the one-day safety training course learners will:

- Know the main legislation regarding health and safety practices on building sites;
- Be able to explain the three reasons for wearing safety hats on the site;
- Be able to operate a wheelbarrow to EU Safety Standards in indoor and outdoor environments.

The next phase (design and delivery) is then deciding which training methods are most suitable for dealing with each of the objectives.

Methods of training and development

A whole variety of methods can be used to address learning needs, but Salas et al. (1995) provide a useful perspective in suggesting that training contains up to four of the following basic instructional elements.

The presentation of information and concepts to be learned

Consider the media used to present the information (face-to-face, written, online, audio only, video and so on) and the ways in which the information is structured and organised.

There should be a clear logic in the order of topics presented and an engaging approach, taking into consideration individual differences. For example, research on cognitive styles (preference for processing information) shows that some people prefer a holistic approach (for example, flicking through a textbook to quickly get an idea of the 'big picture') while others prefer a serialist, step-by-step approach (for example, reading a textbook systematically one chapter at a time to understand its nature before moving on to the next one; Riding and Sadler-Smith, 1997). A good strategy is therefore to give out training manuals and notes before the workshop.

The demonstration of skills to be learned

We often learn new skills by watching how others do it, and Bandura's (1986) social learning theory illustrates the importance of how skills are modelled (see the following section on behaviour modelling training).

The provision of opportunities to practice skills

The opportunity to practice is vital in the early stages of learning a new skill with the returns from practice diminishing as task proficiency increases. However, research highlights that overlearning (practicing a skill even though acceptable levels of performance are reached) can be beneficial in terms of retention in the longer-term (Hagman and Rose, 1983; Taylor et al., 2009), the rationale here is that the more you practice a skill, the more automated it becomes, hence the less likely you are to forget it in the future.

Feedback given to trainees on the skills demonstrated

Requesting feedback on how well you are doing is important, and the timing and nature of this feedback can be highly influential (Druckman and Bjork, 1994; Patrick, 1992). It is most useful when given just after performance of the task (so the trainee can remember what they were doing), is detailed enough to make it clear where the disparity is between current and desired performance, and is done in a constructive manner (for example, highlighting the positives and negatives of the trainees' performance) so as not to demotivate the trainee.

Training methods can therefore vary in their emphasis on the four elements. We will classify our discussion of the range of training methods into five broad classes: on-the-job training; simulations; information presentation and processing; technology-based instruction; and team training and development.

On-the-job training

By far the most common approach to learning at work is on-the-job training (OTJT), where learning is conducted in the actual work setting. This typically involves a novice being paired with a more experienced employee for a period of one-on-one tutelage in how to carry out the desired work. Novices observe all duties and gain 'hands on' experience with progressively more responsibility being given, while receiving constant feedback and coaching until a desired level of performance is reached. The advantages and disadvantages of this approach can be found in Table 10.3.

Where on-the-job training is not appropriate, then a number of off-the-job methods can be considered.

Training through using simulations

Simulations are where training is conducted in an artificial environment designed to reproduce or emulate selected job tasks. A simulator attempts to *represent* a real situation in which operations are carried out, provides users with certain *controls* over that situation and is deliberately designed to *omit* certain parts of the real operational situation (Gagné, 1962). For example, aircraft simulators allow trainee pilots to practice take-offs, flying and landing in a specially built mock-up of a cockpit with a screen providing a computer-generated representation of what they would naturally see out of the window. Table 10.2 shows some common simulation methods and Table 10.3 highlights the advantages and disadvantages of training through simulations.

Table 10.2 Common simulation methods

Type of simulation	Features
Vestibule training	Trainees practice on real plant equipment installed in a separate training area.
Equipment simulators	Trainees practice on equipment mock-ups, e.g. aircraft flight simulators.
Role-playing	Trainees are provided with a scenario and assigned roles to act out, e.g. how an employee in customer services would deal with an angry customer.
In-basket exercises	Derived from assessment centre exercises. Trainee assumes management role and handles assorted in-basket letters, memos or email inboxes. Discussion and feedback from trainer on how well this activity carried out.
Syndicate games	Groups of managerial trainees are assigned roles within a hypothetical organisation. Given information on which to base decisions and fed back results on their decisions.
Behaviour Modelling Training (BMT)	Trainees observe a skilled model before playing role themselves.

Simulation: behaviour modelling training

It is worth spending a little more time on behaviour modelling training (BMT) since there is good research evidence on its effectiveness (Taylor et al., 2005). BMT is based on social learning theory (Bandura, 1977), which outlines how we learn by observing others through four central processes. First, before a behaviour can be modelled, a person must notice it (*attention*). Second, the observer must encode the behaviour into their memory (*retention*). Third, the observer needs to translate the symbolic represen-tations in their memory into their physical actions and check their own behaviours against the model in memory (*reproduction*). The fourth element is the *motivation* of the observer to engage in the observational learning process itself; the motivation can come from the observer persuading themselves this a good thing to do, receiving positive signals from the environment or even seeing that the model is receiving ben-efits as a result of displaying the desired behaviour (vicarious association).

In practice, during a BMT session:

1   a model (for example, an expert) demonstrates the behaviour and skills the trainee has to learn. This can be live or through video;
2   the trainee is encouraged to rehearse and practice the model's behaviour;
3   feedback or reinforcement by the trainer, and possibly other trainees, is provided to approximate the trainee's behaviour that closer to that of the model.

The BMT approach in essence covers all four of the Salas et al. (1995) instructional elements (outlined in the methods of training section earlier) and evidence over the last 30 years has demonstrated its utility in developing skills (Bandura, 1977; May and Kahnweiler, 2000). A meta-analysis of 117 studies by Taylor et al. (2005) showed that BMT effects were largest for learning outcomes (about 1 standard deviation (SD) in performance between BMT and non-BMT groups) and smaller for job behaviour (0.25 SD difference between the groups); these effects on skills and job behaviour remained stable over time. The above research has also pro-vided some useful additional insights:

- Gradual modelling is more effective than one-shot modelling, especially for novel behaviours.
- Individuals can learn completely through symbolic modelling that is, by watching actions and mentally rehearsing them.
- Participative reproduction (actual practice) is more effective, in general, than symbolic processes.
- Skill development is greater when learning points are used (for example, hand-outs also provided which illustrate the main aspects to consider about the modelled behaviour) and there is a longer training time.
- Transfer of skills back to the workplace is greater where mixed models (nega-tive and positive) are used. This comparison helps clarify more precisely for participants which aspects of behaviour make a difference.

- Transfer is greater where goal-setting, training of superiors and rewards/sanctions are used since these provide additional motivation and role modelling for participants.

Although effective, BMT approaches can be resource-intensive since close monitoring and feedback is required, so costs need to be weighed up against other options.

Table 10.3   Methods of training and development: advantages and challenges

Method	Advantages	Challenges
On-the-job training (OTJT)	- Practical principles and applications taught in actual ways used in work: removes issue of transfer of training - Cheap option as no extra facilities used/needed and work is actually done at the same time - New employees acclimatise to both physical and social work environment while learning new skills - Useful approach for simple job tasks and small numbers of new recruits (e.g. production line jobs/bar work)	- Novices only become as good as person they are monitoring – bad habits can be transferred - Experts can often find it difficult to explain what they are doing - Just because trainers are experts, it doesn't mean they are good facilitators/teachers of others - Hence OTJT trainers should be provided with appropriate coaching skills - OTJT may not be amenable to some jobs (e.g. nuclear power plant operator) - Cannot be done for non-existent jobs
Training using simulations	- Useful where costs and consequences of error are too great to deal with in real life - Useful where tasks are inaccessible in real operational situations - Useful where it is too expensive to practice on the job - Ability to provide advice during the task - Ability to manipulate the dimensions of the tasks to become more/less complex - Reduces the stress of the tasks for trainees as no real consequences at stake	- Major issues around fidelity – how accurately the simulation represents the real-world task - The less realistic the simulation the more difficult it is to transfer learning into workplace - Can be expensive to set up - Important to focus realism on structural components that replicate the underlying cognitive/physical functions required rather than surface similarity - Best to replicate conditions under which tasks are done
Reading/direct study	- Simple strategy – direct learners to relevant books, articles and papers - Personalised focus to match individual's needs	- Influenced by motivation to study and skills to extract relevant information

Lectures	• Large numbers of people can be taught at same time • Cost effective • Meta-analysis of training method effectiveness indicate lectures are reasonably effective (Arthur et al., 2003)	• May fail to hit the specific needs of individuals in audience • Problems of pace and one-way communication as little opportunity for discussions of individual problems • Talking about a topic not the best way to acquire skills
Seminars	• Stimulate two-way discussions	• Success dependant on willingness of learner to prepare and participate and the leader's facilitation skills
Case studies	• Complexity of assignment encourages deeper thought	• Concern whether individuals/groups ascertain the general principles desired
Audio visual material	• Holds interest of trainee • Contextually rich • Allows control	• Expensive to produce initially • Material can become outdated and difficult to change
Technology – mediated instruction	• Cost-efficiency of delivery • Trainees can engage in training when and wherever they want • Flexibility of software to allow practice on tasks to support trainer • Computers have the potential to manage majority of the learning experience themselves through Intelligent Tutoring Systems (ITS)	• Technology may not be accessible to, or adequate for, all learners • May mean social interactions are omitted as part of the learning process

Information presentation and analysis approaches

The third category of training methods involves presentation, analysis and discussion of information. Common approaches are outlined below with their concomitant advantages and disadvantages listed in Table 10.3.

Reading/directed study

A very simple strategy is to direct learners to read relevant books, articles and papers.

Lectures

The most common approach in this category is to verbally present the material with visual aids to large numbers of people, with minimal opportunity for interaction.

Seminars/conferences

A more interactive mode of group learning is through seminars or conferences, where participants prepare and present material for discussion by their peers.

Case studies

Case studies involve learners receiving a written report that describes an organisational dilemma or problem (of an actual or fictitious organisation). Learners are expected to analyse the problem and offer solutions based on a number of factors including people, environment, strategic and physical parameters. The idea is therefore to apply knowledge in a realistic context or derive underlying principles through guided discovery. This can be done individually and then taken to group discussion. There is often no single correct solution and trainees are encouraged to be flexible, with the focus on building skills in analysis and problem-solving.

Audio-visual material

The use of audio or video is a good way of engaging learners since participants can see and/or hear the relevant material with added contextual richness and sometimes have the flexibility of using it in their own time.

Technology-mediated instruction

Technology does of course play a role in many of the aforementioned activities but here we will discuss its role in more detail. From CD-ROMs, Internet, intranets, videoconferencing to virtual reality systems, technology-mediated learning has been pushed as the future of workplace training. The annual CIPD surveys of training and development in UK organisations have shown significant usage of technology-based methods in the 21st century (CIPD, 2011). These approaches can have a number of potential advantages in terms of flexibility but also some challenges and these can be found in Table 10.3.

Programmed instruction (PI) machines were developed in the 1950s and probably the first step forward in technology-managed learning. They were based on using the psychological principles of reinforcement where learners were presented with information in a carefully planned sequence and asked questions on each step. The trainee had to respond correctly to each question before being allowed to move on to the next step. The method conveys information, provides practice and allows flexibility through self-pacing. Although learners might finish more quickly, PI was found to be no more effective for learning or retention than traditional methods (Hall and Freda, 1982). However, the PI approach did provide benefits in terms of emphasising the importance of setting discrete training objectives, having the learner as an active participant and utilising a closed-loop training system. Many e-learning programmes these days still follow the basic principle of presenting information, asking a question and only letting the learner move on if they get it right.

Intelligent tutoring systems (ITSs) are at the other end of the technology-managed learning continuum. They are designed to provide more individualised, adaptable and effective learning experiences for students. In essence, they contain three components:

- domain expertise, the rich material that is to be learned in terms of knowledge and procedures;
- a representation of the student's level of knowledge which is gained by the software continually testing the students to see which questions he or she gets right or wrong;
- a teaching expertise component which contains different types of strategies for encouraging learning in users.

The three components interact in such a way that if one approach to training a user is not working (as evidenced by lack of progress in getting questions on the topic right), the ITS can switch to a different approach to teaching the material. Also, learners are given material which is continually matched against their learning needs, providing a more efficient experience. An early example of organisational practice was the learn, explore and practice (LEAP) ITS project developed by US WEST in 1992 as a means of training its new customer telephone contact employees. Other applications since have been in the realms of language teaching, mathematics tutoring and military applications. Since ITSs are fundamentally the incorporation of artificial intelligence approaches in a training context, they are very expensive and time-consuming to develop, hence the current lack of their presence in the mainstream.

Virtual learning environments (VLEs) really took off with the introduction of the Internet, particularly Web 2.0. These are computer-based environments that are relatively open and allow networked interactions with other people. These activities can be synchronous where people engage with tutors and each other in real-time. Second Life™ is one example of an online social environment which has come to be used for a variety of training purposes, for example, teaching medical procedures and helping teams planning for different disaster scenarios. Interactions can also be asynchronous (not in real–time) and these are represented by emails, bulletin boards, discussion forums and so on. Many educational establishments are utilising VLEs to complement or even replace traditional pedagogical/teaching activities. VLEs can offer a truly global reach, but the experience for learners will be heavily affected by access to technology that is capable enough to deal with the relevant demands.

Mobile learning technologies, encompassing wireless and cloud computing coupled with increasingly powerful smartphones and laptops, are making it easier to undertake learning wherever you are. For example, iTunes U from Apple currently has over 350,000 educational lectures, videos and resources from around the world to download on to mobile devices.

Although the potential of technology to enhance learning is exciting, it is telling that in the CIPD 2011 Learning and Talent Development survey, e-learning still came out as 12th in effectiveness out of 13 training methods HR members were asked to rate. We do therefore need to ensure that employees can access the technology, that there are still social interactions between employees and that the material is engaging enough (Noe, 2010).

Team training and development

Work teams are identifiable as a coherent group of two or more people engaged in the completion of a common and valued goal, and who have to work on tasks together in order to reach that goal (Allen and Hecht, 2004). According to researchers (Cannon-Bowers et al., 1995), effective teams:

- have highly skilled members who can effectively complete the tasks the team must perform (taskwork skills);
- have highly developed skills related to working in a team in general, for example, co-ordination, conflict management (teamwork skills);
- develop processes to continually diagnose and address issues that constrain performance, for example, problem-solving skills (process improvement skills).

Various methods are used to enhance taskwork, teamwork and process improvement skills, and we shall discuss common team training and team building approaches.

Team training activities

Involve a systematic effort to improve group effectiveness by enhancing task-related knowledge, skills and attitudes.

Cross training

- Where individuals learn two or more of the jobs that must be performed by the team.
- Often a more experienced team member trains the others.
- Allows increased flexibility for the team, enhances employees' input/value, and facilitates self-management.
- More time consuming to do, the more complex the team jobs become.

Interpositional training

- Less resource intensive.
- The aim is for individuals to acquire a working knowledge of the tasks performed by team-mates and the interconnections between them.

- To build a 'shared mental model' of the tasks between team members and improve cooperation and communication.
- Meta-analysis research highlights that teams with better shared cognition showed better team behaviour processes, were more motivated and performed better (DeChurch and Mesmer-Magnus, 2010).

Teambuilding activities

- Focus on analysing and improving team interactions and processes.
- Most popular approach is sending teams on adventure learning/outward bound activities. Participants are given difficult and unfamiliar physical and mental challenges in an outdoor setting, for example, helping each other over river crossings and other obstacles, constructing shelters out of natural materials or navigating unfamiliar terrain. The aims include improving co-ordination, trust, risk management strategies, creativity, problem-solving and support networks in teams.
- Evidence shows that team building activities can have a moderate positive effect on how people feel about the team and how the team works but issues remain on how well this translates to improved performance back in the workplace (Hattie et al., 1997; Klein et al., 2009).

In summary, the key issue is to match the right training methods to the appropriate objectives. Lectures may be a good, quick way of developing knowledge about health and safety legislation, but practicing on a simulated worksite would be a better way of developing safe working skills like using a wheelbarrow. Beyond the methods used, we also need to weigh up the materials and facilities needed, ensure training facilitators are well-equipped, and create a learning intervention appropriate to the time and resources available to us.

Evaluation

Evaluation is the systematic collection of data relevant to the selection, value or modification of training and development activities (Goldstein, 1986). The data can therefore provide information on whether the training or development activity is effective in achieving its aims and demonstrate the overall value and worth of development activities. Furthermore, we can use it to provide information on how to increase the effectiveness of current or later development activities. From the learner's point of view, we can also assess and specify the areas individuals need to focus on for further development. It is crucial that appropriate evaluation is conducted for training and development activities, given the time and money invested in their design and delivery (Bramley, 1996). We will discuss a variety of models and methods for evaluating the effectiveness of training and development activities.

Formative versus summative evaluation

The first distinction to make in types of evaluation is illustrated in Figure 10.3. Formative evaluation is where data is continually collected and analysed course-by-course during the roll-out of the training programme with the aim of continually improving it. For example, we may run a pilot course and collect feedback from participants to ascertain where learning objectives were or were not being met. We would then take this information to redesign the next course to ensure that unmet objectives would be better addressed. We would again collect feedback data after that to check objectives were being met and so on. The course therefore continually evolves until it reaches a state where the outcomes are at desired levels. Our collection of evaluation data would then recede to more periodic sampling or until an aspect of our input changes significantly (for example, we have a new facilitator).

In contrast, summative evaluation has a long time cycle and is about assessing the overall impact of a programme by comparing the state of functioning of organisations, groups and individuals before the programme ran at all with the state once everyone has been through the programme. For example, if we ran the one-day safety training programme 10 times at BuildOrg between April and September, we could compare accident and absence rates from January to March (before the programme ran) with levels from October to December to compare if there had been any meaningful changes (after the programme had finished). From a practitioner point of view, the formative approach is favoured since the aim is to continually improve the programme. From an academic point of view, the summative approach is favoured where there is no change in the course since researchers like to assess the impact of the same learning activity on many groups of learners.

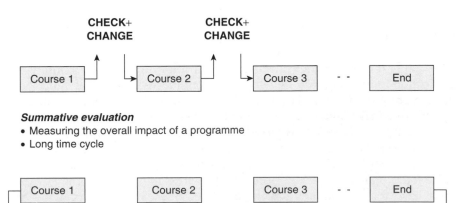

Figure 10.3 Formative versus summative evaluation

Formative can of course be combined with summative evaluation, but be aware that changing the course during the programme means it can be harder to tell which parts of the course are actually generating the meaningful impact picked up by summative comparisons.

Training evaluation models

The Kirkpatrick four-level model

Kirkpatrick's (1959a, 1959b, 1960a, 1960b, 1996) framework is one of the oldest yet still most popular training outcome evaluation models. This is probably because of its simplicity in stating that training effectiveness can be evaluated at four levels as follows.

Level 1 – reactions

- What are trainees' opinions about the training in general and about specific aspects?
- This data is acquired typically through end-of-course questionnaires or interviews. Reaction data can be useful if it provides specific enough feedback on which changes can be made (for example, which parts of the course were useful, which course objectives were met).

Level 2 – learning

- Do trainees acquire the knowledge and skills for which the training was developed?
- This data is acquired through knowledge and skill-based tests.

Level 3 – work behaviour

- Do trainees apply their new knowledge/skills back in the workplace? (Transfer of training.)
- Behavioural data can be gathered through questionnaire ratings by peers, supervisors, customers, self or others, or more objective job performance measures.

Level 4 – business results

- Do the expected changes in organisational performance (for example, increased productivity) appear as a result of the training?
- Data can be collected through tracking existing performance information, gathering new sources of information (for example, customer satisfaction over time), structured interviews with management or even trainee self-reports of examples of impact.

Although a sound basis for developing evaluation strategies, a number of issues need to be considered about the Kirkpatrick model. Many organisations only evaluate at level 1 or level 2 and fail to follow up trainees back in the workplace to assess changes in work behaviour at level 3. This can be partly because problems in deciding who should do level 3 follow-up evaluation (trainer or line manager) means usually neither accept the responsibility. Even less effort is expended at level 4 since there is a logical difficulty in attributing distant organisational outcomes to training, although there is increasing pressure to do so.

The Kirkpatrick model has been criticised (Bates, 2004; Beech and Leather, 2006) in only covering part of the story and three other approaches will be discussed which address these gaps.

Warr, Bird and Rackham's CIROP model

The Kirkpatrick approach focuses only on outcomes of training, whereas the CIROP (Warr et al., 1970; Warr, 2002) model emphasises evaluation information needs to be collected from the earliest stages of training design. Five different types of evaluation are therefore described which cover the training cycle as a whole.

Context evaluation

Within the needs analysis stage, three levels of objectives are outlined:

- Ultimate objectives (what problem in the organisation is the trainer hoping to ultimately change or what organisational objective is the trainer aiming to achieve?).
- Intermediate objectives (what changes in individual work behaviour would the trainer like to influence?).
- Immediate objectives (what immediate knowledge, skills or attitudes do individuals need to acquire to meet the intermediate objectives?).

Input evaluation

The next phase addresses the issue of what is likely to bring about the desired changes. Here, considerations are thus made of available resources (for example, budget, personnel) and possible training techniques, taking into account trainee and organisational factors.

Reaction evaluation

Similar to Kirkpatrick's model, this type of evaluation asks about trainees' feelings about the course, such as overall enjoyment, perceived utility and experienced difficulty.

Outcome evaluation

- Immediate outcomes refer to changes in knowledge, skills and attitudes as measured immediately after the training (Kirkpatrick's level 2).

- Intermediate outcomes cover changes in trainees' on-the-job behaviour (similar to Kirkpatrick's level 3).
- Ultimate outcomes refer to how the department or organisation has changed, similar to Kirkpatrick's level 4 results. This is not generally to be measured at the individual level but to be indicated by changes in the entire department or organisation (for example, improvements in productivity). Again, traditionally, this is seen as very difficult to do.

Process evaluation

- Retrospective view of how well the training development and delivery system has worked once the programme has finished.
- Concerned mainly with the trainees' actual experience of training rather than the intended experiences and so can capture unintended consequences.

The CIROP approach is therefore more wide-ranging than Kirkpatrick in also including contextual, input and process considerations, as well as outcomes.

Kraiger, Ford and Salas' cognitive, skill-based and affective learning outcomes approach

The seminal paper by Kraiger et al. (1993) criticised Kirkpatrick's level 2 for treating learning too simplistically and instead offered a multi-dimensional perspective with three types of outcomes. Cognitive learning outcomes concern verbal knowledge, the organisation of knowledge and cognitive strategies. Skill-based outcomes (involving technical or motor skills) concern how quickly, accurately and easily tasks are carried out. Most interestingly, the authors added affective outcomes as the third category, covering both attitudes and motivational aspects. This latter feature was not really addressed in the original Kirkpatrick model. Although enlightening, the Kraiger approach only focused on learning outcomes, whereas the following model addresses a much wider range of potential impact areas.

Birdi's Taxonomy Of Training And Development Outcomes (TOTADO) model

Birdi (2000, 2010) addresses the issue that past outcome evaluation frameworks focus on certain levels more than others and fail to specify the types of dimensions within those levels clearly enough. TOTADO therefore outlines how training and development activities may be assessed in terms of their impact at the *individual, group, organisational* or *societal* level (see Figure 10.4). Within each level, outcomes can be grouped into conceptually meaningful categories. For instance, individual-level outcomes are separated into affective (for example, attitudes), cognitive (for example, knowledge organisation), behavioural (for example, quality of task performance), physiological (for example, fitness) and instrumental (for example, events such as gaining promotion) dimensions. The majority of the individual-level outcomes can also be applied by aggregation to the work-group context, although there is more focus on measuring interpersonal behaviours and group cognition and affect (for example, shared mental models). The organisational-level outcomes build on the work of organisational performance researchers (for example, Kaplan and Norton, 1996) and can be described under four headings: outputs (for example, quantity and quality of goods produced), financial (for example, profitability), resources (for example, skills of employees), and internal processes (for example, efficiency of systems). Finally, the societal-level considers the wider impacts of training on the community in terms of economic, health and social care, educational, law and order and environmental criteria.

The TOTADO approach offers a number of theoretical and practical advantages:

- It acknowledges that the effectiveness of training and development participation should be assessed on a number of levels, using a range of relevant criteria within

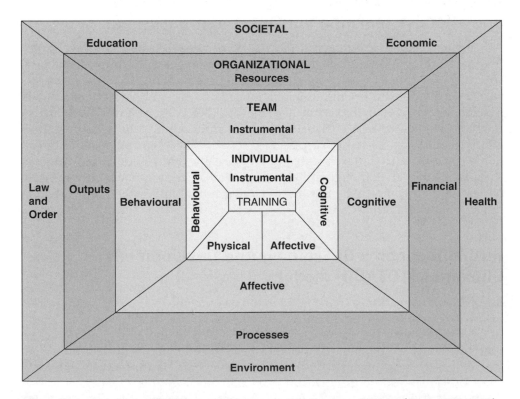

Figure 10.4 Taxonomy of Training and Development Outcomes – TOTADO (Birdi, 2000, 2010)

each level. Conceptually, it integrates the traditional Kirkpatrick training evaluation approach with the wider evaluation perspective offered by other literatures.

- The taxonomy clearly distinguishes between individual, team, organisational and societal measures of organisational effectiveness. Approaches such as Kirkpatrick's have tended to remain vague about measures of individual work behaviour and organisational results and seemed to have ignored team-level or societal analysis altogether.
- The nature of the taxonomy also allows detailed and comparative examination of the types of outcomes produced by different learning activities. For instance, how much impact does participation in formal training compared to work-based development activities have on employees' general job satisfaction?
- The evaluation taxonomy provides a common format for assessing learning and development impact from a diverse range of theoretical approaches. The TOTADO framework is intuitive enough to be applied in practice. For example, in the authors' experience, it has already been used to evaluate a wide variety of programmes, including creativity training, management development, coaching initiatives, quality problem-solving and developing empathic and communication skills in general practitioners.

Box 10.3 provides an evaluation interview schedule based on the TOTADO framework which you can apply to your own training programmes.

Box 10.3

OP IN PRACTICE

How to ... conduct a training evaluation follow-up interview using the BIRDI (2000, 2010) TOTADO framework

The following interview schedule is a good way of collecting data from training participants on the impact of the training on the individual, team/group, organisation or society. Treat the interview as a 'menu' from which you can pick the questions relevant for your training programme. As well as identifying change at each level, within each section we also probe for reasons why desired changes did not occur as a way of understanding how to increase training effectiveness in the future. Please note that the questions can be adapted for other stakeholders apart from the trainee (e.g. supervisors, senior managers, clients) to provide a more rounded view.

TOTADO INTERVIEW SCHEDULE

'In the following interview, I shall be asking you to describe any changes that you think have arisen because of programme X.'

(Continued)

(Continued)

A. INDIVIDUAL OUTCOMES

GENERAL LEAD IN
As a result of taking part in X, how do you think you have changed?

AFFECTIVE
How has taking part in the X changed the way you FEEL about things?

COGNITIVE
What type of things have you LEARNED as a result of taking part in X?

PHYSICAL
How has taking part in the X changed your LEVELS OF HEALTH AND FITNESS?

BEHAVIOURAL
What can you DO now that you couldn't do before taking part in X?

How has taking part in X changed your JOB PERFORMANCE?

INSTRUMENTAL
Has taking part in X led to any changes in the type of work you do?

Has taking part in X led to any changes in your job status or conditions of employment?

Has taking part in X helped you form new relationships at work or changed existing relationships?

Has taking part in X led to any other changes in your work that we haven't discussed yet?

Has taking part in X led to any changes for you outside work?

IDENTIFYING BARRIERS TO CHANGE IN INDIVIDUAL OUTCOMES

Has anything in particular stopped or hindered you changing personally the way you wanted after the training / taking part in programme X?

Is there anything that could be changed about programme X, your organisation or other aspects that could help you achieve these desired changes?

B. TEAM / GROUP OUTCOMES

GENERAL LEAD IN
As a result of taking part in the X programme, how do you think your team has changed?

AFFECTIVE
How has taking part in X changed the way your team FEELS about things?

COGNITIVE
What type of things has your team LEARNED as a result of taking part in X?

BEHAVIOURAL
What can your team DO now that they couldn't do before taking part in X?

How has taking part in X changed your team's WORK PERFORMANCE?

INSTRUMENTAL
Has taking part in X led to any changes in the type of work your team does?

Has taking part in X led to any other changes in the type of work your team does?

Has taking part in X helped your team form new relationships at work or changed existing relationships?

Has taking part in X led to any other changes in your team's work that we haven't discussed yet?

IDENTIFYING BARRIERS TO CHANGE IN TEAM/GROUP OUTCOMES

Has anything in particular stopped or hindered your team or teams changing the way that was wanted after the training / taking part in programme X?

Is there anything that could be changed about programme X, your organisation or other aspects that could help you achieve these desired changes?

C. ORGANISATIONAL OUTCOMES

GENERAL LEAD IN

As a result of running the X programme, how do you think your organisation has changed?

OUTPUTS

Has running X led to any changes in your organisation's outputs, e.g. its productivity, quality levels, variety of products/services offered and so on?

RESOURCES

Has running X led to any changes in your organisation's employees, e.g. their performance, morale, absenteeism?

Has running X led to any changes in your organisation's material resources, e.g. reductions in wastage?

PROCESSES / OPERATIONS

Has running X led to any changes in your organisation's efficiency or the way work is carried out, e.g. speed of production, turnaround on project times?

FINANCIAL

Has running X led to any changes in your organisation's financial performance, e.g. its profitability, balancing of budgets?

Has taking part in X led to any other changes in your organisation that we haven't discussed yet?

IDENTIFYING BARRIERS TO CHANGE IN ORGANISATIONAL OUTCOMES

Has anything in particular stopped your department or organisation changing the way that was wanted after the training / taking part in programme X?

Is there anything that could be changed about programme X, your organisation or other aspects that could help you achieve these desired changes?

D. SOCIETAL OUTCOMES

GENERAL LEAD IN

What types of general impact would you say the X programme has had on communities or groups outside the organisation?

(Continued)

(Continued)

ECONOMIC

What types of general impact would you say the X programme has had on the economy in your region?

E.g. £ investment in geographic region, unemployment rates in area

HEALTH AND WELFARE

What types of general impact would you say the X programme has had on the health or welfare of the community in your region?

E.g. number of deaths from heart disease, alcohol-related illnesses in local population

EDUCATIONAL

What types of general impact would you say the X programme has had on the education levels of the community in your region?

E.g. level of qualifications of local population, % social inclusion of minorities

LAW AND ORDER

What types of general impact would you say the X programme has had on law and order issues in the community in your region?

E.g. number of robberies in the area, % reduction in drug crime

ENVIRONMENTAL

What types of general impact would you say the X programme has had on the geographical environment of your region?

E.g. pollution and waste levels in the region

Has taking part in X had any other impacts on the local or national community that we haven't discussed yet?

IDENTIFYING BARRIERS TO CHANGE IN SOCIETAL OUTCOMES

Has anything in particular stopped or hindered your organisation's impact on the community or society in the way you wanted after the training / taking part in programme X?

Is there anything that could be changed about programme X, your organisation or other aspects that could help you achieve these desired changes?

Assessing the value of training

In this final section, we focus on different methods of assessing the worth of training. Many of the evaluation models above presented different types of outcome data to be collected, but here we will discuss the various advantages and disadvantages of when that data is collected. Figure 10.5 shows three alternative strategies for timing of data collection:

- Strategy 1 – the advantage here is that we can see whether trainees have reached a desired standard of knowledge and 'passed' the course. However, the disadvantage is that we do not know how much they knew before they came on the course and hence how much they actually improved during the training. We may well have been teaching them many things they knew already.
- Strategy 2 – this does allow us to see how much trainees improve by the end of training. Unfortunately, as the period between the pre- and post-training measures increases, the likelihood of non-training factors influencing the improvement increases. For example, trainees' knowledge of a topic may increase not because of the training course they receive but rather a new set of manuals has been produced for them to use in the workplace over the same period of time.
- Strategy 3 – the best test for teasing out the impact of the training compared to other factors. Using a traditional experimental design, pre-and

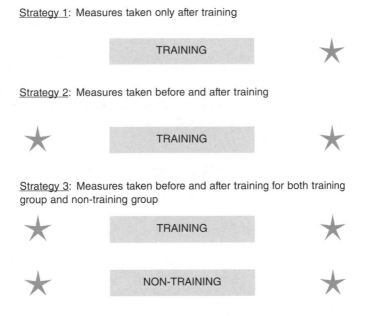

Figure 10.5   Three strategies for timing of evaluation data collection

post-training measures are taken both of trainees and a similar non-trained group over the same time period, that is, the only difference between the two groups is the training. All things being equal, any difference in knowledge, skills behaviour, performance and so on, between the trained and non-trained groups will be due to the training. Typically, organisations react negatively to the idea that certain individuals will not be trained in strategy 3 so a good tip is to have the non-trained group instead as one that is waiting to be trained at a later date. A number of courses usually have to be run for everyone to take part in the training programme so it makes sense to make comparative use of those who will come later.

The control group arrangement in strategy 3 is the best way of assessing the bottom line impact of training versus other factors on organisational performance (level 4 of Kirkpatrick). If that approach is not possible, then Bothell and Cullen (2002) suggested a number of alternative strategies that could be used. The first involves analysing performance data for changes in trends before and after training or comparing between departments that have and have not received training. The second approach is to ask key stakeholders (trainees, supervisors, managers, customers and so on) to estimate the impact the training has had on changes in organisational performance, either through percentage ratings or through provision of examples. The third approach is examining existing studies to ascertain performance differences that would be expected due to training. For example, we have already discussed the meta-analysis by Taylor et al. (2005) on skills and performance differences generated by behaviour modelling training. Case study 2 (Box 10.4) gives an example of an evaluation study conducted in a vehicle manufacturing company to illustrate the application of a selection of the above principles.

Finally, we should briefly discuss the financial return on investment (ROI) from running a training programme, which Phillips (1996) considered should be added as the fifth level to Kirkpatrick's evaluation framework. This cost-benefit analysis is most simply represented by the following equation:

$$\text{ROI} = \frac{\text{TRAINING BENEFITS} - \text{TRAINING COSTS}}{\text{TRAINING COSTS}} \times 100$$

Training costs should be continually monitored and include:

- personnel and labour costs involved in design, delivery and development of the training programme;
- personnel costs in actually taking people off the job to spend time on the training or development activities;
- training materials (for example, handouts, manuals, presentation materials);
- delivery costs (for example, rental of rooms/equipment, travel).

Training benefits are harder to assess but need to be quantified in some manner. For example, these may be related to improvements in performance (productivity, sales, accidents and so on) or reductions in cost (for example, cheaper materials, less machine downtime). Although difficult to do in certain cases, there is now greater organisational pressure than ever to justify investment in training and development activities.

Box 10.4

CASE STUDY 2: Evaluating the impact of quality improvement training in a car manufacturer

The first author of the chapter was asked to evaluate the impact of a major quality improvement training programme conducted in a car manufacturing company. The firm was faced with poor levels of quality in a number of its vehicle ranges and so instigated a programme to improve the quality problem-solving skills of production line team leaders. The course was two and a half days long and involved a mixture of lecture, discussion and practical simulations of shopfloor activities. Over 750 staff took part in the programme over a six month period (April to August) and hence this represented a significant investment in time and money.

Four methods were used to evaluate the training programme. First, a questionnaire was given out to participants at the beginning and the end of the course (Time 1 and 2) then three months (Time 3) and six months later (Time 4). The questionnaires collected information on trainees' reactions to the course (Time 2 and 3), their level of self-rated competence in a range of quality problem-solving skills (all four time points) and their use of those skills in the workplace (Time 1, 3 and 4). Statistical analyses showed trainees responded positively to the course and showed significant improvements in both their competence and reported skill use after the training. The second method was designed to provide a more objective measure of learning and consisted of a multiple-choice knowledge test given to participants at Time 1 and Time 2. Again, analyses showed significant improvements in knowledge with an average pre-course score of 40% correct answers compared to 80% by the end.

With regards to assessing the bottom-line impact of the training, the third method was simply to collect the existing monthly quality performance information (the number of faults found per vehicle) over the period of the year during which the programme ran. Plotting a line through the data showed a clear improvement in quality performance trends once the programme started running and that levels were significantly better after the programme finished compared to the beginning of the year before it ran. There is an issue here that any improvements in quality over this time period could have been due to other things going in the company. Therefore, the fourth evaluation method involved conducting interviews with the senior managers responsible for the 10 main manufacturing areas, both before the programme ran and after it had completely finished. The post-programme interviews asked the managers to rate the impact the training had had on levels of quality in their area (and why) plus identify other activities that were also influencing quality levels over the same time. The interviews clarified that although the creation of new job roles and tools had improved quality, the training did have a substantive role in improving bottom-line performance in that domain.

1   How else could the impact of the training on bottom-line performance have been assessed?
2   What do you think are the practical difficulties of carrying out this type of extensive evaluation and how can they be overcome?

Factors influencing short-term and long-term effectiveness (transfer of training)

Some people learn more than others by the end of training, and others apply their learning to a greater extent in the workplace compared to their peers (known as the transfer of training in the latter case). A significant body of research has emerged which has attempted to identify why this may happen (for example, Aguinis and Kraiger, 2009; Baldwin et al., 2009; Burke and Hutchins, 2007; Colquitt et al., 2000; Tannenbaum et al., 1993). In this section, we shall briefly summarise the five main types of influence on the short-term acquisition of learning by the end of a course and the longer-term transfer of training to work (see Figure 10.6).

The bullet points are of course illustrative and other factors can also be placed under those headings.

Training features – the various advantages and disadvantages of instructional methods have already been discussed above but a number of additional aspects need to be considered. Pre-training activities cover tasks or materials given to participants either before or at the beginning of training sessions. These include advance organisers/previews that outline the content of the course in summary form (and interestingly have been shown to be positively related to the transfer of training in the long term (Blume et al., 2010)), setting pre-work (to get learners up to the same standard before training), having pre-tests to screen out underprepared individuals or even having briefings

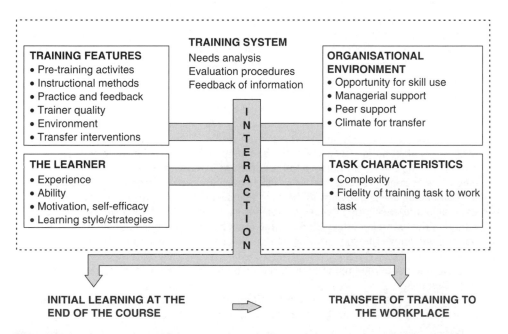

Figure 10.6   Framework of influences on short-term and long-term training effectiveness

with line managers before attendance. Other important features include the amount of practice and feedback participants get in developing skills, plus the quality of the trainer's content and facilitation skills (Burke et al., 2006; Hesketh, 1997). Post-course interventions to improve the transfer of learning include setting goals for application in the workplace, generating strategies for enhancing the likelihood of implementing new skills (known as behavioural self-management) and encouraging self-coaching in the workplace (Tews and Tracey, 2008).

Learner characteristics – naturally, the pre-existing experience, knowledge and skills of participants should influence their learning success, but an individual's general cognitive ability has also been shown to be a key predictor of performance (Blume et al., 2010). Stable personality traits have also shown some relationship with training performance. Out of the Big Five personality traits, various meta-analyses have shown conscientiousness and openness to experience to be related to better training outcomes while findings on other dimensions have been more mixed (Barrick and Mount, 1991; Colquitt et al., 2000; Salgado, 1997). Much more malleable than the latter is somebody's motivation. This can be in terms of attending training, engaging fully in learning activities while on the training or willingness to apply what has been learned back in the workplace. These three types of motivation are distinct and trainers should consider how to maximise each type of motivation (for example, through outlining the benefits of acquiring and applying the taught skills) as they are influential on both short-term learning and long-term transfer (Birdi et al., 1997; Colquitt et al., 2000; Zoogah, 2010). Building up learners' self-efficacy/confidence and reducing their anxiety regarding the topics to be learned are also important issues to consider. Finally, people do differ in their preferences for how they learn (for example, some people like reading material systematically step-by-step while others skim through to get a 'big picture'), so you need to ensure a variety of learning activities are included that appeal to different learning styles (Holman et al., 2001).

Organisational environment – the nature of the workplace becomes particularly important for the transfer of training. The opportunity to use learned skills is an obvious influential factor, but social support also plays a key role. Supervisors can provide instrumental support to allow trainees the time and resources to apply their skills, but they are also important in terms of providing explicit verbal encouragement and implicit role-modelling of desired behaviours (Birdi, 2007; Blume et al., 2010; Ford et al., 1996). Interpersonal support from peers may also be required for an individual to feel comfortable utilising their training in their job, especially where the new behaviours are challenging the status quo (Pidd, 2004). Roullier and Goldstein (1993) have even suggested that there is a general transfer of training climate in organisations, which they characterise in terms of the existence of situational cues to apply learning in the workplace and presence of feedback on use/non-use of skills.

Task characteristics – the more complex the tasks being learned, the greater the mental load on the learner, hence the need for training to be more systematic and longer in these contexts. When it comes to transfer, the fidelity (similarity) of the trained task to the real-world task becomes influential. This focus on fidelity should be more on structural task components (related to task attainment) rather than surface components (not related to task objectives) (Singley and Anderson, 1989). However, it is good to also replicate the conditions under which the task is to be carried out.

Training system – finally, we must restate the importance of the general training cycle steps we have spent the majority of this chapter discussing. Have the relevant needs analyses been done and the objectives appropriately specified? Are the appropriate training methods used given the nature of the task, the audience and the resources available? Saks and Burke (2012) recently found that organisations which undertook more evaluation (particularly around work behaviour and organisational results) were more likely to report higher rates of transfer of training. So, what procedures are in place for evaluating short-term and long-term change, how will this information be fed back to key stakeholders and what actions will be taken if desired changes are not taking place? Deficiencies in any of these areas could also therefore undermine the impact of the learning intervention.

Summary

In conclusion, we can draw together the main themes of this chapter in considering how to introduce more effective training programmes in organisations.

- The training cycle covers the key aspects of needs analysis, design and delivery of training and evaluation of its effectiveness.
- Before starting any training interventions make sure the appropriate organisational (why is learning required), task (what needs to be learned) and person (who needs training) needs analyses are carried out.
- Ensure that training aims and objectives are clear.
- Ensure that the right training methods are matched to the right learning objectives:
  - o on-the-job training is conducted in the actual work setting. It develops the skill in the context in which it is to be used so minimises transfer problems, but there can be issues with the unstructured nature of activity and the tutor role;
  - o simulation training is conducted in an artificial environment designed to reproduce or emulate selected job tasks. This allows practice in a safe context to develop practical skills, and dimensions of the task can be manipulated. However, there can be issues with fidelity of simulation to the real-world task;
  - o information presentation and processing training is conducted in an off-the-job setting in which information analysis is the basis of learning. This is good for conveying knowledge or attitude change, but there are issues with appropriateness for developing skills;
  - o team training activities focus on developing job KSAs, and team building activities focus on team interactions and processes.

- Evaluation needs to be considered from the start of the training design process.
- How much effort and detail needs to be put into evaluation depends on the purpose and availability of resources.
- One needs to be aware of the wide range of outcomes that can be influenced by training and development activities, and develop a strategy to assess the outcomes both in the short-term and long-term.
- There are different approaches to evaluation but there is more of a deficit in checking whether learners actually apply their skills in the workplace (transfer of training) and impact on organisational performance.
- A concluding point, and one we hope clearly emerges from the above discussion, is that when developing training programmes, an interactive design approach is needed which considers the learning objectives and nature of the task being learned, the suitability and viability of different training methods, the attributes of trainees and the organisational context in which trainees operate. Training interventions need to take these issues into account in order to provide the most effective methods of learning and to facilitate the transfer of training to the workplace.

As mentioned at the beginning of this chapter, the use of technology in training is set to increase more and more. The next chapter will focus on the impact of automation on our working lives and cognitive processing. The knowledge from this can be used to inform some thoughts and questions around how to address online or e-learning in the future.

Explore further

- Li, J., D'Souza, D. and Du, Y. (2011). Exploring the contribution of virtual worlds to learning in organisations. *Human Resource Development Review,* 10 (3), 264–85.

A good discussion of the role of virtual technology in influencing future learning.

- Lynton, R.P. and Pareek, U. (2011). *Training for Development*. London: Sage.

This book provides more detailed practical guidance on the training stages.

- Nielsen, K., Randall, R. and Christensen, K. (2010). Does training managers enhance the effects of implementing teamworking? A longitudinal, mixed methods field study. *Human Relations*, 63 (11), 1719–1741.

A good example of implementing an evaluation strategy.

- Noe, R.A. (2010). *Employee Training and Development (Fifth Edition)*. New York: McGraw-Hill.

This book provides more in-depth research and practical coverage of the different aspects of training we have discussed.

- Powell, K.S. and Yalcin, S. (2010). Managerial training effectiveness: A meta-analysis 1952–2002. *Personnel Review*, 39 (2), 227–41.

A useful, wide-ranging review of training impact studies.

- Sadler-Smith, E. (2005). *Learning and Development for Managers: Perspectives from Research and Practice.* Oxford: Blackwell Publishing.

This book also provides more in-depth coverage, with a good focus on management development also.

- Tennant, M. (2006). *Psychology and Adult Learning (Third Edition)*. London: Routledge.

A good overview of different psychological theories of learning.

- Chartered Institute of Personnel and Development, available online at: www.cipd.org.uk

A UK-based professional HR association with lots of useful reports and articles for download.

- American Society of Training and Development, available online at: www.astd.org

A US-based professional HR association with lots of useful reports and articles for download.

- *Personnel Psychology, Journal of Applied Psychology, International Journal of Training and Development, Personnel Review, Academy of Management Learning and Education.*

Good peer-reviewed journals which offer insights into the latest training research.

Discussion questions

1 Why do you think the transfer of training is such a big problem and what do you think could be done about it?
2 Is it better for organisations to just select new people into a job or is it better to train and develop existing employees to do the job?
3 How do you see technology impacting on training in organisations over the next 10 years?

Sample essay questions

1 You have just been employed as the head of training and development for Deskos Ltd, a major furniture manufacturer. The organisation is based on a single site and has a workforce of 8,000 employees. Its main products are tables and chairs for office use. However, it has recently started making a

new product range of specialised beds (known as 'Easi-Beds') in order to diversify and gain greater market share. The beds are specifically designed for people with back problems and can be adapted for different medical conditions. There are more complex versions for hospital use and simpler types designed for private home use.

Deskos originally used its existing sales-force to try selling Easi-Beds to retailers but found that the sales people could not cope with the extra demands and knowledge required by this job. Now, the company has set up a specialised Easi-Bed Sales Division, which consists of 10 of their better existing sales people and 40 new and inexperienced sales recruits. The Managing Director of the company has given you the important task of managing the training and development of these 50 salespeople with the aim of ultimately improving the level of Easi-Bed sales by 10% by the end of this year.

After having conducted a thorough needs analysis, you realise that these sales people would perform significantly better if they improved their communication and negotiation skills, and also had greater knowledge of the types of back conditions that would be helped by Easi-Bed.

What type of training or development interventions would you undertake to ensure the sales-force learned and applied the necessary knowledge and skills? How would you evaluate the effectiveness of your learning interventions? Describe the different types of options you could choose from and justify the particular approach you decide to use. What practical problems might arise from conducting training and evaluation activities this way, and how would you deal with them?

2 Based on the extant literature, critically discuss how different individual, training and work environment characteristics can impact on training effectiveness. What practical recommendations would you therefore make to improve short-term and long-term training outcomes?

Sample examination questions

1 Critically evaluate the usefulness of on-the-job training compared to other training methods.

2 You have been asked to evaluate two training programmes that are run in-house in a manufacturing company. The managing director of the company is unsure if they are effective. The first programme is a one day machine maintenance module for shop floor workers and the second is a one week negotiation skills course for managers. Outline the methods and measures you would use to evaluate these programmes and the actions you would take to present the MD with an effective means of evaluating these programmes.

OP IN PRACTICE: A DAY IN THE LIFE OF ....

Professor Kurt Kraiger, Professor of Industrial Organisational Psychology, Colorado State University, USA

What areas of OP do you work within?	My primary area of interest is training, although I have broadened this to include 'learning in ill-structured environments' to include topics such as leadership development and mentoring. Specific to training, I am interested in what happens when persons try to learn in front of the computer, as it is much less structured (or can be) than the classroom, and the learner is more on their own in terms of choosing topics, measuring progress, and so on. In the past few years, I've expanded this interest to include training older adults.
How did you become interested in this area?	I had a faculty fellowship with a research lab for the US Navy in 1989. They were becoming heavily involved in designing and testing team training, and needed help with the evaluation end of training.
What have been the seminal research papers in this area?	<ul><li>Aguinis, H., and Kraiger, K. (2009). Benefits of training and development for individuals and teams, organisations, and society. *Annual Review of Psychology, 60,* 451–474.</li><li>Baldwin, T.T., Ford, J.K. (1988). Transfer of training: A review and directions for future research. *Personnel Psychology, 41,* 63–105.</li><li>Bell, B.S., and Kozlowski, S.W.J. (2002). Adaptive guidance: Enhancing self-regulation, knowledge and performance in technology-based training. *Personnel Psychology, 55,* 267–306.</li><li>Kraiger, K., Ford, J.K., and Salas, E. (1993). Integration of cognitive, skill-based, and affective theories of learning outcomes to new methods of training evaluation. *Journal of Applied Psychology, 78,* 311–328.</li><li>Noe, R.A., and Schmitt, N. (1986). The influence of trainee attitudes on training effectiveness: Test of a model. *Personnel Psychology, 39,* 497–523.</li></ul>
To what extent does the practical application of your work inform your research?	There is a huge gap between the practice of training and the science of training, so in that sense, there is no link. It doesn't make sense to be chasing training fads. On the other hand, my research on training older workers comes out of a very applied problem. More and more workers are staying employed longer, and may need to be retrained. Since there are known cognitive deficits associated with aging, it's important to understand the effects of these on learning.
What role do ethics have in your work?	I believe that ethics provides a compass that implicitly guides decision-making, perhaps without awareness.
Can you give an example of a day in your working life?	There is no typical day. Across a week, I might spend 3–4 hours in the classroom, 3–4 hours preparing for teaching, 5 hours writing (that's a goal!), 5 hours either meeting with students or interacting with them via email, 3–5 hours reviewing students' proposals, theses, and so on, 4–6 hours in various meetings, 8–12 hours managing email, 6–8 hours handling various administrative tasks.
How do you see your work changing over the next five years?	Clearly, topics such as virtual work, telecommuting, social networks and so forth will be increasingly important. Again, organisations will *implement* these types of interfaces, but the question is whether what they implemented is based on research of what works and why.

OP IN PRACTICE: A DAY IN THE LIFE OF ....

Alastair Wallace, Managing Director at Brainfood Ltd

What areas of OP do you work within?	Transfer of training.
How did you become interested in this area?	I believe it is critical to all learning that transfer takes place, otherwise you are wasting your time, and that of your learner. It is estimated that only 10–15% of training had been shown to result in behavioural changes back in the workplace (Kontoghiorghes, 2004; Baldwin and Ford, 1988; Broad and Newstrom, 1992; Facteau et al., 1995; Georgensen, 1982). This clearly indicates a need for more empirical research into how training is transferred, and the factors that contribute towards successful or unsuccessful transfer.
	More and more organisations are focusing on return on investment in training, and with the advent of greater corporate downsizing and outsourcing, training managers have been spurred on in an attempt to prove efficacy of training, and a demonstrable impact in the workplace (Kearns and Miller, 1996; Easterby-Smith, 1994; Newby, 1992). There is 'intense pressure' applied to trainers and managers to justify spend on training and there are difficulties in measuring efficacy of training departments. I believe there will always be a strong market for training that delivers measureable results, and my organisation, Brainfood Ltd, is committed to providing this as part of our values.
What kinds of organisations are interested in your work and why?	I think it is directly relevant to all organisations that have an interest in successful learning, and high performance. Brainfood works with large multinationals and small businesses alike.
How is your work informed by theory, literature and research?	All my work is informed by theory and research. The past 30 years have seen a massive explosion in the quantity of training research with particular focus on research and theorising in the field of training transfer (Ford and Weissbein, 1997). This has resulted in a large number of new theories, models, reviews and meta-analyses being developed (Salas and Cannon-Bowers, 2001). Although this research is more widely available, trainers have historically often failed to apply the scientific knowledge that does exist.
	It is particularly difficult to identify links between attending training courses and transfer of learning leading to improved managerial performance (Antonacopolou, 1999). Baldwin and Ford (1988) refer to the 'transfer problem' and discuss the problematic nature of measuring transfer of training in the workplace. So we work with organisations to avoid the 'transfer problem'.
What role do ethics have in your day-to-day practice?	Ethics form a critical part of the relationship between the OP practitioner and client, irrespective of their specific discipline. You often have access to highly sensitive commercial information, such as strategies and budgets, and this information could bring down an organisation, or hugely assist its competitors if it is handled carelessly. This is particularly evident when

(Continued)

(Continued)

	working across multiple organisations, where conflict of interest may occur. Often organisations that regularly use OP freelancers will have specific clauses relating to this in their contracts of engagement. On a more personal level, ethics plays a part in working with individuals. When you are helping someone with a development need, they may feel exposed or vulnerable, and it is important that this is handled sensitively and with diplomacy, however ensuring that the organisation's needs are not being compromised.
Can you give an example of a day in your working life?	There is not really a typical day for me! Let me give you a flavour of a typical week instead, which should give you a clearer idea of the type of work that I do and the sheer diversity. • **Monday** – Facilitated a workshop with a small communications agency in London to help them think through the requirements and Key Performance Indicators for their new ERP (enterprise resource planning) system. Quite challenging as the group are very senior and have very definite ideas about what they want! • **Tuesday** – Working from home. Completing the design of a performance appraisal system, and then process mapping the employee and manager's journey before designing an interactive training session to communicate and test it out. • **Wednesday and Thursday** – Fly to Nice to deliver two day conflict management training for large IT firm. 12 delegates from 8 different countries – variable abilities to speak English! Write up evaluation report and course refinements on the flight home. • **Friday** – Carrying out psychometric assessments for a large international drinks manufacturer and giving feedback as part of a development centre.
How has your work changed in the last five years?	Training and development has seen many changes over the last five years. Organisations are becoming less willing to permit long periods of abstraction from duty to attend full or multiple day training events, preferring the learning to take place at desks or in short bursts. This trend has manifested itself in two key ways: e-learning and short session learning. Many industry big-hitters were talking about the 'evolution' – where e-learning would overtake classroom training about ten years ago. Interest in e-e-learning (while still present) seems to have quietened somewhat. However, it has been replaced with movement towards a more blended and multi-component approach. The term 'blended learning' is still misunderstood by many practitioners, with many believing it to mean classroom training + e-learning. The most successful blended learning programmes take Baldwin and Ford's transfer model as a start point, and use this to leverage a truly blended learning programme that is weaved into the fabric of an organisation. It is less likely that training practitioners will turn up and deliver an 'off the shelf, chalk and talk'

training event (although this does still happen in certain organisations!) Clients expect practitioners to engage at a much earlier point in the process of development, using diagnostic tools such as surveys, interviews and focus groups to establish learning needs before beginning a high level programme architecture and approach. The detailed design for training events is changing dramatically also as part of the move towards blended learning, incorporating pre-engagement activities, delegate-centred and discovery based learning, assessment and post-course reinforcement activities. All of these are having a positive impact on the delegate experience, with many organisations reporting a higher take up for training and better overall satisfaction scores. Sadly, although satisfaction with training seems to be increasing, practitioners and organisations still have a very poor relationship with proving bottom line impact. Evaluation processes do not seem have moved on very far, since Kirkpatrick, with many organisations still only evaluating at the most basic levels of delegate experience and learning (Level 1 and 2) at best.

Over the last five years, another of the notable themes within training has been the move towards short session or 'bite size' learning. The growth and success of companies like The MindGym, offering 90 minute 'workouts', where participants learn and practice one isolated skill or technique, is testament to this trend. MindGym now operate in over 30 countries, having trained over 500,000 delegates in over 400 of the world's most successful companies such as Google, Pepsico and Pfiser. Many other large training companies are following suit and developing similar short session propositions to compete for the ever decreasing amount of time and money that is made available for staff training.

How do you see your work changing over the next five years?	Technology will undoubtedly play a part in how training develops over the next five years. The huge increase in the number of smartphones and tablet computers such as the iPad (and the 100 or more imitators already available now), has caused some to forecast that most web searches will take place on these devices by 2014. The potential of these devices is growing exponentially, in terms of both processing speed and graphics capability, and this in turn is leading to new and exciting ways of incorporating their use in a training environment to run events such as 3D virtual simulations for trainee surgeons and electronic performance support systems (EPSS) to provide real time support for complex and highly dangerous roles. All it takes is a simple search on an applications store for your mobile device to find many interesting and diverse ways in which training and learning is taking place, driving theory mock tests, monitoring your expenses and budget, to learning the valves of the heart. As you often hear people say 'There's an app for that!'

Training practitioners are starting to use social networking to set up communities of practice to share ideas and techniques, and also to build cohorts of participants across multi-disciplinary long term programmes, where delegates are often geographically dispersed.

Cloud computing is also set to revolutionise the way we store and share information, with both Apple and IBM launching major new infrastructures |

(Continued)

(Continued)

in late 2011 that will allow organisations and social groups to share everything from music and photos to business email and organisation data through cloud use. Although this sounds very exciting, and heralds a new age in the way we share knowledge and learn, it is not without its difficulties. The 2010 IBM Global IT Risk Survey showed that 77% of respondents believed cloud would make protecting privacy more difficult, 50% expressed concerns about data breach or loss and 66% overall cited security as their top concern when considering cloud.

Learning practitioners will need to stay abreast of these new technologies and keep an ear to the ground if they are to be part of the new world. Anyone who does not speak this new and sometimes confusing language will certainly be left behind pretty quickly!

References

Aguinis, H., and Kraiger, K. (2009) 'Benefits of training and development for individuals and teams, organisations, and society', *Annual Review of Psychology*, 60: 451–74.

Allen, N.J. and Hecht, T.D. (2004) 'The 'romance of teams': toward an understanding of its psychological underpinnings and implications', *Journal of Occupational and Organisational Psychology*, 77 (4): 439–61.

Antonacopoulou, E. (1999) 'Developing learning managers within learning organizations: the case of three major retail banks', in M. Easterby-Smith, J. Burgoyne and L.Araujo (eds) *Organizational Learning and the Learning Organization*. London: Sage. pp. 217–42.

Arthur, W., Bennett, W., Edens, P., et al. (2003) 'Effectiveness of training in organisations: a meta-analysis of design and evaluation features', *Journal of Applied Psychology*, 88: 234–45.

ASTD (2010) *State of the Industry Report 2010*. Alexandria, VA: ASTD.

Baldwin, T. and Ford, J. (1988) 'Transfer of training: a review and directions for future research', *Personnel Psychology*, 41, 63–105.

Baldwin, T., Ford, J. and Blume, B. (2009) 'Transfer of training 1988–2008: an updated review and agenda for future research', in G. Hodgkinson and J. Ford (eds), *International Review of Industrial and Organisational Psychology*. Chichester: Wiley. pp. 41–70.

Bandura, A. (1977) *Social Learning Theory*. Englewood Cliffs, NJ: Prentice Hall.

Bandura, A. (1986) *Social Foundation of Thought and Action*. Englewood Cliffs, NJ: Prentice-Hall.

Barrick, M. and Mount, M. (1991) 'The big five personality dimensions and job performance: a meta-analysis', *Personnel Psychology*, 44: 1–26.

Bates, R. (2004) 'A critical analysis of evaluation practice: the Kirkpatrick model and the principle of beneficence', *Evaluation and Program Planning*, 27: 371–47.

Beech, B. and Leather, P. (2006) 'Workplace violence in the health care sector: a review of staff training and integration of training evaluation models', *Aggression and Violent Behavior*, 11 (1): 27–43.

Birdi, K. (2000) 'Bigger and smaller pictures: identifying the factors influencing training effectiveness'. PhD thesis, University of Sheffield.

Birdi, K. (2007) 'A lighthouse in the desert? Evaluating the effectiveness of creativity training on employee innovation', *Journal of Creative Behavior*, 41 (4): 249–70.

Birdi, K. (2010) 'The taxonomy of training and development outcomes (TOTADO): a new model of training evaluation', in *The B.P.S. Occupational Psychology Conference Book of Abstracts 2010*. pp. 32–6.

Birdi, K., Allan, C. and Warr, P. (1997) 'Correlates and perceived outcomes of four types of employee development activity', *Journal of Applied Psychology*, 82 (6): 845–57.

Blume, B., Ford, J., Baldwin, T., et al. (2010) 'Transfer of training: a meta- analytic review', *Journal of Management*, 36: 1065–105.

Bothell, T. and Cullen, R. (2002) 'Isolating the effects of training: balancing the practical versus theoretical approach', paper presented at the *American Society for Training and Development 2002 International Conference and Exposition*, New Orleans.

Boydell, T. and Leary, M. (1996) *Identifying Training Needs*. London: Institute of Personnel and Development.

Bramley, P. (1996) *Evaluating Training Effectiveness*, 2nd edn. New York: McGraw-Hill.

Broad, M. and Newstrom, J. (1992) *Transfer of Training: Action-packed Strategies to Ensure High Payoffs From Training Investments*. Reading, MA: Addison-Wesley.

Burke, L. and Hutchins, H. (2007) 'Training transfer: an integrative literature review', *Human Resource Development Review*, 6: 263–96.

Burke, M., Holman, D. and Birdi, K. (2006) 'A walk on the safe side: the implications of learning theory for developing effective safety and health training', in G. Hodgkinson and K. Ford (eds), *The International Review of Industrial and Organisational Psychology (Vol. 21)*. Chichester: Wiley.

Burke, M., Salvador, R., Smith-Crowe, K., et al. (2011) 'The dread factor: how hazards and safety training influence learning and performance', *Journal of Applied Psychology*, 96 (1): 46–70.

Cannon-Bowers, J.A., Tannenbaum, S.I., Salas, E., et al. (1995) 'Defining competencies and establishing team training requirements', in R.A. Guzzo and E. Salas (eds), *Team Effectiveness and Decision Making in isation Organisations*. San Francisco, CA: Jossey-Bass. pp. 333–81.

Chiu, W., Thompson, D., Mak, W.M., et al. (1999) 'Re-thinking training needs analysis – a proposed framework for literature review', *Personnel Review*, 28 (1–2): 77–90.

CIPD (2006) *Learning and Development Annual Survey Report 2011*. London: CIPD.

CIPD (2011) *Learning and Talent Development Annual Survey Report 2011*. London: CIPD.

Colquitt, J.A., LePine, J.A. and Noe, R.A. (2000) 'Toward an integrative theory of training motivation: a meta-analytic path analysis of 20 years of research', *Journal of Applied Psychology*, 85: 678–707.

DeChurch, L. and Mesmer-Magnus, J. (2010) 'The cognitive underpinnings of effective teamwork: a meta-analysis', *Journal of Applied Psychology*, 95 (1): 32–53.

Druckman, D. and Bjork, R. (eds) (1994) *Learning, Remembering, Believing*. Washington, DC: National Academy Press.

Easterby-Smith, M. (1994) *Evaluating Management Development, Training and Education*, 2nd edn. Brookfield, VT: Gower.

Facteau, J., Dobbins, G., Russell, J., et al. (1995) 'The influence of general perceptions of the training environment on pretraining motivation and perceived training transfer', *Journal of Management*, 21 (1): 1–25.

Ford, J.K. and Weissbein, D.A. (1997) 'Transfer of training: an updated review and analysis', *Performance Improvement Quarterly*, 10: 22–41.

Ford, J., Kozlowski, K., Kraiger, E., et al. (1996) *Improving training effectiveness in work organisations*. Hillsdale, NJ: Erlbaum.

Gagné, R. (1962) 'Military training and principles of learning', *American Psychologist*, 17: 83–91.

Georgenson, D. (1982). 'The problem of transfer calls for partnership', *Training and Development Journal*, 36 (10): 75–8.

Goldstein, I. (1986) *Training in Organisations*, 2nd edn. Monterey, California: Brookes/Cole Publishing Company.

Goldstein, I. (1993) *Training in Organisations*, 3rd edn. Pacific Grove, California: Brookes/Cole Publishing Company.

Goldstein, I. and Ford, J.K. (2002) *Training in Organisations*, 4th edn. Belmont, CA: Wadsworth.

Gould, D., Kelly, D., White, I., et al. (2004) 'Training needs analysis. A literature review and reappraisal', *International Journal of Nursing Studies*, 41 (5): 471–86.

Hagman, J. and Rose, A. (1983) 'Retention of military tasks: a review', *Human Factors*, 25 (2): 199–213.

Hall, E. and Freda, J. (1982) *A Comparison of Individualised and Conventional Instruction in Navy Technical Training (No. Technical Report 117)*. Orlando, FL: Training analysis and evaluation group.

Hattie, J., Marsh, H., Neill, J., et al. (1997) 'Adventure education and out of bound: out-of-class experiences that make a lasting difference', *Review of Educational Research*, 67 (1): 43–87.

Hesketh, B. (1997) 'Dilemmas in training for transfer and retention, '*Applied Psychology: An International Review*, 46 (4): 317–86.

Holman, D., Epitropaki, O. and Fernie, S. (2001) 'Understanding learning strategies in the workplace: a factor analytic investigation', *Journal of Occupational and Organisational Psychology*, 74: 675–81.

Kaplan, R. and Norton, D. (1996) 'Linking the balanced scorecard to strategy', *California Management Review*, 39: 53–79.

Kearns, P. and Miller, T. (1996), *Measuring the Impact of Training and Development on the Bottom Line*. Hitchin: Technical Communication (Publishing).

Kirkpatrick, D. (1959a) 'Techniques for evaluating training programs', *Journal for the American Society for Training and Development*, 13: 3–9.

Kirkpatrick, D. (1959b) 'Techniques for evaluating training programs: Part 2 – learning', *Journal for the American Society for Training Directors*, 13: 21–6.

Kirkpatrick, D. (1960a) 'Techniques for evaluating training programs: Part 3 – behavior', *Journal for the American Society for Training Directors*, 14: 13–18.

Kirkpatrick, D. (1960b) 'Techniques for evaluating training programs: Part 4 – results', *Journal for the American Society for Training Directors*, 14: 28–32.

Kirkpatrick, D. (1996) 'Revisiting Kirkpatrick's four-level model', *Training and Development*, 50 (1): 54–9.

Klein, C., DiazGranados, D., Salas, E., et al. (2009) 'Does team building work?', *Small Group Research*, 40: 181–222.

Kontoghiorghes, C. (2004) 'Reconceptualising the learning transfer conceptual framework: empirical validation of a new systemic model', *International Journal of Training and Development*, 8 (3): 210–21.

Kraiger, K., Ford, J. and Salas, E. (1993) 'Application of cognitive, skill-based and affective theories of learning outcomes to new methods of training evaluation', *Journal of Applied Psychology*, 78 (2): 311–28.

Mager, R.F. (1984) *Preparing Instructional Objectives*, 2nd edn. Belmont, CA: David S. Lake.

May, G.L. and Kahnweiler, W.M. (2000) 'The effect of mastery practice design on learning and transfer in behavior modelling training', *Personnel Psychology*, 53: 353–74.

McGehee, W. and Thayer, P. (1961) *Training in Business and Industry*. New York: Wiley.

Newby, A.C. (1992) *Training Evaluation Handbook*. San Diego, CA: Pfeiffer.

Noe, R.A. (2010) *Employee Training and Development*, 5th edn. New York: McGraw-Hill.

Noe, R.A. and Tews, M.J. (2012) 'Realigning training and development research to contribute to the psychology of competitive advantage', *Industrial and Organisational Psychology*, 5 (1): 101–4.

Patrick, K. (1992) *Training: Research and Practice*. London: Academic Press.

Patrick, J., Michael, I. and Moore, A. (1986) *Designing for Learning – Some Guidelines*. Birmingham: Occupation Services.

Phillips, J. (1996) 'How much is the training worth?', *Training and Development*, 50 (4): 20–24.

Pidd, K. (2004) 'The impact of workplace support and identity on training transfer: a case study of drug and alcohol safety training in Australia', *International Journal of Training and Development*, 8 (4): 274–88.

Powell, K.S. and Yalcin, S. (2010) 'Managerial training effectiveness: a meta-analysis 1952–2002', *Personnel Review*, 39 (2): 227–41.

Riding, R. and E. Sadler-Smith (1997) 'Cognitive style and learning strategies: some implications for training design', *International Journal of Training and Development*, 1 (3): 199–209.

Rouillier, J. and Goldstein, I. (1993) 'The relationship between organisational transfer climate and positive transfer of training', *Human Resource Development Quarterly*, 4: 377–90.

Saks, A.M. and Burke, L.A. (2012) 'An investigation into the relationship between training evaluation and the transfer of training', *International Journal of Training and Development*, 16: 118–27.

Salas, E. and Cannon-Bowers, J.A. (2001) 'The science of training: a decade of progress', *Annual Review of Psychology*, 52: 471–99.

Salas, E., Burgess, K. and Cannon-Bowers, J. (1995) Training Effectiveness Research', in J. Weimer (ed.), *Research Techniques in Human Engineering*. Englewood Cliffs, CA: Prentice-Hall.

Salgado, J. (1997) 'The five factor model of personality and job performance in the European Community', *Journal of Applied Psychology*, 82: 30–43.

Singley, M. and Anderson, J. (1989) *The Transfer of Cognitive Skill*. Cambridge, MA: Harvard University Press.

Tannenbaum, S., Cannon-Bowers, J., Salas, E., et al. (1993) *Factors that Influence Training Effectiveness: A Conceptual Model and Longitudinal Analysis* (No. 93–011). Orlando: Naval Training Systems Center, Human Systems Integration Division.

Taylor, P.J., Russ-Eft, D.F. and Chan, D.W.L. (2005) 'A meta-analytic review of behavior modelling training', *Journal of Applied Psychology*, 90 (4): 692–709.

Taylor, P., Russ-Eft, D. and Taylor, H. (2009) 'Transfer of management training from alternative perspectives', *Journal of Applied Psychology*, 94 (1): 104–21.

Tews, M. and Tracey, B. (2008) 'An empirical examination of post-training on-the-job sup-
plements for enhancing the effectiveness of interpersonal skills training', *Personnel
Psychology*, 61 (2): 375–401.

Warr, P. (2002) *Psychology at Work*. London: Penguin.

Warr, P., Bird, M. and Rackham, N. (1970) *Evaluation of Management Training*. London:
Gower Press.

Zoogah, D. (2010) 'Why should I be left behind? Employees' perceived relative depriva-
tion and participation in development activities', *Journal of Applied Psychology*, 95 (1):
159–73.

11 Automation and human–machine interaction

Varuni Wimalasiri

Learning outcomes

The aim of this chapter is to:

- provide an overview of automation and human-machine interaction (HMI): key definitions and scope of the area;
- describe its history within Occupational Psychology;
- outline work carried out in the area of human-computer interaction (HCI);
- explain and discuss learning and performance in interactive procedures and its relationship to human cognition, perception and action;
- explain the concept of human error in organisations and provide insights into preventative measures;
- explore emerging themes and future implications for automation and HMI.

Introduction

The area of automation and human-machine interaction (HMI) in Occupational Psychology seeks to discover and apply information about human behaviour, abilities and limitations, to the design of tools, machines, systems, jobs and the person's environments, to enhance productivity and safety in the workplace (Karwowski, 2006). It looks to understand how people use processes such as perception, cognition and action to deal with equipment. This could be in the context of work, recreation or in domestic use. Set against a backdrop of a broad range of sub-topics, the scope of the subject ranges from machine operating objectives (for example, identifying the best visual displays for a worker in a particular type of job) to system redesign (for example, redesign of equipment, procedures and individual and organisational principles related to a certain aspect of work).

Only the naive believe humans fly airplanes. (Ilgen and Howell, 1999)

Ilgen and Howell (1999) make this interesting statement on the Society of Industrial and Organisational Psychology website (the US equivalent of the Division of Occupational Psychology) to illustrate the impact of automation and technology on the modern workplace. They explain how a modern pilot does not fly an aeroplane on his own to get safely from one destination to another; instead he or she relies heavily on the aircraft's sophisticated navigation system and on ground control systems operated by others. They use this analogy to emphasise the increasingly indivisible boundary between human thinking and the thinking done on our behalf by technology. Ilgen and Howell emphasise that those who are not aware of this thinning boundary inherent in the modern workplace are in danger of being naive to its reality and its risks. The principles they describe do not end at flight navigation systems, but they extend to the more day-to-day aspects of work.

Automation and technology continue to create considerable changes in our daily lives and in our workplaces. They extend our human abilities and allow us to undertake tasks which would otherwise be too complex or too time consuming to complete within the span of a day. Take for example the immediacy and accuracy of phone and email messages, allowing us to relate messages and share knowledge with colleagues across continents within a matter of seconds; or the photocopying systems which allow us to copy documents in seconds and transfer them over the Internet. These are all relatively new technology systems, some of which have only been introduced into the general work environment in the last 20 years. In fact some of you may remember workplaces that were free from technology such as emails and the world wide web. All of these and other advancements help to simplify complex tasks and enable us to complete many more than would otherwise have been possible within a day or even a year.

Toffler (1980) likened the scale and impact of this revolution to the agricultural and industrial revolutions of the past, which transformed the way people experienced and functioned in the workplace. Where in the last two centuries much of the work people undertook involved hands-on experience and face-to-face interaction with other people (for example, taking vegetables to market or assembling products on a conveyor), workers are having to work increasingly on a 'virtual' level where much of their interaction is 'indirectly' with others through some of form of technology (Eason, 2002). This transformation of the workplace also means that the psychological requirements placed on the person and their relations with their environment have undergone a significant amount of transition, which calls on a completely different set of rules to grapple with these changes. We are in what we might call an era of 'techno-dependency' (Harper et al., 2008), where principles of automation and HMI have become an important and unavoidable part of our work environments. This change in the industrial land-scape has also meant that this area of study is gaining increasing importance in work-based disciplines such as Occupational Psychology.

History and background of automation and HMI

The term 'automation and human-machine interaction' implies that this area of work explores only the principles of psychology applied to understanding automation issues and humans interacting with machinery. Let us consider this for a moment: in our workplaces we frequently come across computer systems that have the capabil-ity of thinking like humans or going beyond our own capabilities. These might include space exploration systems and virtual reality. Such changes in the techno-logical landscape form a thinning boundary between the thinking of humans and that of computers (Ilgen and Howell, 1999), which implies that modern investigation into the area of the area of automation and HMI is as much about understanding the subtleties of these boundaries as the design of those systems. Work in the area has closely followed advancements of technology in the workplace. As a result the area has seen a varied history and lacks a neat or consistent trajectory. The first sign of this inconsistency comes from the varying labels given to the area of automation and HMI across time and continents. In America this field is called 'applied experimen-tal and engineering psychology' (Proctor and Vu, 2010) and in Europe the area is called 'ergonomics' (Howell, 2003). There is still a lack of universal agreement of a definitive name and the labels seem to have changed over the years with the evolv-ing needs of people and contemporary trends. HMI is the youngest of all the disci-plines of Occupational Psychology enjoying around half a century of documented work. The first review in the area appears in the Annual Review of Psychology in 1958, which defines the discipline as having 'both a professional and scientific aspect' (Fitts, 1958). In 1960 Occupational Psychology laid its initial claims on the area by indicating that issues relating to automation and computer programming are part of the 'newer' role of the industrial psychologist (Gilmer, 1960).

There is a significant time lag of around 24 years between the documented appearance of the discipline in the USA and in the UK. The term first appears in one of the British Psychological Society's (BPS) archived working party reports on the 'future of Occupational Psychology' in 1984 as 'person-machine interactions', which then was considered as sub-area of 'ergonomics' (Davies and Toplis, 1984). Since then the themes noted under 'ergonomics' have been divided up between two key areas that refer to HMI and 'Design of environments and work: health and safety' (Chapter 7). This may also help to explain the significant overlaps that exist between the two areas in Occupational Psychology syllabi.

Automation and HMI in Occupational Psychology is informed by the areas of 'human factors' and 'ergonomics', which refer to the interdisciplinary field con-cerned with design of systems and products for human use (Proctor and Vu, 2010). Work in the area of human factors and ergonomics dates further back than work in

HMI in psychology, meaning that work relevant to HMI was undertaken well before it was documented by any of the governing bodies of psychology. This also means that the history of these related literatures bear evidence of the roots of significant theoretical paradigms related to this and other areas of Occupational Psychology. For instance, automated target prediction systems on wartime aeroplanes took into consideration psychology alongside mathematics, engineering and physiology in their design (Hayward, 2001: 293). Also the Applied Psychology Unit at Cambridge University was involved in improving the seating structures of war-time control rooms in the UK to improve visibility of the plotting tables; helping controllers to be more efficient at conveying information across to battle field operations; and also in helping to understand pilot fatigue (Bartlett and Mackworth, 1950).

Box 11.1

Definitions

Human Factors: The study of human beings and their interaction with products, environments, and equipment in performing tasks and activities. Work in this area looks at human capabilities and limitations, which the helps to apply these principles and applies these to the design, optimising and evaluating human-machine systems (Czaja and Nair, 2006).

Ergonomics: Examines the nature of the human-artefact interactions within the system to determine the dimensions and requirements of those particular interactions (Karwowski, 2006).

Human and computer interaction (HCI)

Historically a large focus of HMI in Occupational Psychology has been on issues relating to human interaction with computers. It is also perhaps the more obvious contribution of HMI to the area of HCI, which looks to understand the interaction between humans and computers and employs a multi-disciplinary approach to make computing systems useful and usable (Olson and Olson, 2003). Work in this area includes contributions from disciplines such as cognitive, social and organisational psychology; anthropology, sociology and the computer sciences. Given that primary design and development issues are dealt with by those who are concerned with the machine component alone, the task of a psychologist usually involves providing scientific and empirical input into the human element of the system. Such collaborative work has led to significant advancements in computing. In fact it has been said that the evolution of the personal computer was delayed due to the fact that early software development was based on expert usability alone and did not consider the unsophisticated user (Howell, 2003: 542).

We have seen a mass proliferation of computing to assist day-to-day activities in our workplaces such as email systems and the world wide web. These systems are constantly evolving and present new and varied challenges to their designers and users. Take for example the early introduction of computers into the workplace, where some of the design goals at the time were relatively simple compared to the complex systems we have today. A study carried out in the 1980s looked at how improvements can be made to allow someone to produce a two-page business letter in less than ten minutes with fewer than three errors after 30 minutes training (Carroll, 1997). In contrast, the challenges dealt with by HCI specialists today are phenomenal. The introduction of graphical user interphases (GUI – commonly pronounced gooey), which allow users to interact with displays with images rather than words, were a giant leap in computing displays and were influenced much by the early work of psychologists (Carroll, 1997). A GUI gives a user information and actions available to them using graphics, icons and visual images rather than text-based interfaces or text commands. Although this form of display has become a staple in computers, it is likely to be overtaken by others, such as web and mobile applications, immersive environments such as virtual reality, and ubiquitous computing where technology weaves itself into daily life. Some researchers are also looking at the possibility of using HCI to extend and improve people's skills and abilities at work (e.g. Xanthopoulou and Papagiannidis, 2012) (see Box 11.3). As computing becomes a staple of society we are seeing more and more diverse population groups looking to interact with technology. These populations include children, older people, people with disabilities or those with no particular training in technology use.

The need for design to accommodate the diverse skills and abilities of these extended populations drives some of the work of psychologists involved in HCI today. One such example is designing the visual composition of a GUI. The goal is to enhance the efficiency of the system while ensuring ease of use for the user of the programe – a design discipline known as usability. Methods of user-centered design are used to make sure that the graphics and 'visual language' introduced in the design is tailored to the user's needs and the tasks needed to be carried out. Think for example of an iPhone®: the goal was to create a phone that would not need an instruction manual because the design was so easy to use. For further information on user-centred design, see the insight from Dr Chandra Harrison in the 'OP in Practice: A Day in the Life of …' at the end of this chapter.

More recently HCI has seen a shift from the individual cognitive level of interaction with computing to an interest in looking at what impact social and organisational issues have on their use. Attention has turned to how people use computer-supported cooperative work (CSCW) and how to improve these processes. Some of the topics covered look at: how people use emails; meeting support systems; conferencing tools; and instant messaging to communicate with each other. Work by psychologists in these areas include teamwork; trust (Bos et al., 2002; Rocco et al., 2000); work-life balance due to the constant availability of the 'office' through technology (Hill et al., 1998) among others. This trend on focusing on the more macro issues in organisations continues in the wider field of automation and HMI today. The rest of this chapter will focus on this level of work by looking at organisational and social issues considered within the area of automtion and HMI.

Learning and the performance of people in automation and HMI

Decision making in organisations

To be able to understand how people interact with machinery it is first important to appreciate the various human cognitive processes involved in such a process and the benefits and limitations that arise from these. Decision making is one such process. To get by in our day-to-day lives we have to break down a complex amount of information presented to us by our environments. The stark advances in technology mean that a great deal of uncertainty is continuously introduced into our workplaces and our homes. Take for example the following analogy: the new wave of students in higher education use mobile devices for note-taking in lectures. If a student needs further information to solve a problem in class then she or he is likely to link into the world wide web, available immediately to them through their device as well as asking their lecturer. She or he is then able to make a greater contribution to the in-class discussion based on this extended knowledge. This also means that the subject knowledge in that session becomes very complex. The lecturer (who, in the past, would have only needed to know immediate knowledge about the topic) now needs to prepare more widely to serve the changing needs of her or his students, providing more up-to-date answers to the problems discussed in class. Essentially a small improvement in technology has not only changed the circumstances of the immediate student but has transformed the whole classroom environment and its needs.

As human beings, we are governed by our ability to think and reason our way through complex situations. As in the classroom, the workplace is in constant flux and provides a great deal of ambiguity. Modern organisations invest a significant amount of money to bring in new equipment to enhance the efficiency of the workplace. As with the lecturer's environment in the classroom, this introduction of new technology puts new demands on the people in the workplace by introducing a significant amount of new information which requires processing. This holds a potential problem for our human capabilities. Essentially a worker's ability to reflect on their life, to plan and solve problems, provides the basis of their thinking behaviour (Walsh, 1995; Wimalasiri, 2007). This ability is determined by a finite source of higher order cognitive processes. Conversely, these are the key processes that help us to 'think' by solving problems, making decisions, attending to cues and reasoning. Table 11.1 shows these abilities categorised into five main components.

At a more subtle level we overcome our cognitive limitations by producing patterns or templates within our minds which act as starter cues for incoming information.

Table 11.1 Five cognitive processes and their function

Cognitive process	Function
Problem solving	The cognitive activity undertaken when the problem is recognised and steps are taken to draw solutions to that problem.
Decision making	Selecting one out of a number of possible options or possibilities.
Judgement	A component of decision making which attempts to calculate the likelihood of various possible events.
Deductive reasoning	Deciding on what conclusions might be true given that initial assumptions are true.
Inductive reasoning	Deciding certain findings are true based on the information available.

Source: Adapted from Eysenck and Keane (2010: 458).

These have been given various labels including, heuristics (Tversky and Kahneman 1973), schema (Bartlett, 1932) and mental models (Senge, 1993). Essentially we compensate for our limited cognitive abilities by creating these mini storehouses of recurring information. When we are presented with information from our environment we simply process the *additional* information, since our 'mini storehouses' provide us with the standard information. Therefore, we do not have to start from scratch. These 'stores' or patterns are used particularly when information is sparse (Hertwig and Todd, 2003) and gives an advantage of speed of processing. This helps to simplify judgements and decision making within these highly complex work environments (Weber and Johnson, 2009). They also ease the pressure on a person's judgement processes and on other cognitive resources such as attention and memory (Kahneman, 2003; Weber and Johnson, 2009; James, 1890).

To understand this concept a bit better let us take, for example, driving a car. When you first learn to drive, the task seems very complex, made up of many manoeuvres and instructions. However over time it becomes 'second nature' to you and many of the manoeuvres come naturally. You will automatically hit your brake at the right time, use the clutch pedal appropriately and shift gears when coming up to a traffic light. This is because in order to preserve cognitive capability, our minds are able to store routine activity in the form of a 'mental model'. This means that when we are experienced drivers we can attend more to the traffic and the weather conditions rather than the driving activity, which helps us to get from one location to another safely. However, human beings are 'finite-capacity information processors and satisficers' – they are limited to how much they can stretch their abilities by their cognitive resources which are innate to them (Jones, 1999; Simon, 1957). Therefore, as a result of these patterns being based on previous experience they might not necessarily serve the purpose of a decision or judgement at hand. Indeed some of these mental models may have gaps which would only become evident after a decision making event (Besnard et al., 2004). As a result people, even experts, are prone to systematic biases. To go back to the example of the car: where normal activity is disrupted, say if you see that the car behind you is coming towards you at speed, you might panic and accidentally hit the car in front or at least jump a traffic light ending up committing a traffic offence. This is where bias or error is most likely to occur (these will be discussed in a later section in this chapter in more detail).

Research in the area of HMI has made significant advances in their under-standing of how people make decisions in complex environments similar to or perhaps even more complicated than the ones described thus far. Early studies on decision making were carried out in lab settings (Anderson, 1990; Kahneman and Tversky, 1979, 1984; Pennigton and Hastie, 1986; Tversky and Koehler, 1994) where decisions are easier to locate and test. These studies have provided a deep understanding of the 'heuristics' or the rules of thumb that our minds use to make decisions. They have allowed psychologists from various sub-disciplines such as neuropsychology and clinical/Occupational Psychology to understand behaviour in great detail and extend these ideas and understand their applica-tions in more detail (Anderson et al., 2005; Busemeyer and Johnson, 2004; Dijksterhuis, 2004; Gilbert et al., 2006).

Although in reality, the workplace presents a more complex environment. Particularly for human factors researchers, the issue of transferring lab-based findings to the field presents a growing problem. To address, this a movement called the 'the naturalistic decision movement (NDM)' was initiated in Dayton, Ohio, in 1989 with 30 social scientists who had an interest in understanding the context of decision making in applied settings. They had an interest in contexts such as flight decks, emergency control centres and the military, among other environments, which require decision making in critical hazardous situations, to improve work processes such as selection, assessment and training. NDM looks at how experienced people in organisations act when faced with uncertain and changing environments to take accurate actions in a way which makes sense to them (Flin et al., 1997). The work carried out within the area of NDM has allowed us to progress in our understanding of how people deal with the complexities of the workplace. NDM is more concerned with the processes leading up to the final decision as opposed to what occurs at the point of decision itself. As the studies are set in the field setting of the organisation it allows the area of NDM to shed light on how people respond to pressure, uncertainty, stress and teamwork to help design jobs and work environments to accommodate for extreme conditions (Flin et al., 1997), which would not be possible in more controlled environments such as laboratory settings.

The area has informed the work of surgeons, airline pilots, anaesthetists, military personnel and more. One of the key findings has suggested that workers in these environments are provided with regular feedback on their tasks to help overcome the complexity by constantly adding to what they know (Brehmer, 1990; Sterman, 1994). The findings and solutions derived for a problem in an NDM environment might look more complicated and wide ranging than one found in a linear decision making study derived from a lab-based study. Box 11.2 shows a study using Critical

Incident Technique to inform NDM frameworks of surgeons (Yule et al., 2006). The research tools used by Yule and colleagues can also be used in other environments to identify key elements of a job which are affected by the complexity of the environment or the technology being handled as part of the task undertaken for the job.

Box 11.2

CASE STUDY: Using Critical Incident Technique to understand the work of surgeons

Critical Incident Technique (CIT) was developed by Flanagan (1954) and is a set of procedures for collecting direct observations of human behaviour in field settings (in this case organisations). It is described in detail in Chapter 9. The way in which the technique is designed to elicit information from the person gives access to the more implicit information related to the person's day at work. The following provides an example of the method in use.

Surgeons are subjected to pressured work environments within the operating theatre which require a significant amount of complex decision making. Apart from the technical skills learned in training, surgeons also apply a variety of non-technical skills developed through experience to address problems which arise during surgery. Yule et al. (2006) used CIT to develop a systematic evaluation tool to identify non-technical skills to assist in training and selection situations of surgeons. They randomly selected 27 surgeons and used CIT to understand what behaviours were used by surgeons to address complexity in the operating room. Through this they were able to identify a range of behaviours that may be used to understand surgeon's behaviour in different situations. Going a step further, this marker scheme can then be used to measure superior and substandard performance of surgeons. The comprehensive list of behaviours and their characteristics identified is called a 'behavioural marker system'. One section of the marker system for surgeons developed from the study findings is given as an example in Table 11.3. The list of all the main categories derived from a collection of such systems is called the 'skills taxonomy'. The skills taxonomy generated for this study is noted in Table 11.2. The left hand column of that table provides headings for all the key non-technical skills required in the job of a surgeon; the 'elements' in the right hand column, provide summaries of all the behaviours derived from the relevant section of the 'behavioural marker system'. This list would help someone to identify the main non-technical skills required of a surgeon when working in an operating theatre. These kind of lists provide detailed information that goes beyond evidence provided by experience and qualifications of the surgeons alone; giving more detailed information to help in the design of selection and training initiatives (see Chapters 9 and 10 of this book). In the context of surgeons, Yule et al. (2006) propose that such a taxonomy can help to avert the many adverse incidents in healthcare which happen due to failures in non-technical skill sets.

(Continued)

(Continued)

Table 11.2   Adapted skills taxonomy for surgeons (Yule et al., 2006)

Category
Situation awareness: Gathering, understanding information and projecting and anticipating future states
Decision Making: Considering, selecting, communicating and implementing options
Task Management: Planning and preparation; flexibility and responding to change
Leadership: Setting and maintaining standards; supporting others; coping with pressure
Communication and Teamwork: Sharing knowledge, information and understanding; coordinating team activities.

Table 11.3   Adapted selected prototype behavioural marker system for 'situation awareness' (Yule et al., 2006)

Category	Element	Example Good Behaviour	Example Poor Behaviour
Situation Awareness	Gathering Information	Liaises with anaesthetist regarding anaesthetic plan for patient	Does not ask for results until the last minute or not at all
	Understanding information	Looks at CT scan and points out relevant area	Overlooks or ignores important results
	Projecting and anticipating future state	Plans operating list taking into account potential delays due to surgical or anaesthetic challenges	Gets into predictable blood loss before telling anaesthetist

- What are some of the non-technical skills required in your role as a student or practitioner?
- What are some good and bad examples for each of these skill sets?

Learning in organisations

Understanding how people learn in organisations is a helpful insight into how higher order cognitive processes might be enhanced in those settings. In Occupational Psychology and management literature, the term 'organisational learning' is derived from the idea that the organisation is a goal-oriented social structure that is able to learn like an organism (Maier et al., 2003; Cyert and March, 1963). As we well know, as an organism grows it changes form; similarly, as a person or an organisation learns there is a change to its cognitions and behaviours. Learning helps us to overcome some of the problems posed by our immediate cognitive limitations (explored earlier in this chapter). Research into understanding how organisations learn has increased significantly in the last two decades. On a macro-level this reflects the measures of organisational capability shifting from tangible products, such as the volume of goods produced, to a more knowledge-based economy where organisations compete with each other based on how much they know (Easterby-Smith and Lyles, 2005; Wimalasiri, 2007). This 'knowing' essentially helps an organisation to stay abreast of their competition. For example, car manufacturers supplying the same market might boost their sales on their competitive product based on an improvement in design knowledge. On a more micro or person level, learning provides a base on which a person can forego their previous actions to provide more effective solutions to new problems.

The psychological perspective was among one of the earliest that helped to provide insights into learning. For example Pavlov in his keystone experiments on 'Classical conditioning' in the 1900s used dogs to show how learning happened through pairing sets of stimuli (that is, pairing a bell with giving food to a dog will later stimulate saliva production in the dog even when the food is absent); and Skinner who showed a more active role played by organisms in learning demonstrated using rats and mazes (Gross, 2010). DeFillipi and Ornstein (2005) identify four dominant areas of learning which are frequently cited in organisational literature; their headings and their assumptions are noted below.

- Information processing – implementing the solutions to organisations which mimic the process of computation found in humans and computers.
- Behavioural – assumes organisations learn through experiences throughout their respective histories.
- Social construction – assumes that learning is grounded in the environment and relationships and people.
- Applied learning – assumes that learning exists in the lived experience of the person and needs facilitation for improvement.

DeFillipi and Ornstein also identify the five psychological perspectives from which the principles cited in these areas are drawn, their headings and assumptions are listed as follows:

- Biological – assumes that a comprehensive understanding of learning must rely on knowledge of the biochemistry and genetic makeup of the human brain.
- Learning theories – assumes that human behaviour happens as a result of learning.
- Cognitive – assumes that people understand and learn by using their thinking, reasoning and memory.
- Socio-cultural – understands people through the context in which they live and work.
- Psychodynamic – much of the person's behaviour is seen as having roots in their past and their childhood.

Through an extensive review of the organisational literature, DeFillipi and Ornstein were able to identify key theories of learning used to explain learning in the workplace. Table 11.4 shows an updated version of DeFillipi and Ornstein's 'psychological perspectives' in theories in organisation. Table 11.4 is

Table 11.4 Psychological perspectives and theories of organisations

Psychological perspective in organisational learning	Information processing: Implement solutions to organisations which mimic the process of computation found in humans and computers	Behavioural/ evolutionary: Assume organisations learn through experiences throughout their respective histories	Social construction: Assumes that learning is grounded in the environment and the relationships between people	Applied learning: Suggests learning exists in the lived experience and requires facilitators to improve practice
Biological: A comprehensive understanding of learning must rely on knowledge of the biochemistry and genetic makeup of the human brain	Storage and memory are distributed across organisations (March, 1991)			
Learning: Human behaviour happens as a result of learning	Learning as computation (Huber, 1991); Stimulus-response refers to lower level learning (Fiol and Lyles, 1985)	Consequences shape learning (Lant and Mezias, 1990)	Social learning is embedded in relationships (Orr, 1990; Wenger, 1998) The person is the scientist and their environment their experimental lab (Polanyi, 1966)	
Cognitive: Attempts to understand people through their thinking, reasoning and memory	The process of making sense refers to higher level learning (Fiol and Lyles, 1985)	Trajectory results from cumulative prior learning (Nelson and Winter, 1982)	Cognition is derived through collective sensemaking (Weick, 1991) Cognition helps to broaden the immediate information derived from the environment (Weick et al., 2012)	Learning comes through the processing of experience (Kolb, 1984) as well as from reflection (Lewin, 1946). Cognition is derived from shared mental models (Salas and Canon-Bowers, 2001; Kim, 1993)
Socio-cultural: Understanding people through the context within which they live			Communities socially construct meaning (Brown and Duguid, 1991)	
Psychodynamic Much of a person's behaviour is seen as having roots in their past and their childhood		History matters (Nelson and Winter, 1982)		Individual and group defensiveness undermines organisational learning (Argyris and Schon, 1974)

Source: Adapted from Easterby-Smith and Lyles (2005).

a helpful tool to navigate the vast literature on organisational learning and understand how learning might be implemented in organisations to help people overcome their immediate cognitive limitations which were discussed before in this chapter.

There are various methods which are employed by organisations to allow organisational learning to occur and for members to share knowledge with each other. Among these methods are knowledge management initiatives such as the use of information and communication technology (ICT) systems. These might include intranet systems and web-based software to traditional telephone and teleconferencing facilities. Other informal knowledge sharing initiatives include using open-plan offices, break-out rooms, team away days and a 'friendly area' around water coolers where workers are most likely to gather and share ideas informally (Wimalasiri, 2007). Virtual systems are starting to be used to enhance communication and learning in organisations, and human factors specialists have a role to play in improving their usability (Stanney et al., 1998). These technologies help people to visualise and train to be able to attend to situations which are otherwise too complex to imagine (e.g. Xanthopoulou and Papagiannidis, 2012 – see Box 11.3).

Box 11.3

OP IN PRACTICE

Using Second Life to improve learning and performance at work

The advances in virtual technology provide an opportunity to extend the world we live in by using imagined forms and opens us to a whole new way of existing and working. Second Life is one such tool which was initially developed by Linden Labs in the USA to allow users to design an avatar representing themselves to live a 'second life' online (BBC, 2009). These are essentially platforms for role playing games that provide a parallel, three-dimensional landscape where players are able to interact with others through their avatars and can engage with and adapt the virtual environments according to their preferences. A recent longitudinal study set out to find whether these virtual games are able to provide deep insights into and improve work related performance of players by examining spillover effects from gaming (Xanthopoulou and Papagiannidis, 2012). Spill over effects refer to the transfer of skills and psychological states of a person from one environment to another (Edwards and Rothbard, 2000). Among other factors, the study looked at how learning in the virtual environment spilled over to the person's real life work environment and what impact this had on their work performance. The study found that those who achieve high scores in learning within the gaming environment were able to transfer those learning skills into their work environment, showing that those who were able to engage in learning activity in the virtual environment were similarly able to do so outside of that environment. Also those who

(Continued)

(Continued)

perform less well refrain from transferring those learning skills to their work environment. The key advantage of using virtual platforms to practice work behaviours is that it allows trial and error which is a key element in learning. Using such technology is particularly useful in work settings where trial and error is not an option. Earlier use of virtual technology can be found in the military to plan and carry out virtual war scenarios and training (Dix et al., 1993) and in medical settings (Stytz, frieder and Frieder, 1991).

What might be some key problems of becoming reliant on virtual technology for training for work performance?
Can you see a use for virtual technology in your own workplace?

Organisations as systems

Organisations are complex environments. As well as being complex, each organisation is dependent on various other subsystems that share a common goal and perform a number of tasks while interacting with its environment (Clegg and Dunkerley, 1980: 190). As with any other organism, organisations then have to adapt to their environment and evolve to certain requirements in order to survive and any understanding of the system would need to demonstrate a consideration of the various subsystems involved.

Most modern organisations are seen as 'open systems' which have interdependent subsystems. Systems theorists define an 'open system' as one which is interdependent on its environment and once created evolves dynamically alongside its environment (Mingers and White, 2010). Such a system requires very little control once it is created (Sanders and McCormick, 1993). Conversely, a 'closed system' is one which is unable to exchange information and processes with its environment and is one that is a highly controlled and isolated organism which has no dependence on its environment. As a result it is dependent on feedback from its operating environment in order to survive. More recently systems theory has been extended to recognise that systems are inherently uncertain (Weick, 1995, 2012). Systems theory was also referred to in Chapter 8. This idea is encapsulated within chaos or complexity theory (Anderson, 1999; Kauffman, 1995; Waldrop, 1992). Within this approach is the understanding that there may be sudden and dramatic changes to the system due to other internal or external changes. Take for example the 9/11 terrorist attacks which provide a good insight into the impact of a sudden introduction of ambiguity into a complex system:

The attack on the twin towers in New York City in 2001 involved a novel model of destruction that had people scrambling for ways to label it. 'Suicide hijacking' and 'aircraft as explosives' were two of the labels that stuck [to the unravelling situation]. The idea of suicide hijacking … had been imagined by the Federal Aviation Administration. It was on a short list of plausible terrorist scenarios, but it was judged unlikely because it did not offer an opportunity for terrorists to have a dialogue in order to gain the release of captive extremists being held in the US. Unimagined was the possibility that terrorists might not be interested in dialogue at all, but only in destruction. (Weick, 2005: 425)

Essentially the federal government of the USA was able to predict the separate events and their interactions, but not necessarily their collective outcome. Although this is an extreme example, it provides a good explanation of a tightly coupled system (Anderson, 1999). In order to counteract the effects which arise from such tightly coupled systems which are inflexible to disaster, complexity theorists suggest that organisations should hold flat structures with autonomous agents to better absorb the impact of such disasters (Mingers and White, 2010). These flat structures help people forego red tape presented by hierarchical boundaries and have more autonomy in decision making to be flexible and time efficient in the way they make their decisions. In the case of 9/11 this would have allowed quicker communication between the hierarchies and between aerospace and military that would have given way to more collective decision-making process. This could have also helped enhance people's imagination to go beyond the known to help prevent the escalation of such similar situations in the future (Weick, 2005). More recent disasters have provided even more practical ways of overcoming complexity by using the public 'bird's eye view' accounts to obtain a broader view of unfolding situations: for example by the use of Twitter and web based blogs. The recent London riots in 2011 and the BBC utilised these methods rather effectively to locate perpetrators and limit damage.

Human error

Knowing both that organisational systems are complex and are operated by human beings who are by nature fallible is to recognise that there is room for error to occur. Human error refers to 'all those occasions in which a planned sequence of mental or physical activities fails to achieve its intended outcome and when these failures cannot be attributed to the intervention of some chance agency' (Reason, 2009: 9). Human factors research recognises that error is the result of a mismatch between the task and human mental and physical capabilities (Sharit, 2006). Within organisations it is well acknowledged that error ultimately leads to incidents and in some cases includes death and destruction of whole or parts of the organisation. Certainly the number of casualties accrued on the ground in the 9/11 attacks discussed above was partly attributable to human error (Weick, 2005). Needless to say that some of the major accidents that have happened owing to error have provided major turning points in research in the area and have helped to advance knowledge about human and system-wide error and help improve error avoidance in other similar work environments (Box 11.4).

Box 11.4

OP IN PRACTICE

Three major disasters and what lessons we have learnt from them

Piper Alpha disaster: was a catastrophic explosion on an offshore oil platform which happened in 1988 and the first one of its kind. The disaster happened because someone failed to replace a valve which was removed during cleaning (human error). The resultant gas leak caused the explosion and the death of over 100 people on the platform, also causing much damage to related infrastructure.

Learning points: Years on much investigation and evaluation of the disaster has taken place. Out of this one of the key recommendations have helped to improve communication during handover during shift change in other similar work environments (Lardner, 1999).

Ladbroke Grove disaster: was a train collision which killed 31 people and injured hundreds of others in 1999. Initially the cause of the accident was attributed to the driver of one of the trains who passed a red light colliding into another train.

Learning Points: The major investigation into the accident completed by Lord Cullen, in 2000 showed that the accident happened due to more system-wide errors rather than to error of the end-user alone. Some of these system-wide factors related to the visibility of signals and driver training and management issues. The recommendations that came out of this investigation have helped to improve awareness about safety culture to reduce accidents and error in other similar environments (Cullen, 2000).

Columbia Disaster: was a space shuttle accident where the shuttle disintegrated while re-entering earth's atmosphere in 2003. The accident caused the death of all of the 7 crew members on board and irrecoverable damage to the shuttle as well as damage to the reputation of NASA.

Learning points: Surprisingly the investigation into this accident showed it had similar characteristics in flight risk management procedures to the Challenger disaster at NASA which had happened in 1998. The NASA investigation report aptly stated the following with regards to their learning points: 'The Board recognised early on that the accident was probably not an anomalous, random event, but rather likely rooted to some degree in NASA's history and the human space flight program's culture. Accordingly, the Board broadened its mandate at the outset to include an investigation of a wide range of historical and organisational issues, including political and budgetary considerations, compromises, and changing priorities over the life of the Space Shuttle Programme' (NASA, 2003: PP9).

There are two key strands of error research which inform human error: one which sees the person using the system as the source of error and another which sees the system the person is in as the source of error (Wimalasiri et al., 2010). Prior to the Cullen report into the Piper Alpha disaster in 1990 (Cullen, 1990) most of the attention focused on finding the users (person or people) of systems and machinery responsible for causing an error which lead to the final accident. Here the emphasis lay on appropriating the blame and for finding root causes (Dorner, 1996). However, following more recent investigations such as the Baker report (Baker et al., 2007) it is now more readily accepted that errors arise due to faults which exist within systems. However, causes for error further up the supply chain are not so clear-cut either until an investigation has taken place. Fear of blame and facing litigation are still often attributed to the under-reporting of errors. This can lead to an incubation of errors in a system which lie dormant until the correct conditions come together to create disastrous outcomes.

This progression of system wide errors to disaster stage is often described through Reason's (1990) 'swiss cheese model'. The model illustrates that organisations exist in layers which have many defences whose function is to protect potential victims and the organisation's assets from local hazards. Some are engineered (for example, alarms, physical barriers, automatic shutdowns) and others rely on people (for example, surgeons, pilots, machine operators) while still others rely on procedures and administrative controls (for example audit processes). In an ideal world all these defence mechanisms are intact and work in unison with each other to protect the system and keep it running efficiently.

However, we live in a world that frequently behaves in a manner which is not ideal and as we discussed is complex and holds a high degree of ambiguity. To explain these uncertainties, Reason (1990) suggests that the layers in his error model have holes in them (akin to a slice of Swiss cheese. These holes refer to faults in the system that are likely to lead to errors when the right conditions come together. These are known as latent errors. Their existence in the system does not necessarily cause errors, but problem are likely to arise when the layers with their various combinations of holes line up to form a trajectory, bringing the accident into contact with the final outcome – usually resulting in a death or a major accident. Take for example the following scenario: a design engineer unknowingly places a 'start' button (with the appropriate 'start' label) on a design drawing of a piece of equipment in a place which usually houses a 'stop' button. When this piece of equipment is finally commissioned, and if the error or mistake gets through to the final build undetected by audit procedures, during an emergency an end-user is likely to press the 'start' button when they actually mean 'stop', owing to their normal reflex reaction (if you remember back to the idea that we are 'finite-capacity information processors and satisficers' discussed earlier in this chapter – this is a very likely reaction). This is called an active failure and can usually to be traced to the end users of a system. It is perhaps the easiest error to identify.

The case study in Box 11.5 helps to illustrate the system-wide implications for error further up the supply chain and how this impacts on the end user. The study demonstrated that end-user error is influenced significantly by the system.

Box 11.5

CASE STUDY 2: Error and the offshore design engineer.

Design engineers working to develop design drawings for offshore oil and gas platforms play a vital role in eliminating risk to the end users of those platforms. Designers use their engineering knowledge to transform a set of performance

(Continued)

(Continued)

criteria into the end product that eventually becomes the functioning oil platform. Therefore design engineers play a key role in imagining and designing what eventually becomes the technology that holds and is operated by end users who work on those oil and gas platforms. An important requirement at all stages of the design and construction of the platform therefore is to eliminate any possible errors which might give rise to end user error, and therefore to accidents and fatalities during day-to-day work on those platforms. Although the design is conceptualised in the minds of the individual and groups of designers, essentially these designers are subject to system-wide influences, many of which are hidden from direct awareness.

Human error is caused by a multitude of factors both at the individual and systems level. To understand designer error it is important to understand the interaction between the multitude of factors which influence the design process. These range from the tools they use, their interactions with their colleagues, socio-political aspects of the system, socio-cognitive factors, political as well as cultural factors relating to both the designer and related stakeholders who support the design construction process of the oil and gas platforms.

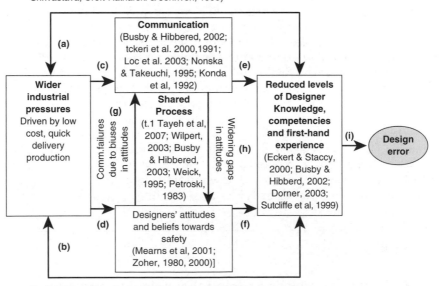

Factors effecting designer error from (from Wimalasiri et al., 2010)

> The diagram shows the complex interplay of factors which impact on the off-shore platform designer and then the process of design which essentially has implications for transferring risk to the end construction and to the possibility for causing accidents and errors.
>
> - What personal and system-wide factors influence possible error causation in your role at work?
> - How might these be reduced?

The way in which errors materialise vary markedly from one situation to another and from one person to another. The types of errors that can occur then would be very different depending on a work situation. Errors can be translated as 'actions-not-as-planned'. For example if you consider putting butter in your tea and milk on your toast at breakfast time to be an error, then this type of error would be relatively easy to detect. You either watch yourself for memory lapses at breakfast time more carefully or get someone else to warn you when you are about to repeat that error. Other errors and their sources are not so obvious. Reason (2008) suggests that the detection of error can be improved by the provision of a generic error classification system, where a number of behaviour categories can be used to identify and mitigate error producing actions by interpreting a the list of error classifications from a simple list as below, as it relates to your own work situation.

- Omissions – a necessary step in a sequence is omitted accidentally. An example here is forgetting to use hot water when making a cup of tea; it is likely the tea will not infuse in cold water to make your cup of tea.
- Intrusions – an unnecessary act is introduced into prescribed sequence of actions an example would be using. A blow-torch to make a boiled egg; it is likely to break the shell. (This is not far from the truth in real world examples, as we found out in one of our studies (Wimalasiri et al., 2010) that someone reported an injury which happened as a result of a person using a hand-drill to pick their nose while it was still plugged in.)
- Repetition – unnecessary repetition of tasks. For example, if you keep putting tea bags into your cup of tea, then you are likely to have a very bitter cup of tea which is undrinkable.
- Wrong objects – right actions in the wrong context. An example here would be if you wish to make french toast and put a tea bag and milk into a frying pan; the result will be inedible.
- Misorderings – right actions wrong sequence. An example here would be if you break your egg into your egg cup and the shells into the boiling water to make a boiled egg for your breakfast; again you will end up with something inedible unless you like raw eggs for breakfast!
- Mistimings – right actions wrong time; an example here is if you put your toast into the toaster after it has ejected.

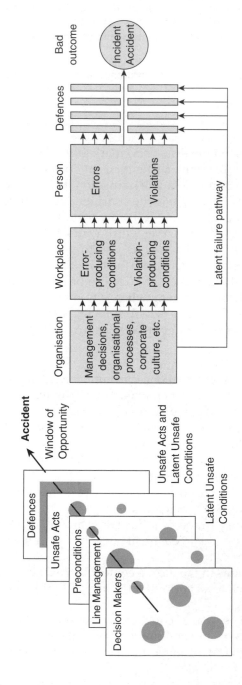

Figure 11.1 Reason's Swiss cheese model

- Blends – unintended merging of two actions meant to serve separate goals. An example here is if you put bread, milk, egg, sugar, tea bags into a frying pan at the same time when intending to make French toast and tea; you will neither get tea nor French toast.

There is a reason that these breakfast time examples are used to explain Reason's error classifications system – it is simply to illustrate that they can be applied to any situation however complex or simple to help identify likely errors which could happen in that system. If you are likely to use this system to detect errors at breakfast time then a note on your fridge in the breakfast area at home can help bring your attention to the errors which are likely to happen every morning. Similarly, having a good understanding of what daily errors are likely to take place in a work place can help to mitigate the simplest of latent errors helping to avoid more significant disasters down the line as suggested by the 'swiss cheese' model. Recent research has shown that jobs can be designed in ways to reduce designer error in system (Daniels et al., 2008, in press).

The major role of the human factors specialist is to determine the human issues within the design process of the system. This would entail understanding the requirements of the person, their role within the department or the organisation, the needs of the person and the immediate and wider system and the relationships between the components and the stakeholders of the system and their interrelationships. The optimisation of the system might come in the form of: improvements to the tasks to be undertaken by the personnel; design of the interphase or the technology; developing new training material to support users design of jobs and evaluation and audit tools used to assess the effectiveness of actions.

The future of automation and HMI

It is fair to say that we are in an era of 'techno-dependency' which has become almost second nature to societies all over the world (Harper et al., 2008). Today many of us have the option to buy our groceries, check our bank balances and make travel arrangements through our mobile phone; sophisticated computer systems manage most of the navigation on the airplanes we fly on from one destination to another; robotics are making their way into the home to help clean and cook; and voice automated systems enable those who are less able to navigate their homes more safely and take care of themselves. There are equally dramatic changes which are happening in the world of work. These are due to factors such as the speed of advance of technology, advances in knowledge owing to the globalisation and thinning of cross-disciplinary boundaries, the rapidly changing climate and limits in traditional sources of energy. Some of the current issues faced by those working in automation and HMI include the following.

- The drastic changes in the climate is setting off a need for an area called 'green ergonomics' which is leading to a fundamental shift in how we think about living, working and consuming. Owing to the requirement of alternate energy sources there is now an increase in the construction of wind farms (Institute of Ergonomics and Human Factors, 2011).
- There is also new branch of ergonomics called neuro-ergonomics, which looks to learn from how neural activity at the genetic level can inform the design of technological systems (Parasuraman and Wilson, 2008; Proctor and Vu, 2010).
- A recent strand of work (Harper et al., 2008) has integrated human emotion and body posture relevant to interactions into virtual reality systems. The intention is that such systems would be used to help people interact more effectively across continents without being present and carry out more complex tasks together.
- Space travel is also becoming an activity which might be available on a large scale and those sysems would present a totally new set of automation and HMI issues.
- Virtual reality is increasingly being used in work settings to overcome thinking limitations or to help train people for complicated situations.

All these advances may mean that the expertise of automation and HMI specialists is called upon to help with the development of new work environments and jobs requiring new operating systems, premises, safety cultures and training requirements. These are only a handful of examples and it may be that by the time this book reaches you some of these might already be old news.

   These significant advances in technology have implications for the area of automation and HMI. For one, the pace of change of technology makes it that much harder to keep up with problems which might arise through human-machine interaction, and as we find solutions we might find that technology has moved on and that those solutions become redundant. Also the integration of technology into day-to-day living requires a 'finer eye' to evaluate the true nature of the problems arising from the interaction between humans and machines. Harper et al. (2008) suggest the following recommendations to accommodate for the complexity of the ever changing human-computer landscape:

1 Constantly revisit research and design methods in HMI.
2 Reconsider the boundaries of use of technology and the multiple possible applications of that technology (including in varying environments).
3 Keep links with other disciplines and consider their role in the current status and future of technology.

4 Consider the implications of technology to all of society as changes may have wider ethical and societal implications to groups beyond immediate use.
5 Engage with government, policy and society to help with the above.
6 Always look ahead at least 14 years at the global level.
7 Consider these wider implications and qualities in training of future HMI specialists.

Summary

This chapter has provided a broad understanding of the sub-discipline of automation and HMI. The area is the youngest of all the sub-disciplines of Occupational Psychology and has its roots in engineering. It has adapted and evolved to suit the needs of those working in the discipline and more importantly to reflect the technological advances in work environments. Encompassing human factors and ergonomics during its early days, HMI has gathered the support and interest of many other disciplines through its journey to where it is today. From humble beginnings, where psychologists were recruited to help the war effort, HMI is now spearheading work in up-and-coming areas such as alternate work forms and helping people to understand and work in increasingly complex and technology driven environments. Given we live in a society which is driven by technology, we are likely to see this area grow rapidly and significantly and perhaps be awarded a more prominent status among the other key areas of Occupational Psychology.

Explore further

- The Human Factors and Ergonomics Society is an interdisciplinary, non-profit organisation promoting the understanding of human characteristics which are applicable to machine and system design. Further information about the Society can be found through following the web link: https://www.hfes.org//Web/Default.aspx
- *Journal of Human Factors and Ergonomics Society.* This is a bi-monthly peer reviewed journal presenting original scientific works that contribute to the understanding and advancement of the systematic consideration of people in relation to machines, systems, tools, and environments.
- Salvendy, G. (2012) *Handbook of Human Factors and Ergonomics*, 4th edn. Chichester: Wiley.

This is a comprehensive book and covers various topics in human factors and ergonomics in great detail: from fundamentals to applications.

- The Health and Safety Executive is the national independent watchdog for work risk, safety and work-related health in the UK. The governing body's website has an informative section about the application of HMI principles to the workplace, including policies and procedures. More information can be found by following this web-link. You can also find various accident investigation reports on this website. http://www.hse.gov.uk/humanfactors/

- A more in depth understanding of the history and development of human factors and ergonomics can be found in comprehensive reviews of the areas (Hendrick, 1991; Proctor and Vu, 2010; Waterson and Eason, 2009).

- See special issue on complexity theory in *Organisation Science*, Volume 10(3), for a good explanation of complexity theory and a review of the relevant literature.

- Weick, K. and Sutcliffe, K. (2009) *Managing the Unexpected: Resilient Performance in an Age of Uncertainty*. Chichester: Wiley.
  The book explains of the defining characteristics of risky organisations and how to apply those principles to more conventional workplaces.

- Some key disaster investigation reports noted in this chapter provide extensive accounts of investigations and information about possible root causes of incidents. You may be able to apply the knowledge you have gained in this chapter and from your reading to evaluate some of the conclusions drawn in those reports.
  Cullen, W.D. (Lord) (2000) *The Ladbroke Grive Rail Inquiry (Part 1 & 2)*. Norwich: HSE Books.
  NASA (2003) Columbia accident investigation board, volume I, National Aeronautics and Space Administration and the Government Printing Office Washington, D.C. (http://www.nasa.gov/columbia/home/CAIB_Vol1.html).
  Commision Report (2004) The 9/11 commission report. National Commission on Terrorist Attacks upon the United States. (http://www.9–11commission.gov/report/index.htm).

- An extensive list of some key developments and lessons learnt following the offshore oil platform, Piper Alpha, disaster are noted on the HSE wesbite's offshore safety cases: (http://www.hse.gov.uk/offshore/safetycases.htm)

Discussion questions

1 What are the significant points in the history of the development of HMI?
2 What contributions have psychologists made to the area of HMI?

3 What is human error? How might you limit human error in a system?
4 What are some of the advances that are pushing the boundaries of HMI? How is this likely to affect the sub-discipline in the future?

Sample essay questions

1 Organisations have to design systems to accommodate the chance of error: discuss.
2 How does organisational learning help people to overcome complexity in the work environment? Discuss.

Sample examination questions

1 What does an Occupational Psychologist working within the field of automation and human-machine interaction automation and (HMI) do?
2 Critically evaluate the use of the term automation and HMI in the field of Occupational Psychology and its ability to describe the actual breadth of the work involved in the field.
3 What lessons do complex organisations teach us?

OP IN PRACTICE: DAY IN THE LIFE OF ...

Dr Chandra Harrison, Freelance Researcher

What areas of OP do you work within?	My formal job title is user experience researcher. But the title encompasses a variety of different roles that address human-centred design of products and services. Fundamentally, I help companies to make their products better by doing formative and or summative research as part of the design process (see Figure 1). I conduct strategic stakeholder workshops in the planning stages of product development to identify the methods and business needs; conduct ethnographic research to discover user needs; create user requirement documents including personas, user scenarios, wireframes, information architecture etc. to help inform design; conduct qualitative research on prototypes to help inform the design; and conduct final evaluations to assess whether the product has achieved the requirements. I also provide consulting and training on usability and accessibility on a variety of different platforms (mobile, web, software, products). My job involves applying human-centred design principles to make products more effective, efficient and satisfying for all people involved in the use of the product.

(Continued)

(Continued)

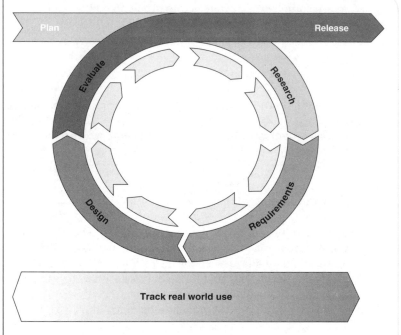

Figure 1   The phases of human-centred design

How did you become interested in this area?	When I was younger I loved to see how things worked, from engines to garden gates. I'd pull things to pieces and see if I could put them back together in a better way that made them more effective, efficient or satisfying to use. Whenever I interacted with any product, service or website, I could see all the ways it could be improved.
	I was also aware of how difficult it was for a huge part of the population to use mainstream computer products, especially older people and those with disabilities. The frustration experienced by so many people (like my Dad trying to use a computer) motivated me to explore why technology caused different negative emotions. The cognitive workload required to work out how to use technology (such as the controls of heavy machinery) motivated me to explore how to make products easier to use. The lack of independence for people with disabilities and presence of social stigma of medical devices motivated me to help design assistive technology that was not only easy to use but also reduced dependence and social stigma.
	After discovering human factors as part of my undergraduate psychology studies I realised this profession offered a way to help people by making technology more intuitive and easier to use. My first major project was working with a company that makes low vision reading aids, working with elderly people with visual impairments to figure out how to make the products easier to use.

What kinds of organisations are interested in your work and why?	Every type of organisation benefits from applying human-centred design principles. For example:
	• Broadcasters such as BBC use human-centred design to help ensure their products are presented in an accessible way, for example making sure their website is accessible to people with disabilities.
	• Manufacturers use human-centred design to help ensure their products fit the skills and (physical, cognitive and emotional) constraints of users, for example ensuring that mobile phones are small enough to be held and operated one handed.
	• Software producers use human-centred design principles to ensure that software matches the mental models of the user to ensure that the software is easier to use, for example making accounting software match with the way accountants actually do their job.
	• Travel companies apply human-centred design principles to help make the purchasing process simpler, for example making it easier to find flights that match the cost and timing needs of the user.
	• Government agencies use human-centred design to help the general public access information quickly and easily, for example working out what the informational needs are surrounding flood mitigation.
	• Charitable organisations might use human-centred design principles to help optimise their website to make it easier for users to make donations.
	• Medical equipment companies apply human-centred design principles to their products to reduce the chance of errors, for example testing whether nurses are able to operate safety critical technology under psychological stress.
	The list is endless. What they all have in common is that they apply human-centred design to make their products better, safer, easier, quicker, more enjoyable for all the people involved in their use.
How is your work informed by theory, literature and research?	Most practitioners in my area have a post graduate degree. Many come from a psychology, computer science, design or interactive media background. The theory of human-centred design is firmly based in a solid understanding of behaviour, cognition, emotion, social psychology and human factors.
	Because of the massive growth in the area in recent years there has been a plethora of popular texts that superficially cover the theory. This has provided some understanding for many practitioners in the web domain. However a more theoretical and solid knowledge is needed for applying human-centred design to more complex systems. It is important for people designing things like air traffic control rooms to have a thorough understanding of the needs of the user. It is important to know how much information, on which sensory channels, at which frequency can be processed before errors become unacceptable. A solid knowledge of psychology and other human factor principles is vital.
	It is also important for us to consider the business, task and environmental needs of any project. As researchers, we consider the physical, organisational and technical environmental needs as well as the human requirements.

(Continued)

(Continued)

What do you think have been the major developments in this area?	Human-centred design is not new. However, the biggest changes in the past ten years have been that the discipline has moved away from focusing on a purely work based systems analysis to considering softer human factors such as emotion and from the physical product to a more digital arena. Emotional elements of design now receive a large amount of focus. The plethora of non-work-based systems (such as gaming and web) has created a desire to move beyond assuring effectiveness and efficiency of products to exploring the satisfaction of products to a much greater extent. While in safety critical environments the functionality, reliability and usability are the most important aspects of design, in a less risk sensitive environment there is a lot more focus on pleasure, desire and personal meaning.
Can you give an example of a day in your working life?	Because I'm a consultant and work on a variety of different projects no day is the same. But there are five basic types of day that I have, depending on where in the process I am with a project. **Business Development** days might consist of • Talking to clients about their research needs • Preparing or presenting pitches to clients about possible research work we could do • Writing proposals for clients about the research work that is planned • Attending and presenting at conferences and industry talks to raise profile of profession • Schmoozing with clients Once the work is won the next days would be **preparation** which might consist of: • Further meetings with clients to clarify research parameters • Researching the product so we know what to be looking for • Writing a discussion guide for interviews • Setting up the research environment • Preparing materials for diary studies • Finding research participants Once everything is in place then we do the **data gathering** for research and this might involve: • Interviewing participants • Testing products such as when doing accessibility audits • Observing or shadowing participants • Compiling data from data loggers or web analytics Once all the data is gathered then we need to **analyse the data** and this includes: • Exploring data for trends • Reviewing and coding video or audio files • Crunching numbers if we are doing large surveys • Workshops with clients to focus research findings • Clarifying discrepancies in the data • Determining recommendations

- Creating personas, wireframes, sitemaps, taxonomies
- Creating video highlights

The final phase would be **presenting** the findings to the client and might include:

- Writing reports which are typically PowerPoint presentations
- Delivering the reports to various stakeholders
- Workshops with clients to discuss how they could implement the recommendations made

References

Anderson, J.R. (1990) *The Adaptive Character of Thought*. Hillside, NJ: Lawrence Erlbaum Associates.

Anderson, J.R., Albertm M.V. and Finchman, J.M. (2005) 'Tracing problem solving in real time: fMRI analysis of the subject process tower of Hanoi', *Journal of Organisational Neuroscience*, 12: 1261–74.

Anderson, P. (1999) 'Complexity theory and organisation science', *Organisation Science*, 10 (3): 216–32.

Argyris, C. and Schon, D.A. (1974) *Organizational Learning: a Theory of Action Perspective*. Reading, MA: Addison Wesley.

Baker, J.A., Leveson, N., Bowman, F.L., Priest, S., Erwin, G., Rosenthal, L., Garton, S., Tebo, P.V. Hendershot, D., Wiegman, D.A. and Wilson, L.D. (2007) The report of the BP U.S. oil refineries independent safety review panel. Available at: http://www.bp.com/bakerpanelreport (accessed 9 October 2012).

BBC (1999) 'What happened to 2nd life?'. Available at: http://news.bbc.co.uk/1/hi/8367957.stm (accessed 1 November 2012).

Bartlett, F.C. (1932) *Remembering*. Cambridge: Cambridge University Press.

Bartlett, F.C. and Mackworth, N.H. (1950) *Planned seeing, Air Ministry publication*. London : His Majesty's Stationery Office.

Besnard, D., Greathead, D. and Baxter, G. (2004) 'When mental models go wrong: co-occurances in dynamic, critical systems', *International Journal of Human-Computer Studies*, 60: 117–28.

Bos, N., Olson, J., Gergle, D., Olson, G. and Wright, Z. (2002) 'Effects of computer-mediated communications channels on trust development', in *Proc., CHI (Compuetr Human Interaction)*. New York: ACM Press.

Brehmer, B. (1990) 'Strategies in real-time: dynamic decision making', in R.B. Hogarth (ed.), *Insights in Decision Making: A Tribute to Hillel J. Einhorn*. Chicago: The University of Chicago Press.

Brown J.S. and Duguid, P. (1991) 'Organizational learning and communities of practice: towards a unified view of working, learning and innovation', *Organization Science*, 2: 40–57.

Busemeyer, J.R. and Johnson, J.G. (2004) 'Computational models of decision-making', in D.J. Koehler and N. Harvey (eds), *Blackwell Handbook of Judgement and Decision Making*. Malden, MA: Blackwell.

Carroll, J.M. (1997) 'Human-computer interaction: psychology as a science of design', *Annual Review of Psychology*, 48: 61–83.

Clegg, S. and Dunkerley, D. (1980) *Organization, Class and Control*. London: Routledge & Kegan.

Cullen, W.D. (Lord) (1990) *The Public inquiry into the Piper Alpha disaster*. London: Department of Energy.

Cullen, W.D. (Lord) (2000) *The Ladbroke Grive Rail Inquiry (Part 1 & 2)*. Norwich: HSE Books.

Cyert, R.M. and March, J.G. (1963/1992) *A Behavioral Theory of the Firm*, 2nd edn. Englewood Cliffs, NJ: Prentice Hall.

Czaja, S.J. and Nair, S. (2006) 'Human factors engineering and systems design', in G. Salvendy (ed.), *Handbook of Human Factors and Ergonomics*. Chichester: Wiley.

Daniels, K., Beesley, N., Cheyne, A.J.T. and Wimalasiri, V. (2008) 'Coping with demands – it's what you do with control and support that counts: an experience-sampling study of affect and cognitive functioning', *Human Relations*, 61(6): 845–74.

Daniels, K., Beesley, N.J., Wimalasiri, V.P. and Cheyne, A.J.T. (in press) 'Problem solving and well-being: exploring the instrumental role of job control and social support', *Journal of Management*.

Davies, J.G.W. and Toplis, K.C.F. (1984) 'The British psychological society scientific and professional affairs board's working party on the future of occupational psychology report', Internal report of the British Psychological Society.

DeFillipi, R. and Ornstein, S. (2005) 'Psychological perspectives underlying theories of organisational learning', in M. Easterby-Smith and M.A. Lyles (eds), *Handbook of Organisational Learning and Knowledge Management*. Malden, MA: Blackwell. pp. 19–37.

Dijksterhuis, A. (2004) 'Think different: the merits of unconscious thought in preference development and decision making', *Journal of Personality and Social Psychology*, 87: 578–98.

Dix, A., Finlay, J., Abowd, G. and Beale, R. (1993) *Human–Computer Interaction*. Harlow: Pearson.

Dorner, D. (1996) *The Logic of Failure: Recognizing and Avoiding Error in Complex Situations*. New York: Metropolitan Books.

Easterby-Smith, M. and Lyles, M. (2005) 'Introduction: watersheds of organizational learning and knowledge management', in M. Easterby-Smith and M.A. Lyles (eds), *Handbook of Organisational Learning and Knowledge Management*. Malden, MA: Blackwell. pp 1–16.

Eason K.D. (2002) 'People and computers: emerging work practice in the information age', in P.B. Warr (ed.), *Psychology at Work*, 5th edn. London: Penguin.

Edwards, J.R. and and Rothbard, N.P. (2000) 'Mechanisms linking work and family: clarifying the relationship between work and family constructs', *Academy of Management Review*, 25 : 178–99.

Eysenck, M.E. and Keane, M.T. (2010) *Cognitive Psychology: A Students Handbook*. Hove: Psychology Press.

Flanagan, J.C. (1954) 'The critical incident technique', *psychological Bulletin*, 51(4): 327–59.

Fitts, P.M. (1958) 'Engineering psychology', *Annual Review of Psychology*, 9: 267–94.

Fiol, C.M. and Lyles M.A. (1985) 'Organizational learning', *Academy of Management Review*, 10(4): 803–13.

Flin, R., Salas, E., Strub, M. and Martin, L. (1997) 'Introduction', in R. Flin, E. Salas, M. Strub and L. Martin (eds), *Decision Making Under Stress*. Aldershot: Ashgate.

Gilbert, S.J., Spengler, S., Simons, J.S., Frith, C.D and Burgess, P.W. (2006) 'Differential functions of lateral and medial rostral prefrontal cortex (area 10) revealed by brain-behavior associations', *Cereb Cortex*, 16 (12): 1783–9.

Gilmer, H. (1960) 'Industrial psychology', *Annual Review of Psychology*, 11: 323–50.

Gross, R. (2010) *Psychology: The Science of Mind and Behavior*. Abingdon: Hodder.

Harper, R., Rodden, T., Rogers, Y. and Sellers, A. (2008) *Being Human: Human-Computer Interaction in the Year 2020*. Cambridge: Microsoft Research Ltd.

Hayward, R. (2001) 'Our friend electric: mechanical models of mind in postwar Briatin', in G.C. Bunn, A.D. Lovie and G.D. Richards (eds), *Psychology in Britain: Historical Essays and Personal Reflections*. London: The Science Museum and the British Psychological Society.

Hendrick, H.W. (1991) 'Ergonomics in organisational design and management', *Ergonomics*, 34 (6): 743–56.

Hertwig, R. and Todd, P.M. (2003) 'More is not always better: the benefits of cognitive limits', in D. Hardman and L. Macchi (eds), *Thinking: Psychological Perspectives on Reasoning, Judgment and Decision Making*. Chichester: Wiley. pp. 213–31.

Herzberg, F. (1964) 'The motivation-hygiene concept and problems of manpower', *Personnel Administration*, 27 (1): 3–7.

Hill, J.E., Miller, B.C., Weiner, S.P. and Colihan, J. (1998) 'Influences of the virtual office on aspects of work/life balance', *Personnel Psychology*, 51 (3): 667–83.

Howell, C. (2003) 'Human factors and ergonomics', in I.B. Weiner, W.C. Borman, D.R. Ilgen and R.J. Klimoski (eds), *Handbook of Psychology*, Vol 12. Chichester: Wiley.

Huber G.P. (1991) 'Organizational learning: the contributing processes and the literatures', *Organization Science*, 2(1): 88–115.

Ilgen, D.R. and Howell, W.C. (1999) The National Research Council's Committee on Human Factors (or "Human Factors: It's More Than You Think"), Society of Industrial and Organisational Psychology. Available at: http://www.siop.org/tip/backissues/TipJuly99/5Ilgen.aspx

Institute of Ergonomics and Human Factors (2011) *Green Ergonomics: Embracing the Challenges of Climate Change*. Available at: http://www.ergonomics.org.uk/articles/green-ergonomics-embracing-challenges-climate-change (accessed 9 October 2012).

James, W. (1890) 'The consciousness of self', in W. James (ed.), *The Principles of Psychology, Vol I*. New York: Diver Publications.

Jones, B.D. (1999) 'Bounded rationality', *Annual Review of Political Science*, 2: 297–321.

Kahneman, D. (2003) 'A perspective on Judgement and choice: mapping bounded rationality', *American Psychologist*, 58 (9): 697–720.

Kahneman, D. and Tversky, A (1979) 'Prospect theory: an analysis of decision making under risk', *Econometrica*, 47(2): 263–91.

Kahneman, D. and Tversky, A. (1984) 'Choices, values and frames', *American Psychologist*, 39: 341–50.

Karasek, R.A. and Theorell, T. (1990) *Healthy Work*. New York: Basic Books.

Karwowski, W. (2006) 'The discipline of ergonomics and human factors', in G. Salvendy (ed.), *Handbook of Human Factors and Ergonomics*. Chichester: Wiley.

Kauffman, S. (1995) *At Home in the Universe: The Search for the Laws of Self Organisation and Complexity*. New York: Oxford University Press.

Kim, D.H. (1993) 'The link between individual and organizational learning', *Sloan Management Review*, 35(1): 37–50.

Kolb, D.A. (1984) *Experiential Learning as the Source of Learning and Development*. Englewood Cliffs, NJ: Prentice-Hall.

Lant, T. and Mezias, S. (1990) 'Managing discontinuous change: a simulation study of organizational learning and entrepreneurial strategies', *Strategic Management Journal*, 11: 147–9.

Lardner, R. (1999) 'Effective shift handover'. Available at: http://www.hse.gov.uk/research/otopdf/1996/oto96003.pdf (accessed 1 November 2012).

Lewin, K. (1946) 'Action research and minority problems', *Journal of Social Issues*, 2(4): 34–46

Maier G.M., Prange, C. and von Rosenstiel, L. (2003) 'Psychological perspectives of organisational learning', in M. Dierkes, A. Berthoin Antal, J. Child and I. Nonaka (eds), *Handbook of Organisational Learning and Knowledge*. New York: Oxford University Press.

March, J.G. (1991) 'Exploration and exploitation in organizational learning', *Organization Science*, 2(1): 71–87.

Mingers, J. and White, L. (2010) 'A review of the recent contribution of systems thinking to operational research and management science', *European Journal of Operational Research*, 207: 1147–61.

NASA (2003) *Columbia Accident Investigation Board, Volume I*. Washington, DC: National Aeronautics and Space Administration and the Government Printing Office.

Nelson R.R. and Winter S.G. (1982) *An Evolutionary Theory of Economic Change*. Cambridge, MA: Harvard University Press.

Olson, G.M. and Olson, J.S. (2003) 'Human-computer interaction: psychological aspects of the human use of computing', *Annual Review of Psychology*, 54: 491–516.

Orr, J. (1990) 'Sharing knowledge, celebrating identity: war stories and community memory in a service culture', in D.S. Middleton and D. Edwards (eds) *Collective Remembering: Memory in Society*. Beverly Hills, CA: Sage Publications.

Parasuraman, R. and Wilson, G.F. (2008) 'Putting the brain to work: neuroergonomics past, present, and future', *Human Factors, 50:* 468–74.

Pennington, N. and Hastie, R. (1986) 'Evidence evaluation in complex decisions making', *Journal of Peronality and Social Psychology*, 51: 242–58.

Polanyi , M.E. (1966) *Personal Knowledge: Towards a Post-critical Philosophy*. Chicago, IL: University of Chicago Press.

Proctor, R.W. and Vu, K.L. (2010) 'Cumulative knowledge and progress in human factors', *Annual Review of Psychology*, 61: 623–51.

Reason, J. (1990) *Human Error*. Cambridge: Cambridge University Press.

Reason, J. (2008) *The Human Contribution: Unsafe Acts, Accidents and Heroic Recoveries*. Aldershot: Ashgate.

Rocco, E., Finholt, T., Hofer, E.C. and Herbsleb, J. (2000) 'Designing as if trust mattered', CREW Tech Report, University of Michigan.

Salas, E. and Canon-Bowers, A. (2001) 'Special issue, preface', *Journal of Organizational Behavior*, 22: 87–8.

Sanders, M.S. and McCormick, E.J. (1993) *Human Factors in Engineering and Design*, 7th edn. New York: McGraw-Hill.

Senge, P.M. (1993) *The Fifth Discipline: The Art and Practice of the Learning Organisation*. New York: Doubleday.

Sharit, J. (2006) 'Human error', in G. Salvendy (ed.), *Handbook of Human Factors and Ergonomics*. Chichester: Wiley.

Simon, H.A. (1957) *Models of Man*. New York: Wiley.

Stanney, K.M., Mourant, R.R. and Kennedy, R.S. (1998) 'Human factors issues in virtual environments: a review of the literature', *Presence*, 7 (4): 327–51.

Sterman, J.D. (1994) 'Learning in and about complex systems', *System Dynamics Review*, 10: 291–330.

Toffler, A. (1980) *The Third Wave*. New York: Bantam.

Trist, E., Higgin, G., Murray, H. and Pollock, A. (1963) *Organisational Choice*. London: Tavistock.

Tversky, A. and Kahneman, D. (1973) 'Availability: a heuristic for judging frequency and probability', *Cognitive Psychology*, 5 (2): 207–32.

Tversky, A. and Koehler, D. (1994) 'Support theory: a non-existential representation of subjective probability', *Psychological Reviews*, 101: 515–18.

Waldrop, M.M. (1992) *Complexity: The Emerging Science at the Edge of Order and Chaos*. New York: Simon Schuster.

Walsh, J.P. (1995) 'Managerial and organisational cognitions: notes from a trip down memory lane', *Organisation Science*, 6 (3): 280–321.

Waterson, P. and Eason, K. (2009) '"1966 and all that": trends and developments in the UK ergonomics during the 1960's', *Ergonomics*, 52 (11): 1323–41.

Weber, E.U. and Johnson, E.J. (2009) 'Mindful judgement and decision making', *Annual Review of Psychology*, 60: 53–85.

Weick, K.E. (1991) 'The non-traditional quality of organizational learning', *Organization Science*, 2(1): 116–24.

Weick, K. (1995) *Sensemaking in Organizations*. London: Sage.

Weick, K.E. (2005) 'Organising and failures of imagination', *International Public Management Journal*, 8 (3): 425–38.

Weick, K.E. (2012) 'Organised sensemaking: a commentary on processes of interpretive work', *Human Relations*, 65 (1): 141–53.

Wenger, E. (1998) *Communities of Practice: Learning, Meaning and Identity*. New York: Oxford University Press.

Wimalasiri, V. (2007) 'A cognitive psychological perspective to knowledge sharing in organisations', PhD thesis, University of Nottingham, 2007.

Wimalasiri, V., Beesley, N., Cheyne, A. and Daniels, K. (2010) 'Social construction of the aetiology of designer error in the UK oil and gas industry: a stakeholder perspective', *Journal of Engineering Design*, 21 (1): 49–73.

Xanthopoulou, D. and Papaginnidis, S. (in press) 'Play online, work better? Spillover of active learning and tranformational leadership', *Technological Forecasting*.

Xanthopoulou, D. and Papagiannidis, S. (2012) 'Games-work interference: the beneficial effects of computer games for work behaviors', in D. Derks and A.B. Bakker (eds), *Digital Media at Work*. New York: Psychology Press.

Yule, S., Flin, R., Patterson-Brown, N. and Rowley, D. (2006) 'Development of a rating system for surgeons' non-technical skills', *Medical Education*, 40: 1098–104.

Part III

Considering the future

12 Emerging trends and future directions in Occupational Psychology

Lara Zibarras and Rachel Lewis

Learning outcomes

On completion of this chapter you should:

- appreciate what Britain might 'look like' in the future;
- have an understanding of some of the emerging trends in the workplace;
- appreciate how these changes may influence the future of Occupational Psychology.

Introduction

There is little doubt that the work environment is changing and that work life has undergone a dramatic transformation during the 20th century. With this in mind, it is probable that the future of work will also look remarkably different; but making 'predictions' regarding future directions in Occupational Psychology will most likely be inaccurate. Think, for example, that in the 1970s it was suggested that human intelligence would soon be replaced by computer technologies and that all offices would be paperless (Sellen and Harper, 2003); yet neither prediction came true. What we can say with certainty is that work in the future will look radically different to what we know today, or could even imagine. So even if it is difficult to predict what will actually happen, in anticipating the future, Occupational Psychologists may be able to plan for the changing expectations of employees, organisations and the implications that this may have for the future workplace. Thus, in this chapter we aim to introduce you to some general directions of Occupational Psychology, given the emerging and (possible) future trends in the workplace.

What might the UK look like in 2020?

A good place to start thinking about 'the future of Occupational Psychology' is to consider what the UK might look like in 2020 (with the caveat that it is virtually impossible to make accurate forecasts). We outline here some of the projected statistics relating to the UK and then consider how these might influence the workplace.

In 2011, the Office for National Statistics (ONS) projected that the UK population will increase by 4.9 million between the years 2010 to 2020, with the UK population reaching 70 million by mid-2027. The ONS also indicates that the population is steadily aging (ONS, 2011). Currently, life expectancy at birth in the UK has reached its highest levels for both males (78.5 years) and females (82.6 years); and it is anticipated to increase (ONS, 2011). In fact, life expectancy is anticipated to increase by nearly five years between 2010 and 2035, when it is projected to reach 83.4 years for males and 87.0 years for females.

In 2010, those over 60 years old in the UK accounted for 22.6% of the population, and by 2020 this is projected to rise to 23.9%. The total number of people of state pension age (SPA) is likely to increase by 28% from 12.2 million today to 15.6 million in 2035. Between the years 2010 and 2020, SPA will change from 65 years for men and 60 years for women to 65 years for both sexes. Between now and 2046, SPA is projected to rise to 68 also for both sexes. So for those of you entering the workplace today, you can expect to be working well into your 60s, and possibly into your 70s.

The ONS also suggests that there will continue to be significant net migration into the UK over the coming years. Migrants are said to be people who change their country of usual residence for at least one year, so that the UK becomes their country of residence instead. The current estimate (ONS, 2011) is that over 200,000 people will migrate to the UK each year, with the majority of these expected to be aged between 20 and 39 years.

Thinking about all these changes that will take place in the UK generally, what might an organisation of 2020 look like? It is likely to be characterised by an aging workforce, but also have an influx of younger employees (who may be termed Generation Y [Donkin, 2009]) and, given the steady flow of migration, we are likely to see increasingly multicultural organisations. Indeed, Donkin (2009) suggests that changing demographics will be an important force for change in the future – in the next 10 years we are likely to see the proportion of the population over 65 to exceed those aged less than 16. People will increasingly be working in organisations for longer to reach state pensionable age; once they leave work, since life expectancies are increasing, they are likely to spend an increasing proportion of their lives *not working* as well. Not only will population growth and the aging population be significant in the workplaces of the future, but also the impact of migration and the likely growth of new and different industries.

> If you cannot accurately predict the future then you must flexibly be prepared to deal with various possible futures. (Edward de Bono)

Recession and current financial/political situation

We have been, and still are in early 2013, experiencing a global recession that started in 2008. Generally, in the UK, this has led to higher unemployment particularly among the young; less consumer spending; a decline in house prices (although London remains less affected); an increase in bankruptcies; and increasing food and petrol prices. While 'every day' people have been hard hit by the recession, remarkably many large corporations and even banks (some of whom had been bailed out by the UK government) were reporting record profits and paying huge bonuses to their CEOs and senior executives in 2009.

Nevertheless, throughout the world, there has been evidence of political instability arising from the global recession. Indeed, the 'Arab Spring' is said to have been sparked by general discontent caused by high inflation, unemployment and corruption (Spencer, 2011). Many countries have been implementing significant 'austerity measures' – felt here in the UK and throughout Europe. This has led to political unrest, for example, there was a huge general strike in Greece because of the economic situation and schools, airports and other services were closed. Later there were riots on the streets of Athens. Currently there is uncertainty over whether Greece (and perhaps Portugal and Spain) will remain within the Eurozone. It may be that the time that this book goes to press, the Greeks have exited the euro and are back using drachmas. If this happens, perhaps we will see pesos in Spain and escudos in Portugal.

There is no doubt that the political landscape is changing and with it the world in which organisations operate. It remains to be seen the extent to which this will impact the employees working within them. In these challenging times, it certainly seems harder for young people to get jobs and many more people are being made redundant. This is likely to influence culture and climate, and with significant numbers of people out of work, we may face a situation in the UK where people have been out of jobs for longer than in them. How will these issues effect organisations of the future? These issues may significantly influence many of the emerging trends and future directions of Occupational Psychology.

Emerging and future directions of work and Occupational Psychology

Here, we summarise some of the emerging and future changes anticipated in the workplace as suggested by the authors in Part II. In so doing we will draw on many of the authors' insights as to how these might influence the future of Occupational Psychology. First, you might wish to use the technique outlined in Box 12.1 to imagine for yourself what the emerging and future directions of work and Occupational Psychology might be.

Box 12.1

Stretch Imaging (Patterson and Zibarras, 2009)

The following technique encourages you to consider how the world might look like in the future. Using this technique might help you decide for yourself what some of the future directions in Occupational Psychology might be.

    There are three stages to this process, outlined below.

Stage 1

First imagine that the year is 2020 and then focus on what the world might look like by then – it might help you to consider some of the demographic changes that we have outlined in the previous section. Consider some of the following questions in order to create your image:

- What types of social policies exist in the UK?
- What does a 'working week' look like?
- Which industries are most successful?
- Which country is the most economically powerful in the world?
- What does the 'average' family look like now?
- Is the importance placed on 'work' in a person's life changed? If so, in what ways?
- Have communications and personal interactions at work changed? If so, in what ways?
- Have the education and health systems changed? If so, in what ways?

You should be able to provide a rationale based on your current knowledge as to why certain things have changed in the way you suggest.

Stage 2

Now that you have developed a vision of the world in 2020, apply this to Occupational Psychology. You may want to consider the following questions:

- In 2020, what have been the key changes to the economic and social environment?
- In 2020, what have been the key changes to the workplace?

> - How has this influenced the eight areas of Occupational Psychology?
> - Are there still eight areas of Occupational Psychology?
> - Have there been any political changes that have influenced this as well?
> - What impact might this have had on your role as an Occupational Psychologist?
>
> *Stage 3*
>
> In the final stage, consider what Occupational Psychology might do in order to meet these particular challenges in the future. The idea here is to generate novel ideas that might be useful in a rapidly changing environment.

Impact of technology

Overwhelmingly, the chapters in Part II highlighted technology as the key area that is likely to impact our future working environments. In fact, many of those influences are already being seen with many changes in technology emerging currently. As we emphasised in Chapter 1, there have been huge technological advancements in the previous hundred years or so. This has resulted in rapid changes in organisations, such as alterations in job requirements and the ways in which people work. So the impact that technology has been having on people's working lives and Occupational Psychology is already evident, and there is very little doubt among the authors of the chapters in this book that technology will continue to have a significant influence. A number of key areas have been identified in each of the chapters and here we outline some of the main themes.

As was highlighted by the author of Chapter 11 on automation and human–machine interaction (HMI), we might say that we are currently in an era of 'techno-dependency' where many of us, all over the world, rely on various technologies to do things both at work and in the home. The examples given in Chapter 11 included buying groceries and checking bank balances on our mobile phones and using voice automated systems to help those who are less able to take care of themselves. All of these technological changes – of which there are sure to be many more over the coming decades – will require the expertise of Occupational Psychologists expert in the field of HMI to ensure that these technologies are easy to use; and support rather than hinder employees in the workplace.

Dr Chandra Harrison, Freelance Researcher

' As technology becomes more and more pervasive in our lives and in our work, the need for better human-centered design becomes more apparent. '

The impact of technology was highlighted in Chapter 9, 'Selection and assessment'. Here, the authors suggested an increase in the use of online testing, which has both benefits and drawbacks for applicants and organisations. For applicants, they can have access to testing at a time and place that suits them, but access relies on having a good Internet connection. From an organisation's perspective, there is greater access to applicants from around the world but online testing may increase the potential for cheating. The authors also suggested the increase in the use of different types of media in selection, such as video-based CVs and multi-media SJTs. The use of these technologies may have the positive effect of improving the fidelity (or reality) of selection methods, but Occupational Psychologists must ensure that appropriate research accompanies practice to confirm that these methods are appropriate (with good predictive validities and that they are acceptable to candidates).

For those of you who have applied for jobs in organisations, you will see that technology is often a key part of the process – many organisations use their website to give information to potential applicants and ask that CVs or application forms are completed online or submitted via email. However, organisations of the future will need to be aware that poor website design can have a negative influence on recruitment outcomes; stylistic features have been shown to influence an applicant's attraction to the organisation and their decision to accept the job (Cober et al., 2003), and website usability is positively related to organisational attractiveness (Pfieffelmann et al., 2010). It is in this area where HMI and selection and assessment will no doubt meet; thus HMI may be particularly important in addressing how people interact with and use organisational websites.

Another interesting area where selection and assessment might be different in the future is the extent to which we might use other ways to select employees. Consider, for example, the potential use of genetic testing. Might this be a way in which organisations choose to select people? However, this is likely to open up a huge area of potential for discriminatory practices if people are selected based on genetic tests. Currently the Ministry of Defence uses biochemical screening for sickle cell disease. It is argued (Ernsting et al., 1999) that this prevents potentially catastrophic sickling that can be brought on by low oxygen pressures in flight. It may be possible here to justify selecting out people with this disease, but at what point would this be a form of eugenics?

It is also likely that our interaction with social networking sites will continue to grow in importance in relation to selection and assessment. In January 2012, Facebook Timeline was launched, which is a feature that enables a user to scroll through an individual's history – for instance seeing what an individual did in a particular year. An article by Philip Landau (2012) in the *Guardian* suggests that this will have important effects from an organisational point of view. Already it is suggested (careerbuilder.co.uk) that over one-half of employers use social networking sites to research employees and applicants; and it is likely that this will only increase with a higher percentage of individuals using the sites, and with sites having more accessible and organised information. Although there are implications for employers using this information with regard to the Data Protection Act, Landau suggests that 'it is unlikely that an employer viewing a personal social media site without printing it off or forwarding it would be caught by the Act'. The increased use of this form of 'pre-application vetting' by employers opens opportunities for Occupational Psychologists to advise on how best organisations might use these resources effectively and ethically. We would also predict that the vetting will become more sophisticated. With a recent article by Back et al. (2010) finding that Facebook profiles represent actual personality (rather than an idealised self-perception, which may be a criticism of use of personality psychometrics in selection), we can start to see how these social networking sites may continue to grow in importance for organisations.

Professor Kurt Kraiger, Professor of Industrial Organisational Psychology, Colorado State University, USA

> Clearly, topics such as virtual work, telecommuting, social networks, and so forth will be increasingly important in the future for Occupational Psychology. Although organizations may *implement* these types of interfaces, as Occupational Psychologists we must question whether what they have implemented is based on research of what works and why.

In Chapter 10, the authors outlined a number of ways in which technology is already being used to deliver different training programmes, for instance, through the use of the Internet, virtual learning and mobile technologies. As the authors highlighted, the annual CIPD survey of training and development shows that there has been a significant increase in the usage of technology-based methods, with the advantages of such methods being flexible for trainees since people can complete training programmes at any time from any place in the world. However, currently, e-learning is still considered less effective than other training methods and so future workplaces may use 'blended' learning solutions, which mix technological and non-technological approaches to build on the advantages of both approaches. Again, it is possible to see how the concepts drawn from human–computer interaction (Chapter 11) will be important in this domain.

Alastair Wallace, Managing Director of Brainfood, also has some very interesting points to make about the impact of technology on training as follows:

The huge increase in the number of smartphones and tablet computers has led to new and exciting ways to incorporate their use in a training environment to run events such as 3D virtual simulations for trainee surgeons, and electronic performance support systems (EPSS) to provide real time support for complex and highly dangerous roles, such as offshore crane operators.

Social networking is going to have a much more profound influence on the way we train and develop in the future. Practitioners are already using social networking to set up communities of practice to share ideas and techniques, and also to build cohorts of participants across multi-disciplinary long term leadership programmes where delegates are geographically dispersed.

Sarah Lewis, Managing Director at Appreciating Change

‘ I think the impact of social media, cloud technology, interconnectedness, instant access has great implications for our notions of how organisations will be designed, organised and managed. Leaders who work with the concept that they can control the information in their organisation, and, even more pertinently, the sense people make of what is going on, will find their ideas increasingly at odds with what is actually happening. Organisations have yet to work out how best to work with and benefit from this changed world of information and connection. ’

In Chapter 5, technological developments are considered in the field of counselling, specifically concerning e-based counselling. There has been an emergence of counselling through email whereby the client and counsellor email each other through a secure web portal. Other technologies that may increasingly be used in the future are those of live chat, Skype and MMS. Indeed the use of virtual environments may facilitate counselling encounters where the client and therapist meet in a virtual room. The use of technology was also explored in Chapter 7, 'Design of work environments'. Here, the author shows how the use of technology needs to be considered when thinking about workplace design. Indeed, as technology becomes increasingly complex in future organisations, the design of technology-based tools used at work must consider the abilities and limitations of a person's skills (perceptual, cognitive and motor). If there are significant mismatches, the potential for human error and subsequent accidents will rise.

The increase in technological capability within our environment and within organisations specifically means that increasingly employees are able to work remotely. Teleworking (also called telecommuting or virtual working) is defined by Baruch as 'An alternative work arrangement by which employees perform tasks elsewhere that are normally done in the primary or central workplace, for at least some proportion of their work schedule, using electronic media to interact with others inside and outside the organisation' (2001: 114). The increase in 'working from anywhere at anytime' (Kurland and Bailey, 1999) has been immense. In 1994, Wilkes et al. stated that forecasts suggested teleworking would involve 90 million people worldwide by 2030. In 2007, Sudan et al. stated that the teleworker population in 2006 was actually 758.6 million – and forecast that this would rise to over 1 billion by 2011. To put this into context, this would represent nearly one-third of the worldwide employee population engaging in telework.

The rise in the mobile worker population has significant implications for Occupational Psychology in terms of both theory and practice. Many researchers have noted that working away from the central organisation has an impact on the employee's motivation for work, their attitudes, their organisational perceptions, and their perception and belief about work relationships (Morganson et al., 2010). These differences for both the individual and the organisation can be both positive (for instance, the increase in autonomy and reduction in overheads) and negative (for instance, social isolation, reduced organisational commitment and lack of support). A meta-analysis by Gajendran and Harrison (2007) recently aimed to develop a model of teleworking, however, researchers argue that evidence is still contradictory and interdeterminate – meaning that the jury is still out on when and in what context teleworking may be beneficial or adverse for employees, the organisation and the wider society. Occupational Psychology has a real part to play academically by conducting more research to explore the impact of teleworking, and in practice to develop guidance and interventions for organisations in order to create effective teleworking policies and practices.

Professor Frank Bond, Professor of Occupational Psychology and Head of Department, Goldsmiths, University of London

' The trend in teleworking and flexible working will continue to grow. This has already presented opportunities for Occupational Psychologists in terms of how leaders lead, team working and work design. Certain sectors, such as the financial services, have not adopted these new ways of working to the extent that others have (e.g. marketing and PR); we expect this will change. '

Impact of ageing workforce

As outlined earlier in the chapter, the age demographics of the UK will look significantly different over the coming years. Additionally, within Europe it has been estimated that by the year 2050, the proportion of workers aged between 55 to 64 will increase to 60% (Carone et al., 2005). This represents a significant shift in the age composition of the future workforce and it will be important for Occupational Psychology to understand the role of age in the workplace. Occupational Psychology has only just begun to touch on the issue of age in the workplace and advances will certainly be needed both in terms of theory and practice.

Nevertheless, some recent research has begun to investigate how age may influence certain work outcomes (Kanfer and Ackerman, 2004; Ng and Feldman, 2010). For example, in Ng and Feldman's (2010) meta-analysis of over 800 empirical articles, the authors found a positive relationship between age and many job-related attitudes. For example, older workers had higher job satisfaction, they were more satisfied with the work itself and were more satisfied with their levels of pay. Additionally, older workers were more motivated at work and made more positive assessments of their work environment. Findings also showed that older workers were more committed at work. These types of findings may influence how certain Occupational Psychology interventions are designed to account for age.

In future, organisations will need to address some crucial questions regarding the extent to which there might be stereotypes about age or biases against certain age groups, what human resource policies might be needed to motivate and manage different ages of employees, whether different age groups have different work–life balance tensions and how jobs can be designed to take into account the needs of different ages of workers. These are among the types of issues that are likely to be addressed by Occupational Psychology in the future.

There are some interesting points in Chapter 5 regarding the 'theories of career development' which touch on the concept of age in the workplace. Many of the theories put forward consider career development as something that evolves throughout different stages of a person's life. So the life or career stage that Occupational Psychologists might explore in future workplaces are the 'late adulthood' stage (Levinson et al., 1978) or the 'maintenance' stage (aged 45–64) as considered by Super (1980).

The potential impact of the ageing workforce on Occupational Psychology is highlighted succinctly in this quote by Professor Frank Bond:

> I think that the ageing workforce will present a number of challenges and opportunities for Occupational Psychologists. Many people will want to work well into their 60s; others will be forced to, owing to increases in the pension age – all over the Western world. In addition, at least in the UK, there is no longer a mandatory retirement age. All of these changes will have an impact on Occupational Psychology; for example, in terms of training and development, ergonomics, counselling and personal development, and performance management. In addition, we do not yet know how our current middle-aged portfolio workers will approach their work, as they get into their 60s.

Globalisation

In a globalised economy and increasingly globalised organisations, managing diversity may be a complex issue for individuals and organisations. Organisations are likely to face challenges of managing a multicultural workforce. We highlighted in Chapter 1 that many workplaces in the UK are increasingly bringing together different cultures, both physically in offices or virtually via different branches of an organisation being based in different countries around the world. There is a growing challenge for organisations to develop human resource systems (for example, selection, development and training) that take into consideration different cultures and ethnicities. Being part of a multicultural working environment is likely to be increasingly evident as the 21st century progresses.

In some of the chapters in Part II, the authors highlight how globalisation will influence the future of work. For example, in Chapter 5 the authors outlined how employee assistance programmes (EAP) in an organisation may 'look' different depending on the country they are based in. For example, because the concept of the 'counsellor' does not necessarily exist in many countries, it may be social workers in one country, psychiatrists in another and psychotherapists in yet another. Thus the development of EAPs may vary, unlikely to necessarily replicate the UK model. Employee selection (Chapter 9) might also be significantly influenced as organisations become increasingly globalised. A key issue to be addressed will be how organisations can ensure that selection and assessment methods are used fairly for the same job level in different countries. For example, would organisations choose to use exactly the same selection method across countries – say, the UK and the UAE. The challenge here would be to ensure that the selection methods are translated and then used across countries in a best-practice way. But would this be fair, given that the local context in each market would be so different? Would it be more fair to develop entirely different selection methods that take into account different contextual (social, cultural and religious) issues that might significantly impact an applicant's ability to complete a selection method that was originally developed in another country. It is likely that Occupational Psychologists will tackle this issue when working in organisations that operate in different countries.

Other areas to consider in the future of Occupational Psychology

There are also a number of research areas and practice that are currently emerging in Occupational Psychology, which are not necessarily addressed by the BPS syllabus, and may grow in the future. We outline here some key areas employee engagement; resilience; pro-environmental behaviour in the workplace; and methodological advancements such, as multi-level modelling.

Employee engagement
As discussed in Chapter 4, employee engagement is becoming increasingly important in terms of our understanding of employee relations and motivation. It is the

case that despite a proliferation of work in practice, academic literature has not yet caught up. As Saks states 'employee engagement is rarely studied in academic literature and little is known about its antecedents and consequences' (2006: 600).

Future research by Occupational Psychologists must work to understand further both the antecedents, and moderators, of employee engagement in organisations in order to provide the most effective and evidence-based interventions in practice. In particular, Lewis et al. (2011b) suggest that exploring and understanding the leadership or management behaviours that drive employee engagement are crucial.

Resilience

Following the recent financial downturn, organisations are much more likely to be asking questions such as the following:

- What can we do to protect our organisation during this downturn to ensure we can survive?
- How can we perform effectively despite the financial crisis?
- How can we bounce back as an organisation once the situation improves?
- How can we ensure our employees 'weather the storm'?
- How can we keep a healthy workforce in this unhealthy climate?

The answer to all these questions may lie in the understanding of resilience.

Resilience is a very hot topic in practice. If you search online for 'Resilience in organisations' you will see millions of search results with organisations and individuals offering to provide solutions for the problems of developing, improving, measuring and promoting resilience within businesses. In the academic world, the study of resilience in individuals has a rich and compelling history from both the psychology and psychiatry literature. This began with the study of children who were developing well despite poor living conditions, moved on to a focus on resilience in coping with trauma and then expanded to explore the factors that both promote resilience and protect individuals from adversity. A succinct definition of what is meant by individual resilience comes from Windle, describing it as 'the successful adaptation to life tasks in the face of social disadvantage or highly adverse conditions' (1999: 163).

At an organisational level, Lewis et al. (2011a) suggest it is conceptualised in a similar way to individual resilience, but the focus is upon how well the organisation can 'weather the storm' or adapt to challenges it faces. Therefore organisational resilience is concerned not only with the individuals (employees) within the organisation, but also the culture and processes that make up that organisation.

It has been suggested that, perhaps as a result of the literature spanning a number of domains, the understanding of resilience, particularly at the organisational

Table 12.1

Individual resilience	
Resilience is conceptualised as:	Resilience is ...
A Personality/individual characteristic	A part of an individual's innate personality (such as internal locus of control, self efficacy and optimism)
Environmental	Dependent on the experiences that individual has had (for instance how much social support there is)
Person-environmental	A product of both personality characteristics and the environment
Organisational Resilience	
Key to resilience is:	Resilience is dependent on ...
Job design	The features of an individual's job (for instance how much control they have)
Organisational culture and structure	The culture, processes and procedures of the organisation
Leadership	Engaging, supportive leadership
Systemic/external environment	External environment and social relationships

Source: Adapted from Lewis et al. (2011a).

level, is confused and complex. In 2011, Lewis et al. (2011a) conducted a literature review to understand how both individual and organisational resilience was conceptualised in the literature. A summary of the review is included in Table 12.1.

The range of conceptualisations, and lack of agreement in terms of clear definitions of both individual and organisational resilience, has resulted in an even wider range of approaches in both academia and practice towards addressing the issue of resilience in organisations. Lewis et al. (2011a) also found that there is a real lack of research on organisational resilience. It seems that despite a huge body of literature on resilience in general psychological literature (and from other domains), within Occupational Psychology there has been little interest.

In order to provide clear guidance to practice on tackling resilience, further research within organisations is needed. It is also essential that Occupational Psychologists are able to translate the existing extensive literature on resilience into effective, evidence-based guidance and interventions for organisations. As the literature base is already present, and as the need for resilience in organisations is likely to grow ever stronger over the coming years, both Occupational Psychology and Psychologists are in a unique position to be able to have a significance impact on this area in both academia and practice.

Environmental sustainability

The context within which businesses operate is changing: water scarcity; energy supply problems; a depletion of natural resources; and increased waste may soon have a negative impact on the way organisations function. It is widely accepted that human and industrial activity are largely responsible for creating these types of environmental problems, and thus it has been argued that changes in human behaviour are an essential part of the solution (Oskamp, 2000). Indeed, governments worldwide have increasingly challenged organisations to address their environmental performance in addition to economic performance, with the UK government stressing the importance of employee behaviour change in attaining the UK's environmental targets (Parliamentary Office for Science and Technology, 2010).

In addition to the responsibility that organisations have for addressing environmental issues, more and more companies are beginning to acknowledge the business case for integrating sustainability into their business strategies and are taking a strategic approach to environmental management (Govindarajulu and Daily, 2004). This means we may start to see organisations committing to environmental policies to facilitate a shift towards more sustainable business practices (Jabbour and Santos, 2008). Although behaviour change is recognised as a key part of the solution to the environmental problems that we face, the role of employee behaviour in delivering improvements to an organisation's environmental performance has been largely overlooked (Davis and Challenger, 2009) and it is likely that future organisations may become more savvy in this respect.

Recently, research by Zibarras and Ballinger (2010, 2011) explored the extent to which different environmental initiatives were being implemented in UK organisations to encourage staff to behave pro-environmentally. Of 147 organisations surveyed, most (86%) indicated that they recycled waste materials and 69% of organisations indicated that they had an environmental policy in place within their organisation. Findings also showed that the most prevalent methods used to encourage employee pro-environmental behaviour had significant management involvement, and that these practices were generally perceived to be the most successful approaches to encouraging pro-environmental behaviour, after internal awareness campaigns. The findings highlighted the importance of senior and line management support and commitment, which were rated as the most important facilitators for effective environmental practices within 86% of organisations. Also, lack of senior management commitment was identified as the most significant barrier to effective environmental practices in 70% of organisations. Another key finding from the research was that the environmental practices used in organisations were Occupational Psychology practices which either directly or indirectly fell under the remit of HR departments. These findings suggest that for organisations to achieve environmental targets, both line manager and employee involvement are crucial, and it is here that Occupational Psychologists may have a significant influence in workplaces of the future.

Methodological advances

There have also been significant methodological advances in psychological research over the preceding decades. Techniques, such as structural equation modelling (SEM), are increasingly emerging in Occupational Psychology research and have enabled Occupational Psychologists to predict and explain causal relationships between variables. SEM (as introduced in Chapter 3) allows exploratory and confirmatory modelling and thus is suited to both theory development and testing. In confirmatory modelling, the researcher starts out with a hypothesis that is represented as a causal model and the relationships between the constructs in the model are tested. The model is then checked against the obtained data to see how well the model fits the data. For example, we may theorise that fairness perceptions are influenced by perceptions of job relevance of a specific selection method (say, a psychometric test), but that this relationship is mediated by both a trait (neuroticism) and a state (test-taking self-efficacy). We could use SEM to test this relationship, as shown in Figure 12.1. If we were to use SEM to test this relationship we might, for instance, find that there is significant mediation via self-efficacy, but less mediation via neuroticism.

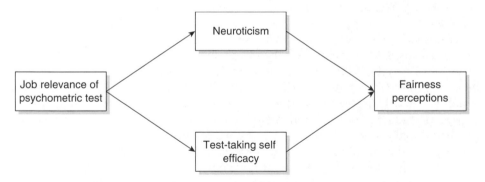

Figure 12.1   Model of relationship between job relevance perceptions of test and fairness perceptions

Other methods such as multi-level modelling (MLM) are also being increasingly used and are useful in Occupational Psychology because they allow researchers to explore the influence of variables at different levels (that is, individual, group, team and organisational level variables) on specific outcomes. This is a particularly effective method to use in organisational research because it enables researchers to identify where an intervention has been successful and at what level. This change follows current trends in occupational research for more contextual understanding of sample and environment. To illustrate this, leadership was originally studied in terms of what *the leader did or said* (where the employees were not considered). It then moved to a study of *the conditions under which what the leader did or said would be effective* (taking a more situational approach). Later, studies explored the impact of the relationship between the employee and the leader (such as LMX) and *the consequence of what they said or did upon that employee* (such as transformational leadership). Now we are seeing an emergence of literature that explores the effect of the wider team, and both the organisational and external environment, upon leadership and its outcomes (such as complex leadership theory and team LMX). In research we are increasingly seeking to understand more about the mechanisms by which (or conditions under which) variables interact in the workplace – and with this trend, analytical methods will need to become more complex.

Additionally, there has also been an increasing acceptance of the use of qualitative research methods. Many Occupational Psychology researchers and practitioners agree that they can be extremely useful for certain research questions and also to explore the meaning behind patterns of data. Indeed, as King states: 'the goal of any qualitative research ... is ... to see the research topic from the perspective of the [individual], and to understand how and why they have come to this particular perspective' (2004: 11). It is possible to understand why qualitative research can be considered useful in organisational contexts because data gathered is likely to be salient and personally relevant to the employees, and explanations for events are provided from the employee and *not* the researcher's point of view. Indeed, qualitative research methods allow participants to expand on responses and discuss certain issues, adding detail that they consider relevant to the topic (MacKenzie-Davey and Arnold, 2000). This is not possible when closed-response questionnaire items are used (Symon et al., 2000). Indeed, there has certainly been an increasing synergy between researchers advocating either quantitative or qualitative techniques (Patterson, 2001). Often mixed methods approaches are used since in organisational research there might be a need to both examine the patterns of data and explore the meaning behind the pattern of data. For example, an organisation might find that a high percentage of their new recruits are leaving after only six months on a particular job. The organisation might use quantitative techniques to explore the pattern of data and find that a higher percentage of younger than older employees are likely to leave after a few months and also that male employees were statistically more likely to leave than female. Without using any qualitative techniques, such as exit interviews, it would be impossible to understand why so many people are leaving. So, in this instance, qualitative methods would provide contextual meaning and further understanding of the initial finding. To read further about analytical techniques, see Chapter 3.

Summary

This chapter started out by exploring what the UK might 'look like' in the future in order to highlight how this might affect the workplace. We have also summarised the key emerging trends and possible future directions in Occupational Psychology, based on information from all our authors and contributing practitioners and academics.

Our key areas that we have explored included:

- the impact of technology;
- the impact of the ageing workforce;
- globalisation;
- employee engagement;
- resilience;
- the impact of the 'green' agenda;
- methodological advances.

In the Explore Further section at the end of this section we have indicated where you can get more information on any of these new trends and emerging areas. This is of course not an exhaustive list and, as we have suggested, the world is changing so rapidly that it is likely that new areas will have emerged and grown in importance even before this book is published. Continue to read and gather information from a wide number of sources in the business world and externally in order to keep connected. To refresh on some of these sources, refer back to Chapter 3.

In the next chapter we will conclude by exploring what impact these new and emerging trends may have on the work of Occupational Psychologists in the future, and therefore what the associated skill and knowledge demands may be.

Explore further

- The Office for National Statistics provides interesting research and publications on the state of the UK, including labour market, population, economy and the environment. You can download these articles here: http://www.ons.gov.uk/ons/publications/index.html.
- The Work Foundation is an independent authority on work and its future. It publishes a range of reports that focus on what the future of work might look like. These can be found here: http://www.theworkfoundation.com/Research.
- Gajendran, R.S. and Harrison, D.A. (2007) 'The good, the bad and the unknown about telecommuting: meta-analysis of psychological mediators and individual consequences', *Journal of Applied Psychology*, 92 (6): 1524–41.
- Lewis, R., Donaldson-Feilder, E. and Pangallo, A. (2011) 'Developing resilience: an evidence based guide for practitioners', project report. London: The Chartered Institute of Personnel and Development.
- Lewis, R., Donaldson-Feilder, E., and Tharani, T. (2011) 'Management competencies for enhancing employee engagement', project report. London: The Chartered Institute of Personnel and Development.

- Zibarras, L. and Ballinger, C. (2010). Promoting environmental behaviour in the workplace: A survey of UK organisations. Available at: http://www.sbcscot.com/programmes/climate-change/mayday-network-newsletters/pro-environmental-behaviour-a-survey-of-uk-organisations.pdf (accessed 10 January 2011).

Discussion questions

1 What impact do you feel the recession has had upon the work environment here and globally?
2 Consider implications of each of the future trends upon employee's experience of the workplace.
3 How might these future trends impact upon the role of Occupational Psychologists in the future?

References

Back, M.D., Stopfer, J.M., Vazire, S., Gaddis, S., Schmukle, B.E. and Gosling, S.D. (2010) 'Facebook profiles reflect actual personality, not self idealisation', *Psychological Science*, 21: 372–74.

Baruch, Y. (2001) 'The status of research on teleworking and an agenda for future research', *International Journal of Management Reviews*, 3 (2): 113–29.

Carone, G. Costello, D, Guardia, N.D., Mourre, G., Przywara, B., Salomaki, A. (2005)' The economic impact of ageing populations in the EU25 Member States'. European Economy Economic Papers, 236.

Cober, R., Brown, D., Levy, P., Cober, A. and Keeping, L. (2003) 'Organisational web sites: web site content and style as determinants of organisational attraction', *International Journal of Selection and Assessment*, 11 (2–3): 158–69.

Davis, M.C. and Challenger, R. (2009) 'Climate change – warming to the task', *The Psychologist*, 22: 112–14.

Donkin, R. (2009) *The Future of Work*. Basingstoke: MacMillan Publishers.

Ernsting, J., Nicolson, A.N. and Rainford, D.J. (1999) *Aviation Medicine*. Oxford: *Butterworth–Heinemann*.

Gajendran, R.S. and Harrison, D.A. (2007) 'The good, the bad and the unknown about telecommuting: meta-analysis of psychological mediators and individual consequences', *Journal of Applied Psychology*, 92 (6): 1524–41.

Govindarajulu, N. and Daily, B.F. (2004) 'Motivating employees for environmental improvement', *Industrial Management & Data Systems*, 104 (4): 364–72.

Jabbour, C.J.C. and Santos, F.C.A. (2008) 'The central role of human resource management in the search for sustainable organisations', *The International Journal of Human Resource Management*, 19 (12): 2133–54.

Kanfer, R. and Ackerman, P.L. (2004) 'Aging, adult development, and work motivation', *The Academy of Management Review*, 29 (3): 440–58.

King, N. (2004) 'Using interviews in qualitative research', in C. Cassell and G. Symon (eds), *Essential Guide to Qualitative Methods in Organizational Research*. London: Sage. pp. 11–22.

Kurland, N.B. and Bailey, D.E. (1999) 'Telework: the advantages and challenges of working here, there and everywhere', *Organisational Dynamics*, 28: 53–67.

Landau, P. (2012) 'What if Facebook timeline was read instead of your CV?', *Guardian*. Available at: http://www.guardian.co.uk/money/work-blog/2012/jan/30/facebook-timeline-employers-applications.

Levinson, D., Darrow, C., Klein, E., Levinson, M. and Braxton, M. (1978) *The Seasons of a Man's Life*. New York: Random House.

Lewis, R., Donaldson-Feilder, E. and Pangallo, A. (2011a) 'Developing resilience: an evidence based guide for practitioners', project report. London: The Chartered Institute of Personnel and Development.

Lewis, R., Donaldson-Feilder, E. and Tharani, T. (2011b) 'Management competencies for enhancing employee engagement', project report. London: The Chartered Institute of Personnel and Development.

Mackenzie-Davey, K.M. and Arnold, J. (2000) 'A multi-method study of accounts of personal change by graduates starting work: self-ratings, categories and women's discourses', *Journal of Occupational and Organizational Psychology*, 73 (4): 461–86.

Morganson, V.J., Major, D.A., Oborn, K.L., Verive, J.M. and Heelan, M.P. (2010) 'Comparing telework locations and traditional work arrangements: differences in work-life balance support, job satisfaction and inclusion', *Journal of Managerial Psychology*, 25 (6): 578–95.

Ng, T. and Feldman, D. (2010) 'The relationships of age with job attitudes: a meta-analysis', *Personnel Psychology*, 63 (3): 677–718.

ONS (2011) National population projections, 2010-based projections. Available at: http://www.ons.gov.uk/ons/rel/npp/national-population-projections/2010-based-projections/index.html (accessed 6 December 2011).

Oskamp, S. (2000) 'Psychological contributions to achieving an ecologically sustainable future for humanity', *Journal of Social Issues*, 56: 373–90.

Parliamentary Office for Science and Technology (2010) Climate change: engagement and behaviour. Available at: http://www.parliament.uk/documents/post/postpn347.pdf (accessed 21 July 2011).

Patterson, F. (2001) 'Developments in work psychology: emerging issues and future trends', *Journal of Occupational and Organisational Psychology*, 74 (4): 381–90.

Patterson, F. and Zibarras, L. (2009) 'Creative problem-solving at work', *General Practice Update*, June: 48–51.

Pfieffelmann, B., Wagner, S.H. and Libkuman, T. (2010) 'Recruiting on corporate web sites: perceptions of fit and attraction', *International Journal of Selection and Assessment*, 18 : 40–7.

Saks, A.M. (2006) 'Antecedents and consequences of employee engagement', *Journal of Managerial Psychology*, 21: 600–619.

Sellen, A. and Harper, R. (2003) *The Myth of the Paperless Office*. London: MIT Press.

Spencer, R. (2011) 'Tunisia riots: reform or be overthrown, US tells Arab states amid fresh riots', *Telegraph*. Available at: http://www.telegraph.co.uk/news/worldnews/africaand indianocean/tunisia/8258077/Tunisia-riots-US-warns-Middle-East-to-reform-or-be-overthrown.html (accessed 31 May 2012).

Sudan, S.K., Ryan, S., Drake, S.D., Sandler, M., Broggs, R. and Giusto, R. (2007) 'Worldwide mobile worker population 2007–2011'. *Forecast 37*.

Super, D. (1980) 'A life-span, life-space approach to career development', *Journal of Vocational Behavior*, 16 (3): 282–98.

Symon, G., Cassell, C. and Dickson, R. (2000) Expanding our research and practice through innovative research methods. *European Journal of Work and Organizational Psychology*, 9(4), 457–462.

Wilkes, R., Frolik, M. and Urwiler, R. (1994) 'Critical issues in developing successful telework programmes', *Journal of Management Systems*, 45 (7)30–34.

Windle, M. (1999) 'Critical conceptualisation and measurement issues in the study of resilience', in M.D.E.J Glantz and J. Johnson (eds), *Resilience and Development, Positive Life Adaptations*. New York: Kluwer Academic/Plenum. pp. 161–78

Zibarras, L. and Ballinger, C. (2010) Promoting environmental behaviour in the workplace: a survey of UK organisations. London. Available at: http://www.sbcscot.com/programmes/climate-change/mayday-network-newsletters/pro-environmental-behaviour-a-survey-of-uk-organisations.pdf (accessed 10 January 2011).

Zibarras, L. and Ballinger, C. (2011) 'Promoting environmental behaviour in the workplace: a survey of UK organisations', in D. Bartlett (ed.), *The Psychology of Sustainability in the Workplace*. London: BPS. pp. 84–90.

13 Future directions for Occupational Psychologists

Rachel Lewis and Lara Zibarras

Learning outcomes

On completion of this chapter you should have:

- considered the roles that Occupational Psychologists may increasingly occupy as a result of the financial crisis;
- considered the new opportunities afforded by the emerging trends in the workplace, as discussed in Chapter 1 and Chapter 12;
- reflected upon what these changes and opportunities might mean for the future skill requirements of Occupational Psychologists.

Introduction

As we have seen described in each chapter of this book, the work environment continues to change at an increasing and dramatic rate. These changes have many implications for the work that Occupational Psychologists undertake both within organisations and in research. In this chapter we will seek to consider how the work that we may do as Occupational Psychologists (as explored in Chapter 2) may differ as a result of the changes in the world of work (as explored in Chapter 12). In particular we will identify the opportunities that may arise from changes brought on by the current financial crisis and by emerging trends in the workplace. The chapter will then move towards a consideration of the new and emerging skills needed by Occupational Psychologists. First, briefly revisiting the skills content from Chapter 2 and, second, integrating our discoveries from writing the book towards a suggestion of current and future skill demands. In summary, it is intended that this chapter will provide 'food for thought' for a new generation of Occupational Psychologists, making sure that, when you are ready, you are at the cutting edge of practice and research.

What roles will Occupational Psychologists increasingly occupy?

Since 2008, the modern world has been in the grip of a serious financial crisis. In Chapter 2, we explored where Occupational Psychologists worked. Perhaps the biggest change since the financial crisis has been in terms of Occupational Psychologists working as external consultants (working in a consultancy for a range of different organisations and environments). We have seen many such organisations cut the number of salaried consultants on their payroll and instead employ associates if and when project work comes in. This has resulted in a decline in consultancy roles for those entering the profession of Occupational Psychology but an increase in opportunities for, and availability of, associate work (where you work on temporary projects for other consultancies or organisations). It is also true that there will have been cuts seen for Occupational Psychologists working as internal consultants, as has been reflected across the whole job market.

Rather than dwelling on the negative impact of the financial crisis for our profession, we asked our authors, eminent academics and leading practitioners to consider what opportunities may actually arise from this situation. We have summarised their ideas below.

Delivering evidence-based practice

What leaders of organisations need when times are hard is to know, as far as possible, that any budget spend is done so wisely. In our profession, we are ideally placed, by using our research skills and an existing body of research and literature, to be able to access and use an evidence base for the solutions that we offer to organisations. These skills offer us opportunities over and above our competition.

By using evidence-based practice, we can demonstrate to organisations both that our solutions have been shown to work and also the financial impact of that solution (such as impact on return on investment). As Alastair Wallace, Managing Director at Brainfood states:

> OPs really need to improve the bridging of the academic–practitioner divide, and really start to promote sound evidence-based practice in order to develop true and lasting change. Accurate insights and demonstrable results are the

only way to convince leadership within an organisation of the true value of the OP contribution.

Using evidence-based practice does not just have to mean finding and using evidence from the wider body of research literature, but also being able to use and understand existing data within organisations. This could mean for instance combining data from staff surveys and appraisal results to explore links between employee engagement and management competence. As Rob Briner, Professor of Organisational Psychology at the University of Bath succinctly puts it:

> What will become extremely important in the future is that we start to use, in a critical way, the research evidence we already have, as well as working with organisations to better understand and use the data and evidence they have.

Predicting performance

Perhaps related to the previous point, as organisations become more discerning in their use of resources, there will be an increasing opportunity for Occupational Psychologists to use their evidence base, research and analytic skills to predict performance at the individual, team and organisational levels. It may be that this could involve the use of more sophisticated analytical methods (as discussed as an emerging trend in Chapter 12) to demonstrate patterns in organisational data. This may involve the development of and advice on the use of more objective criteria for measuring performance. It could also involve the evaluation and validity testing of interventions around leadership and in the wider HR and OD sphere. Frank Bond, Professor of Occupational Psychology and Head of Department, Psychology, at Goldsmiths, University of London, also suggests that there is an opportunity for further academic research in this area:

> It is important for researchers to identify individual characteristics and psychological processes that are good at predicting performance *and* that we can also influence. Currently, traits such as the Big 5 are used to predict work behaviours fairly effectively, but the problem is: you cannot fundamentally change them. This limits the extent to which you can develop certain aspects of an individual's behaviour. It is early days, but we are beginning to find that an important psychological process that underpins mental health and behavioural effectiveness – psychological flexibility – may be one such variable. Research has shown that it predicts mental health and performance over the course of at least one year, and it can also be enhanced through a brief training programme. I think that researchers will attempt to identify other such characteristics.

Talent management

Globalisation has brought an increased 'war for talent' with competition from both local and global organisations for the best employees. This also coincides with organisations having fewer available funds to reward, motivate and develop employees – the recognised ways to retain employees. With our knowledge and evidence base around motivation (explored in Chapter 4) and also emerging constructs such as employee engagement (explored in Chapters 4 and 12), again, Occupational Psychologists are in a strong position to occupy and 'own' this area within organisations. Further, by the use of evidence-based practice, our advice to organisations can be made all the more persuasive.

Although it is recognised that the marketplace for talent management solutions is highly competitive and cluttered, Kurt Kraiger (Professor of Industrial Organisational Psychology, Colorado State University, USA) suggests there is a real opportunity for Occupational Psychologists in the future in this space:

> Historically, these systems [talent management], would be built from scratch organisation by organisation. Increasingly, you see not only large consulting firms offering customisable, downloadable applications, but HR managers with the capacity to 'google' the applications they want and customise them with little or no understanding of best practices. This could mean a dramatic drop in the demand for skilled OPs, but instead what I think it will mean is that OPs can move in the direction of being change agents (or organisational development specialists) who are there to answer the question of *why* we need such tools, and how the organisation needs to change, instead of supplying tools. It's more interesting work!

Managing change and increasing resilience

With increasing levels of change, organisations are going to need to seek professionals to help them to understand the impact of that change on their organisation and, in particular, upon their employees. As discussed in Chapter 12, one of the emerging trends in the workplace is resilience – both of organisations and individuals within those organisations. With a huge body of psychological literature exploring ideas and interventions aimed at tackling, measuring and creating resilience, and with a real appetite within organisations for clear guidance and solutions, this trend represents a real opportunity for Occupational Psychologists both in academia and practice.

It is also likely that the organisational interest in managing change will offer opportunities more widely across the profession. As Julianne Miles, Director of Career Psychologists, a career counselling consultancy, states:

> In my field, for many organisations career counselling is still equated with outplacement and remedial assistance. I can envisage Occupational

Psychologists having increased involvement in workplace training and coaching for a broader base of employees, helping individuals with career management and transition, and with the development of skills in resilience and flexibility. [We] are ideally placed to help employees to develop the psychological attitudes to negotiate the continually changing working environment, with reduced job security and a high degree of unpredictability.

Workplace health initiatives

In the last 10 years, there has been an increased interest in academic literature around employee health and well-being. This has resulted in a range of clear and consistent findings in the literature relating to both the psychosocial hazards in the workplace that can cause ill health (for instance, poor working relationships, lack of autonomy or high job demands as described in Chapters 4 and 7) and those factors in the organisation and external environment that promote well-being and that buffer against the impacts of psychosocial hazards (for instance, employee engagement, as described in Chapter 12). From the academic literature, and a variety of practitioner publications, there is now a strong business case for organisations to focus upon improving employee well-being. For an example, see the section on employee engagement in Chapter 12. This offers the opportunity for Occupational Psychologists to provide advice, guidance and interventions to organisations on managing well-being for their employees.

As well as working with organisations and the employees in work, there will also be more opportunities for Occupational Psychologists to work with employees who are out of work and, with an improvement in the economic situation, are looking towards returning to work. This may involve supporting the employee through training and development, or through coaching and counselling, or through working with the target organisation to develop a return to work plan. Professionals who can effectively equip the long-term unemployed with the skills and confidence to return to work will be much in demand in the financial recovery.

In Chapter 12 we explored emerging trends that may be pertinent and important for Occupational Psychology as a profession. Each of these emerging trends will represent new role opportunities for Occupational Psychologists in the future. Table 13.1 includes some suggestions, but we would urge you to take some time to think for yourself about what the possibilities and therefore gaps might be for future research and practice.

Table 13.1   Role and research opportunities suggested by emerging trends

Emerging trend	Research opportunities	Practice role opportunities
Technology	• HMI research to ensure new technologies are easy to use and fulfil organisational objectives • Research to establish validities of new methods of selection (such as video-based CVs) • Research exploring impact of social media on employee engagement, attitudes to selection, team building, workplace relationships and so on • Impact of new technologies on psychosocial aspects of work and the work environment • Research on comparative methods in efficacy of/response to counselling • Further research on context within which teleworking is beneficial and adverse • Research on 'technology overload' and its management • Further research on impact of technology on team working and on leadership	• Support/training and development provided to employees in the workplace • Facilitating the introduction and management of new technologies to increase user acceptance and satisfaction • Introduce the use of different types of media in selection processes • Advice on best practice around use of social networking/social media • Increased use of technology in training including use of social media • Use of e-based counselling, including Live Chat, Skype and MMS • Guidance and interventions around teleworking policy and practices • Guidance around managing virtual teams • Helping individuals to manage the demands of technology in professional and personal life
Ageing workforce	• Further research needed to understand the role of age in the workplace • Research on 'late adulthood' to understand how current middle-aged workers might approach work in their 60s	• Focus on ergonomics to ensure the work environment takes into account age • Design of interventions to account for age • Development of HR policies to motivate and manage different ages of employee • Re-design of jobs to take age into account • Interventions to address stereotyping and discrimination by age • Advice and guidance around Equality Act • Helping individuals and organisations to manage transitions out of work and/or re-designing roles in late adulthood

Globalisation	• More research exploring global acculturation, cultural norms within organisations and diversity • More truly global research (rather than mainly US/Europe based)	• Development of HR systems to take into consideration cultural and ethnic diversity • Interventions around managing diversity • Training around cultural norms/practices to enable effective cross cultural working
Employee engagement	• Academic research around employee engagement including conceptualisation, antecedents, moderators and mediators of engagement • Focus on understanding engagement in context of other variables such as new technology	• Provision of evidence based interventions to foster and create employee engagement • Provision of measurement tools and organisational diagnostics around engagement • Training and development of 'engaging' managers • Guidance around creating organisational cultures of engagement
Resilience	• Research within organisations needed to develop OP specific literature • More long term intervention based research • Development of organisational resilience measures	• Advice and guidance to organisations to provide clarity around resilience • 'Weatherproofing' organisations at the strategic level • Measurement/conducting resilience diagnostics within organisations • Provision of evidence-based interventions to foster resilience at individual, team and organisational level • Counselling and coaching focusing on building resilience and developing psychological attitudes to negotiate the continually changing work environment
Environmental sustainability	• Research to understand role of employee behaviour in delivering improvements to an organisation's environmental performance • Research to understand the influence of managers and organisational culture on the 'green' behaviour of employees	• Provision of consultancy to build sustainability into business strategy • Development of interventions to change employee behaviour around sustainability in the workplace • Involvement of line managers in environmental practices

(Continued)

Table 13.1 (Continued)

Methodological advances	• Increased use of real-world research • Increased use of longitudinal, cross lagged or time series research • Increased use of complex analytics such as HLM and SEM to be able to predict and explain causal relationships between variables, and explore the influence of variables at different levels on specific outcomes	• Advanced analytical practices used on organisational data in order to provide evidence based practice • Training and development provided to practitioners around research and analytical skills • Increased use of statistical skills to provide 'bottom line' support for interventions and solutions in the workplace

Box 13.1

Exercise

Consider Table 13.1 – can you think of any other role applications for the emerging trends? With regards to your personal experience and aspirations, which areas particularly interest you? Are there implications for your skill needs?

What skills will Occupational Psychologists need in the future?

In Chapter 2, we explored the skills that were likely to be useful to Occupational Psychologists. Within this, we included Table 2.1 that provided an overview of the key skills. A summary of that table has been replicated in Table 13.2.

Reflecting upon the predictions for future roles, it is likely that in the coming years, some of those skills will increase in importance, and other skills are likely to emerge as important for Occupational Psychologists. Again, we consulted with our authors and contributing academics and practitioners for their thoughts on the key skills that would increase in importance in the future. Their thoughts fell into three key areas.

Research and analytical skills

It has been much repeated throughout the book, in particular in this chapter and Chapter 12, that organisations will increasingly be turning to consultants that provide and offer solutions that can be *proven* to be effective.

Table 13.2 Summary of core skills table presented in Chapter 2

Critical thinking skills
Problem solving skills
Consultancy skills
Communication skills
Data management and analysis skills (e.g. knowledge of SPSS and/or qualitative research)
Scientist-practitioner model: using evidence-based research
Working with people
Planning and organising
Active listening skills
Relevant technical skills

Rob Briner, Professor of Organisational Psychology, University of Bath, believes that this will require skills in three areas:

First, a much deeper level of critical thinking. Critical thinking about research, about their own practice, and the problems and issues they see in organisations.

Second, skills around reviewing and using existing research evidence will be essential: in particular learning the skills that are required to undertake systematic reviews of existing evidence that address practice questions of relevance to organisations.

Third, the data analysis skills necessary for making sense of the often large quantities of data organisations already have but don't use to help make informed and evidence-based decisions.

Perhaps the most repeated assertion within this is the need for, in particular practitioners, to be up to date with statistics and analytical methods. This does not just mean learning statistics during your undergraduate or post-graduate degree but also proactively continuing to develop and update those skills across your career with training, reading and development. Ivan Robertson, Director of Robertson Cooper Ltd and Professor of Organisational Psychology, Leeds University Business School:

It is even more important than ever for OPs to develop (during their training and keep up to date after that) a sound grasp of the contemporary quantitative methods that are used by researchers to analyse data. I don't believe that practitioner OPs need to use these techniques in their everyday work – but they do need to be able to read the relevant literature! For several decades now the trend has been for researchers to use more and more complex methods of data analysis – not because complex is better – but somewhat paradoxically – because these more complex forms of analysis enable clearer and simpler conclusions to be drawn from research. Falling behind in understanding the quantitative analyses used by researchers makes it more or less impossible to draw on the science base.

With fewer opportunities and more competition for jobs, it is important that Occupational Psychologists differentiate themselves from other consultants or practitioners such as HR professionals and management consultants in the marketplace. As discussed in Chapter 2, it may not be that we do different roles, but where we differ is in our methodologies, in other words our use of evidence-based practice. It is therefore by use of these methodologies and analytical methods that we can both differentiate ourselves and stay ahead of the competition in the marketplace. This view is upheld by Dr Maura Kerrin, Director, Work Psychology Group:

> Our biggest threat is that other areas look like they do similar stuff to us, and they take human based data in organisations and link it to certain outputs, but yet they have no training in 'humans'. We need to retain those skills.

Creativity and innovation

> Given the recent meltdown, the areas of creativity and innovation in organisations will become really important. (Professor Fiona Patterson, Cambridge University and Director, Work Psychology Group)

In Chapter 8, the idea of aligning a business strategy with the structure of the organisation levels was introduced. The suggestion was that if a business strategy was to enable innovation and creativity, the organisational structure would aim to be correspondingly organic (low levels of formalisation and centralisation). It is likely, in the constantly moving business environment, that organisations will increasingly need to be set up so that they can operate flexibly and creatively – with the outcome of keeping up with the change, and staying ahead of the competition.

The same is true of individuals – with change at both the job and organisational levels occurring constantly, individuals need to be equipped with the skills to be flexible and to adapt and innovate according to the dynamic environmental demands. As Occupational Psychologists this means from a personal practice perspective continuing to develop our skills across our profession, for instance, updating our research knowledge and being able to develop creative and innovative solutions to problems for organisations. It also, however, means that we will need to use these skills to help others, be they employees, managers or clients, develop creative skills and think more creatively about their own issues in the workplace. It may also involve increasing use of change management and OD skills. As Kurt Kraiger stated when asked what new skills Occupational Psychologists will need in the future: 'More classic OD skills – diagnostics, encouraging and supporting change, evaluating impact.'

Wider business knowledge and skills

Perhaps the most commonly mentioned skill need by our practitioner and academic contributors was that of greater, stronger and wider business and consultancy skills. It is often mentioned that Occupational Psychologists tend to practice at the individual rather than strategic level, and are involved in interventions that sit outside of wider business goals and initiatives. Further, they are often seen as purveyors of 'soft skills' rather than solid tangible financially based solutions and benefits. Additionally, it has also been suggested that psychologists need to know more about the general functioning and practice of an organisation in order to understand the issues – and be able to recommend clear evidence-based solutions that are also firmly business based. The following quotations provide more thoughts on this issue.

> It is essential that OPs focus more on the organisational aspect of OP, bridging the theory–practice gap by increasing commercial understanding, strategic perspective and awareness of key business drivers. OPs are sometimes seen as theoretically driven, rather 'ivory tower'. We need to demonstrate a clear understanding of business realities. (Julianne Miles, Director of Career Psychologists)

> Developing a good understanding of business skills and consulting skills is something that is useful regardless of what specific role someone holds. Developing a better grasp of these things will help practitioners to do their job better – and researchers will be better able to focus their research and get it used if they are more connected with the day-to-day problems and opportunities that arise in organisations. (Ivan Robertson, Director, Robertson Cooper Ltd and Professor of Organisational Psychology, Leeds University Business School)

> We need to be more commercial as a practice. Until we can talk pounds and pence in the boardroom with any semblance of rigour, it will be difficult to be perceived as anything else other than another cost line on the annual budget statement. (Alastair Wallace, Managing Director of Brainfood)

It is only when Occupational Psychologists start to place an increased importance on these skills that they will be able to start having a greater influence within organisations. Perhaps it is the case that MSc courses will need to include a greater focus on strategic management, business management and other aspects of commercial functioning. It may also be that, along with experience of working within the eight areas of Occupational Psychology (as explored in Part II of this book), it will be fundamental for Occupational Psychologists in training to gather commercial and strategic experience. It is also important to note that, again in a continuing refrain from this book, Occupational Psychologists will be required to constantly update their business skills in order to stay ahead of the game. Sarah Lewis, Director of Appreciating Change, puts this point succinctly:

> I'm not sure we need any 'new' skills, we just need to keep the present ones that make a difference up to scratch in a changing world. As people who want to influence what other people do and how they behave, we have to keep developing our skills in these areas.

Reflecting therefore on these insights, how might these influence the list of core skills provided in Chapter 2 (and revisited earlier in this chapter)? Table 13.3 attempts to translate the future skills suggestions into the table presented previously. New skill requirements are shown in bold.

Using this information proactively

Having read this book, it is likely that you are at the start of your career in Occupational Psychology. It may be that you have lots of other previous experience (perhaps in a different area) and you are changing careers, or it may be that you are a student starting out in the world of work. Either way, before completing this book, we would recommend taking some time to reflect upon the contents of the book and what you would like to do next – for instance, you may want to start by asking yourself some of these questions:

- Do I want to become a chartered and registered Occupational Psychologist?
- Which area of Occupational Psychology really interests me?
- What type of roles will I be aiming for in the future?
- What skills and experience are going to be important for me to reach my career goals?
- What further experience do I need to develop the necessary skills?
- What action do I need to take to reach my career goals?

You may want to read more about the psychometrics and career theories introduced in Chapter 5 to help you with the answers to the questions. It may be that you would like to contact a career counsellor or coach yourself, or you may want to conduct your own research to increase your self awareness about your needs

Table 13.3   Summary of core skills table presented in Chapter 2 along with updated skill predictions for future Occupational Psychologists

Core skills needed by OPs (as shown in Chapter 2)	Skill necessity/impact in the future
MSc in Occupational Psychology or similar	Will continue to be important particularly to provide theoretical underpinnings for practice, and research and analytical skills ***May also be a requirement for skills education at the level of business, strategic and financial management and consultancy**
Critical thinking skills	Will continue to be key
Problem solving skills	Will continue to be key, and may rely more heavily on evidence-based practice, i.e. using the evidence base from literature, and data from organisational evidence to create solutions that will be effective
Consultancy skills/ **Wider business and strategic skills and experience**	Will increase in importance with the need for OPs to have a greater, stronger, all-round business knowledge and understanding ***Will also be important to have influencing skills and be able to consult and relate to senior management. Consultancy offerings will need to be based on evidence-based practice and be financially astute – and consultants will need to be able to deliver solutions credibly and with influence**
Communication skills	Will continue to be key and will increase in complexity ***Occupational Psychologists will not only be required to have communication skills dealing with different audiences from employees through to board level organisational members but will also need to communicate through use of various new and emerging technologies. Further, OPs will need to be aware of research to enable the most effective communication for each particular medium and technology**
Data management and analysis skills	Will grow in importance ***Occupational Psychologists will be required to develop and maintain analytical skills in current and emerging techniques (such as multi-level modelling) in order to offer unique solutions, and firmly evidence-based practice**
Scientist-practitioner model	Will grow in importance ***It will become a core skill requirement for practitioners to use relevant research and academic knowledge in order to provide cutting edge solutions to organisations; and for academics to conduct research to address organisationally relevant and focused issues**

(Continued)

Table 13.3 (Continued)

Core skills needed by OPs (as shown in Chapter 2)	Skill necessity/impact in the future
Working with people	Will continue to be key *Occupational Psychologists will be required to build skills in working with people across all levels of the organisation, through use of multiple technologies and medias, and with influence and credibility. Occupational Psychologists should be able to work cross functionally and operate as a strategic partner
Planning and organising	Will continue to be key
Active listening skills	Will continue to be key
Relevant technical skills	Will continue to be key *The need to update and refresh technical skills will become more urgent and move towards being continuous
Creativity and innovation skills	Will be a new core skill requirement

and wants. In order to start to consider the skill priorities and gaps, you may want to use the Box 13.2 as a template for discussion.

To access skill development, you may find it useful to gain information from Chapter 2 which surrounded preparing for a job. You may also find Chapter 3 useful for sources of information related to Occupational Psychology. However, what is going to be key for all is thinking about your resources and opportunities flexibly. Perhaps after graduating from your MSc, you cannot find a job in a related discipline; however, if that job provides you with understanding of business or financial management it could be very useful to you. The job may equip you with skills and experience communicating with different groups of employees; or even communicating via different technologies. It may be a sales job – which will equip you with important influencing and credibility skills. Try to think flexibly and consider opportunities in terms of the skills that they will provide.

Another fantastic way of accessing skill development is through use of your networks, both in the field of Occupational Psychology (your tutors, peers, consultants and academics you met through the course of your studies, relevant groups on social media) and personal connections. This may be through work shadowing, project work, internships – or conducting 'barter' work where you help develop a skill gap of theirs that you are an expert in and vice versa.

Box 13.2

Skills gap exercise

Current and future core skills	Do you currently have these skills?	Where can you access appropriate skill development?
MSc in Occupational Psychology or similar		
Financial/wider business management education		
Strategic business experience		
Critical thinking skills		
Problem solving skills		
Creativity and innovation skills		
Consultancy skills		
Communication skills		
Data management and analysis skills (e.g. knowledge of SPSS and/or qualitative research)		
Scientist-practitioner model: using evidence-based research		
Working with people		
Planning and organising		
Active listening skills		
Relevant technical skills		

Summary

In Chapter 1 of this book, we explored the history of Occupational Psychology and started to look towards the future of the discipline, looking more deeply at this in Chapter 12. What is clear is that we as a profession need to keep developing in order to keep up with the changes happening within the economy, within organisations and within technology. What we also need to do however is increase our 'voice' as a profession. It is the case that the majority of the public, as discussed in Chapter 2, will not have heard of the profession and those that will have heard of Occupational Psychologists will not know what we do.

Having influence at the boardroom level within organisations is one way to do this; another is having influence on government policy by adding to discussions and advising. As Emma Donaldson-Feilder discussed, getting the OP perspective recognised as significant and valuable is a really key step in this, as the advisory positions are currently dominated by economists. Finally, it is about using your own networks (personal and professional) to spread the word about Occupational Psychology and demonstrating, through ethical, evidence-based practice, what an important and unique role we fulfil.

Explore further

- Keep up to date with news, current affairs and business events in order to spot implications and changes in the workplace. Ideas of sources of information are included in Chapter 3.
- Increase your network by using social media and making contacts with academics and practitioners who are working in the area of work that you are attracted to. For instance, if you want to go into the area of diversity as a practitioner, contact and introduce yourself to all the consultancies and organisations that work in this area. Starting a dialogue can only be a positive thing.
- Become as knowledgeable about the profession as possible. This will be formally through BPS and HPC communications and informally through networks, publications, such as *The Psychologist*, and social media (for examples see Chapter 3).
- Explore ways to address your skill gaps.

Discussion questions

1 Do you agree with the future skills that we have identified? Are there any additional skills that you think will be increasingly necessary?
2 Given your understanding of the profession of Occupational Psychology, where do you see the future and how do you feel the profession can stand out from others?

Author index

Subject index